VATICAN CITY

Editing and supervision to the texts
Carla Cecilia

Translation from Italian
Eugene Rizzo and Lisa Dasteel

Cover design and restyling
Alessandra Murri

© Edizioni MUSEI VATICANI
Vatican City
www.museivaticani.va

ISBN 978.88.8271.021.7

1st Edition   2001
2nd Edition   2007
1st Reprint   2010

Photographs
© Photographic Archive Vatican Museums (A. Bracchetti, P. Zigrossi); C. De Grazia, M. Maranzano, G. Ricci Novara, M. Sarri, G. Vasari courtesy of Musei Vaticani; P. Oszwald, D. Schwille (Kunst und Ausstellungshalle Bonn) courtesy of Musei Vaticani; Vatican Secret Archives; Vatican Library; Fabric of Saint Peter; Photo Service by «L'Osservatore Romano»; Alinari Archives; Scala Archives; F. Mayer Magnum; Metropolitan Museum of Art (New York); Musées Royaux d'Art et Histoire (Bruxelles); Nationalmuseum (Stockholm); Pubbliaerfoto; Kupferstich-kabinett (Berlin); ATS Italia Editrice.

Printed by
Vatican Typography

Orazio Petrosillo

VATICAN CITY

EDIZIONI MUSEI VATICANI

PREFACE

Any visitor to Rome standing in St. Peter's Square cannot help but be struck by the stunning basilica with its façade by Maderno and cupola by Michelangelo—the latter harmoniously crowning the whole with an effect at once soaring and elegant.

Inevitably, the visitor's eye moves spontaneously to the imposing series of sober Renaissance buildings (not without their own air of defensive fortresses) which comprise the Apostolic Palaces or the "Home of the Pope".

Thanks to television and other means of communication, these two images—St. Peter's Basilica and the adjoining palaces—are known throughout the world. The cupola, or as the locals say in the colorful Roman dialect, "er cuppolone", is the very symbol of Roman Christianity, just as the Colosseum is of Imperial Rome.

From his window on the third floor of the Apostolic Palace, the pope speaks every Sunday to the entire world. This familiarity has become even more direct since the existence of television. Tirelessly, he seeks to sow moral values, exhort people to peacefulness, and offer a ringing message of hope.

These two architectural complexes are at the heart of Vatican City, a tiny independent state composed of a mere 108 acres. Universally known and respected for its spirituality, its ethical values and for the religious faith that it represents, the Vatican is also the custodian of an astonishing collection of historical, cultural and artistic treasures.

For all that, the public's familiarity with the inner workings of this mini-State is sketchy at best. For obvious reasons, much of what is within its walls is not directly accessible to the public. Aware, however, that "the Vatican belongs to all of us" and that its artistic treasures are part of the patrimony of all humanity, we have tried to render them accessible to everyone. This means bringing these treasures into the homes of all those who haven't the chance to visit Rome, whose only knowledge of the city was provided by those televised views we mentioned earlier.

This attractive volume, published by Edizioni Musei Vaticani, is part of such a cultural undertaking. The author is Orazio Petrosillo, a noted journalist on Vatican affairs whose writing is both informative and graceful. And true to its proven tradition, the Vatican printing press has produced an impeccable editorial format, one that is blessed moreover with abundant color illustrations. Taken as a whole, the book offers the reader a marvelously detailed visit within the walls of this tiny State, permitting him to penetrate its secrets and to savor its countless artistic treasures.

History and theology form the thread that runs through the author's exposition. The reality of the Vatican, in fact, is grounded in both. Everything goes back to the tomb of St. Peter, the apostle upon whom Christ built his church. Above Peter's tomb, which is the object of immense Christian devotion, two successive basilicas have arisen: that built by Constantine in 322 A.D., and the present one, begun by Julius II in 1506 and completed in 1615 during the pontificate of Paul V. Peter's tomb, then, was the ideal point of reference around which "Vatican Hill"—with a connection at once spatial and spiritual—took shape and evolved to its present-day configuration.

It is a fascinating story, told in a manner that is both instructive and accessible. I have no doubt that the reader will emerge with a knowledge and appreciation of the Vatican. Distant and mysterious for many, fascinating for all, the Vatican in the course of centuries has been transformed by towering artists into an immense museum. At the same time, the presence of the pope means that it is the visible center and eternal point of reference for all those who profess the Catholic faith.

Rosalio José Cardinal Castillo Lara
President of the Pontifical Commission
for Vatican City State (1990-1997)

INTRODUCTION

This book is not intended as a guide to the Vatican in the strict sense of the term. There are no minutely detailed descriptions of the artistic treasures, no listings of all the historical implications of each monument. The aim has been simply to keep company with the visitor, to provide notes which will serve later to revive the feelings and impressions experienced during his or her days in Rome.

It occasionally happens that we are brought somewhere by a friend who knows a particular place well, can relate details about its history while at the same time communicating his love for what he's talking about. The result is a genuine spiritual impact with the reality of the place, a familiarity with the persons encountered, a sense of excitement generated by all the beauty contemplated. With our curiosity so keenly aroused, we are surprised by the web of historical coincidences and cultural cross-references that seemingly emanate from every stone.

I hope these pages will be a bit like that friend. Only in this case, he is accompanying you into the mysterious "sacred island" that is the Vatican. Everything there is kept up admirably. Everything there—spanning twenty centuries and yet enclosed within a few hundred meters—is connected to the same mission that brought Peter to Rome where he was martyred and buried on Vatican Hill. The "mystery" of the Vatican consists of the extraordinary rapport between this hill and the events of Jerusalem. It is a place imbued with spirituality, but not of the sort whereby cloistered monks silently contemplate the Kingdom of God in the hereafter. Rather, it is a spirituality well grounded in history, one that perpetuates the mission Christ entrusted to Peter. Throughout history, much of humanity has looked—and looks now—toward this hill. Thanks to the Vatican, Rome has become heir to Jerusalem. "Whence Christ is Roman...", as Dante wrote with brilliant theological intuition. Incredibly, the secret of Rome's eternity is perched on this tiny strip of land.

The hidden aspiration of this volume is to transform—respectfully and tactfully, to be sure—the tourist into a pilgrim. This is also because anyone who remains stubbornly closed to the superhuman message that emanates from these stones would have failed to grasp the meaning of the Vatican. "It's not earth, but a piece of the sky!," cried the Humanist scholar Emanuele Crisolora at the beginning of the fifteenth century. Being able to recall this phrase to those of the three million annual visitors who come to Rome and happen to choose this book as their companion is something deeply satisfying to the author.

Our visit is organized in a logical progression which begins at the tomb of the apostle, passes through the basilica which houses it, ascends to the palaces from which the pope guides the Church, traverses the museums with their numerous masterpieces, covers the magnificent papal gardens and comes out again on the stunning piazza which was our point of departure.

To the unity of place we've added unity of time. Starting at daybreak in the mysterious subterranean world of the Vatican's grottoes we will progress to early-morning prayers at the sanctuary. Mid-morning will be reserved for the incessant multiple activities of the pope. At noon we will bask in the sunlight of artistic masterpieces. A restful afternoon will be spent outdoors in the gardens of the tiny city-state, after which will follow a thought-filled sunset in the incomparable piazza.

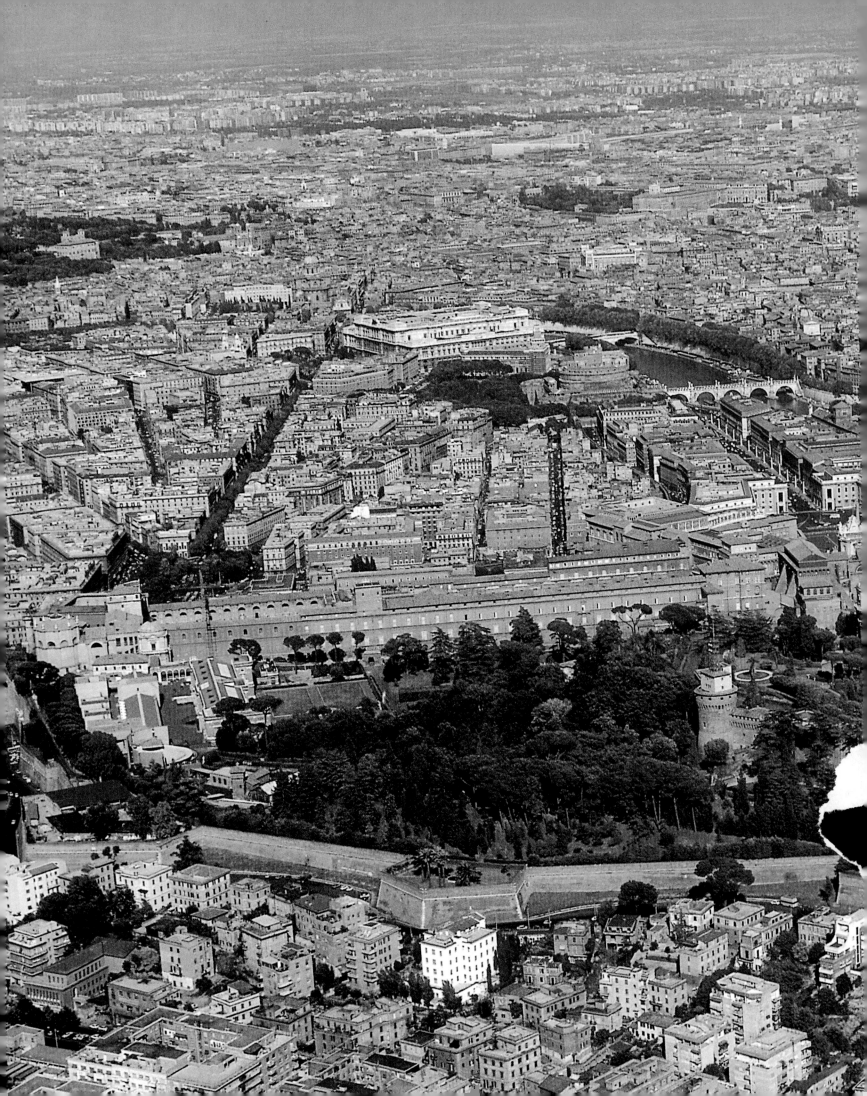

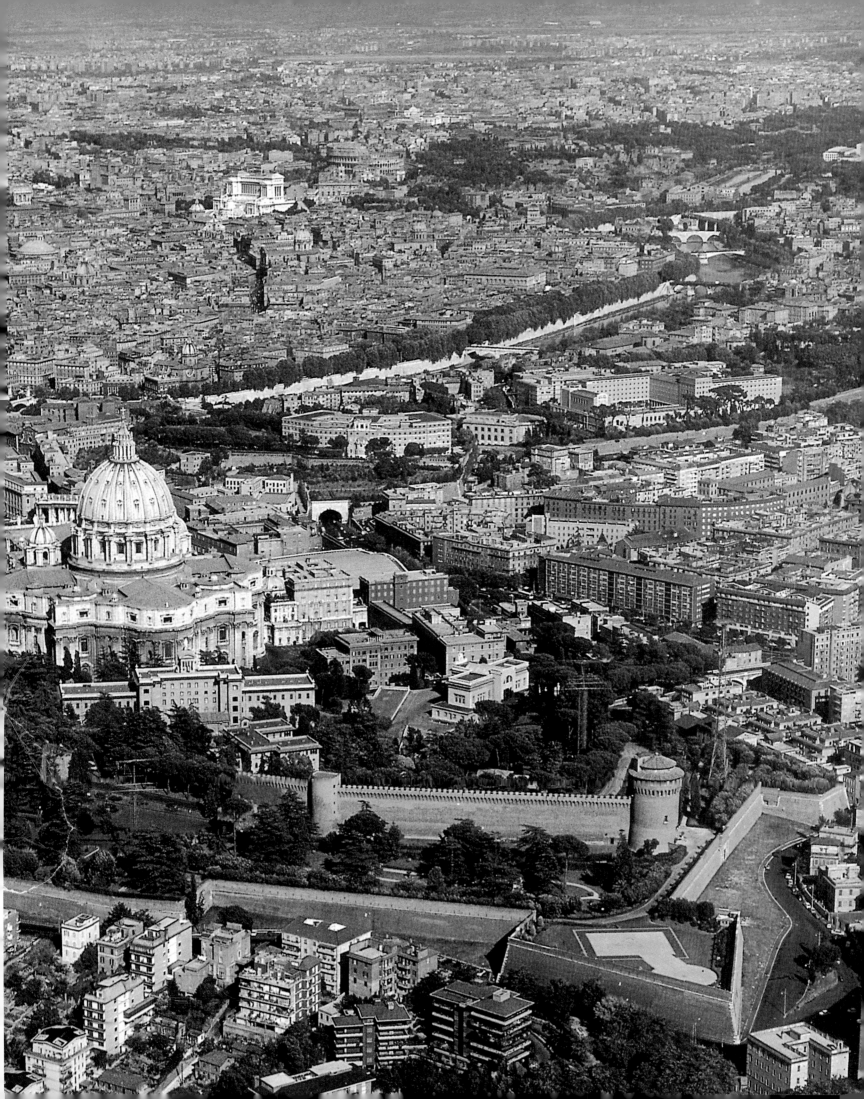

General Overview

A Miniature State

"The smallest state in the world at the center of the largest spiritual kingdom." So the Vatican has been defined. Comprising barely 44 hectares (108.6 acres), the whole of it can be easily viewed from the top of the cupola of St. Peter's. By comparison, the Principality of Monaco, which is the next smallest independent state, is nearly three-and-a-half times larger. Shaped like a trapezoid, the Vatican is enclosed within walls (completed between 1540 and 1640) which join on the piazza. The maximum length of the tiny state is 1,045 meters, from the opening of the Bernini colonnade to the heliport; its maximum width is 850 meters, from the auditorium where papal audiences are held to the entrance of the museums. The perimeter of the entire state is 3,420 meters.

The whole of the Vatican is within the city of Rome. With respect to the city which surrounds it, it is located to the west of the Tiber and hence close to Rome's historic center. It derives its name from the Vatican Hill, dating back to the time of the Etruscans (5th century B.C.).

As an independent state, it is so tiny that all essential services do not fit within its walls. In fact, the Vatican possesses more territory outside its walls than within, such as the 136 acres of the Pontifical Villas and the 1,086 acres of the transmission center at Santa Maria di Galeria.

Equally few in number are its inhabitants. There are around 500 citizens—half of whom represent the Holy See abroad—plus just over 300 persons authorized to reside there while maintaining their original citizenship.

What really makes the Vatican unique is that it exists to guarantee the independence of a universal organization like the Holy See—in other words, the central government of the Catholic Church. "Just big enough to keep together body and soul," was Pius XI's comment upon the establishment of the mini-state that came with the signing of the Lateran Treaty on February 11, 1929. That was the pact that finally resolved the "Roman Question"—first opened with the capture of Rome by the republican armies of Garibaldi on September 20, 1870.

Spread gently across Vatican Hill, rising from the twenty meters' elevation of Piazza San Pietro to a peak of 78.5 meters (highest point in the gardens), the city-state is made up one-third of buildings, one–third of tiny squares and courtyards, and one-third of gardens. All in all, there are 10,000 rooms, 12,000 windows and 997 staircases. Viewed from above, it looks like a vast architectural complex, airy and orderly, almost the product of a single mind. It is truly "the artistic patrimony of all mankind" as UNESCO defined it. And indeed it seems a sacred work of art, with Michelangelo's cupola as its gleaming crown. In the midst of the urban tumult of Rome, the Vatican is an island of peace and tranquility—a "regal miniature", as the English Catholic writer G.K. Chesterton so charmingly expressed it.

Capital of a Spiritual Realm

If it were judged by normal criteria, the Vatican would surely appear insignificant as a state. And yet this little city is the capital of no less than the largest spiritual "kingdom" in the world. A kingdom of which 950 million Roman Catholics, spread throughout all the world's continents, are full-fledged members. The Vatican is their "communal home" not only because it is the center of the Holy Apostolic Roman Church, but because the pope, their visible head, resides there.

The place is so small that it could be the property of a single family. In fact, during the day it is impossible to enter the Vatican without a specific reason. By 8:30 pm all five entry gates are shut, with the exception of the St. Anne Gates which remain partially open until midnight. But on the side facing the main square (which is always open), the city can be said to be the most visited in the world. No other capital can claim such a level of interest because none can compete with its extraordinary concentration of art works. It was here, after all, where artists of the caliber of Bramante, Raphael, Michelangelo and Bernini had their workshops.

And yet, the tens of thousands of masterpieces kept in the basilica, in the Apostolic Palaces and in the museums—not to mention the vast patrimony contained in the libraries and archives—cannot wholly explain the inordinate hold that the Vatican exercises over hundreds of millions of people around the globe. For this is truly "an

Vatican City, *seen from west to east (previous pages). The 16th–century fortified walls are clearly visible. Behind them are the medieval walls of the Leonine City; the section between the Radio Tower (to the left) and the Tower of St. John was restored and renovated at the time of Nicholas V.*

immense state of souls rather than persons"—a point of reference to which humanity turns for its spiritual bearings.

"From St. Peter to the present day, there has been a direct line through the winding history of humanity,"wrote Paul VI. "No other voice but that of the apostle has spoken more coherently of brotherhood, liberty, human respect, disarmament, love, moral and civil progress." Pilgrims come here in order to pray in St. Peter's Basilica and to see the Holy Father. *Videre Petrum*—that is, seeing Peter, is an aspiration of faith that springs from the deepest regions of the soul; it connects the Prince of the Apostles to each of his successors. To each of them in turn the Lord made his sublime promise: "Thou art Peter and upon this rock I will build my Church."

No one is a foreigner in this city. Everyone feels at home inside these walls and within the embrace of the great colonnade. At the same time, each of the more than ten million pilgrims who journey here every year is aware of a sense of mystery that hovers over everything. It is something far bigger than these stones, bigger than the spacious square, the immense basilica, all the gilded palaces. The Vatican lifts the soul. Its solemn and sacred sites give us the feeling that there is something superior to the man-made world.

The basilica and its connected palaces are the outer garment, as it were, of a spiritual reality; similarly, the visible structures of the Church contain the invisible sources of grace within. Here we cannot be tourists simply viewing art works. We are walking in the steps of generations of Christians who have preceded us in the course of centuries. We are never alone in the Vatican. We are in spiritual company that extends back over two thousand years.

Aerial view of the Vatican complex.

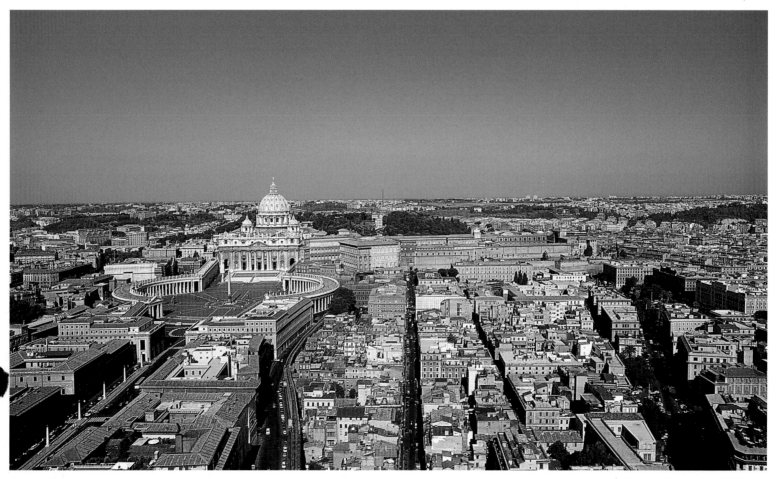

THE TOMB OF PETER

Our Point of Reference Within the Vatican

The key to understanding the Vatican can be found in the mystery of the keys. This is no mere play on words. It has to do with the mandate given Peter by Christ to guide the Church throughout all history. God entrusted Peter with the keys to Heaven. We must examine closely the providential design which, around the year 42 A.D., brought the prince of apostles to Rome, the capital of the Roman Empire. Here, sometime between 64-67 A.D., he was martyred in Nero's Circus, at the foot of the Vatican Hill, and entombed in a nearby burial ground. His body was placed in the nude earth, barely covered with a few scattered bricks.

In order to understand the mystery of the Vatican, we must begin with this moment of absolute humility: the plain burial of an executed man at the height of anti-Christian persecution. A very short distance separated the place where Peter professed his Faith through martyrdom from the spot where he was buried. Just as it was in the case of Christ, who died on Calvary and whose body was entombed in a nearby cemetery belonging to Joseph of Arimathea.

Peter's tomb is our point of reference within the Vatican. It is at the crux of everything, the reason for all that was subsequently built. This magnificent city would not exist; the greatest temple in all Christendom would not have risen here, were it not the burial place of a fisherman from Galilee who bore witness to Christ's Resurrection and whose Faith was so strong that he too accepted crucifixion. He was a poor Jew, rejected by the authorities among his own people, possessing neither Roman citizenship nor a proper use of Latin. The burial of this man was an event that transformed and ultimately exalted Vatican Hill and its necropolis. The city that we observe today was born within the fortification meant to defend that tomb and the church that rose above it.

We can strain our fantasy in an effort to imagine how that place might have appeared two thousand years ago. It was an uninhabitable area to be sure, marshy and filled with grass snakes. The land was infertile and the wine produced there of an inferior quality. In short, a place to avoid, not least because the boggy strip along the right bank of the Tiber was where malaria proliferated. Later the area would be improved with the addition of several grand villas. And when the Roman Empire was established, a circus was constructed in the flat area next to the river, between the Vatican and Janiculum Hills. At the hub of this circus, the Emperor Caligula (37-41 A.D.) placed an Egyptian obelisk, most likely brought on a barge from Alexandria.

During the persecutions between 64-67, the apostle Peter, leader of Rome's Christian community, was martyred in that circus together with a number of his brethren. Their burial at the foot of Vatican Hill was to be the premise for the most extraordinary transformation any site has undergone from ancient times to today. The necropolis is located several meters below the surface of the present-day basilica. We can't be sure, but originally it might have extended from Nero's bridge for several miles along the Via Cornelia.

Peter's Memorial

If we were to walk along the narrow alleyway 70 meters long that separates two rows of burial stones—mostly dating from the second century—it would be as though we were taking up the dare once made by the ecclesiastical writer Gaius. Writing at the close of the second century to the heretic Proclo, Gaius challenged him in these words: "I can show you the memorials erected to the apostles, because if you go to Vatican Hill or to the Via Ostiense, you'll find the memorials of the founders of this Church." He was speaking, of course, of Peter and Paul. The memorial to Peter is located seven meters below the papal altar in St. Peter's Basilica.

There, in the center of a quadrangular area measuring four meters by four, dubbed "Field P" by archaeologists, the humble tomb of the Apostle was dug sometime during the sixth decade of the first century. According to tradition, a terebinth tree originally marked the spot where Peter was buried. Around the year 160, a wall was erected next to the sepulchre (called "the red wall" because of the color of its plaster), separating this burial spot from other parts of the necropolis.

Next to it, a small monument was constructed. It consisted of a slab with two niches, one above the other, divided by a marble shelf supported by two small columns 80 centimeters high. The combination of the two—the slab with its niches and the "red wall" against which it was built—must be what Gaius was referring to with his talk of "memorials". Dating from slightly after the middle of the second century, the structure is exceptionally important.

We know it was the most venerated part of the burial ground. The "red wall" and the modest memorial within "Field P" testify to the wish, as early as the middle of the second century, to conserve and integrate an earlier tomb within the context of an expanded necropolis. And this took place, we should bear in mind, in spite of the extra care that Christians had to take at a time of ferocious persecution.

In order to protect the mortal remains of the Apostle from repeated accumulations of mud and earth, another wall was placed perpendicular to the "red wall". This was named by archaeologists "Wall G" (for Graffiti) because of the numerous messages etched onto the plaster. The invocations to Christ, Mary and St. Peter speak eloquently of the devotion of the first pilgrims.

In a small loculus carved out of "Wall G" and paved with slabs of marble, were deposited what was left of Peter's mortal remains after having been buried for nearly two centuries in the earth.

The fact that all of this was cared for and watched over, even within the context of a constantly expanding necropolis, means that it was a place of veneration from the earliest times. Peter was there. The Emperor Constantine and Pope Sylvester were so sure of it as to encapsulate the whole in a larger monument of white and purple marble with slabs of red porphyry. Built into it was a passageway that allowed one to approach the tomb of the Apostle.

Architectural Folly

The monument stood at the center of the transept within a great basilica, measuring 110 meters by 55, begun around the year 322 A.D.—a decade or so after the famous edict that granted religious freedom to the Christians. Constantine's veneration for Peter's tomb was such that he did not hesitate to embark on what was, by any standards, an architectural folly: building an immense construction largely on clay, at the slopes of a hill that would have to be entirely excavated. So strong was the Emperor's religious sentiment that he risked profaning a necropolis that was still in use.

It is a touching thought for us today to know that the level of the new construction was determined by that humble slab of marble marking Peter's tomb. All the mausoleums that stood higher than the memorial were either opened or destroyed; those which were lower were covered with earth in the same manner that Pompeii and Herculaneum were buried beneath the lava of Vesuvius.

And that was the way the pre-Constantinian necropolis remained until the 1940s, when it was excavated by order of Pius XII. It constituted one of the great archaeological discoveries of our time. Peter's tomb was the ideal cornerstone for Constantine's basilica and—twelve centuries later—for the even more grandiose basilica which succeeded it. The connection between then and now is something that is almost palpable. There is a continuity of tradition, an unchanging veneration for that tomb—which has now been identified with absolute certainty.

In the first centuries after Christ, Constantine's basilica was essentially a combination temple-and-mausoleum dedicated to Peter. Whereas the transept was given over to the veneration of the tomb, the nave and aisles were reserved for liturgical activities. If the celebration of Mass was called for, a portable altar was put there.

At the end of the sixth century, it was St. Gregory the Great who called for the construction of a permanent altar. He had the presbytery raised, thereby creating a semi-circular crypt which permitted the faithful to approach the tomb virtually on their knees. In his turn, Calixtus II created a second altar above that of Gregory in 1120. And above even that, in the new basilica, the papal altar (known as the "confessional altar") was placed vertical to the original tomb. It was consecrated by the Aldobrandini pope, Clement VIII, in 1594.

The same pope ordered the alteration and embellishment of the crypt. Still today we can walk along the aisle that leads to the chapel (named after Clement) in the Vatican grotto. So it is clear that the veneration of Peter's tomb is something which has united all his successors—right up to Pius XII's ordering fresh excavations a half century ago and John Paul II's decision to render Peter's monument more visible to pilgrims by making a new entrance beneath the Confessional Altar.

The New Jerusalem

The close rapport between tomb-altar-basilica resembles the chain of spiritual succession that is similarly enacted with a ritual like the laying of the hands. Such a connection—at once physical and spiritual—keeps Peter "alive" today in his 263rd successor. It amounts to nothing less than a spiritual patrimony that echoes down the centuries, impervious to the vicissitudes of history. Through its most important Bishop, the Church of Rome remains one with its Divine Founder. In this sense, the Vatican becomes a sacred island, a type of new Holy Land. Indeed, it appears like a New Jerusalem, come into being between the two comings of Christ: the first in historic Jerusalem, the second with the Second Coming.

This is what Dante—a pilgrim at the first Holy Year in 1300—alluded to when he had Beatrice declare *E sarai meco sanza fine cive / di quella Roma onde Cristo e' Romano* ("you shall be with me until the end of all things / in that Rome where Christ is Roman"). As we see, the poet sang of Rome as nothing less than the symbol of the heavenly Jerusalem. It is for this reason that the Vatican can never be merely a museum, for all that it is one of the most prestigious in the world.

Next to Peter's tomb, both in the Vatican grottoes and above in the Basilica itself, repose the remains of 147 popes including all those who have reigned in this century. In the spacious church with its nave and two aisles, there are many sarcophagi. Indeed, you can find there a small compendium of European history: the tombs of the German Emperor Otto the Great, Carlotta di Savoia Queen of Cyprus, Queen Christina of Sweden, James III with the last Stuarts. But always and forever, at the center of everything is the sepulchre of the Apostle Peter.

The lower niche of the Monument to Peter is known as the *Nicchia dei Pallii*. We see there the small golden casket

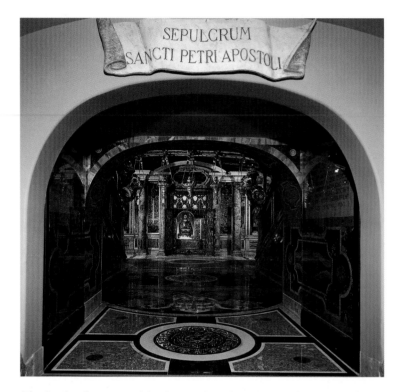

The Confession, *a semicircular, outdoor dugout, was designed and decorated by Carlo Maderno in 1600 between the floors of the old and the new basilica. In 1979 an arch was built so that the Confession would be visible from the Vatican Holy Grottoes as was the case in earlier times when it could be seen from the nave of Constantine's basilica. ("Confession" indicates the burial place of those who continued to "confess" their true faith even though this led to martyrdom).*

containing the *Pallii* (the outer liturgical insignia of the bishops' authority). Below it is visible a small opening in the marble slabs. Through there, pilgrims used to lower little bits of cloth in order to automatically make them relics.

From a small grille in the ceiling of Clement's chapel we can actually look up toward Bernini's baldachin and beyond—all the way up to Michelangelo's cupola. By doing so, one has the impression of observing a vast religious undertaking from its very source; from the place, as it were, that it has both guarded and preserved for two millennia. This is the meaning of the triumph of Faith. And if the greatness of Peter's temple soars over the little tomb, we know it is still the latter which buttresses and exalts everything built above it.

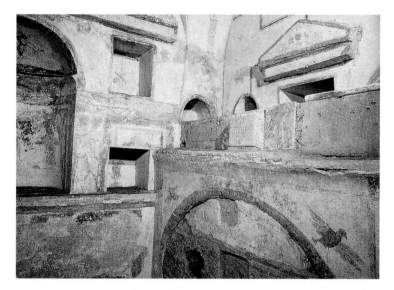

The Necropolis *below the basilica was covered by Emperor Constantine in the year 320 in order to level off the ground on the spot where he wanted to have a basilica built commemorating Peter's tomb. Excavations carried out in the 1940s under Pius XII brought to light about 70 meters of a little pathway with Christian graves on one side, and pagan graves, where some converted Christians were also buried, on the other. These tombs were built between the 2ⁿᵈ and 3ʳᵈ centuries on top of an older graveyard where Peter was buried, not far from the Circus where he was put to death. The ceiling of the Caetenni family mausoleum, as well as the ceilings of other tombs, were destroyed to make room for the foundations of the basilica.*

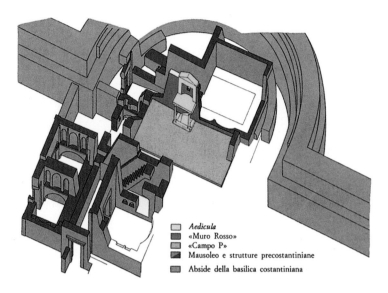

Reconstruction of the Necropolis. *In front of the "memorial" to Peter, against a red wall, is an empty space called "Field P" in the 1951 official report of the archaeological excavation.*

- Aedicula
- «Muro Rosso»
- «Campo P»
- Mausoleo e strutture precostantiniane
- Abside della basilica costantiniana

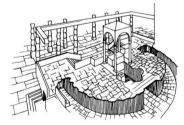

The Crypt of Gregory I. *At the time of Gregory I, towards the end of the 6ᵗʰ century, the floor of the apse was raised a meter and a half in order to place a new altar (the first steady one) above Constantine's Monument. The original "memorial" remained visible from the nave and a semicircular passageway led to a votive chapel behind the monument.*

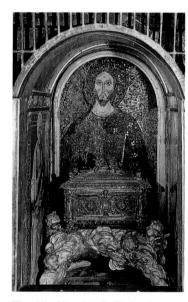

The Nicchia dei Pallii *is the lower niche of the "memorial" to Peter. The Christ figure is a 9ᵗʰ century mosaic. The small casket containing the Pallii (white woolen stoles to be worn by new metropolitan archbishops as soon as they are consecrated) was a gift of Benedict XIV.*

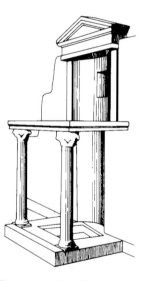

Reconstruction of the "memorial" to Peter. *This small monument (2.7 by 1.75 meters) was built in the second half of the 2ⁿᵈ century to commemorate St. Peter's burial place. The original monument is mentioned in a letter written by Gaius, a Roman high priest, in approximately the year 200.*

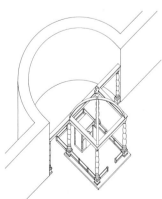

Constantine's Monument. *Emperor Constantine incorporated the original "memorial" to Peter in a larger, rectangular monument with a bronze baldachin supported by spiral marble columns on top.*

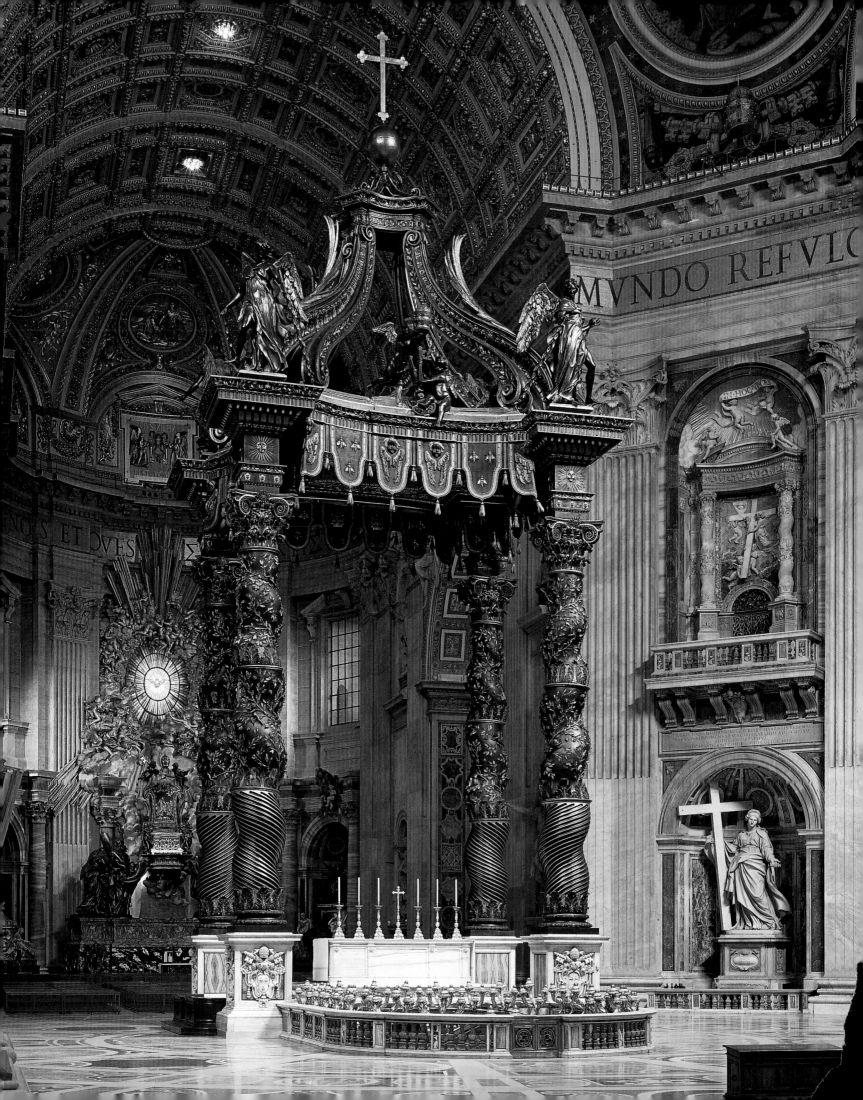

THE BASILICA

Eighteen Popes and Twelve Architects

We've chosen an unusual way to enter the Basilica. What we've done is to come up from the foundations, the very cornerstone. Now we are standing in the midst of the greatest monument of sacred architecture ever built. In a sense, it truly "seals" the Apostle's sepulchre. And as a crowning touch, the cupola by Michelangelo. Taken as a whole, the Basilica is an enormous ciborium or baldachin hovering over Peter's memorial, with the latter at the focal point of the entire architectonic system. In fact, it is located at the crossing of the longitudinal, transversal and vertical axes of the entire edifice.

One is stunned by the monumental size of this great temple. It was erected during the course of a century (1506 to 1616) and under no fewer than eighteen popes, from Julius II to Paul V. Paul, in fact, put his name on the façade. Even afterwards, such popes as Urban VIII and Alexander VII were still promoting important works inside the Basilica, so that work continued straight through to the middle of the 16th century. The tormented course of this vast project—undertaken and later modified by eleven successive architects—is a fascinating story.

Donato Bramante, one of the founding fathers of Renaissance architecture, drew up the initial plan in 1506. He conceived the basilica in the shape of a Greek cross, to be topped by a cupola whose vertical axis would come directly down to the tomb of the Apostle.

Bramante wished to "place the dome of the Pantheon atop the huge vaulting of the Basilica of Maxentius". Which is to say, to outdo the most sublime architecture of the classical world in order to glorify Peter. Both Raphael and Giuliano da Sangallo subsequently objected to Bramante's plan, bringing the designs back to a Latin cross. Antonio da Sangallo perfected the project and made a model in wood of the basilica that is recognizable to us today. In 1545,

Michelangelo radically revised Bramante's plan. The entire edifice, he reasoned, should be like a pedestal for a vast dome that would stand forth from a lofty tambour.

The conception of a curved cupola was transformed by Giacomo della Porta and Domenico Fontana into a pointed arch, which gave to the whole a thrust and spatial harmony that we still admire today. Indeed, we think of it as being inseparable from the Roman skyline. Finally, Carlo Maderno definitively settled on the notion of a Latin cross with a generous lengthening of the central nave. This not only permitted a much greater participation by the faithful; it allowed him to include in the new plan all those art works that were a part of what remained of the original basilica. Finally, between 1612 and 1616, the imposing façade with its immense columns was brought to completion.

For certain stretches of time, as many as 2,000 workers were engaged on the vast project. Eight hundred alone toiled on the tambour. They undertook twenty-two months of frenzied labor, working even at night by torchlight, in order to gratify Sixtus V's pressing desire to bring the whole thing to conclusion. Finally, on May 14, 1590, the cupola was completed. But the official consecration of the "Temple"—as the new St. Peter's then came to be called—was officiated by Pope Urban VIII on November 18, 1626. By all accounts, that date marked the 1,300th anniversary of Constantine's original basilica.

The measurements of all the other great basilicas throughout the Christian world are marked on the marble floor of the central nave. They speak eloquently of the vastness of this one, which covers an area of 44,000 square meters. St. Peter's is 187 meters long, and this figure becomes 219 if you add the portico and the width of the walls. The façade of the church is as big as a soccer field, being 114 meters wide and 46 meters tall. With its diameter of 42.5 meters, the cupola virtually matches that of the Pantheon. At the summit of its cross, it stands 136 meters high.

A "Theological" Construction

Inside, one is overwhelmed by the gold, the sumptuous statues, the solemn funerary monuments of the popes, and above all by the great scenographic triumph of Bernini's

The Altar and the Baldachin. Over the course of the centuries, three altars were placed over the original "memorial" to Peter. The last one, consecrated by Clement VIII in 1594, is a block of marble from Nerva's Forum. The gilt bronze baldachin, which is 29 meters high not including the cross, is the work of Bernini, who finished it in 1633.

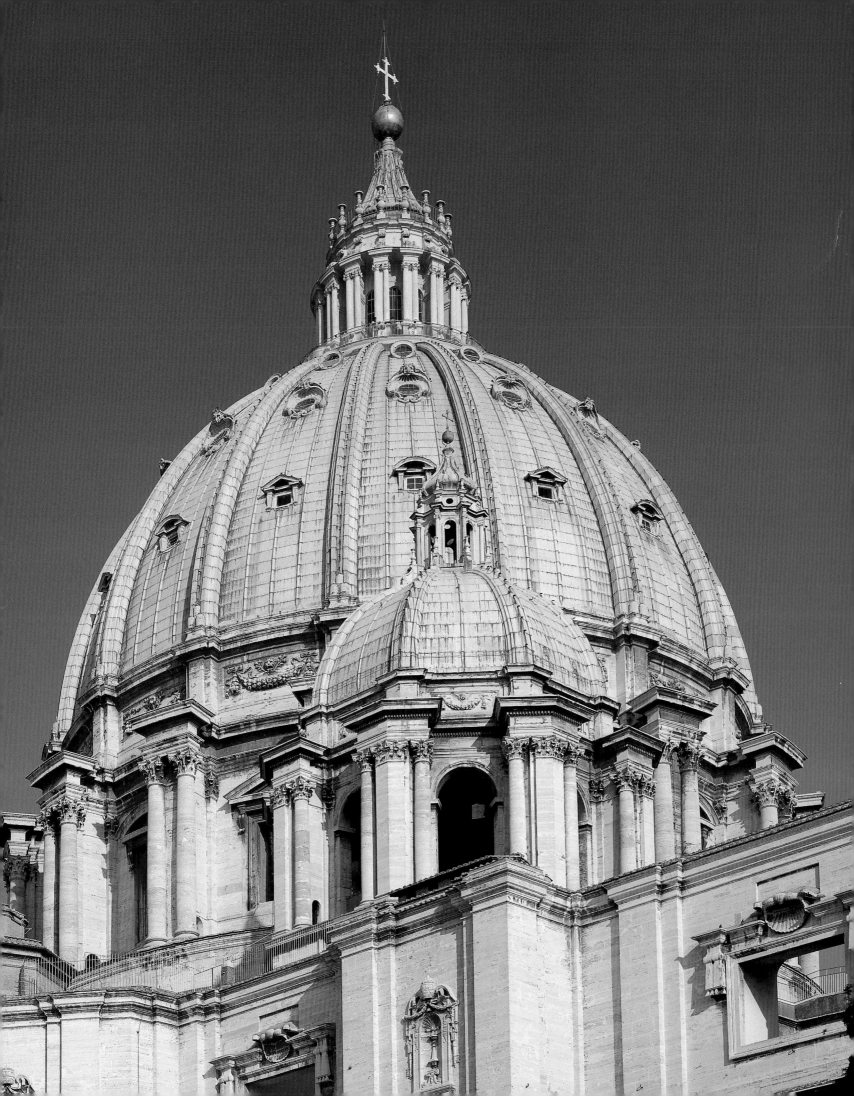

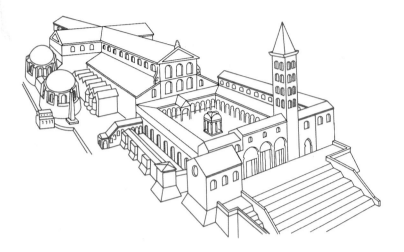

Constantine's Basilica *was probably consecrated in 326 by Pope Sylvester I. In front of the entrance was a vast, outdoor atrium, a rectangular area surrounded by porticoes, with a bronze fountain for holy ablutions standing in the center. It was built in the shape of a pine cone and may be seen today in the courtyard of the same name in the Vatican Museums. To the left of the transept is the rotunda, built under Emperor Caracalla (211-217). Between it and the obelisk, which was later transferred to St. Peter's Square, is another rotunda built during the reign of Theodosius I in approximately the year 400; they both served as mausoleums. The areas marked in red in the drawing indicate later additions to the original basilica.*

baldachin above the confessional altar. Inevitably, we are filled with a feeling of reverence and awe in the presence of so much grandeur. Nor is the interior of St. Peter's, as some have suggested, a purely theatrical experience. After the initial impact, the pilgrim begins to comprehend the sacred message that the building imparts.

The entire construction is dedicated to Peter's special mission. Indeed, the great block letters at the base of the tambour beneath the cupola say as much: "Thou Art Peter, and Upon This Rock I Will Build My Church." We understand then that we are in the presence of an architectural masterpiece that is also a theological edifice. No other church in the world can proclaim itself the visual expression of Christ's words. If Peter is the rock upon which the community of believers was founded, this basilica, rising out of a sublime profession of Faith, is surely its visual

View of the Cupola *from the roof of the Basilica.*

realization. Everything we look at is an artistic expression of Christ's mandate.

If we go to the outside of the apse and study Michelangelo's arrangement of windows, pilasters, geometric panels, cornices and dripstones, we perceive a message that is not merely artistic. We can intuit the solidity of the Church through the great horizontal lines before us. At the same time, the powerful vertical thrust of the mighty pilasters is crowned by corinthian capitals. A tension tending toward transcendence is strongly evoked by the propelling force of the cupola, something made emphatic by the sixteen double columns with vaulting ribs that lead all the way up to the cupola's skylight.

The cupola, with its massive profile, seems to be yearning for universality. Michelangelo wanted it immense, so that it

The Nave *and* Aisles of Constantine's Basilica *were 118 meters long. They can be seen in a fresco by Domenico Tasselli formerly in the Vatican Grottoes; the fresco has been detached and is now in the sacristy of the basilica. It was painted before the nave and aisles were destroyed, and shows the wall that Sangallo the Younger built in 1538 to separate this area from the transept of the new basilica under construction.*

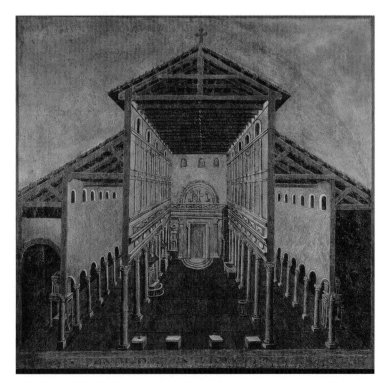

would "embrace all the Christian peoples of the earth." The inside of it could be a pictorial description of Paradise itself.

Through the sixteen large windows, broad ribbons of shimmering light might appear to the visiting pilgrim as if forming a staircase down from heaven itself.

So strong was the writer Stendhal's impression of the place that he made the following entry in his journal. "It would be impossible not to be awed by a religion that has produced such works. Nothing in the world can compare with the interior of St. Peter's. Even after a year's residence in Rome, I would go there for hours to bask in the beauty of it."

The novelist then suggests that the visitor go directly beneath the cupola. "You must sit on a wooden bench and lean back as far as possible. That way, it will be possible to rest while contemplating the immense void that hovers above. However little one might possess of true spirituality, the imagination cannot fail to be staggered by the experience."

Ineffable Lightness

Central to the connection between Michelangelo's cupola and Peter's tomb is the superb bronze baldachin by Gian Lorenzo Bernini. In the midst of the vast basilica, there was the real possibility that Peter's memorial—rather than remaining at the center of everything—might actually disappear.

It was for this reason that Urban VIII, immediately upon his election in 1624, chose "his" sculptor, who he had known from the time he was a youth, to make a dramatic contribution to the Basilica. Specifically, Urban wanted Bernini to create a huge baldachin for the main altar, as if to put a crown over the Apostle's sepulchre.

Bernini conceived this architectural masterpiece as an immense piece of sculpture, a bronze construction fully twenty-nine meters high. Indeed, it was taller than any of the Renaissance palaces in Rome. And yet it somehow communicates a sense of celestial lightness. To our eyes, the twisting movement of the bronze columns suggests a spiralling ascent that loses itself in the bluish-gold light emanating from the mosaics above. These, located in the cupola, depict first Paradise and then (in the very cap of the lantern) God the Father. In effect, the twisting columns of the baldachin repeat the shape of the columns which supported

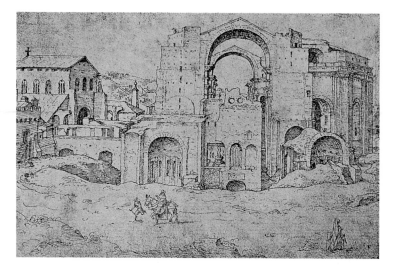

We know what St. Peter's looked like in approximately 1535 because of a drawing by Maarten van Heemskerck. The new construction did not show much progress since Bramante's death in 1514. To the left is a part of the earlier construction in which the nave and aisles are still visible (as well as Sangallo's dividing wall). On the other side of the building site, the top of the obelisk can still be seen in its original location. One of the Confession's spiral columns is visible through a window.

Constantine's ciborium. Eight of these now adorn the four balconies of the pilasters in the cupola, bearing witness to the continuity between the Medieval and the Renaissance ardor in keeping alive the memory of the Apostle.

So far we've been magnetized by the vertical line that rises heavenward from the memorial to the Prince of Apostles. But the horizontal line is no less impressive. Take as an example the entrance to the Basilica. There are five large doors leading into the interior. The door to the far right is the Porta Santa, which is sealed shut and is only opened during a Year of Jubilee. The middle door, with shutters in bronze, was made by Filarete in 1439-45 and was already a part of the earlier basilica. Indeed, the door was the first great work of Renaissance art executed in Rome, although done by a Florentine. Of its six panels, two are dedicated to the martyrdom of Peter and Paul, whereas four horizontal strips narrate the principal episodes in the effort to reunite the Eastern and Western Churches. On the extreme left is the Door of Death (1964), on which the sculptor Giacomo Manzù depicted various ways in which a man might be martyred.

From the very entrance, the main theme of the basilica is evident. The vast central nave with its barrel vaulting 44 meters above ground; the procession of thirty-nine early saints appearing in their niches; the twenty-eight allegorical figures representing the virtues jutting out from the large cornices; the pilasters in precious marbles; the arcade of seemingly triumphal arches—all these draw our gaze in the direction of Bernini's baldachin. It looms before us like a call to prayer above the tomb of the Apostle.

From the baldachin, we naturally look toward the end of the apse and the huge reliquary made by Bernini between 1658 and 1666. Enclosed within is a wooden chair or pulpit believed to have belonged to Peter. In reality, recent studies have revealed that it was a royal throne that the Carolingian sovereign Charles the Bald had made for himself. Probably he presented it to the pope on the occasion of his imperial coronation as Holy Roman Emperor in the Basilica at Christmas in 875.

At the base of the throne are four large statues of early doctors of the Church: the Latin Ambrose and Augustine, and the Oriental Athanasius and John Chrysostom. With their stately gestures they seem to be upholding and sanctioning the authority of the pope, directly inspired by the Holy Spirit. Indeed, the hovering Holy Spirit is depicted as source of all light and wisdom by Bernini's inspired choice of employing yellow-gold Bohemian glass to filter the light.

With the intuition of the genius he was, Bernini was anticipating the times. The placement of the Holy Spirit above the pope seems a prelude to the Dogma of Papal Infallibility, proclaimed in this very basilica during Vatican Council I in 1870. And the presence of the four doctors of the church from East and West would seem to evoke the doctrine of episcopal collegiality affirmed by Vatican Council II in this very setting between 1962-65.

One Holy Catholic and Apostolic Faith

Every work of art within the basilica makes us ponder the unfathomable mystery of the Faith and the Mystical Body of Christ. When the aisles of the Basilica are filled for a papal celebration, everything seems in synchrony between the assembled throngs and the physical fact of the church around them. And it gives us an unequalled emotion to sing out at full volume beneath these vaultings *"Et unam, sanctam, catholicam et apostolicam Ecclesiam"* (one, holy, catholic and apostolic church). How much greater is the emotion of this profession of faith when the ceremony in question is presided over by the successor of Peter, and the crowd before him consists of a multiracial assembly of the faithful!

Here it can be said that the very stones reflect the life of the spirit. "Stones of Light," in fact, is the title of some verses written by the young Bishop Karol Wojtyła in the fall of 1962 when, with 2,300 other bishops, he sat here every morning for the first session of the Council. Some of the lines were inspired by the basilica, whose stones "unify not only the spaces of a Renaissance structure but the spaces within us." "This is the rock," he wrote, "of a massive temple, it is the pasture that brings us to the cross," concluded the future pope.

Nor is it true that it is difficult to pray inside St. Peter's. "Choose any of the chapels," wrote Monsignor Ennio Francia, "and you'll suddenly find yourself alone on this holy land, blessed by the blood of Peter and that of the first Christian martyrs. The building has magic, it has all the splendor that could possibly render homage to the Revelation that toppled paganism and built a new civilization on its ashes."

This vast church was modelled to express greatness, and in so doing to buttress the Counter-Reformation. The central nave was lengthened precisely in order to convey the concept of immensity and to accommodate the grandiose ceremonies and extensive processions. It was inconceivable to abandon a sacred area as rich in religious connotations as the one, amid which rose the nave of Constantine's temple.

In our time, the immense central nave has been turned into the Hall of a Great Council. That great length has become synonymous with universality. The historic events of the Church, the solemn celebrations, the canonizations and beatifications, the councils and synods, have always found there an adequate backdrop. The concrete expression in architecture of Peter's profession of faith helps us to concentrate our gaze on his successor, the visible vicar on earth today. From the Apostle to the Church, from the Church to the pope. The basilica thus serves to connect all this. All three stand beside Christ, whose cross is everywhere triumphant and whose words—spelled out for all to see along the basilica's great horizontal trabeation—serve to fuse forever faith and art.

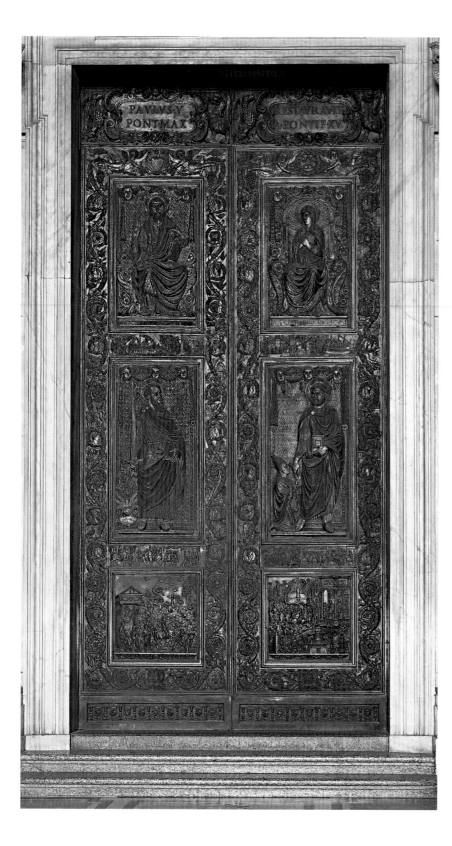

The main door of St Peter's. It was carved in 1445 for Constantine's Basilica by the Florentine artist, Antonio Averulino, called Il Filarete. The six larger panels depict Christ the Savior, the Virgin Mary, St. Paul, St Peter and the stories of their martyrdom. In 1620, additions were made to the top and bottom bringing the doors to a height of 6.5 meters, to fit the entrance of the new basilica. Eugene IV Condulmer, who donated the bronze door, is portrayed at St. Peter's feet. The four decorative bands separating the relief panels depict events from the years of his reign, specifically the 1439 Council of Florence, where the unification of the Orthodox and Catholic churches was discussed. The space surrounding the two saints is decorated with Arabic writing. Carved amidst the acanthus volutes on the borders are scenes of animals and characters from history and ancient mythology, a typical decoration of the Renaissance inspired by classical art. This door is the earliest example of Renaissance art in Rome.

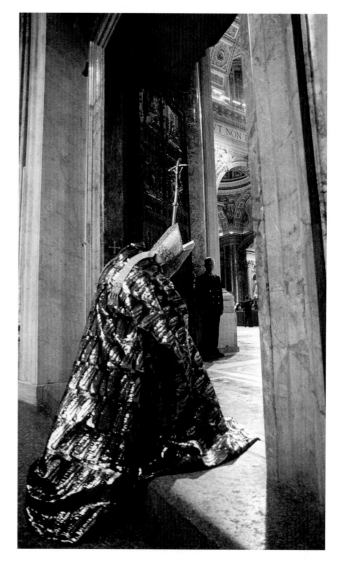

John Paul II crosses the threshold of the Holy Door at the beginning of the 2000 Jubilee. Traditionally, the Holy Door is opened by the pope only at the beginning of a Holy Year, and is closed again at the end of the Jubilee. It remains sealed during the period between one Holy Year and the next.

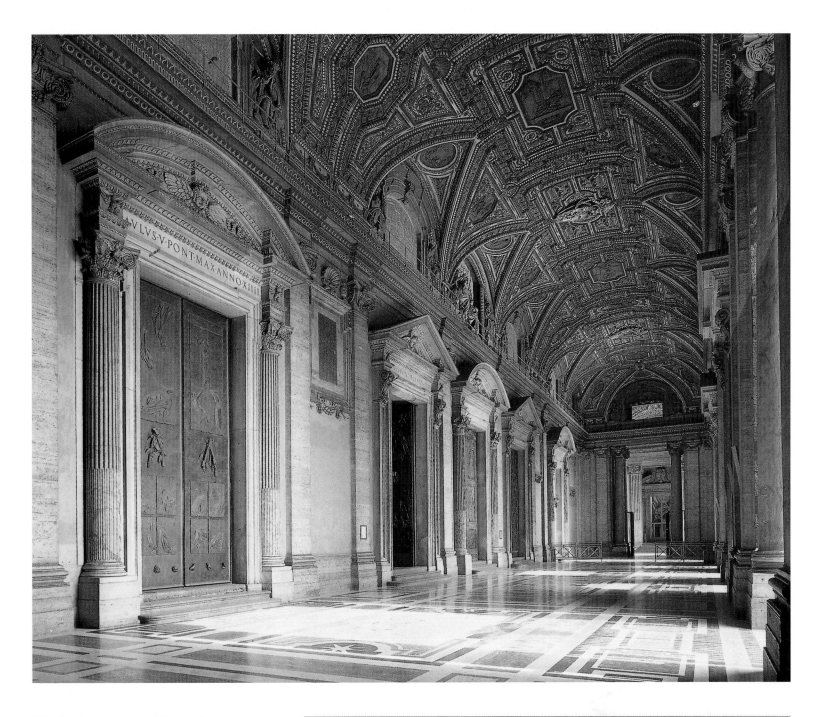

The five bronze doors of the basilica open onto the Atrium: the Door of Death by Giacomo Manzù (1964), donated by Msgr. George of Bavaria, a canon of St. Peter's; the Door of Good and Evil by Luciano Minguzzi (1977); Filarete's door (1445); the Door of the Sacraments by Venanzio Crocetti (1964); and the Holy Door by Vico Consorti, donated by the Swiss Catholics for the 1950 Jubilee.

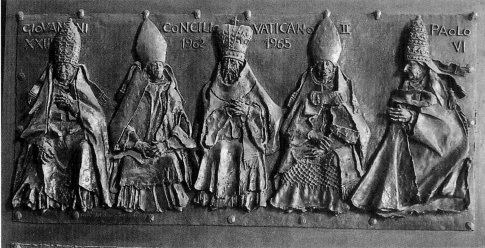

On one panel of the Door of Good and Evil, the sculptor Minguzzi commemorated Vatican Council II (1962-65).

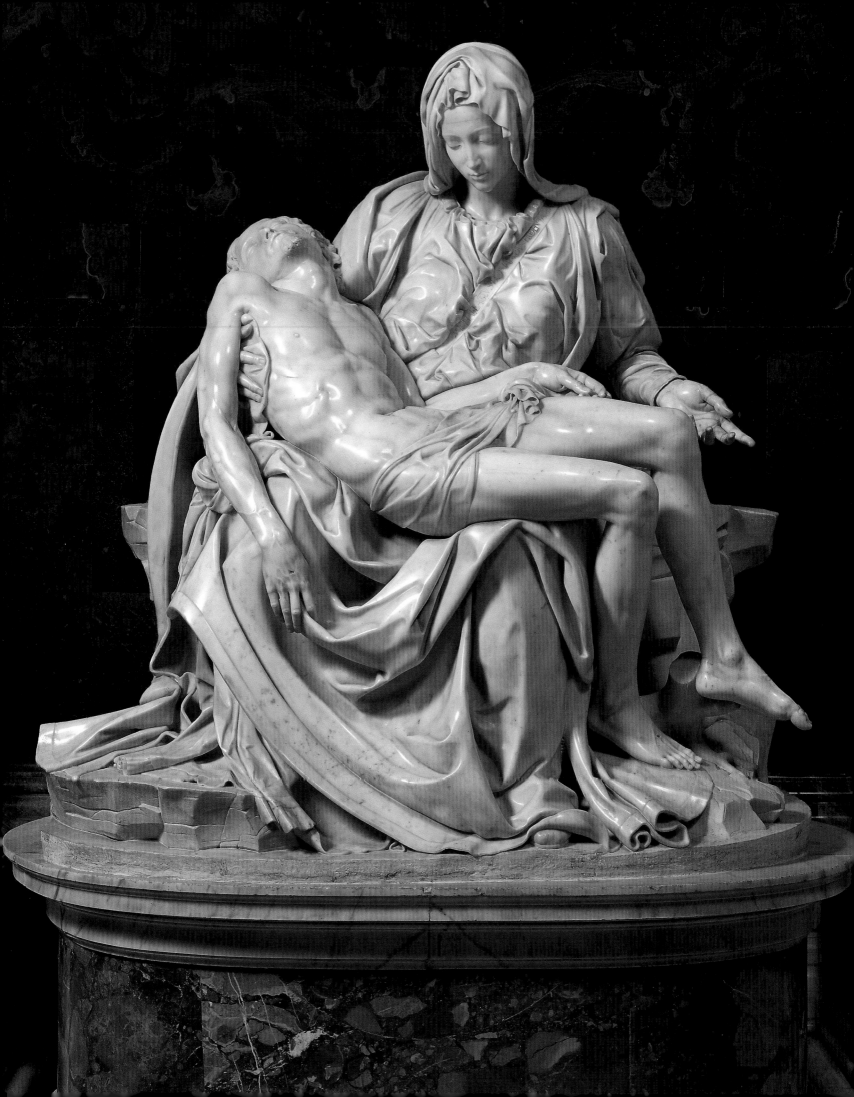

The new nave and aisles of St. Peter's were commissioned by Paul V Borghese and built by Carlo Maderno in 1608-12. The mosaic inscription around the inside of the cupola (above, right) is written in Latin, signifying: "Thou art Peter and upon this rock I will build my Church and I will give to thee the keys of the kingdom of heaven". Peter's mission is also recalled beneath the cornice which runs along the nave and the cross vault. The nave (below), from the entrance to the apse, is 186.36 meters long. The decoration of the basilica, begun during the papacy of Urban VIII Barberini for the 1650 Holy Year celebrations, was designed and supervised by Bernini.

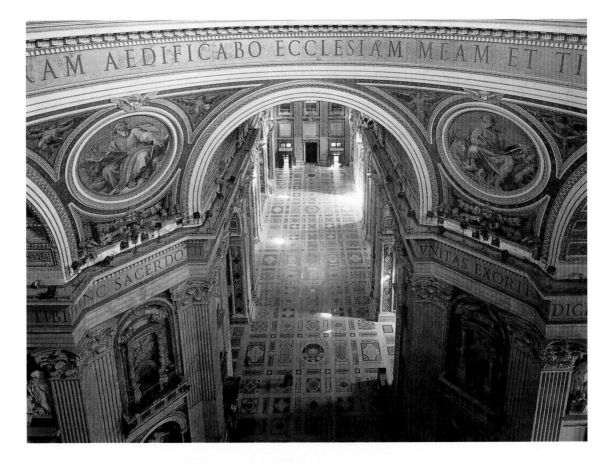

The Pietà was carved out of a single block of Carrara marble by Michelangelo, who added his signature and the adjective "fiorentino" (Florentine) to the Madonna's sash. The Pietà was commissioned by Cardinal Jean de Villiers de la Groslaye, the French ambassador to Rome. The twenty-one year old Florentine artist worked for more than two years, from 1498 to 1500, to complete the statue. Its composition is based on French sculptures of the same subject popular in the previous century, although Michelangelo has created a radically new portrayal of the Mother holding her dead Son. Michelangelo's classical training is revealed in the perfect proportions of the life-size bodies and their relationship to each other, the youthful yet timeless faces, and the Virgin Mary's expression of calm, mournful resignation. The concept of the Redemption, which had previously always been linked to representations of grief, appears to generate a mood of classical serenity in this work.

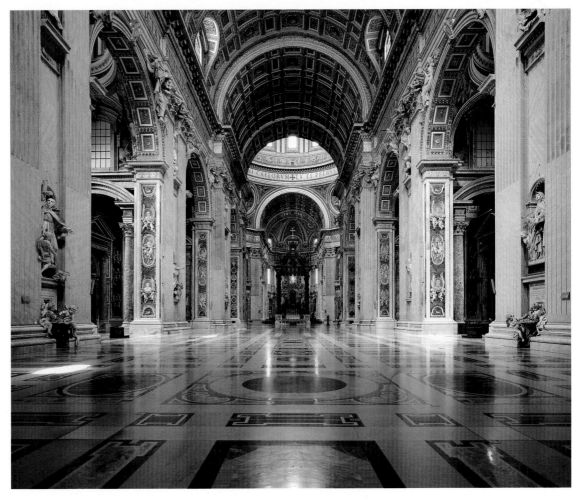

The cupola *designed by Donato Bramante had been included in the original construction plans for the new basilica. The Rovere pope Julius II laid the first stone on April 18th, 1506 below the column of Veronica. At Bramante's death in 1514 only the piers (with a perimeter measuring 71 meters) and the huge connecting arches (44.8 meters high) had been completed. Michelangelo worked on the construction of the dome's tambour from 1546 until his death in 1564. In 1590 Giacomo della Porta and Domenico Fontana completed the vault; the following year they finished work on the lantern. On the inside (right), the mosaics were composed at the end of the century from cartoons by Cavalier d'Arpino; the scenes depict the circles of Paradise with God the Father at the summit. In the eye of the lantern there is an inscription dedicated to Sixtus V, under whose patronage the work was completed. From the floor to the top of the cross the cupola is 136.57 meters high; its interior diameter is 42.56 meters.*

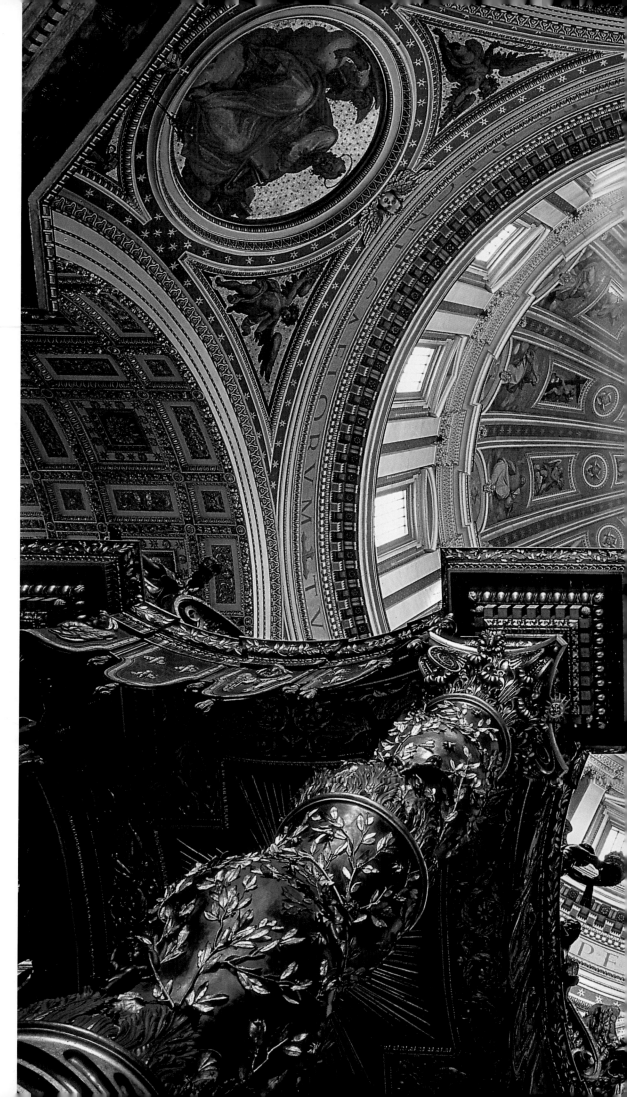

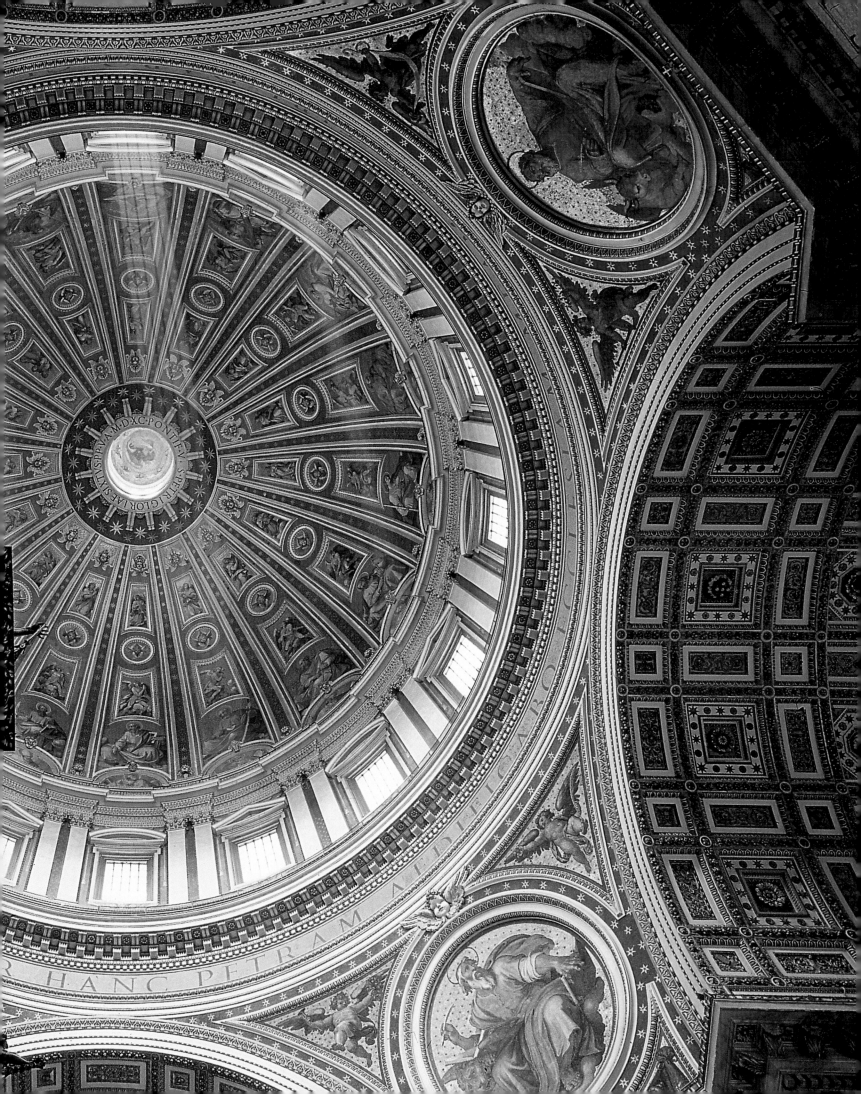

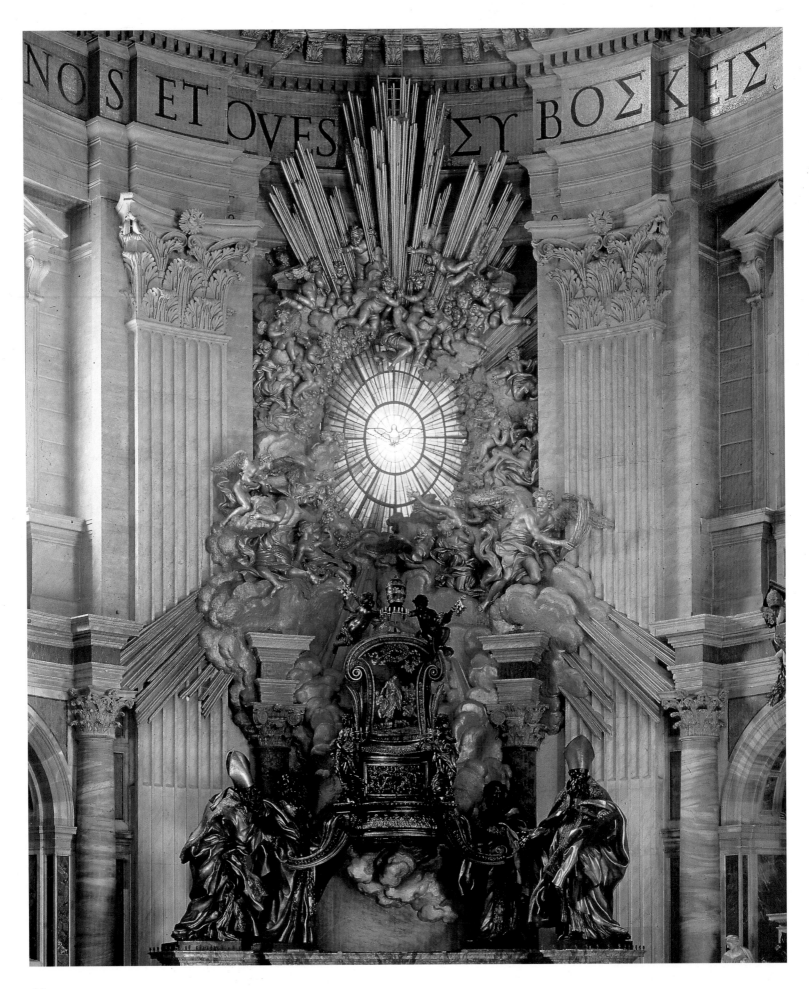

Cathedra of St. Peter in Glory (previous page). *This enormous reliquary, designed and built by Bernini in 1658-66, surrounds the throne that tradition attributed to Peter. The four Doctors of the Church stand at the base of the chair: two Western ones, Ambrose and Augustine (wearing miters), and two Eastern ones, Athanasius and John Chrysostom. With this magnificent, phantasmagoric work, the artist terminated the decoration of the basilica. It was at once a triumph of the Baroque and a celebration of papal primacy. Almost exactly a century and a half had passed since the first stone of the vast temple was laid (April 18, 1506); its construction was the spark that ignited Protestant reaction.*

The Triple Crown *(on the right)* is the papal tiara comprising the three crowns which symbolize the pope's threefold power as Father of Kings, Rector of the World and Vicar of Christ. Dating from the 18th century, it is used to crown the bronze statue of St. Peter on June 29th, St. Peter's feast day. The traditional use of the tiara by the pope during official ceremonies ceased during Paul VI's papacy.

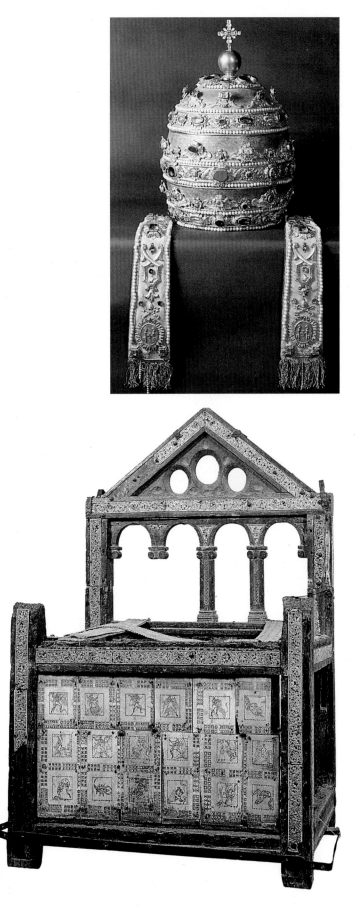

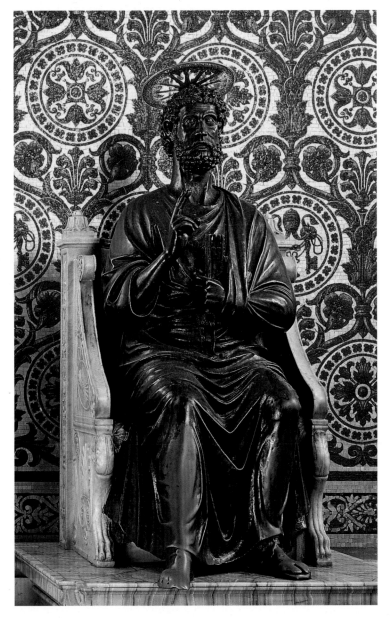

The bronze statue of St. Peter *is traditionally attributed to Arnolfo di Cambio. In recent years some scholars have suggested that it is the work of an unknown Syrian artist of the 4th century.*

St. Peter's Cathedra *was the imperial throne of Charles the Bald which he presented to Pope John VIII in 875, the year he was crowned Holy Roman Emperor in St Peter's.*

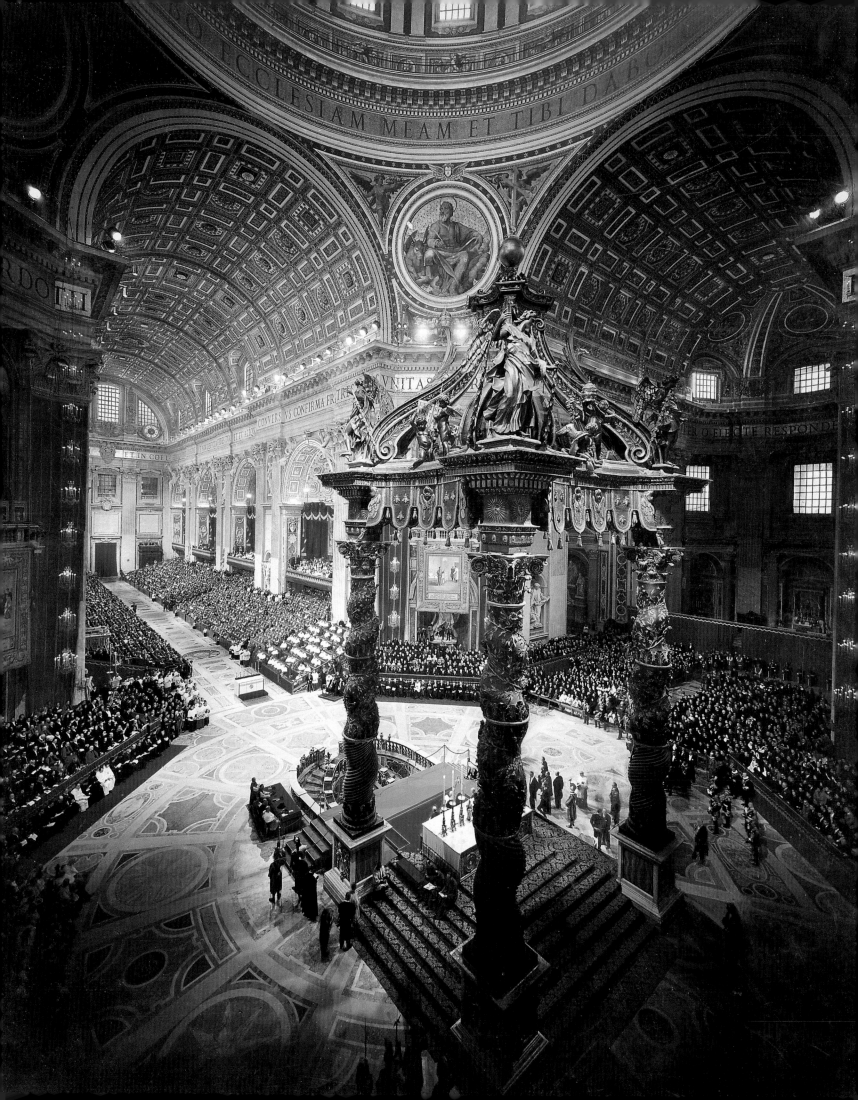

The Synod of Bishops *(an "assembly" of bishops)* was instituted by Pope Paul VI on September 25, 1965 to ensure a more unified and efficient collaboration between the pope and the bishops. Since 1971 the Synods are held in a smaller room in the same building as the Hall of Papal Audiences.

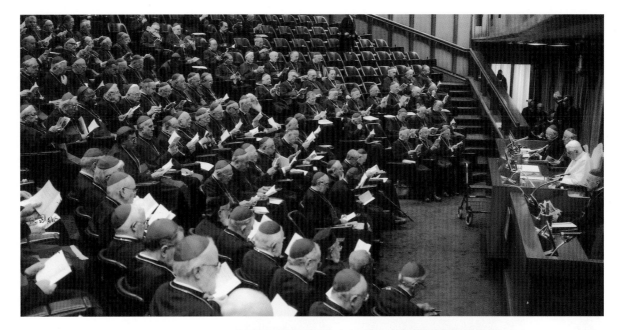

The Sacred College of Cardinals *was instituted in 1150, but from the earliest times, a group of prelates of the Roman clergy has always assisted the Bishop of Rome in governing the church. The pope gathers the College of Cardinals into a consistory (church tribunal) to decide matters of special importance and to grant greater solemnity to specific resolutions. Since 1054 the cardinals have held conclaves (Latin for "closed with a key") in which they elect the new pope. In this picture the College of Cardinals (right) can be seen gathered outside the Basilica for a public ceremony with the Pope.*

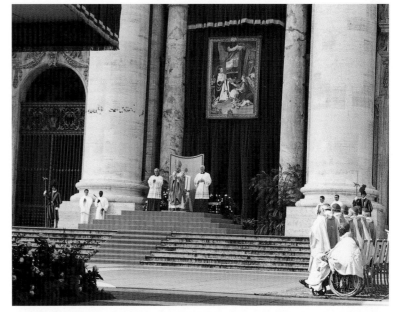

In the exercise of his duties, the pope is assisted by the bishops (more than 4000). As the successors of the Apostles, they are appointed directly by the pontiff and meet with him in Ecumenical Councils (right) to make decisions on matters concerning the Church.

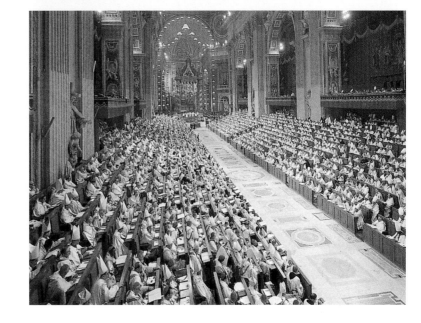

St. Peter's Basilica during a Council. Maderno's semicircular opening in the floor of the basilica so that the faithful can see the Confession is clearly shown in the photo.

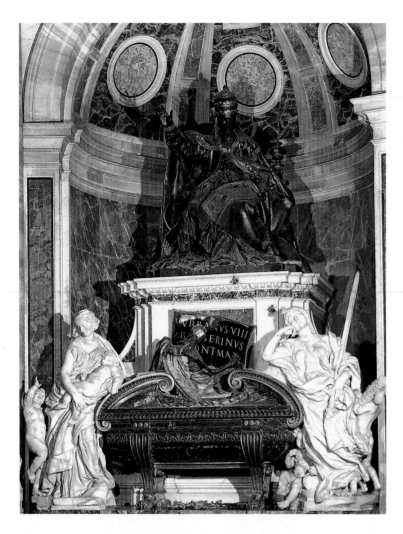

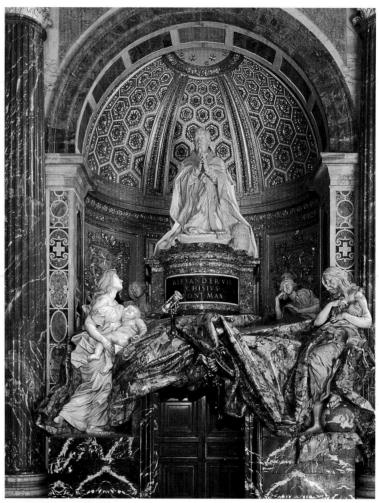

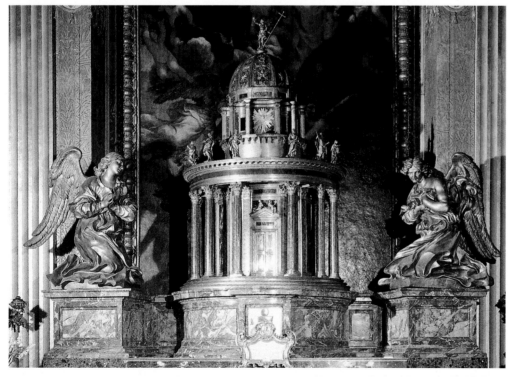

The tomb of Urban VIII *by Gianlorenzo Bernini (above, on the left). Pope Barberini commissioned this splendid portrait, in which the sculptor is clearly exalting the role of the papacy. It blends perfectly with the rest of the decoration of the basilica and was intended to glorify Peter and his successors. Charity and Justice watch over the scene of the triumph of the pope, while Death writes out his name.*

In the tomb of Alexander VII *(above, on the right), Bernini probably intended the pope's gesture to symbolize his devoted asceticism. The artist was nearly eighty years old when he designed this monument (1671-78). Bernini had been one of the innovators of the Baroque style, and this sculpture is a good example of its extravagant ornateness. The figures of Charity and Truth are in the foreground, and Justice and Prudence are placed around the base.*

In the Chapel of the Sacrament, the *ciborium in gilt bronze with the angels are late works by Bernini (1673-74). It clearly shows the influence of Bramante's* Tempietto *in the church of San Pietro in Montorio.*

Four expressive Baroque statues dating from 1629-40 at the base of the piers supporting the dome: *St. Longinus by Bernini (in the center), St. Helen by Andrea Bolgi (right, above), Veronica by Francesco Mochi (right, in the center), St. Andrew by François Duquesnoy (right, below).*

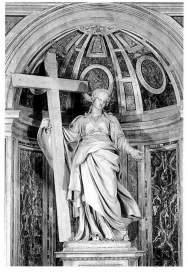

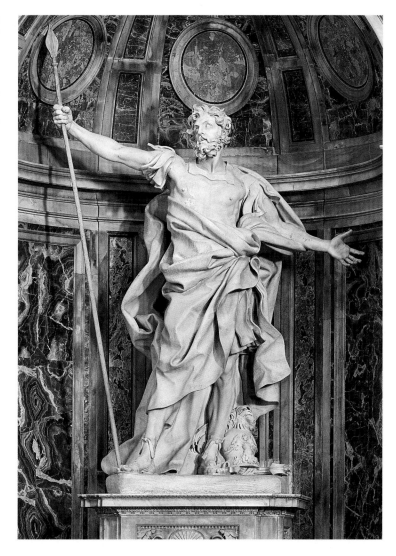

The baptismal font, *(below),* consists of a porphyry basin, measuring four by two meters, which dates from the Roman imperial age. The gilt bronze cover, with the Holy Trinity blessing the world in the center, was designed in the 1690s by Carlo Fontana.

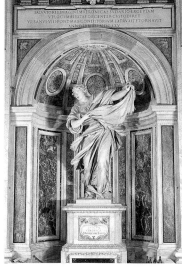

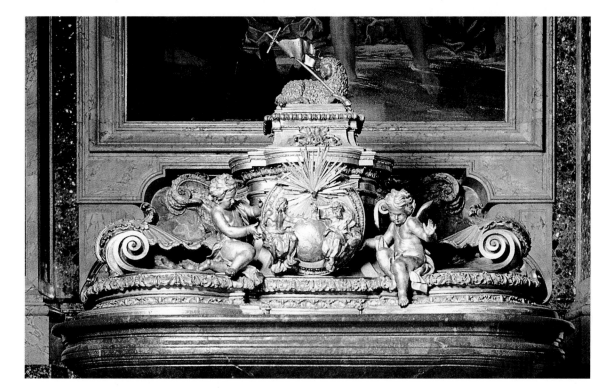

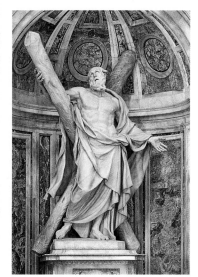

The *Vatican Holy Grottoes*. Besides the crypt, built by Gregory I in the 6ᵗʰ century by raising the presbytery of Constantine's basilica, the grottoes of St. Peter's include a large area between the floors of the old and new basilicas. Popes and kings are buried here. Between 1935 and 1950, it was turned into a burial church with a nave and two aisles. The monument of Pius VI (right), sculpted by Antonio Canova, is at the far end of the Grottoes.

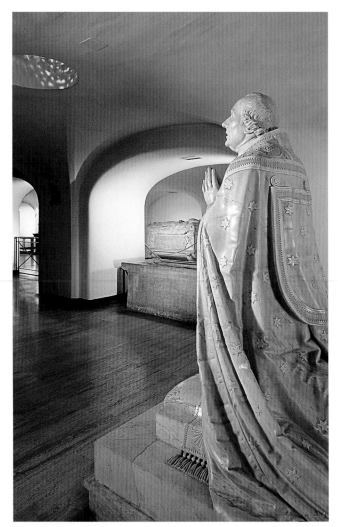

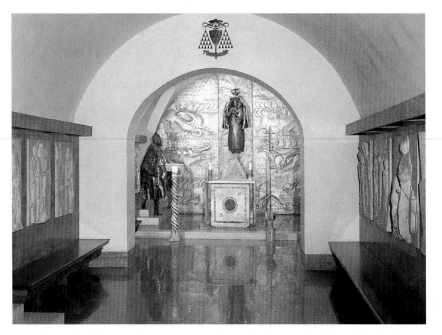

The Hungarian Chapel *was consecrated in 1980. To the left of the altar, the statue of St. Stephen; along the side walls, bas-reliefs depicting stories from the lives of Hungarian saints. All of the decoration was done by Hungarian artists.*

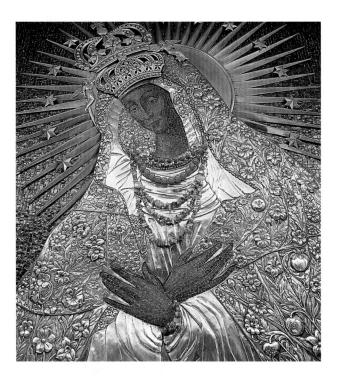

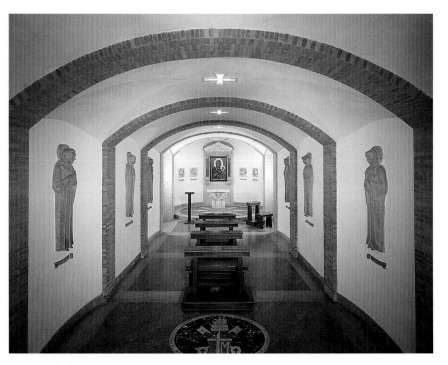

On the periphery of the Vatican grottoes, the Lithuanian Chapel *consecrated in 1970. A portrait of the Madonna of Vilnius is on the altar.*

The Polish Chapel *was consecrated by Pope Pius XII in 1958 and later enlarged in 1982. On the altar is a mosaic reproduction of the Madonna of Czestochowa.*

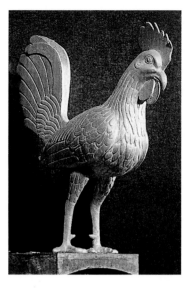

The cockerel (9th century during the reign of Leo IV) that stood on the belfry of the original St. Peter's.

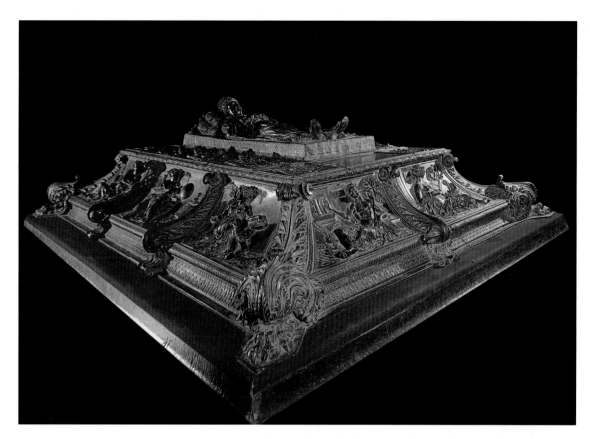

The bronze tomb of Sixtus IV, founder of the Sistine Chapel. A true "manifesto" of Renaissance Christian art, it was carved in 1493 by Antonio del Pollaiolo. The artist has placed the three Theological Virtues and the four Cardinal Virtues on either side of the pope; along the base of the sarcophagus are the seven Liberal Arts and the art of Perspective.

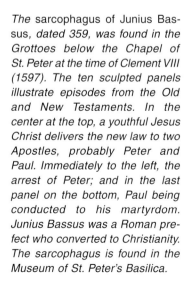

The sarcophagus of Junius Bassus, dated 359, was found in the Grottoes below the Chapel of St. Peter at the time of Clement VIII (1597). The ten sculpted panels illustrate episodes from the Old and New Testaments. In the center at the top, a youthful Jesus Christ delivers the new law to two Apostles, probably Peter and Paul. Immediately to the left, the arrest of Peter; and in the last panel on the bottom, Paul being conducted to his martyrdom. Junius Bassus was a Roman prefect who converted to Christianity. The sarcophagus is found in the Museum of St. Peter's Basilica.

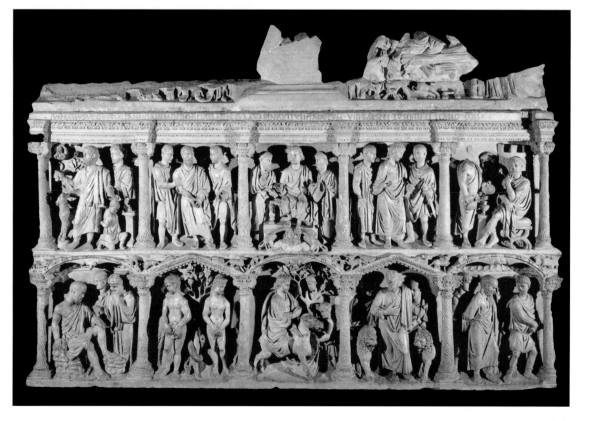

The Palaces

Ubi Papa, ibi Roma

As the basilica is the great custodian of Peter's tomb, so is the Apostolic Palace the building's extension. In a certain sense it is the rectory of St. Peter's. Architecturally, "the pope's house" represents a continuity with the basilica, even if when viewed from above this isn't immediately evident. In effect, it is a whole collection of buildings, the heart of which dates back from the thirteenth to the seventeenth century.

Everything that happens here centers around the pope. As the successor to Peter and the Bishop of Rome, he is the universal shepherd of Christ's flock, helmsman of the mystic ship of the Lord. And, to continue the metaphor, the pontifical palace is like the bridge of this ship.

Observing the Holy Father in his multiple activities as teacher, author of encyclicals, governor of the Church, watching him appear at general audiences and in the performance of the solemn acts of his ministry, one can't help but think of the nine titles that illustrate the offices of every pope. For the pope is at once Bishop of Rome, Vicar of Christ, successor to the Prince of Apostles, Sovereign Pontiff of the Universal Church, Patriarch of the West, Primate of Italy, Archbishop and Metropolitan of the Province of Rome (an area as large as the region of Latium), Sovereign of the Vatican City-State, and Servant of God's Servants. This last title was a humble afterthought coined by St. Gregory the Great in reply to the Patriarch of Constantinople who wished to call himself ecumenical or universal patriarch.

The least important of the pope's many titles regards his territorial sovereignty over the city-state. The Vatican, after all, is but the material infrastructure of the Holy See, which is the juridical expression of the central government of the church. The Vatican exists for the pope and not vice versa. If by misfortune the pope were deprived of it, it is not as though his authority would be in any way diminished. In fact, the more than 160 ambassadors from all over the world are accredited to the Holy See and not to the Vatican. That is what the celebrated jurist Enrico da Segusia, known as Cardinal Ostiense, had in mind when he stated *"Ubi est papa, ibi est Roma"* ("the seat in Rome is wherever the pope is"). The primacy of Peter is invested in him inasmuch as he is the bishop of the seat inherited from the first apostle.

Several Centuries in a Few Meters

Not many visitors are aware that the first residence of the popes was not the Vatican but the Lateran Palace. They lived there for nearly a thousand years, from the time of Constantine to the time of exile in Avignon. Even today, the Lateran basilica is the cathedral of the Bishop of Rome. But few tourists who visit the Vatican manage also to fit into their schedule this medieval edifice to which was added, in Renaissance times, loggias by Bramante and Raphael.

It is an extraordinary experience, going back centuries in time while merely covering a few meters. This is what happens inside the Vatican when we pass from the St. Damasus courtyard, surrounded by buildings erected in the 16th century, and cross through the Parrot, Borgia and Sentinella courtyards. The open spaces grow narrower; there is less light, and severe defensive structures rise all around us. Thus we have gone from the end of the 1500s, when Sixtus V had the present-day Apostolic Palace built, back to the first half of the fifteenth century and even as far back as 1277-1280, the years in which the Orsini pope Nicholas III broke all precedent by taking up residence in the Vatican.

These are two separate worlds in terms of city planning. From the Renaissance splendor with its spacious loggias opening out toward the city, we are catapulted backward to an era obsessed with the necessity of defending itself from external enemies. Between towers and sturdy fortifications with narrow windows, we can speak of a "fortified home" without danger of exaggeration.

In the adjacent *Cortile del Maresciallo* we will see how Bramante and Raphael, in the early years of the 16th century, built the new façade of the Renaissance palace in part by adding onto the prior medieval constructions. The new way of building walls and pilasters marked the transformation into a new epoch. Above the archway in one of the side entrances, walled up to permit the construction of the loggias, we can still see the coat of arms of the Piccolomini pope Pius II (1458-64).

In order to understand the development of the apostolic palaces within the Vatican, it is necessary to go back many centuries. For a millennium, as we said, the popes lived in the Lateran Palace next to their cathedral. In all that time, the basilica next to Vatican Hill remained a cemetery church located in open country. Next to it was a monastery and a few

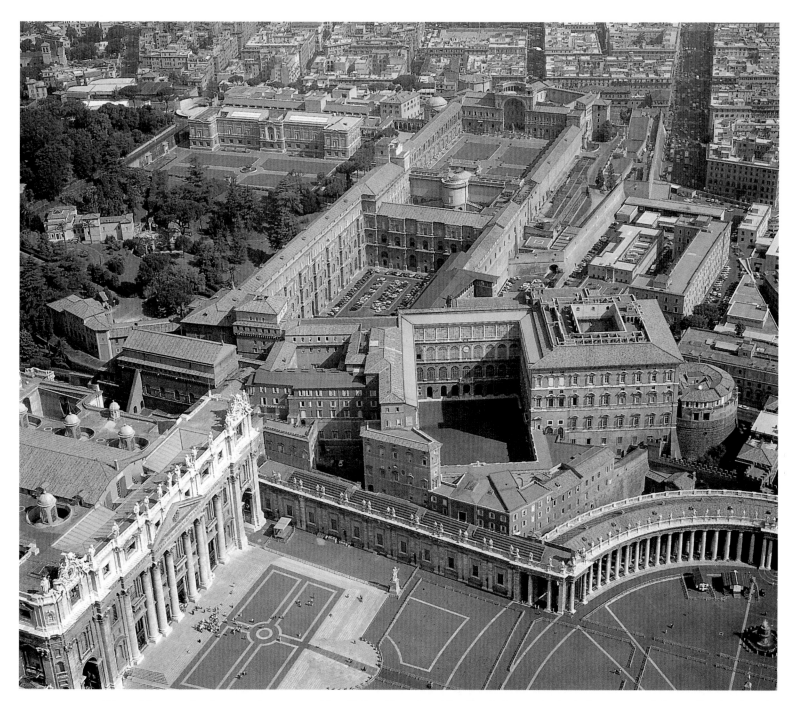

View of the papal palaces and museums. *The Sistine Chapel and the Borgia Tower dominate the square of the medieval palace. In the center, the Courtyard of St. Damasus and the Sistine Palace, with Nicholas V's Tower below. Towards the rear, the two long Belvedere Corridors, with the sloping area conceived by Julius II and Bramante, crossed by the Sistine Library and the* Braccio Nuovo *(new extension) of the museums. In the background is the* Nicchione della Pigna *(large niche of the pine cone). The Tower of the Winds is clearly visible beyond the middle of the left corridor. Also to the left, in the distance, is the* Pinacoteca *(Picture Gallery) and the administrative offices of the Vatican Museums. Among the trees are the* Casina of Pius IV *and the Pontifical Academy of Science.*

The Basilica of St. John Lateran. *Alessandro Galilei's main façade dates from 1735, with the eastern view of the Lateranensis Palace and Clement XII's new layout.*

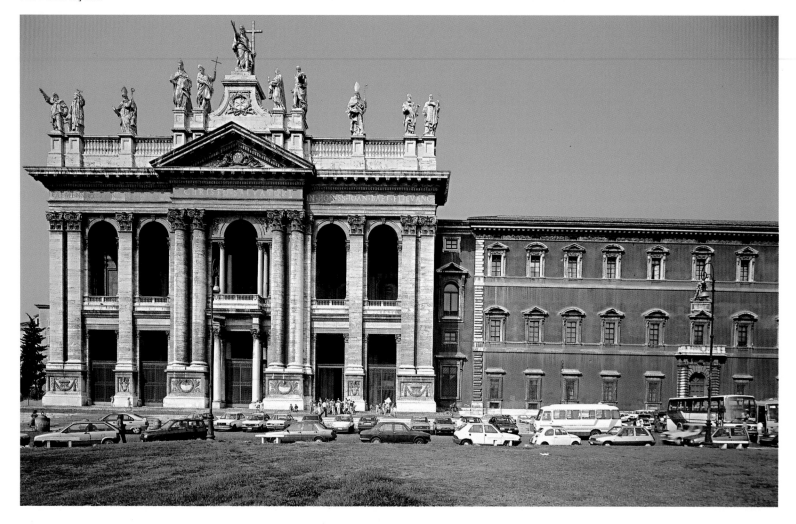

dwellings for the custodian and the clergy who officiated at the basilica. At the same time, precisely because it was across the Tiber and thought to be an unhealthy zone, the little cluster of buildings next to St. Peter's offered safe refuge to the popes during turbulent times.

Pope Symmachus took shelter there during the Laurentian Schism (501-506), building two bishop's residences right next to the basilica. A *Palatium Caroli* was added by Leo III on the occasion of the visit to Rome by Charlemagne (799-800). Three decades later, Gregory IV added guest quarters in order to be able to spend the night there and not

have to return to the Lateran on the vigil of important feasts and commemorations at St. Peter's.

When the Vatican was sacked in 846 by more than 10,000 Saracen pirates, Pope Leo IV decided to erect a wall—twelve meters high and with no fewer than forty-four towers—to protect the basilica and the nearby hill. It ran from the banks of the Tiber and included the Castel S. Angelo fortress. Thus, the "Leonine city" came into being, parts of which are still visible today within the boundaries of the Vatican gardens. This ninth century walled city became the basis for all future development of the area.

The Basilica of St. John Lateran *the cathedral of Rome, before the renovation commissioned by Innocent X in the 17th century. This fresco in the church of San Martino ai Monti dates from the first half of the 17th century and shows the Lateran Basilica in its medieval form.*

Pope Boniface VIII *(on the right), in the Loggia delle Benedizioni of the Lateran Palace, proclaims the year 1300 as the first Holy Year. This is from a manuscript dating from the 16th century (Biblioteca Ambrosiana, Milan) and is a copy of a fresco by Giotto dating from around 1308. Most of it was lost but a fragment remains in the Lateran Palace.*

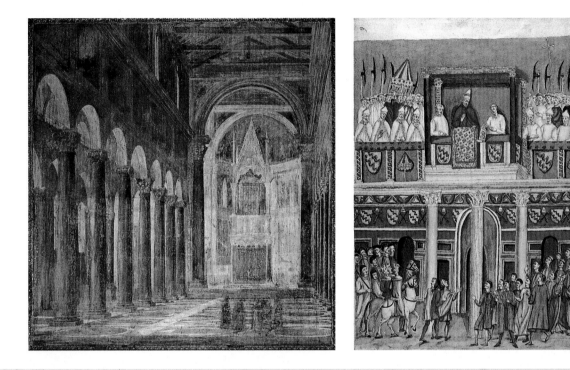

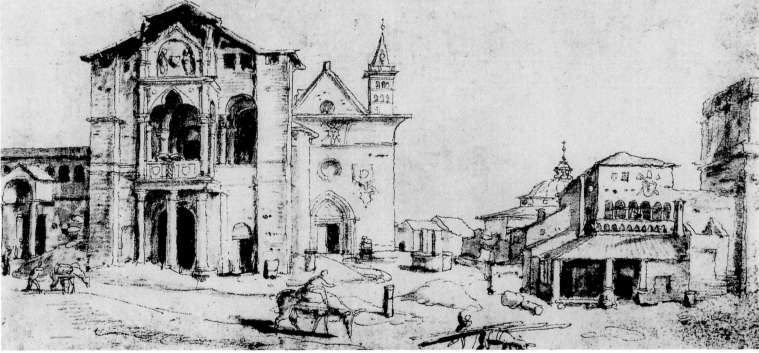

Before their exile to Avignon (1309-77), the pope and the Roman Curia resided in the palace next to the Basilica of St. John Lateran. The Lateran Palace, *with Boniface VIII's* Loggia delle Benedizioni, *as it appeared in a drawing made in 1534 by Maarten van Heemskerck (in the Kupferstichkabinett, Berlin). To the right, the façade of the basilica's transept. After 1309 the Lateran Palace was never again used as the popes' residence.*

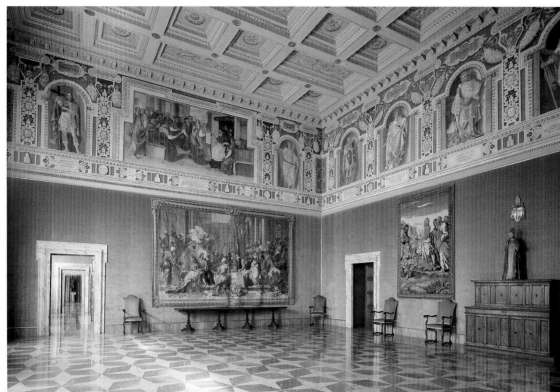

The rooms used for official ceremonies in the Lateran's Apostolic Palace *are a series of frescoed halls, decorated with a rich collection of 17th and 18th century Italian and French tapestries.*

Below, left and right, the open galleries next to the monumental halls have been turned into the Vatican History Museum *displaying relics of the combat forces of the Pontifical State, the lay court, abolished by the 1978 reform, as well as ceremonial objects that were no longer in use. A rich collection of papal portraits dating from the 16th century onwards is also found in this museum.*

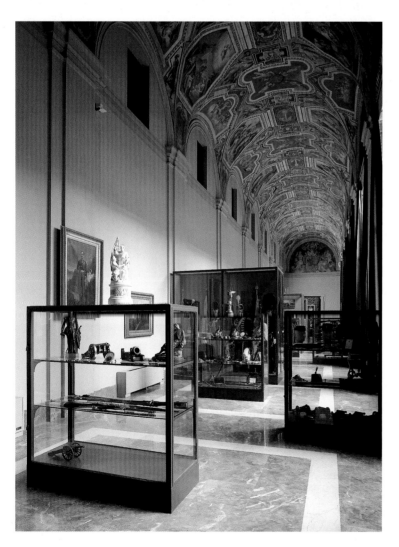

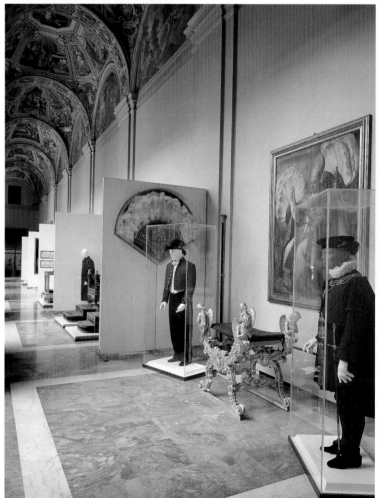

Eugenius III, between 1145 and 1153, had a palace built to the south of the basilica, perhaps adding to one of those constructed earlier by Symmachus. But Innocent III (1198-1216) who brought the Holy See's temporal power to its apogee, dominating the entire Christian world of his day, was oddly victimized by the political factions within Rome itself. Often he had to seek refuge within the Vatican, where he built onto the palace of Pope Eugenius and ordered the construction of a second wall around the city. By now, it had become the alternate residence of the popes.

A Four-sided Fortress

Innocent IV (1243-1254) enlarged the Vatican complex by adding a new palace replete with towers erected on the hill to the north of the church. Subsequently, his home-fortress became a part of Nicholas III's project for a four-sided series of crenelated buildings surrounded by towers. In the three years of his reign (1277-1280), Nicholas lived permanently within the Vatican. Of the four-sided complex, he was able to finish the south side (facing the basilica) and that of the east, giving out toward the city. That view looked out over a garden, now the present-day Courtyard of St. Damasus.

In order to observe the structure of this medieval palace, one must go to the cupola of St. Peter's. From there, everything appears as if it were on a map. First we must locate the Parrot Courtyard, so called because at the top of it there were numerous decorations of mythological birds. Of the fortified square begun by Nicholas III, two of the towers are no longer visible because they were either knocked down or incorporated into successive constructions. Still standing is the fortification that surrounds the Sistine Chapel and the tower built by the Borgia pope.

The four-sided fortress was completed almost two centuries later. The north side was finished in the middle of the fifteenth century by Nicholas V, whereas the west side was concluded still later. Before it was finished, there was first the seventy-year absence in Avignon (1309-1377) and then the nearly four decades of the Great Western Schism (1378-1417), during which there were simultaneously a pope and two anti-popes.

Upon his return to Rome from Avignon in 1377, Gregory XI found the Lateran Palace destroyed by fire. That was the initial reason he and his successors decided to live in the Vatican. But it wasn't until Nicholas V, the Humanist pope who ruled the Church from 1447 to 1455, that a large-scale building program was seriously begun. Nicholas was also the pope who founded the Vatican Library. Not surprisingly, it was said of him that he "spent most willingly on books and buildings."

Though he left untouched the outer fortifications, this pope from Tuscany threw open the rooms of his residence to the artists of the Early Renaissance. Fra Angelico, who covered Nicholas's private chapel with frescoes, opened the way for an array of resplendent artists. From this moment and for more than a century, the papal residence was at the center of all that was most exciting in the production of art. All of the humanistic culture was put at the service of papal authority. The popes saw these artists as "the keepers or guardians on earth of the eternal verities," as Nicholas V was wont to say. The patronage of the popes was fueled by a far-reaching intuition: Truth (that is, religion and science), Goodness (ethics and justice) and Beauty (poetry and music) all flowed from the same divine font, and all could be supremely communicated through the figurative arts. This notion was behind all the papal patronage of the Renaissance period, even if not all of them were irreproachable in their private lives or indeed in their way of governing the church.

A worthy successor to Nicholas V as a humanist was the Della Rovere pope Sixtus IV, who reigned from 1471 to 1484. He reestablished the chapel in the palace, thereafter known as the Sistine, and summoned the greatest painters of the age to decorate it. From October 1481 until the following summer, the coordinator for all this was no less than Perugino. In turn, he brought Botticelli, Pinturicchio, Ghirlandaio, Signorelli and Cosimo Rosselli to execute a vast gallery containing the portraits of the popes, preceded by episodes from the Old and New Testaments.

It is to Sixtus IV that we owe the official founding of the Vatican Library. Established on the ground floor of the pontifical residence, it was opened for the first time to the public during the 1470s. Together with the chapel named after him, Sixtus wished to add an indispensable element of defence to the Vatican. In fact, one of the remarkable things about the Sistine Chapel is the sharp contrast between its exterior—provided even with a fortified patrol route—and its interior with its sublime and unsurpassed Renaissance masterpieces.

The Peak of the Renaissance

It was Sixtus IV's nephew, Giuliano Della Rovere, having taken the name Julius II following his ascension to the papal throne in 1503, who charged Michelangelo with the supreme task of completing work on the Sistine Chapel. The great Florentine artist frescoed the lunettes and the vaulting with the Ancestors of Christ, episodes from Genesis, and a series of prophets and sybils. Buonarroti was above all a sculptor and had had no prior experience with frescoes; all the same, he succeeded in the gigantic undertaking of painting the more than 600 square meters of the ceiling. In the twenty-five consecutive months in which he "labored like a madman," from July 1508 to August 1510, he brought to life 343 figures, doing so with a new vision that made all the works done by those preceding him seem secondary by comparison.

The crux of his vast narrative are the nine episodes of Genesis. Michelangelo interpreted them as a great mythic cycle on the origins of man, the Creation, sin and ultimate redemption. Adam infused with life by the touch of God's finger is perhaps the most celebrated image in all of western art. The magnificent nudes involved in the drama of Sin, the Ancestors of Christ, the prophets and sybils—all these unforgettable figures play a role in the titanic spiritual tale he was unfolding.

We know that Michelangelo's contemporaries took in his masterpiece in "mute astonishment". This includes Bramante and Raphael, who perhaps in their hearts hoped that their great Tuscan rival would fail.

It was from the young and brilliant Raphael from Urbino that the strong-willed Julius then commissioned the decoration of his new living quarters. These were located above those of Alexander VI, previously frescoed by Pinturicchio. The three rooms that Raphael painted constitute one of the towering fresco cycles of the Renaissance, both in terms of doctrine and in the furtherance of the limits of art. The great neo-Platonic concepts of Truth, Goodness and Beauty are exalted in the Stanza of the Signatura; God's protection of the Church is illustrated in the Stanza of Heliodorus; and the consequent political implications are evident in the Stanza of the Borgo Fire.

The decade of Julius II's pontificate (1503-1513) saw an extraordinarily fortuitous fusion of a pope's vast program of works with the amazing creative capacity of a handful of supreme artists. Other than bringing about the decoration of the Sistine Chapel ceiling and Raphael's Stanzas, it was Julius who determined to build a new basilica. This meant resuming the demolition begun by Nicholas V (interrupted for half a century) and erecting a new façade for the papal palace. Both undertakings were assigned to Bramante.

But we must not leave the Sistine Chapel just yet. Twenty-two years after having labored on the ceiling, Michelangelo once again received a papal summons. This time it was the Farnese pope, Paul III (1534-1549), who called him to execute the "Last Judgment". From 1536 to 1541, the visionary artist labored anew, bringing to life 314 figures in a swirling vortex of angels and demons, the redeemed and the damned. At the center of the vast tormented tableau is Christ, depicted in a moment of severe judgment. Vasari hailed Michelangelo's "Last Judgment" as the crowning moment in all art. No less enthusiastic are today's visitors. Thanks to the huge undertaking of cleaning the entire masterpiece, they can now see the original colors in all their glory.

Where the Holy Spirit Acts

Undoubtedly, the Sistine Chapel is of central importance within the Vatican. And it is not only because from the time "all Rome crowded inside to peer at the ceiling" it has remained the most visited monument of all. It is because the Sistine offers us the most sublime and dramatic tale of human history: from the creation to the last day, from sin to redemption to the Final Judgment. And yet, the Sistine Chapel is more than this.

Interestingly, its dimensions—40.5 by 13.5 meters—correspond exactly to those of the Solomon's Temple, offering yet another argument for the perception of Rome as the "New Jerusalem." Moreover, this space is particularly sacred to the Catholic community because it is "where the Holy Spirit acts" during the numerous conclaves that have been held within its walls. It is there that the Holy Spirit has illuminated the cardinals, guiding them in their election of a new pontiff.

John Paul II himself said so on April 8, 1994 when inaugurating Michelangelo's restored frescoes in the Chapel. "Insofar as a pictorial image, given its intrinsic limits, is able to express such a thing," the pope asserted, "everything that can be said about infinite divine majesty is said here."

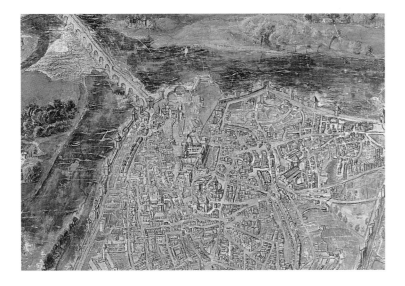

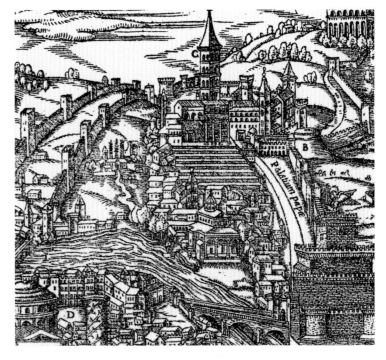

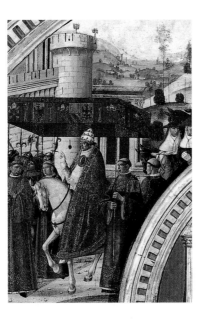

The papal residence at Avignon *(above, detail of Venaissin's map in the Gallery of Maps), built at the time of Clement VI Roger (1342-52).*

Pope Clement V (Bertrand de Got) and the papal court moved to Avignon in 1309 under the protection of the King of France. The papacy returned to the Vatican in Rome in 1377 under Gregory XI (Roger de Beaufort), *who is portrayed (on the right) as he enters Rome in this 1501 fresco by Benvenuto di Giovanni del Guasta (Ospedale di Santa Maria della Scala, Siena).*

We know what the medieval papal palace with its corner towers looked like from a woodcut in Sebastian Munster's Cosmographia Universalis *(1550). It is based on a copper engraving, the work of Florentine artist, Francesco Rosselli, dating from 1480. To the right, on the hilltop, entirely out of proportion, stands the Palazzetto del Belvedere, which was built in the gardens for Pope Innocent VIII. Below, we can see Castel Sant'Angelo (Hadrian's Tomb) as it appeared before the renovations commissioned by Alexander VI.*

Overwhelmed by such magnificence, we come out of the Sistine Chapel in stupefied silence. Before resuming our walk in pursuit of the evolution of the papal palaces, however, we should at least briefly acknowledge some of the glories that we were forced to leave behind. These include the Pauline Chapel with its two frescoes by Michelangelo of the conversion of Saul and the crucifixion of Peter–masterpieces that clearly depict the effect of divine grace on the two apostles.

With the new façade of the papal palace overlooking Rome, Julius wished to transform a dark medieval castle into a luminous Renaissance dwelling. Bramante's highly original concept called for the addition of three orders of airy loggias with arches connected to the existing structure. The work was completed by Raphael who modified the third loggia by substituting the arches and pilasters with a trabeation supported by a series of light semi-columns. This particular loggia, destined at the time for Cardinal Bibbiena, is today the seat of the Secretariat of State.

Great changes were also underway within the pontifical residence. In 1538, under Paul III, Antonio da Sangallo the Younger transformed the *Sala Regia*, designed to receive foreign sovereigns and ambassadors, into a vast hall. Four decades later its walls were decorated by Giorgio Vasari, Taddeo Zuccari and others in a vast fresco cycle celebrating significant episodes in the history of the Church. Their works recalled not only the spiritual but the political supremacy of the papacy throughout Christendom.

Facing the *Sala Regia* are entrances to the Sistine and Pauline chapels as well as that of the *Sala Ducale*. The latter, used in medieval times as an area for formal receptions, now underwent a transformation. As we see it today, the hall is derived from the fusion of two chambers, adjacent but on different axes. Bernini joined them, ingeniously masking the divergence with the addition of a theatrical curtain formed of stucco, which is held aloft by winged cherubs.

On the north side of the papal palace, Gregory XIII (1572-1585) added another building, also furnished with loggias to continue those of Bramante. This in effect closed the north side of the St. Damasus courtyard. The east side was completed in 1589 when Sixtus V called Domenico Fontana to design an austere square building. It too has loggias on the side facing the courtyard, whereas its tall façade reflects less the grace of the Renaissance than the rigors of the Counter Reformation. The whole palace rises up from ramparts and consequently, when viewed from ground level, maintains a military look of defensiveness. When Bernini designed the colonnade, he fixed forever the main entrance to the apostolic palaces. Essentially, he put the Bronze Doorway at the point where the colonnade intersects with the northern portico. From there, we have a superb view of a theatrical staircase leading to the most ancient wing of the medieval palace.

The World's Crossroads

This building, which is the pope's home, is the object of particular attention every Sunday. It is then, when the noontime Angelus is due to be recited, that the pope appears at the window of his private study to be seen by the thousands of pilgrims gathered in the piazza below.

It wasn't always this way. From the end of the sixteenth century until 1870, his predecessors preferred living in the Quirinal Palace—thought to be located in a healthier climate, though only a few kilometers away. Only after the

Republican troops under Garibaldi stormed the city in 1870 did the popes return to the Vatican. Initially, they took up quarters on the second floor of the Apostolic Palace. No doubt the then-reigning pope, Pius IX, considered the move a temporary measure.

His successor Leo XIII (1878-1903) felt quite at home in this vast setting, though it must be said he did arrange to sleep in a smaller room down on the first floor. It was Pius X who made the move to the third floor, ordering an apartment to be decorated. Ever since then, the private quarters of the pope have been located there. The only changes have been those of interior decoration, reflecting the tastes and personal habits of the successive pontiffs.

Paul VI (1963-1978) had a garden created on the roof of the building. There the Pope can stroll, pray, read his breviary and prepare his speeches in the quiet and tranquility the place affords.

In the thirteen rooms of various sizes located on the second floor—the largest being the Library, the Clementine Rooms and the Consistory—the pope "receives" for two hours. This happens every day of the week but Wednesday and Sunday. Visitors include bishops, world figures, select groups from all continents.

Virtually on a daily basis, then, the whole world enters the pope's home to express their hopes, and above all their griefs. What they have to say is transformed into prayer.

The heart and soul of the pope's apartment is formed by his study and his chapel. The chapel is the crossroads of everything, not merely because the pope spends three hours a day there (mostly kneeling in silent colloquium with Our Lord) but because with each change in the day's activity we know he stops there briefly. The other hub of the pope's activity is his private study—the window of which is perhaps the most celebrated in the world. It is toward that window that the gaze of millions upon millions of persons is turned every Sunday at the time of the Angelus.

This room, second from the right on the third floor, is where the pope works on an average of six hours every day. Here he studies, checks documents, prepares new encyclicals, writes speeches and sermons, examines the weighty briefs and dossiers prepared for him by the Secretary of State and by other departments of the Curia.

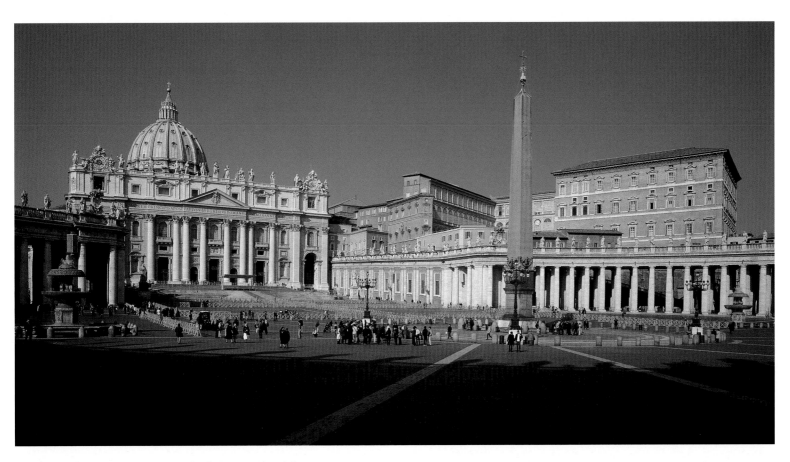

St. Peter's Square with the Apostolic Palace on the right.

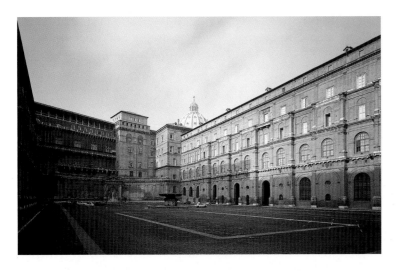

The medieval structures of the papal palace, dating from the time of Nicholas V, are still visible on the north façade. Starting from below, the windows of Sixtus IV's Library (behind the exedra), and above them, the Borgia Apartments and Raphael's Stanzas, which were Julius II's apartments. To the right, the Borgia Tower, commissioned by the Borgia pope Alexander VI, which at the time served as the northwestern corner's bulwark. The exedra below, which marks the opening of the Belvedere Courtyard, was designed and built by Pirro Ligorio (1565). The top two floors were added later, at the time of Pius XII, in order to create offices for the Secretary of State.

The Bronze Door *(on the right), which was the entrance to the Vatican palaces at the time of Pope Paul V, was placed by Bernini at the end of Constantine's Portico.*

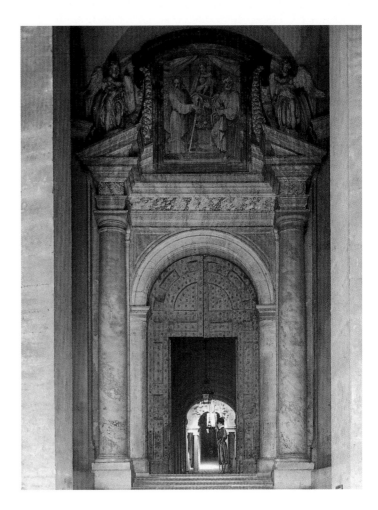

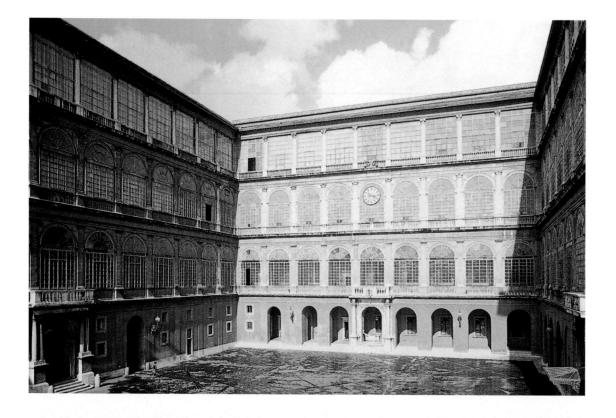

The Courtyard of St. Damasus is the central element around which the three wings of the popes' residence were built over the centuries. To the left are the loggias that Bramante and Raphael added to the medieval structure in 1508-19. The façades of other wings built in later years were modeled on them. In the center is Gregory XIII's wing, begun at the time of Pius IV; to the right is the building designed by Domenico Fontana for Sixtus V. The courtyard is named after the pope who in the second half of the 4th century channeled the water that flowed through this area causing considerable damage to the basilica.

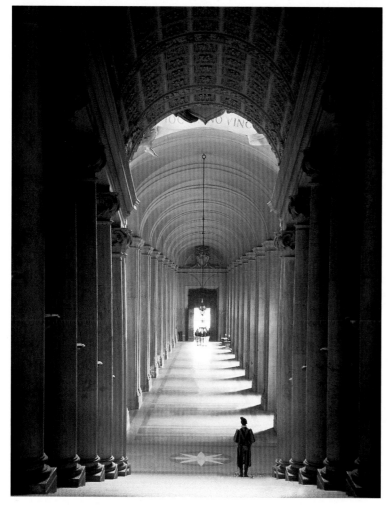

Constantine's Portico which derives its name from the statue of the Roman emperor that Bernini placed here, opposite the atrium of the basilica.

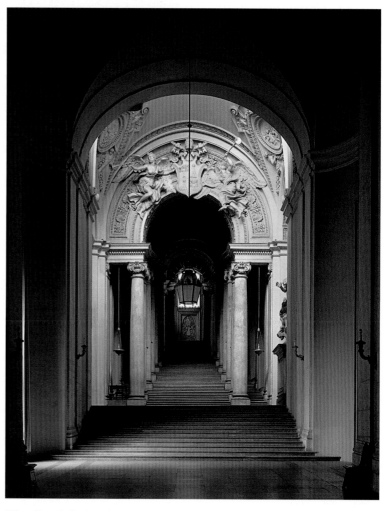

The Royal Stairway constitute the new entrance to the palaces that Bernini designed as part of his reconstruction of St. Peter's Square.

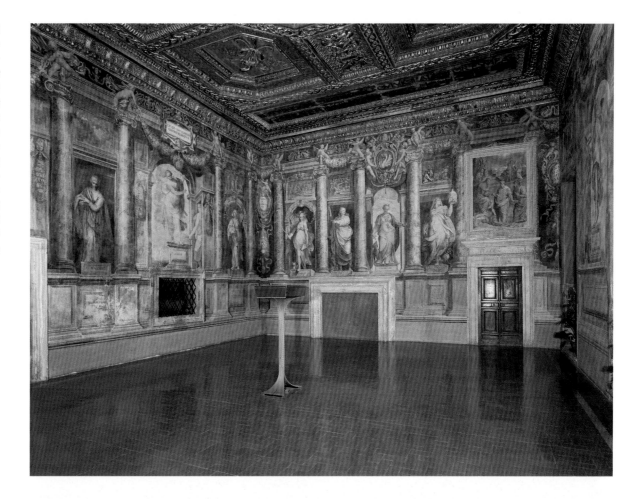

Apostolic Palace. The Old Hall of the Swiss (Sala Vecchia degli Svizzeri). Giovanni Barile's ceiling was probably based on a design by Raphael; the frescoes were done by Marco da Faenza and his school. The allegorical figures of the fifteen Virtues are inserted in a false architectural background, surrounded by garlands of flowers and fruit held by winged cherubs. Part was executed in color and part using the chiaroscuro technique.

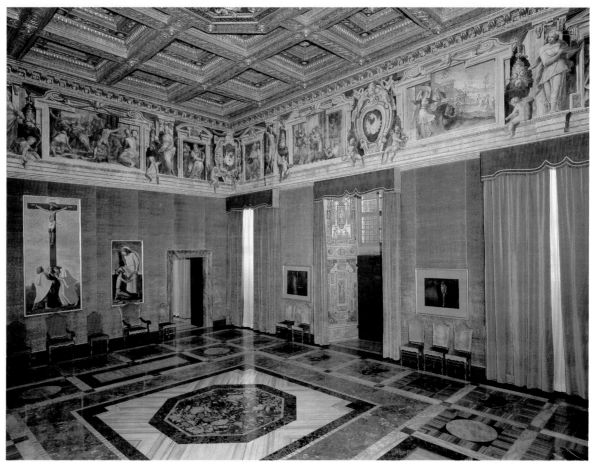

Apostolic Palace. View of the first Hall of Vestments (Sala dei Paramenti). Many artists, including Marco da Faenza, Giovanni Battista della Marta, and Paris Nogari under Mario Sabbatini's direction, worked on the magnificent decorations depicting stories derived from the Acts of the Apostles as well as the virtues and symbolical figures. The splendid gilt carved wooden ceiling was commissioned by Pius IV in 1563, but was restored under Gregory XIII.

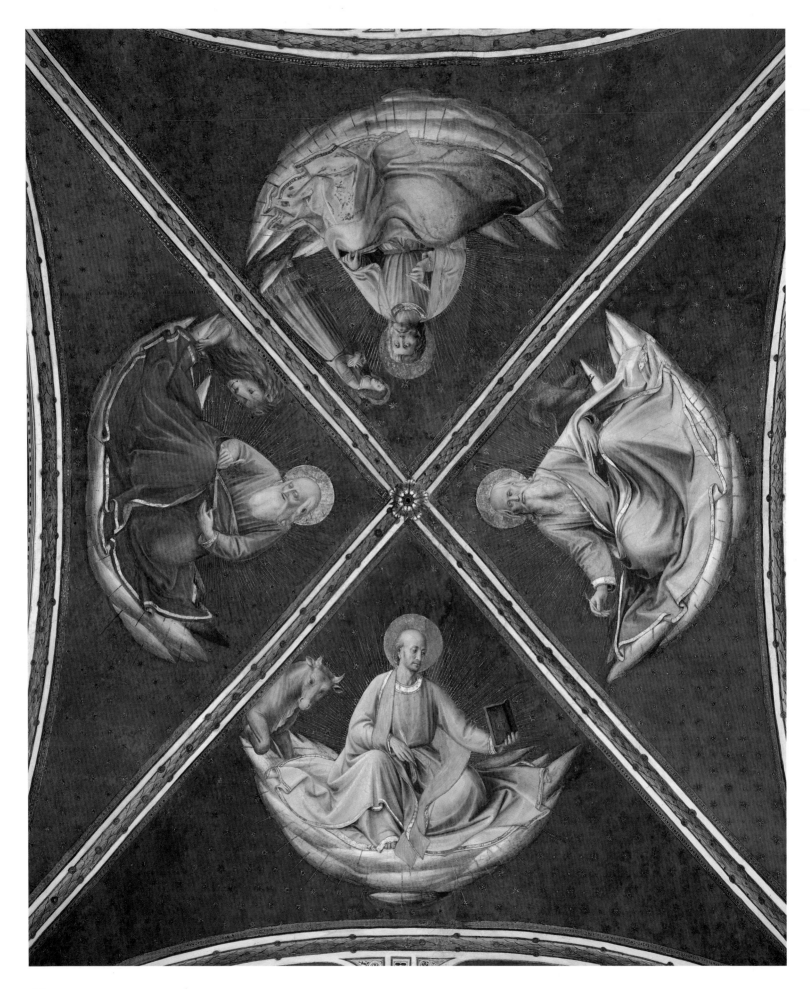

The *Chapel of Nicholas V*. When the Holy See was brought back to Rome after its period of exile in Avignon, the papacy embarked on a vast program of renovation for the city and the Vatican. Between 1447 and 1451, in the private chapel of Pope Nicholas V Parentucelli, the Dominican friar, Giovanni da Fiesole, known as Fra Angelico, painted frescoes illustrating the story of the lives of St. Stephen (in the lunettes) and St. Lawrence (in the lower panel). The use of perspective in the composition is typical of early Renaissance painting in Florence.

Fra Angelico's Ceiling in the Chapel of Nicholas V *(on the left). In the cells of the vault against the backdrop of a starlit sky, the four evangelists are portrayed: St. Luke, with a bull, is reading; St. John, with an eagle, is depicted in a moment of meditation; St. Mark, with a lion, is writing; and St. Matthew, with an angel, is depicted in a moment of inspiration.*

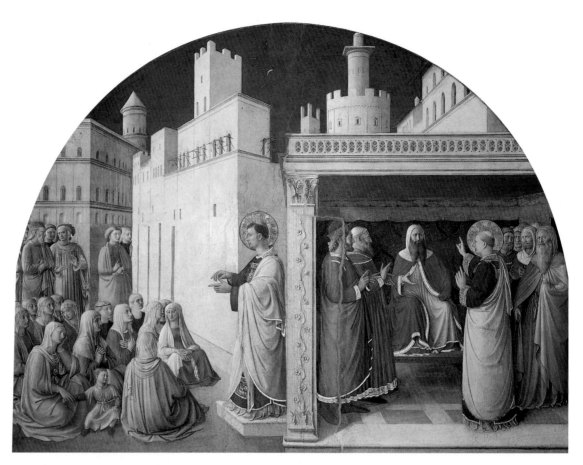

St. Stephen preaching, and the disputation in the Sanhedrin.

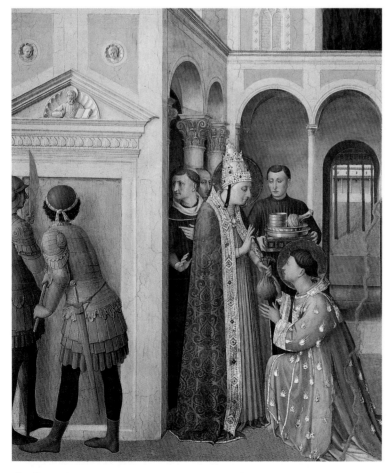

St. Sixtus handing the church's treasures to St. Lawrence.

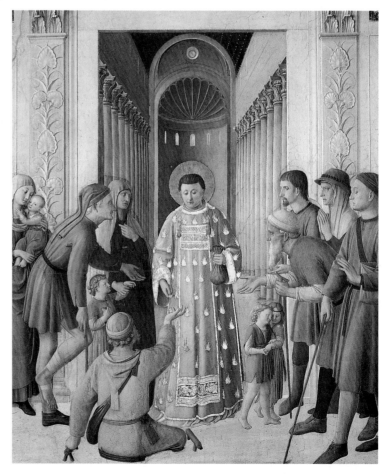

St. Lawrence distributing alms to the poor.

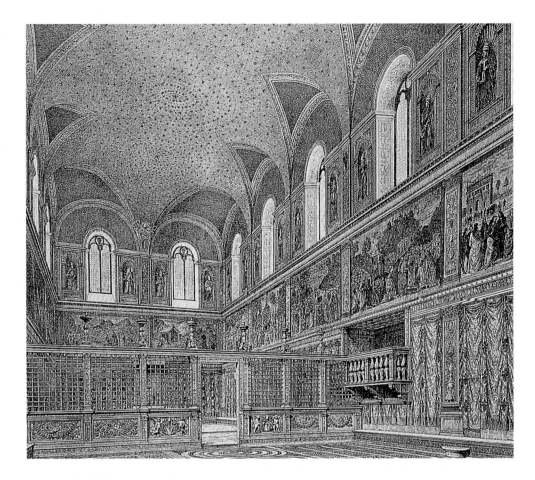

The *Sistine Chapel*, looking towards the altar wall, as it appeared before the decoration commissioned by Julius II. The ceiling, later frescoed by Michelangelo, was decorated with gold stars against a blue background painted by Pier Matteo d'Amelia. The floor plan of the chapel is a rectangle measuring 40.5 by 13.5 meters, the same size as Solomon's temple. It is 20.7 meters high. The lower part of the side walls is decorated with frescoes that imitate hanging tapestries. The upper part, between the windows, contains a gallery of the first 31 sanctified popes (the genealogy of the Bishops of Rome); these portraits were painted at the same time as the scenes from the Old and New Testaments below them. The popes' portraits as well as the scenes depicted in the middle row begin at the altar wall; later they were painted over by Michelangelo in his "Last Judgment". The splendid geometric pattern of the floor inlay is modeled on the multicolored pavements of medieval churches. The choir stall and the marble balustrade (a kind of iconostasis) are the work of Mino da Fiesole and assistants. In the second half of the sixteenth century, the balustrade was moved back several meters to make room for the presbytery.

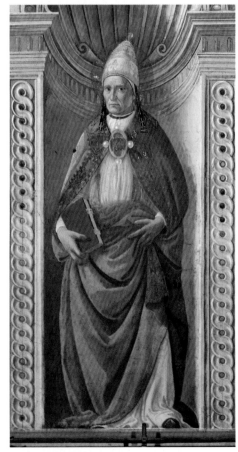

Sistine Chapel. Domenico del Ghirlandaio's St. Victor I *(189-199).*

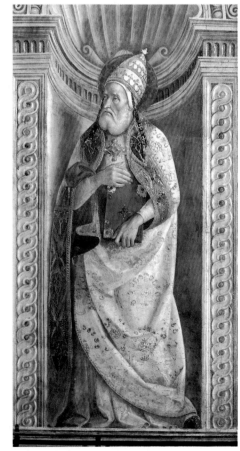

Sistine Chapel. Fra Diamante's St. Urban I *(222-230).*

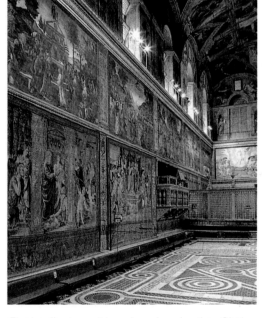

Raphael's tapestries *hanging in the Sistine Chapel for the celebration of Easter, 1983.*

A view of the Sistine Chapel after the restoration of Michelangelo's frescoes.

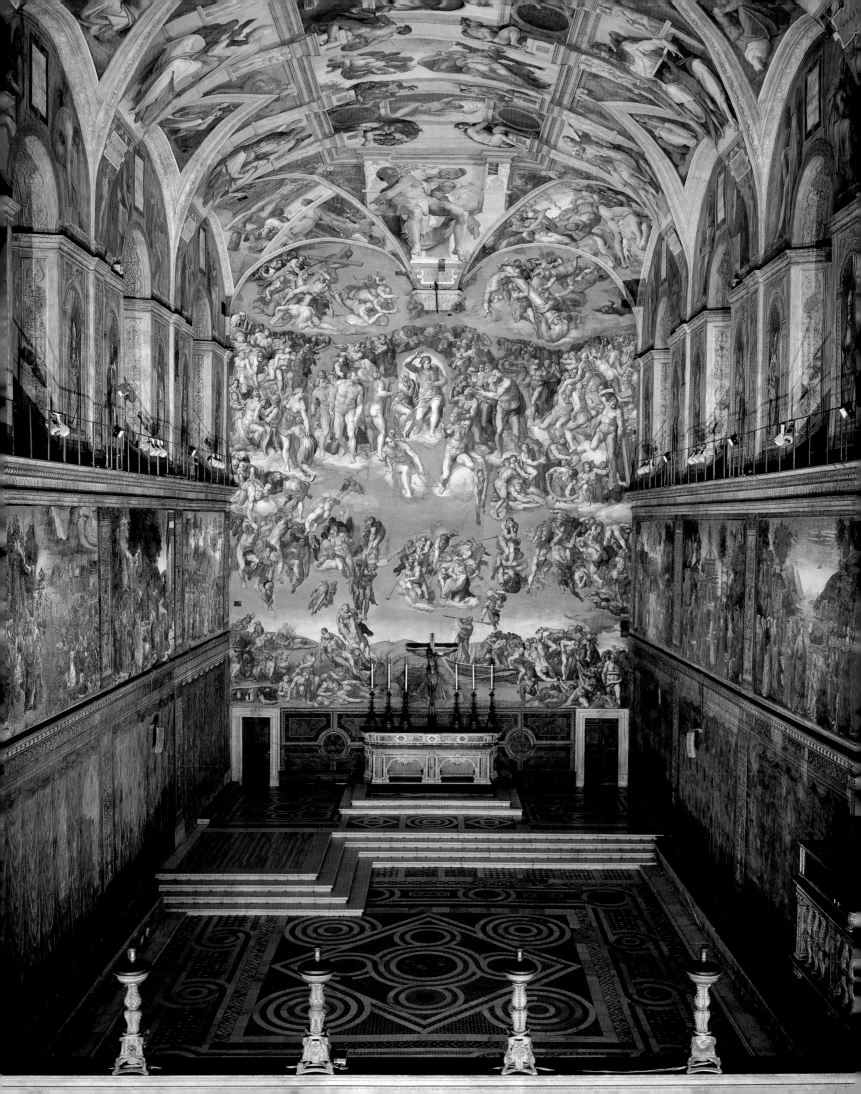

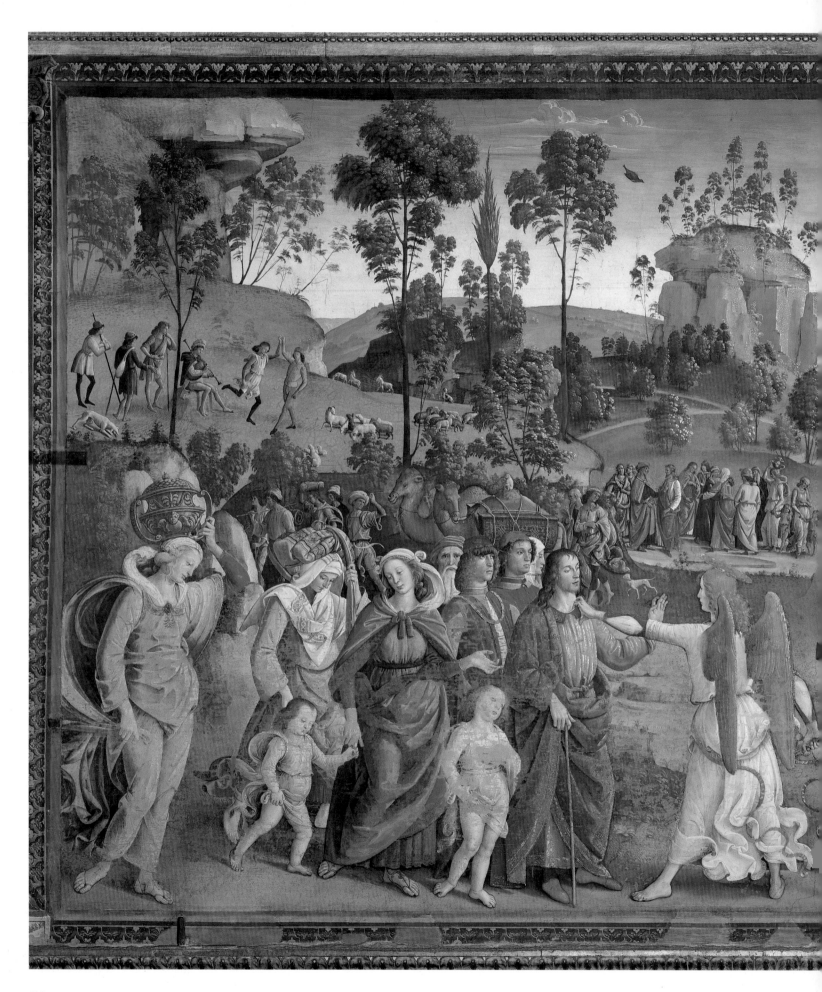

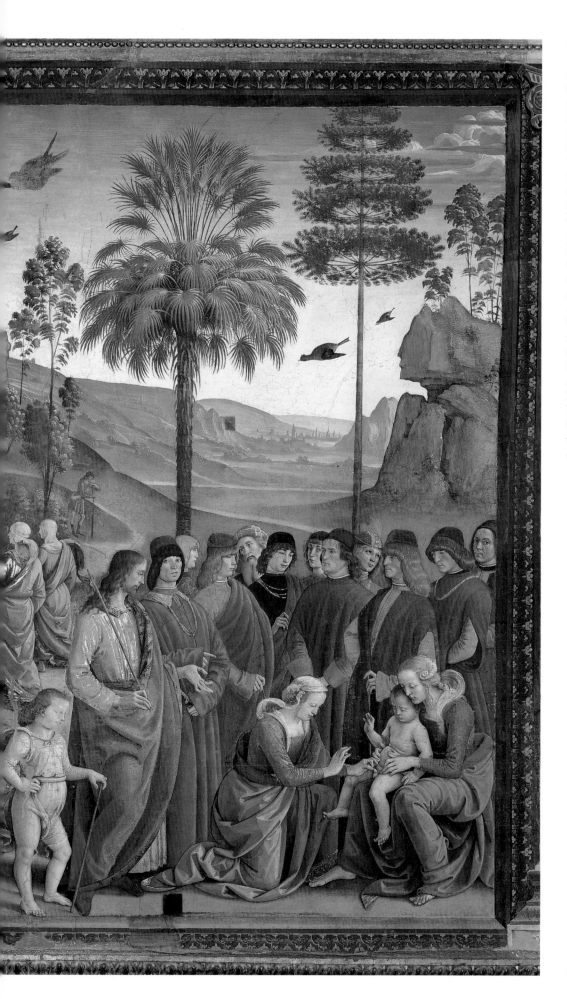

Sistine Chapel. *Stories from the Old and New Testaments*. Covering the long walls of the chapel, the two pictorial cycles consist of seven frescoes each illustrating episodes from the lives of Moses and Christ. Begun late in 1481, the paintings represent a mature synthesis of Umbrian-Tuscan figurative styles of the early Renaissance. The four frescoes on the altar wall and on the entrance wall were destroyed: the first two were covered by Michelangelo when he painted his "Last Judgment", and the others were lost when the wall collapsed in 1522 (Luca Signorelli's "Dispute over the Body of Moses" and Ghirlandaio's "Resurrection of Christ" were repainted in the late 16th century by Matteo da Lecce and Arrigo van den Broek, called *Il Paludano*). Sixtus IV certainly dictated that the iconography of the fresco cycle should emphasize the universal supremacy of the Roman pope over any other power. Sixtus IV entrusted the work to Pietro Perugino, who was assisted by Pinturicchio, Cosimo Rosselli, Piero di Cosimo, Sandro Botticelli, Domenico del Ghirlandaio and Luca Signorelli. On August 15, 1483 the chapel was inaugurated and dedicated to Our Lady of the Assumption.

Perugino, Moses' Journey into Egypt.

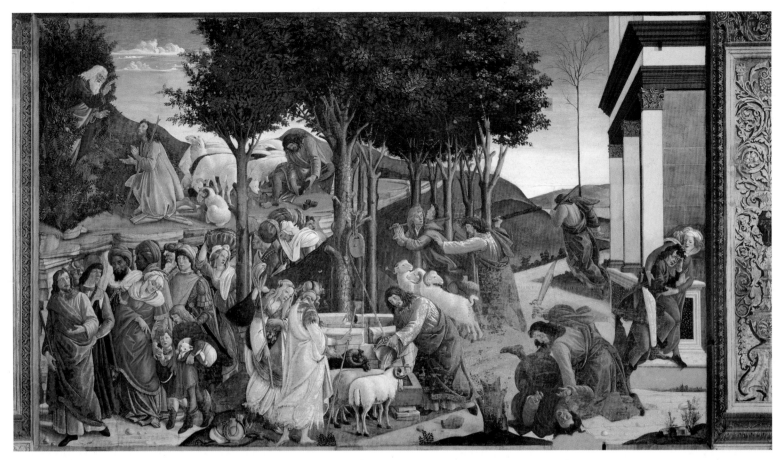

Sandro Botticelli, Episodes from the life of Moses.

Biagio di Antonio, The Crossing of the Red Sea.

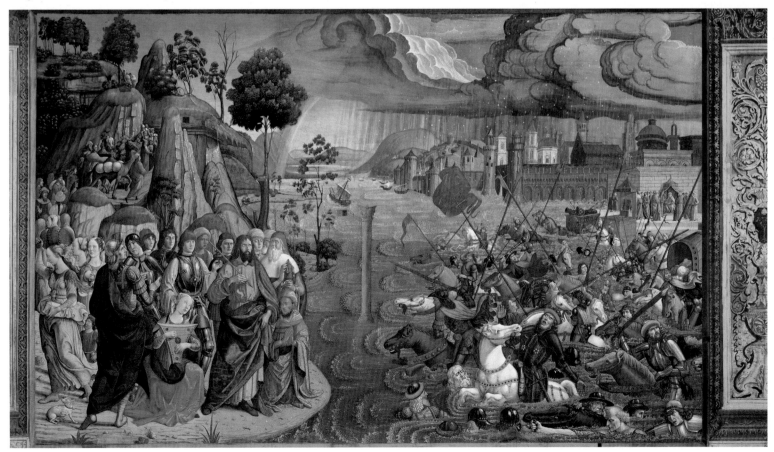

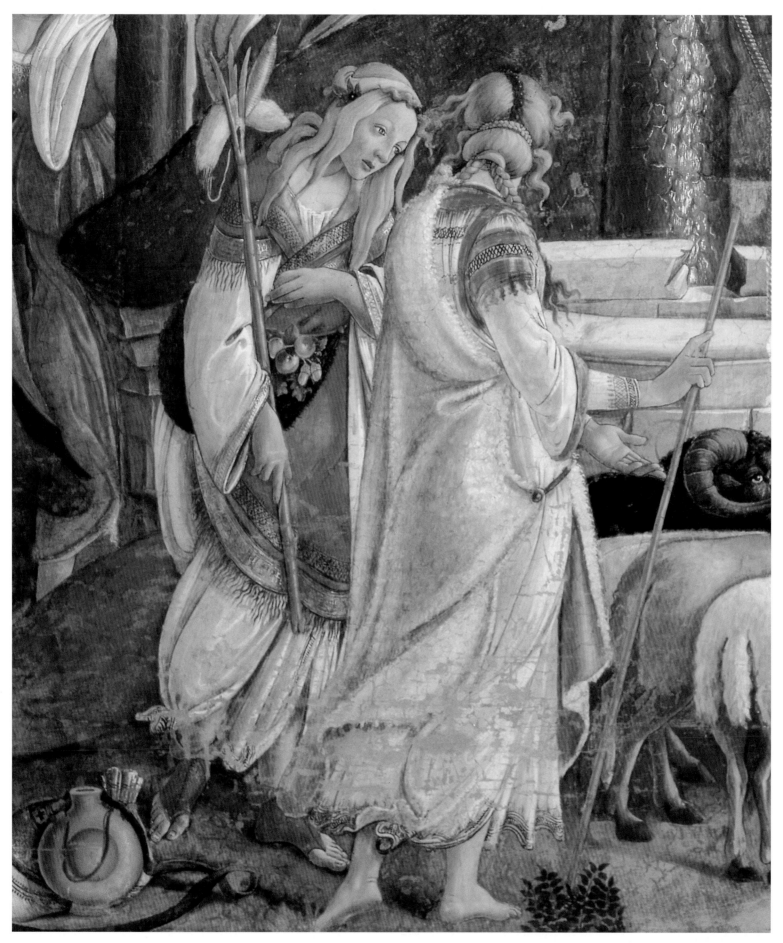

Sandro Botticelli, Episodes from the life of Moses, *detail.*

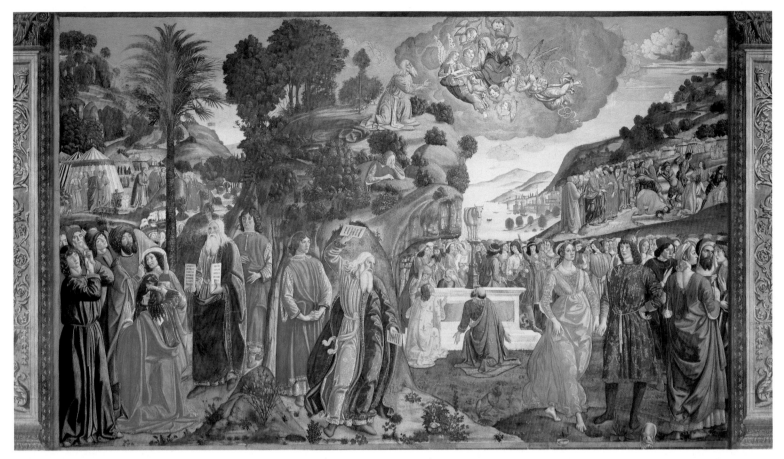

Cosimo Rosselli, The Handing Over of the Tables of the Law.

Sandro Botticelli, The Punishment of Korah, Dathan and Abiram.

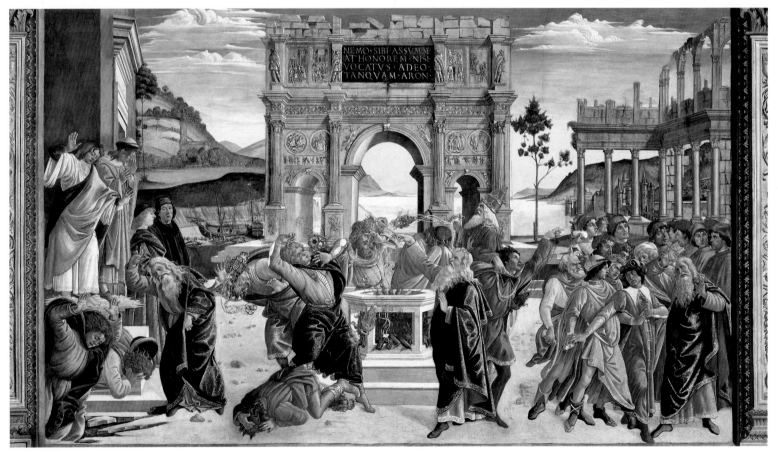

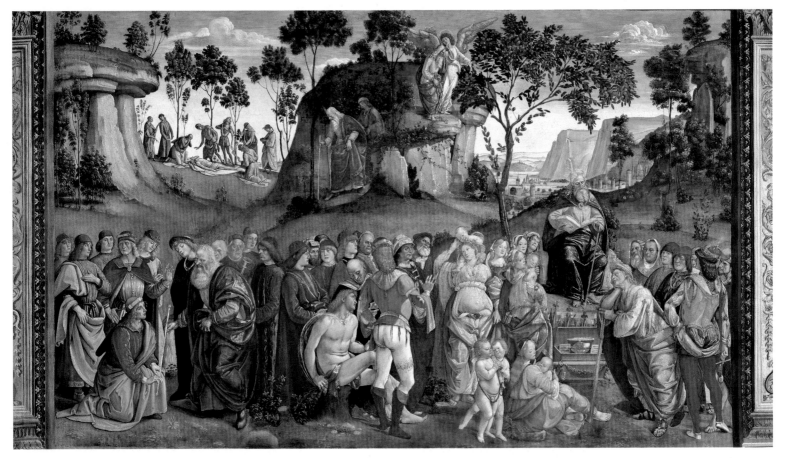

Luca Signorelli and Bartolomeo della Gatta, The Last Days of Moses.

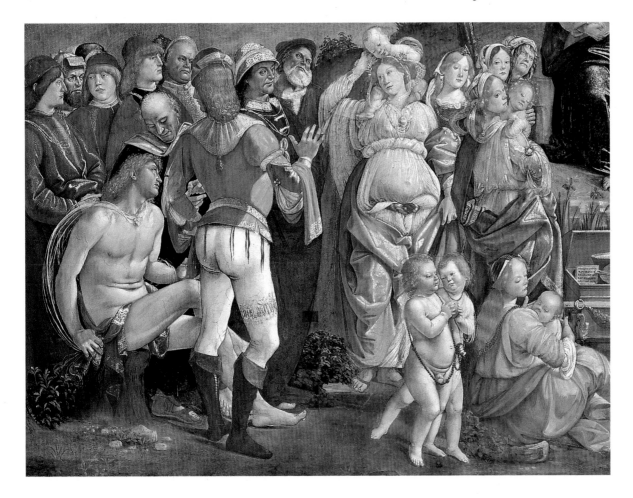

Luca Signorelli and Bartolomeo della Gatta, The Last Days of Moses, *detail*.

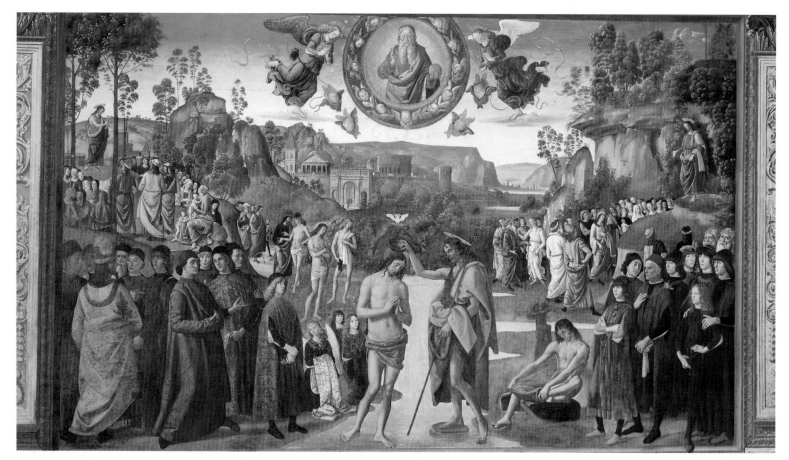

Perugino, The Baptism of Christ in the Jordan.

Sandro Botticelli, The Temptations of Christ and Purification of the Leper.

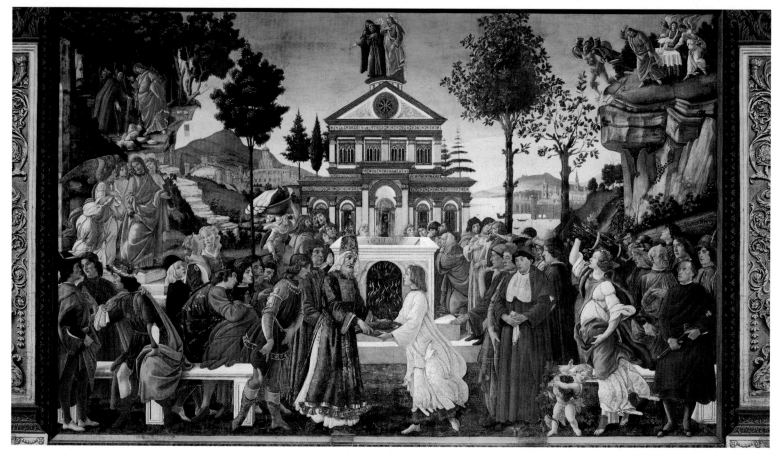

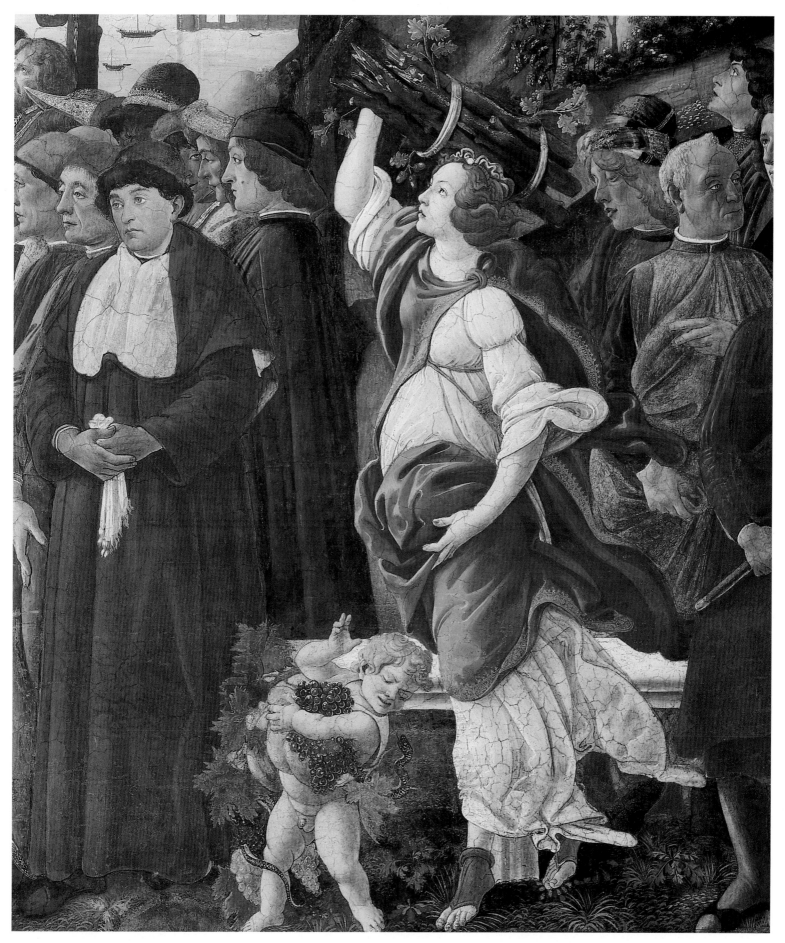

Sandro Botticelli, The Temptations of Christ and Purification of the Leper, *detail.*

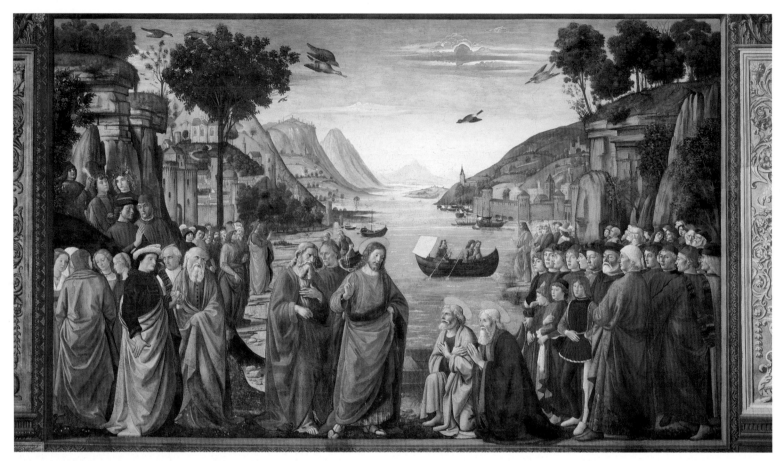

Domenico Ghirlandaio, The Call of St. Peter and St. Andrew.

Cosimo Rosselli, The Sermon on the Mount and Christ Heals a Leper.

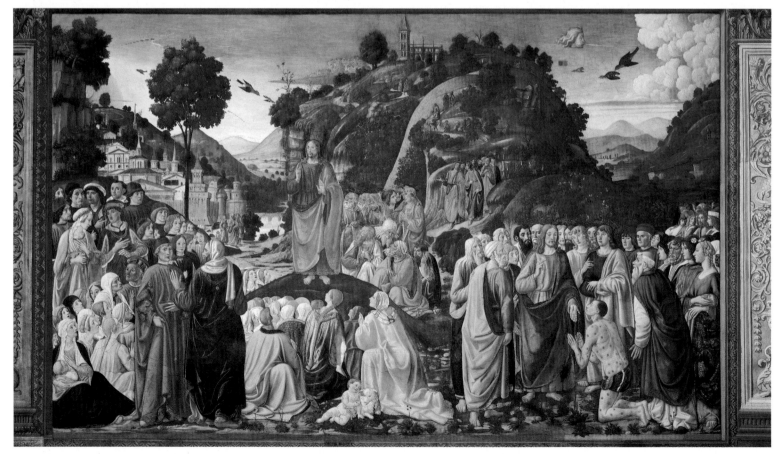

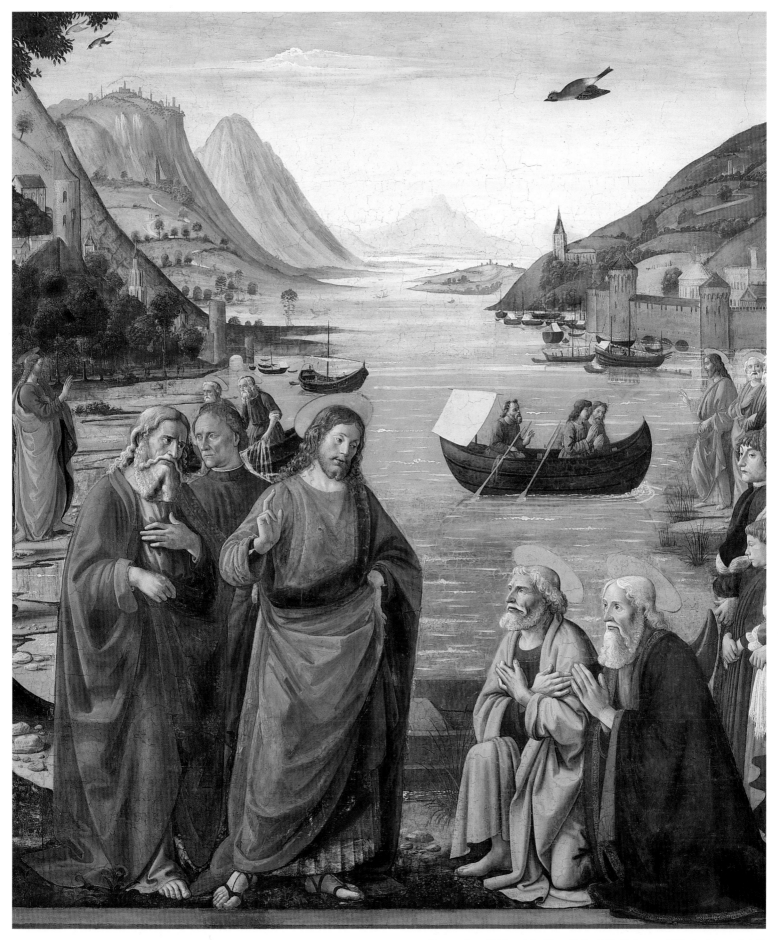

Domenico Ghirlandaio, The Call of St. Peter and St. Andrew, *detail.*

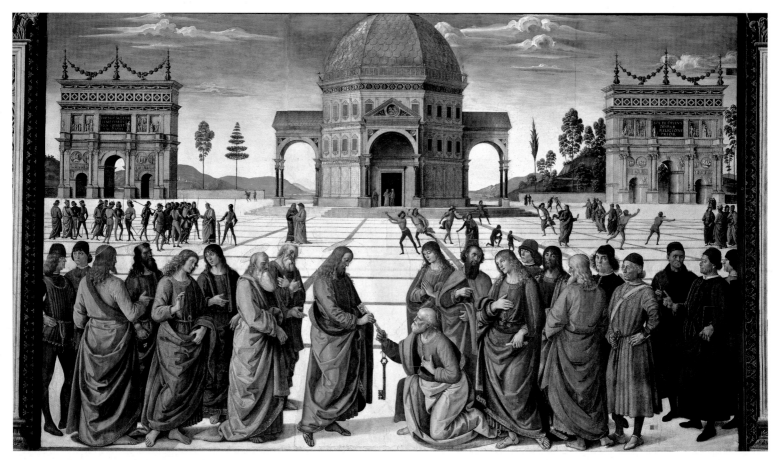

Perugino, Jesus handing the Keys to St. Peter.

Cosimo Rosselli, The Last Supper.

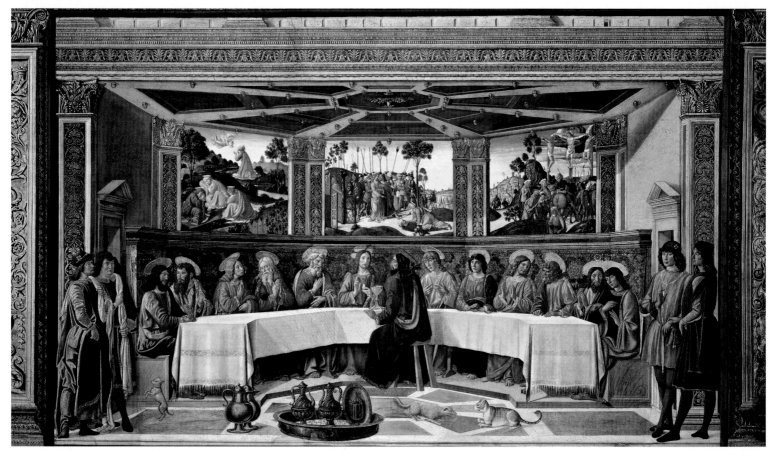

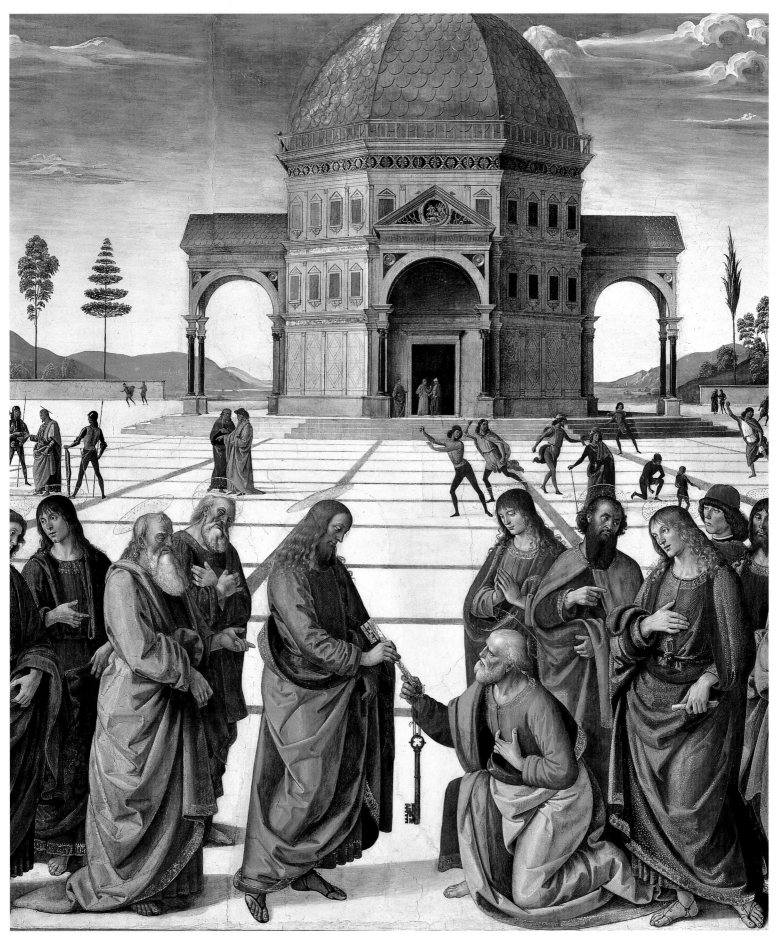

Perugino, Jesus handing the Keys to St. Peter, *detail.*

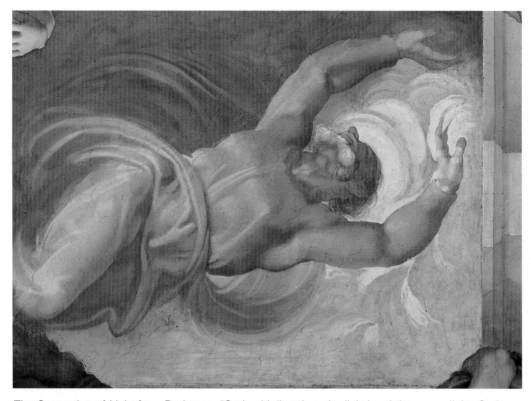

The Separation of Light from Darkness: "God said, 'Let there be light,' and there was light. God saw that light was good, and God divided light from darkness. God called light 'day', and darkness he called 'night'" (cf. Genesis 1: 4-5).

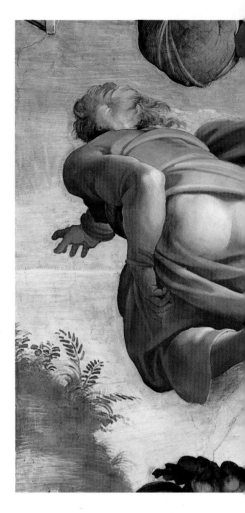

The Creation of the Sun and Moon and the Plants (above): "God said, Let there be lights in the vault of heaven to divide day from night, and let them indicate festivals, days and years. ... God made the two great lights: the greater light to govern the day, the smaller light to govern the night, and the stars. ... God saw all he had made, and indeed it was very good." (cf. Genesis 1:14-15,31) Michelangelo uses a very original visual device to portray God from both the front and the rear, as if He could see all He had created around Him and thus express satisfaction.

Ceiling of the Sistine Chapel. Michelangelo was commissioned by the Rovere pope Julius II (1503-1513) on May 10, 1508 (the date on the contract). The Pope had originally planned for him to paint the figures of the 12 Apostles on the corbels of the lunettes, but the artist did not consider that such a project would be grand enough. Thus Michelangelo obtained the Pope's authorization to execute his own plan which proved to be on a much vaster scale from both an architectural and an iconographical point of view. In all likelihood, the artist followed precise directions given to him by scholarly theologians of the papal court in producing such a solid project from a theological viewpoint. The nine episodes from Genesis are depicted in the central part of the ceiling. In the middle, the presence of the thrones of the Seers (Prophets and Sibyls) is more meaningful than the "historical" images contained in the Old Testament. The gift of prophecy, granted to the seers by divine inspiration, permits the interpretation of the Old Testament scenes with a new key, that of the Redemption: thus, Noah's drunkenness becomes a metaphor for Christ scorned; the flood for the baptism; Noah's sacrifice for the Passion, etc. The Ancestors of Christ, portrayed on the spandrels and lunettes, follow the sequence in the opening of the Gospel according to St. Matthew. Christ's descendants through Abraham are excluded from the higher world because they are unaware of the Revelation, and thus represent, with the succession of generations, the hope and the expectation of the Redemption. The scenes portraying the miraculous liberation of the chosen people, depicted in the spandrels of the four corners, also refer to this new interpretation (Judith and Holofernes, David and Goliath, the Brazen Serpent and the Punishment of Haman). Once the decoration was complete, on November 1, 1512, Pope Julius II was able to celebrate Vespers in the Chapel dedicated to the Assumption.

The first three Biblical scenes are clearly presented as a triptych portraying the creation of the universe. It is dominated by the imposing presence of the Creator who, hovering in the air supported by a strong wind, molds the limitless space beneath him.

Dividing the Waters from the Land: "God made the vault, and it divided the waters... God called the vault 'heaven'" (cf. Genesis 1: 7-8).

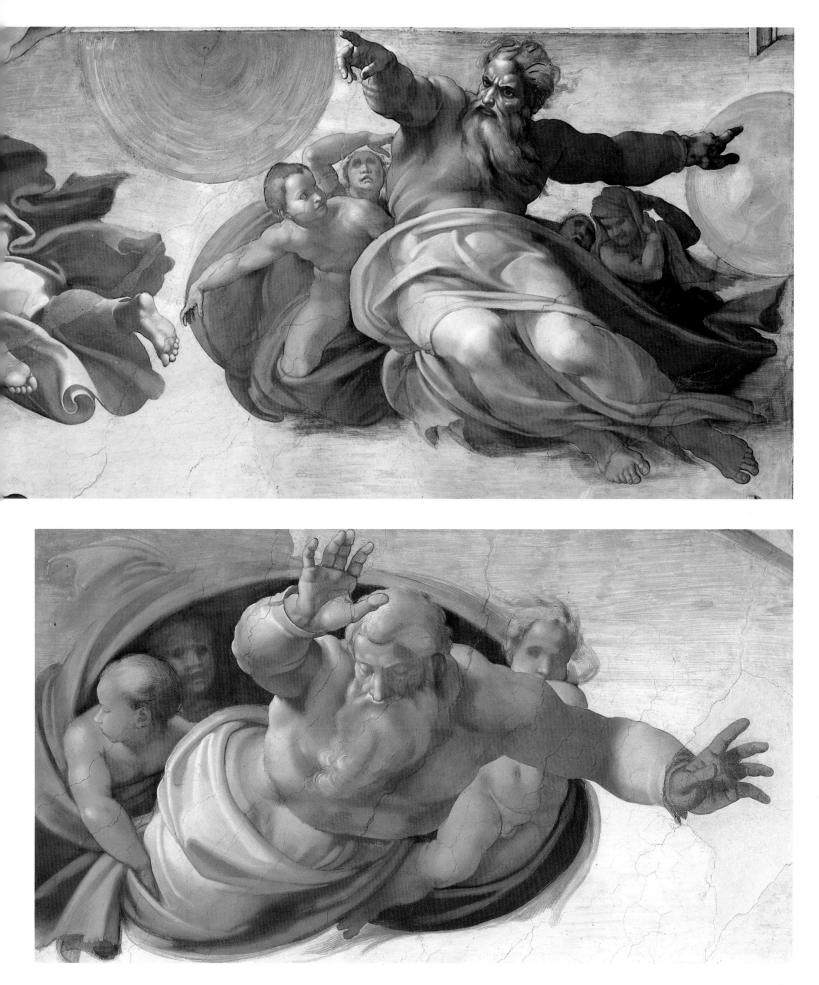

Michelangelo dedicated another triptych (illustrated in these pictures) to the creation of man and woman and the original sin in the center of the ceiling.

In the centerfold, a complete view of the ceiling in the Sistine Chapel.

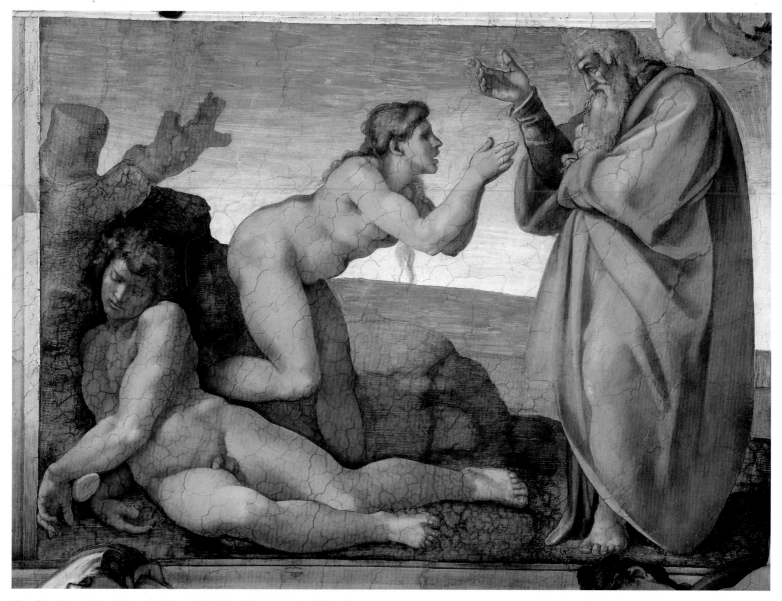

The Creation of Eve *(above):* "It is not right that the man should be alone. I shall make him a helper. ... Then, Yahweh God made the man fall into a deep sleep. And, while he was asleep, he took one of his ribs and closed the flesh up again forthwith. Yahweh God fashioned the rib he had taken from the man into a woman. ... both of them were naked, the man and his wife, but they felt no shame before each other." (cf. Genesis 2:18,21-22, 25).

The Creation of Adam *(next pages).* "Yahweh God shaped man from the soil of the ground and blew the breath of life into his nostrils, and man became a living being." (cf. Genesis 2: 7) Painted on the ceiling of the Sistine Chapel by Michelangelo in 1512, the Creation of Adam is one of the incontrovertible masterpieces of all time. The Creator, held by angels in the sky, is seen as he instils life into Adam, naked and inert, by grazing his hand. The expressive power of Michelangelo's composition contrasts God's power with Adam's vulnerability, thus lending visual reality to the Father, a pure spirit, who creates by thought alone. From a compositional viewpoint, we must also admire Michelangelo's ability to animate the physicality of the bodies of Adam and God, placed on a horizontal plane, so that the axes of their outstretched arms do not quite coincide.

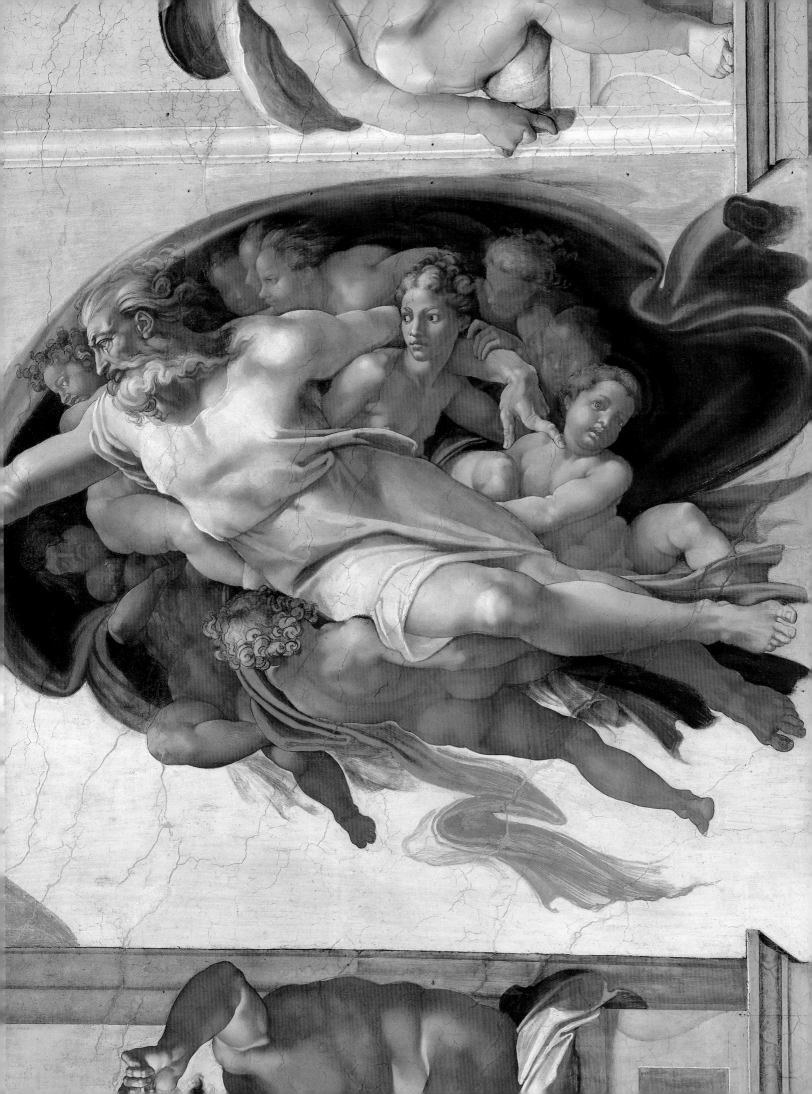

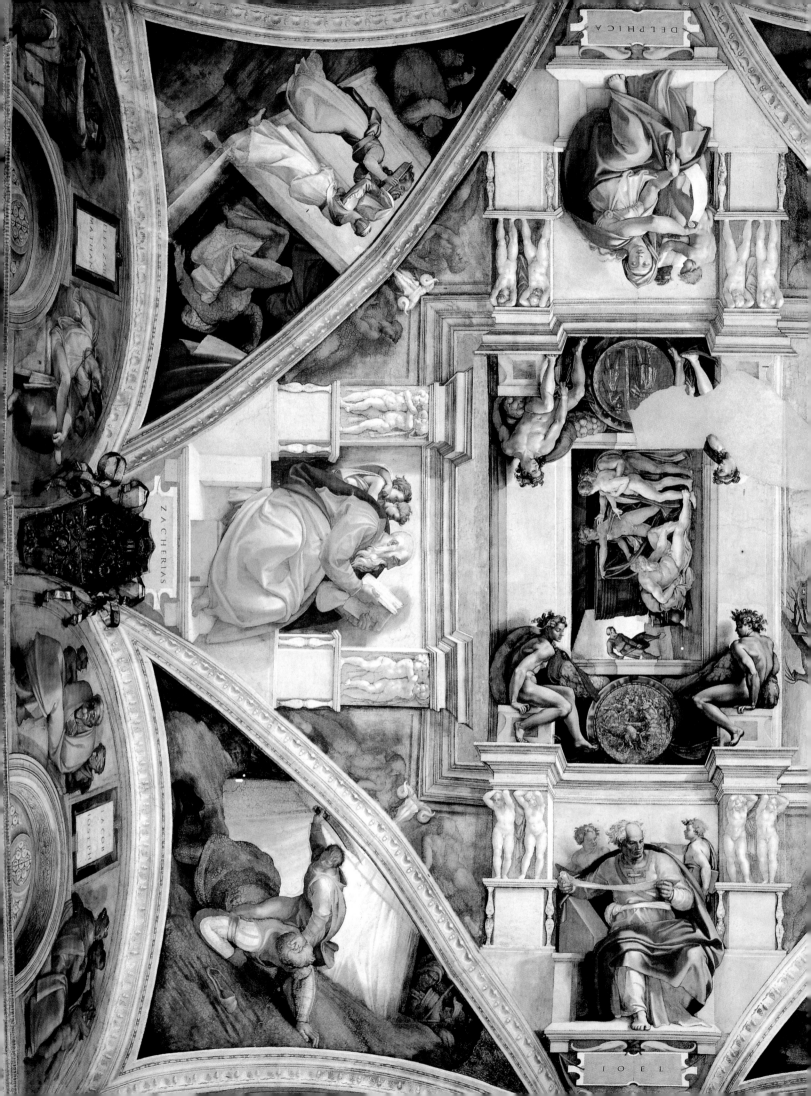

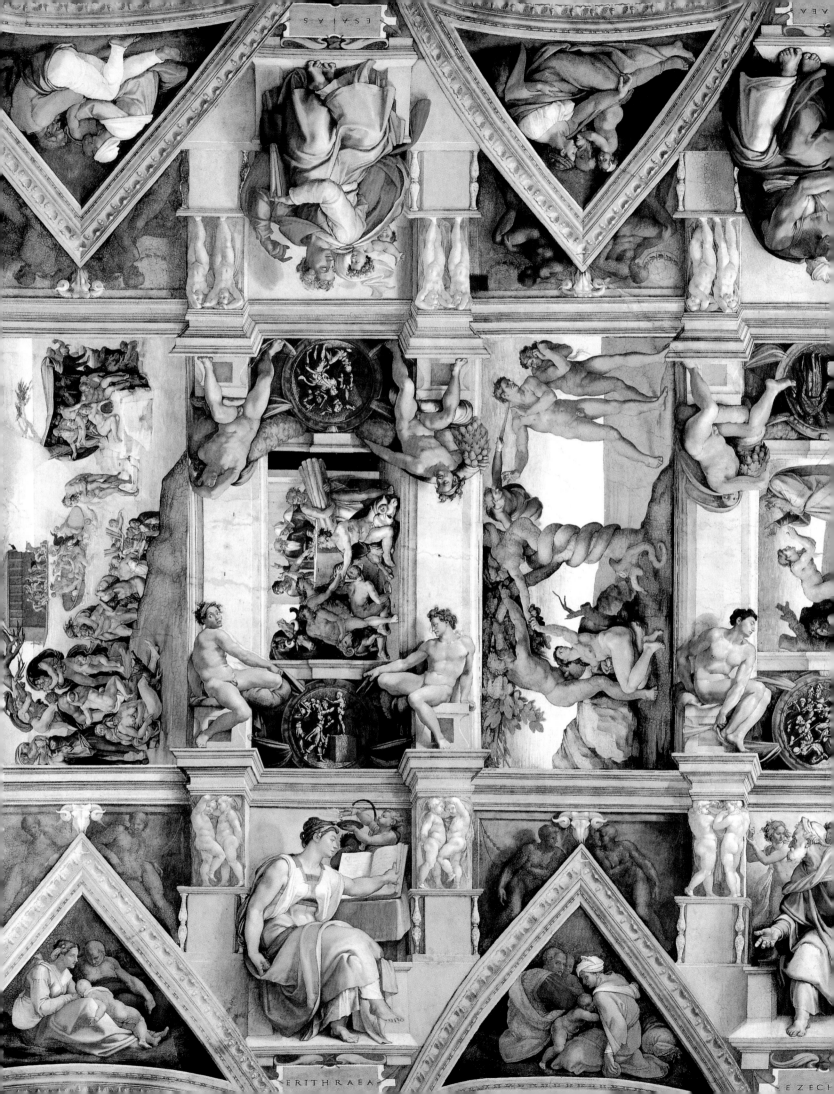

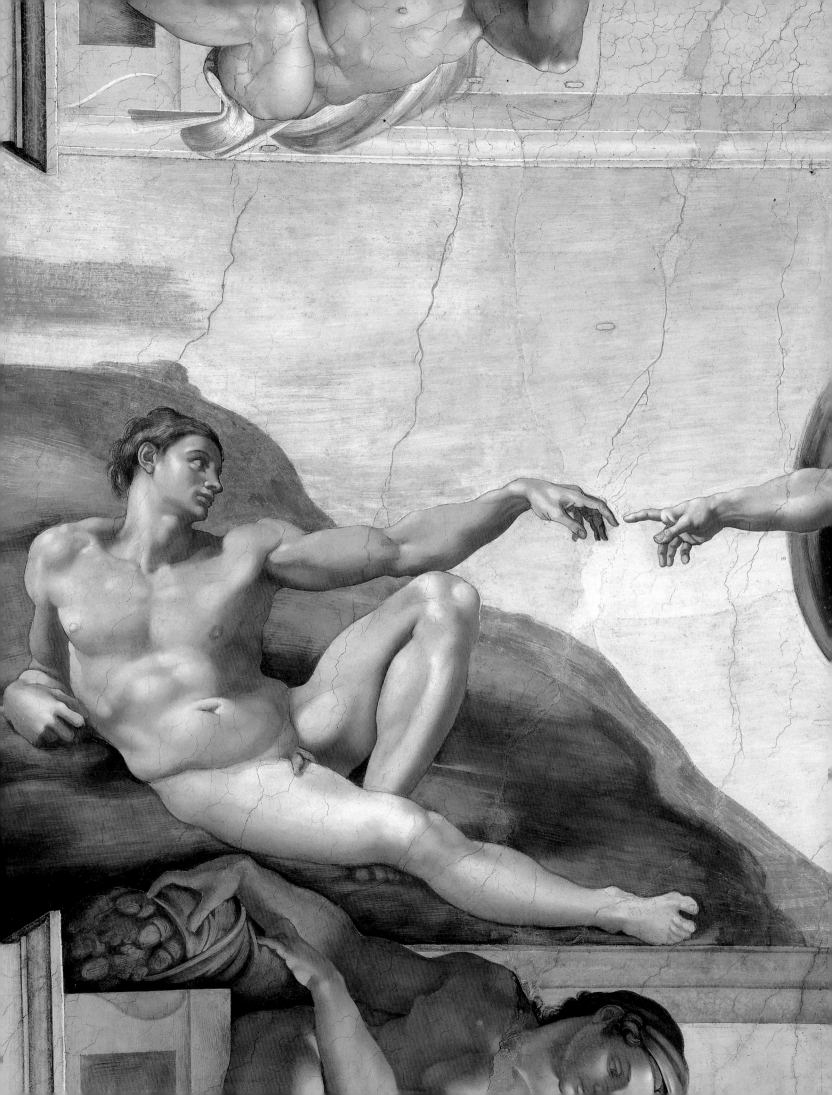

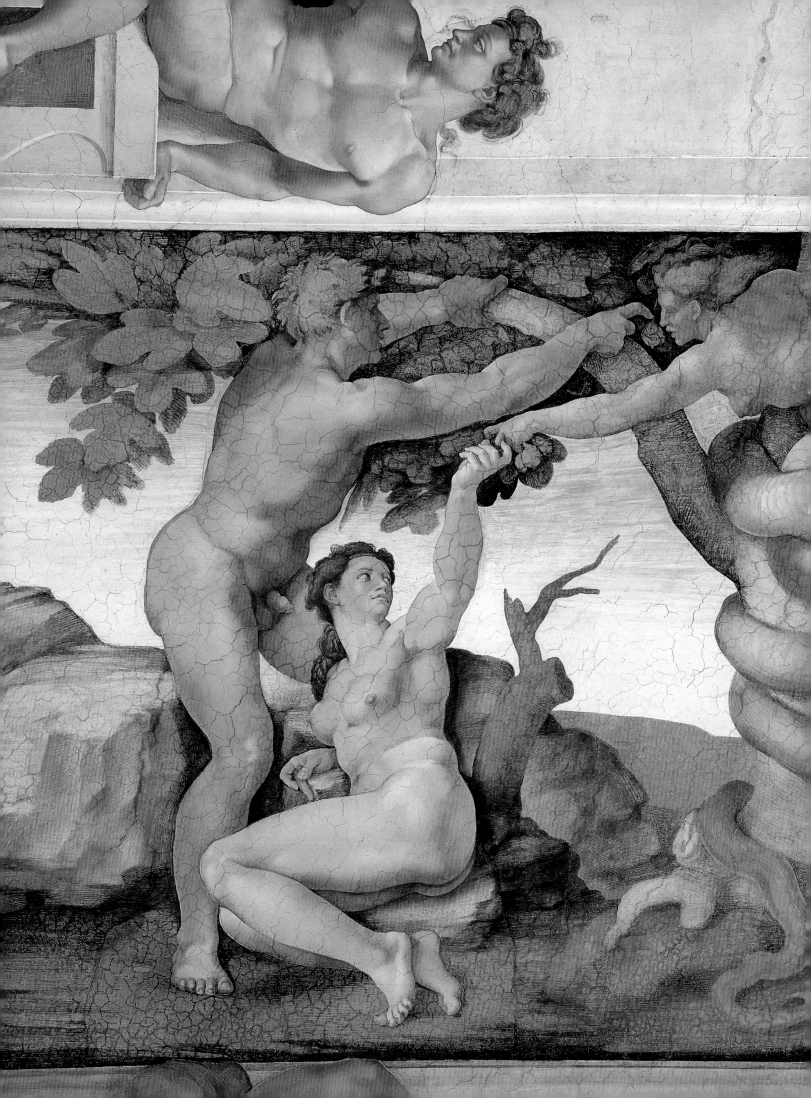

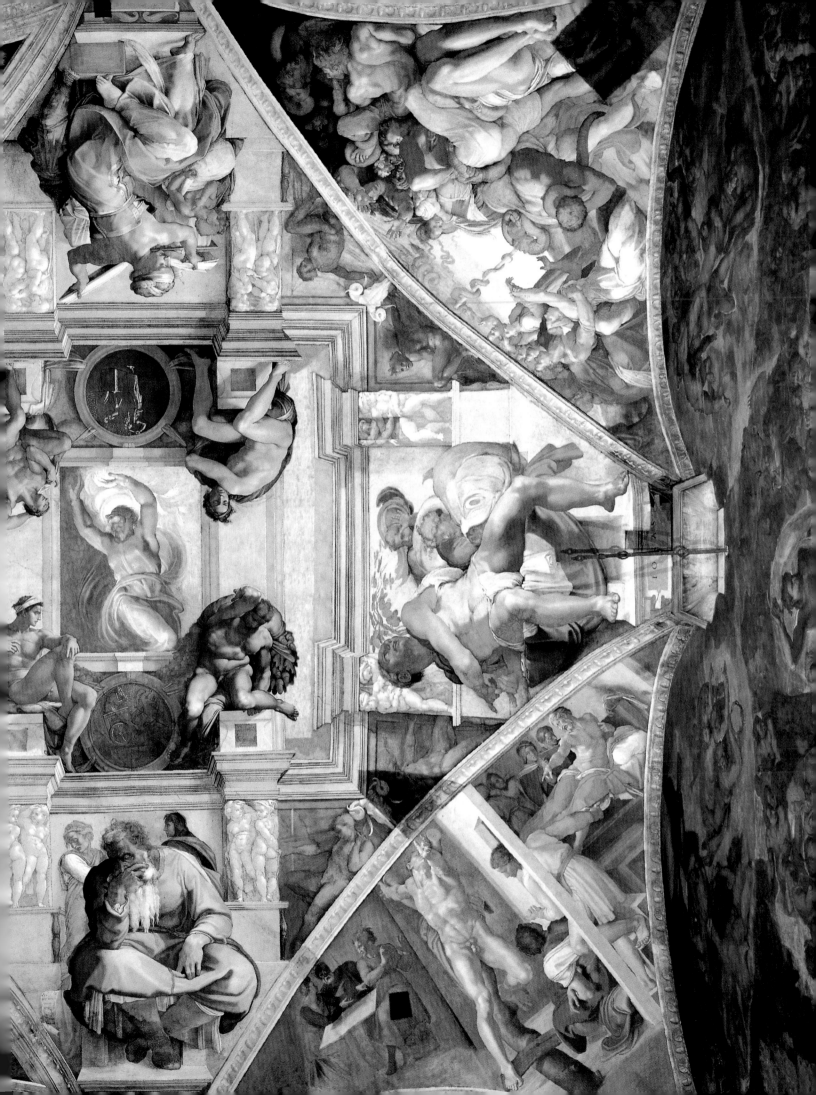

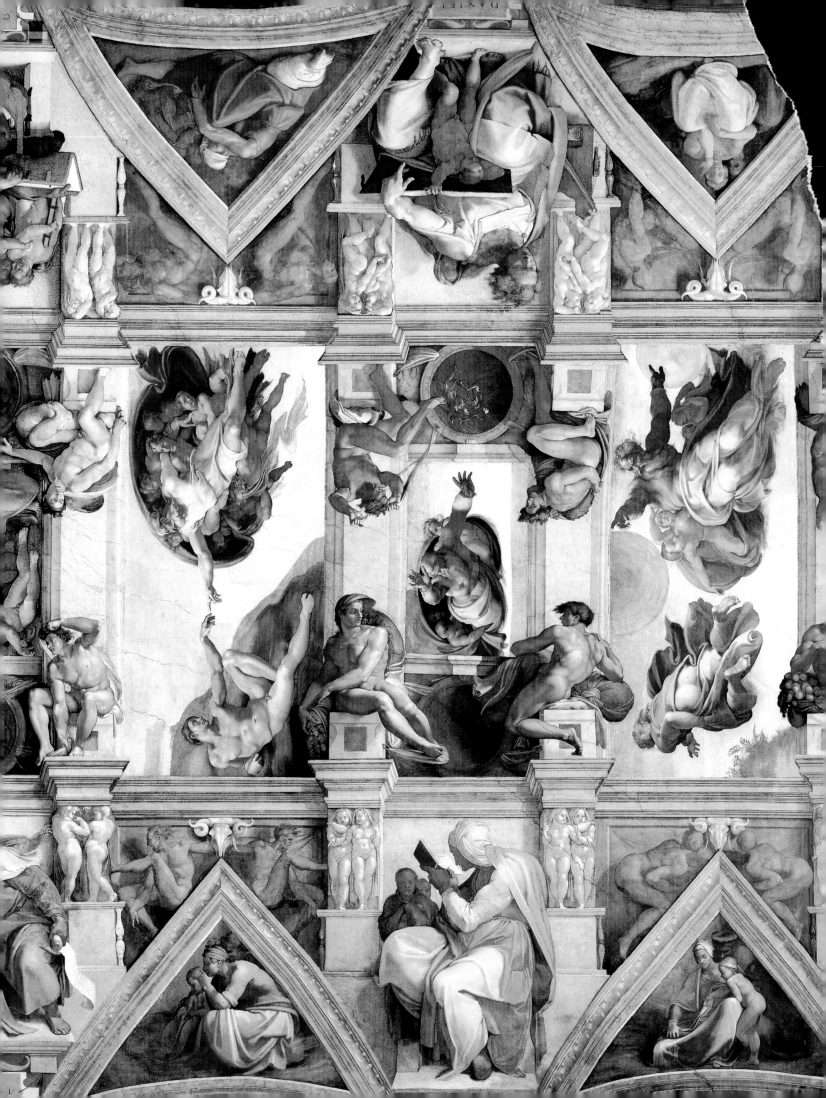

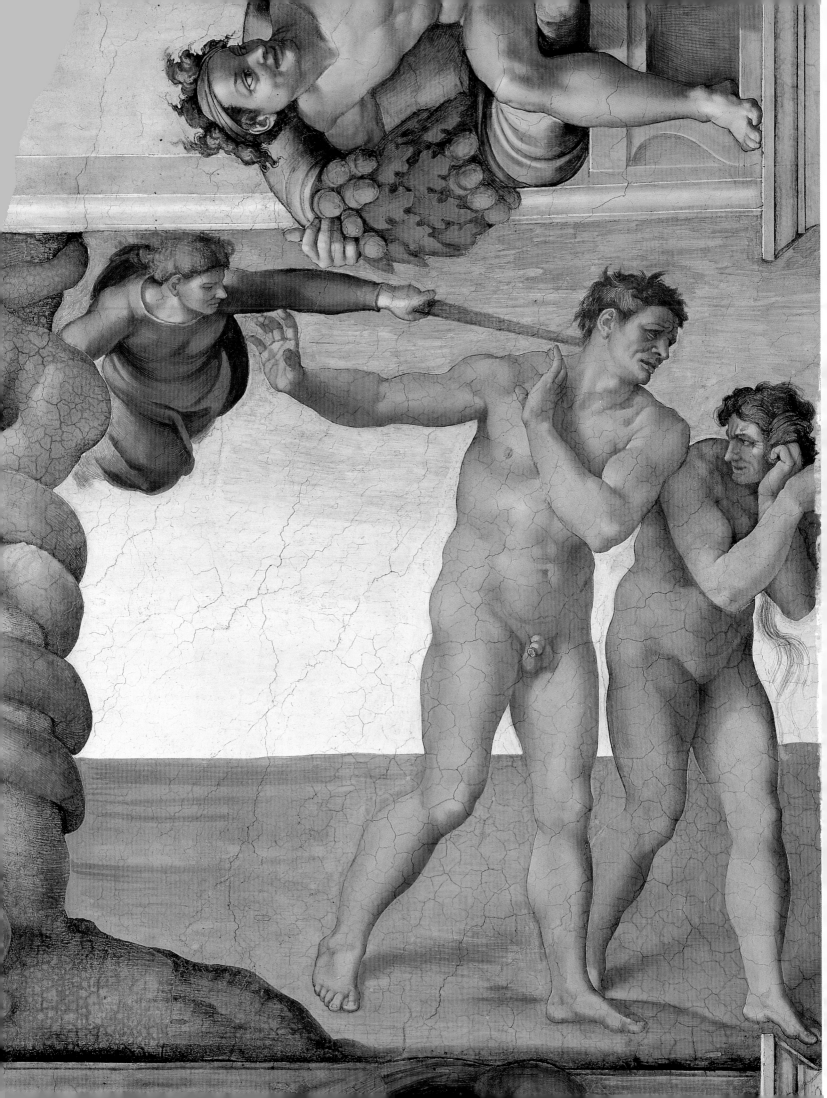

The Original Sin and the Expulsion from Eden *(previous pages).* Michelangelo's interpretation of the scene of the Original Sin portrays the characters in an untraditional way. Adam is the one who plucks the forbidden fruit from the tree, while Eve, reclining and passive, accepts it from the serpent. In an entirely new way, Michelangelo depicts the episodes of the Temptation and the Expulsion from the Garden of Eden in the same scene: cause and effect are separate, but they are also intimately joined together by the Tree of Good and Evil, around which the demon tempter, portrayed in the shape of a woman, is coiled.

The Drunkenness of Noah: *"Noah, a tiller of the soil, was the first to plant the vine. He drank some of the wine, and while he was drunk, he lay uncovered in his tent" (cf. Genesis 9: 20-22).*

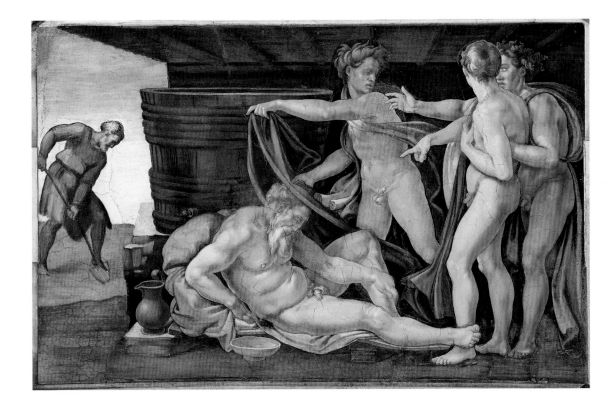

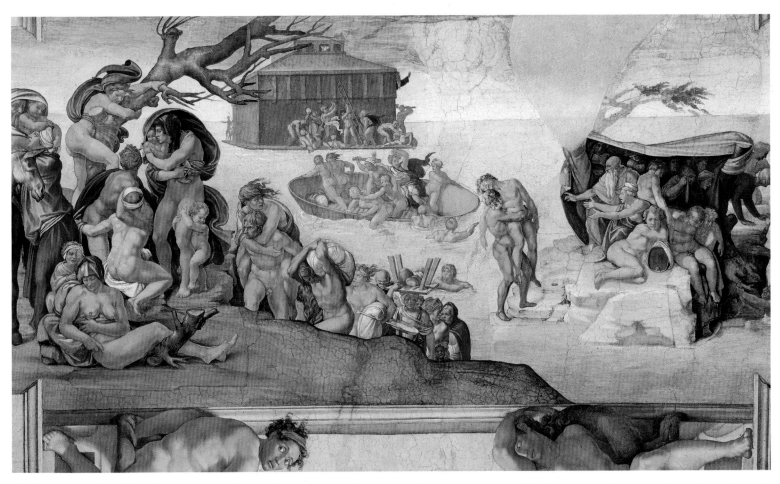

The first scenes that Michelangelo painted were the stories narrating the main episodes of Noah's life. They should be observed starting from the entrance: "The Drunkenness of Noah" (above), "The Deluge" (below), and "The Sacrifice of Noah" to God (following page).

The Deluge *(above): "And heavy rain fell on earth for forty days and forty nights. ...Every living thing on the face of the earth was wiped out ... and only Noah was left, and those with him in the ark" (cf. Genesis 7: 12, 20-22).*

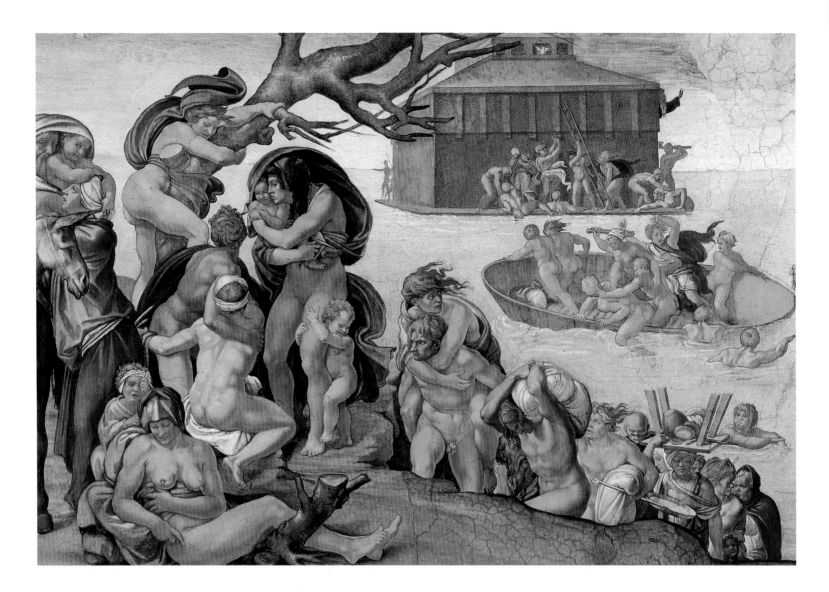

The Deluge, *detail (above):* Michelangelo imagined that the ark was built like a cathedral, a device that is clearly a reference to the Church, the "new ark" for the salvation of all peoples.

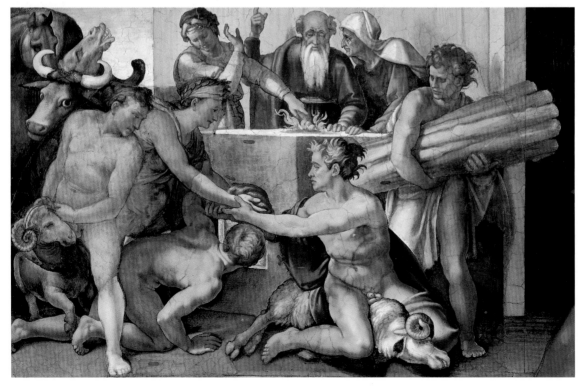

The Sacrifice of Noah *(left):* "Then Noah built an altar to Yahweh and, choosing from all the clean animals and all the clean birds he presented burnt offerings on the altar" (cf. Genesis 8:20).

Judith and Holofernes: *Judith is one of Israel's heroines because, in a critical time for the history of her people, she was able to use a stratagem to kill the head of the enemy forces that were besieging the city. Michelangelo depicts the conclusive moment in her act of liberation: "Twice she struck at his neck with all her might and cut off his head. ... After which, she went out and gave the head of Holofernes to her maid..." (cf. Judith 13: 8-10).*

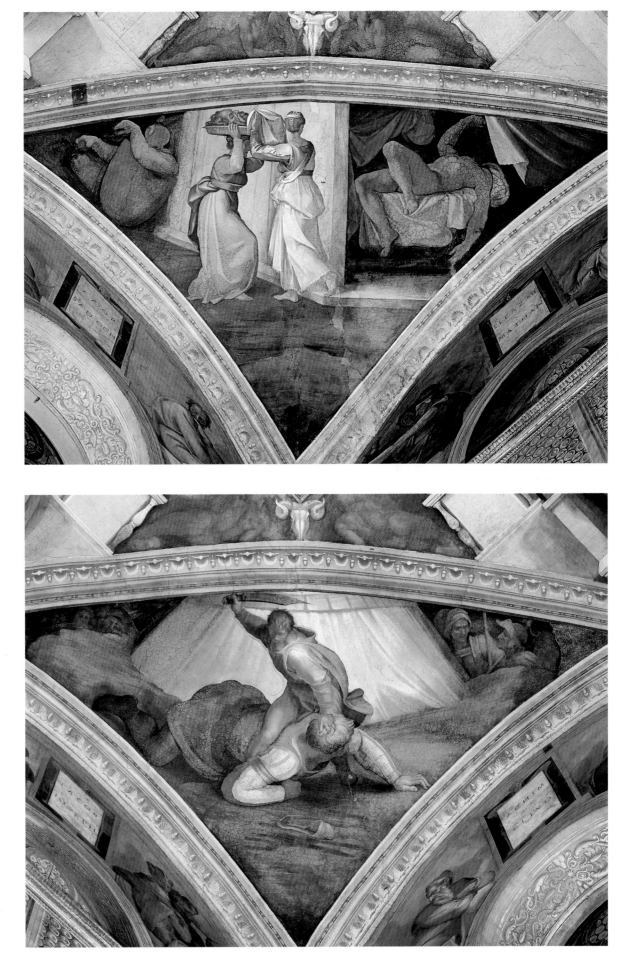

David and Goliath: *"Thus David triumphed over the Philistine with a sling and a stone; he hit the Philistine and killed him, though he had no sword in his hand. David ran and stood over the Philistine, seized his sword, pulled it from the scabbard, despatched him and cut off his head" (cf. Samuel 1:17, 50-51).*

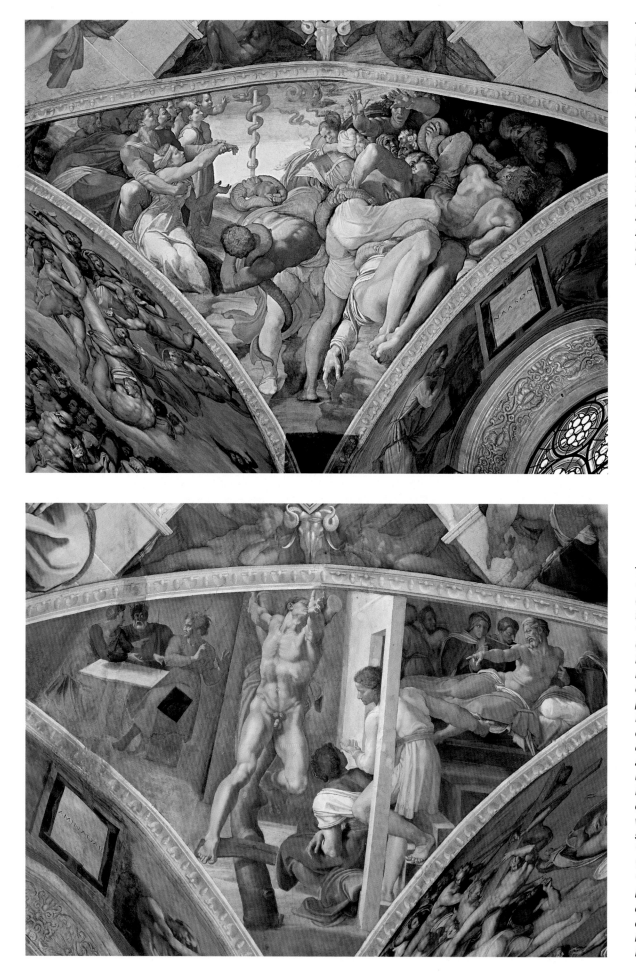

The Brazen Serpent: "They left Mount Hor by the road to the Sea of Suph, to skirt round Edom. On the way the people lost patience. They spoke against God and against Moses. ... At this, God sent fiery serpents among the people; their bite brought death to many in Israel. ... Moses interceded for the people, and Yahweh replied, 'Make a fiery serpent and raise it as a standard. Anyone who is bitten and looks at it will survive'" (cf. Numbers 21: 4-8).

The Punishment of Haman: "The king and Haman went to Queen Esther's banquet... the king again said to Esther, 'Tell me your request...' Queen Esther replied, 'and if it please your majesty, grant me my life—that is my request; and the lives of my people—that is what I want. For we have been handed over, my people and I, to destruction, slaughter and annihilation... King Ahasuerus interrupted Queen Esther, 'Who is this man?' he exclaimed. 'Where is the man who has thought of doing such a thing?' Esther replied, 'The persecutor, the enemy? Why, this wretch Haman!' ... 'Hang him on it', said the king. So Haman was hanged on the gallows which he had erected for Mordecai, and the king's wrath subsided" (cf. Esther 7: 1-3, 6, 9-10).

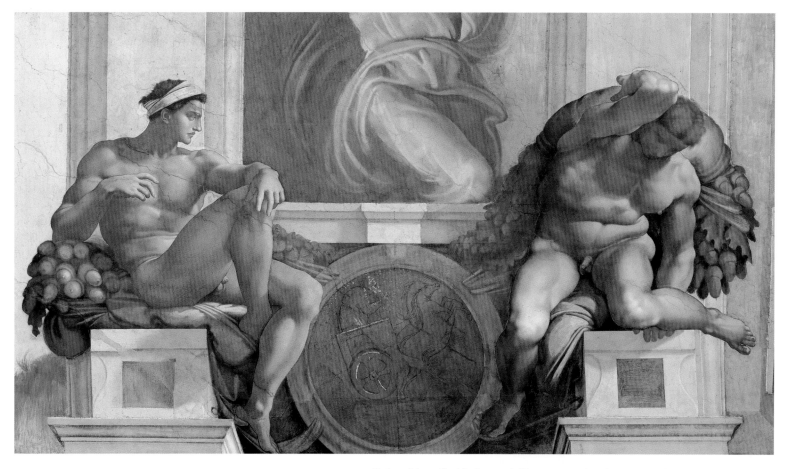

Pairs of Ignudi with the medallions portraying the prophet Elijah carried skyward in a chariot of fire (above) and Abraham's sacrifice of Isaac (below).

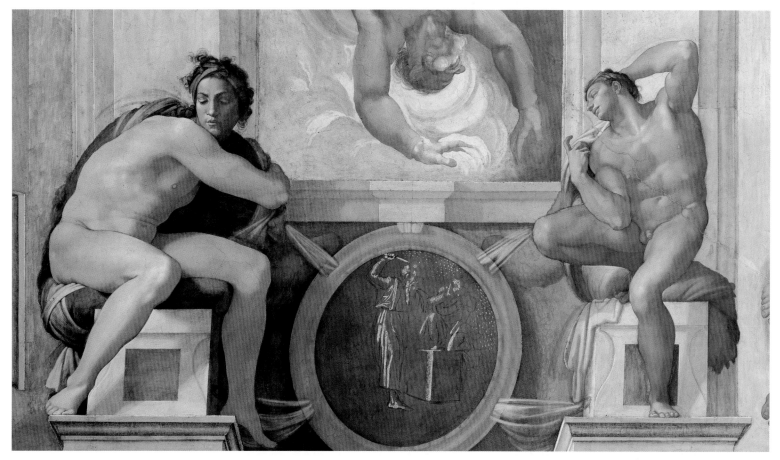

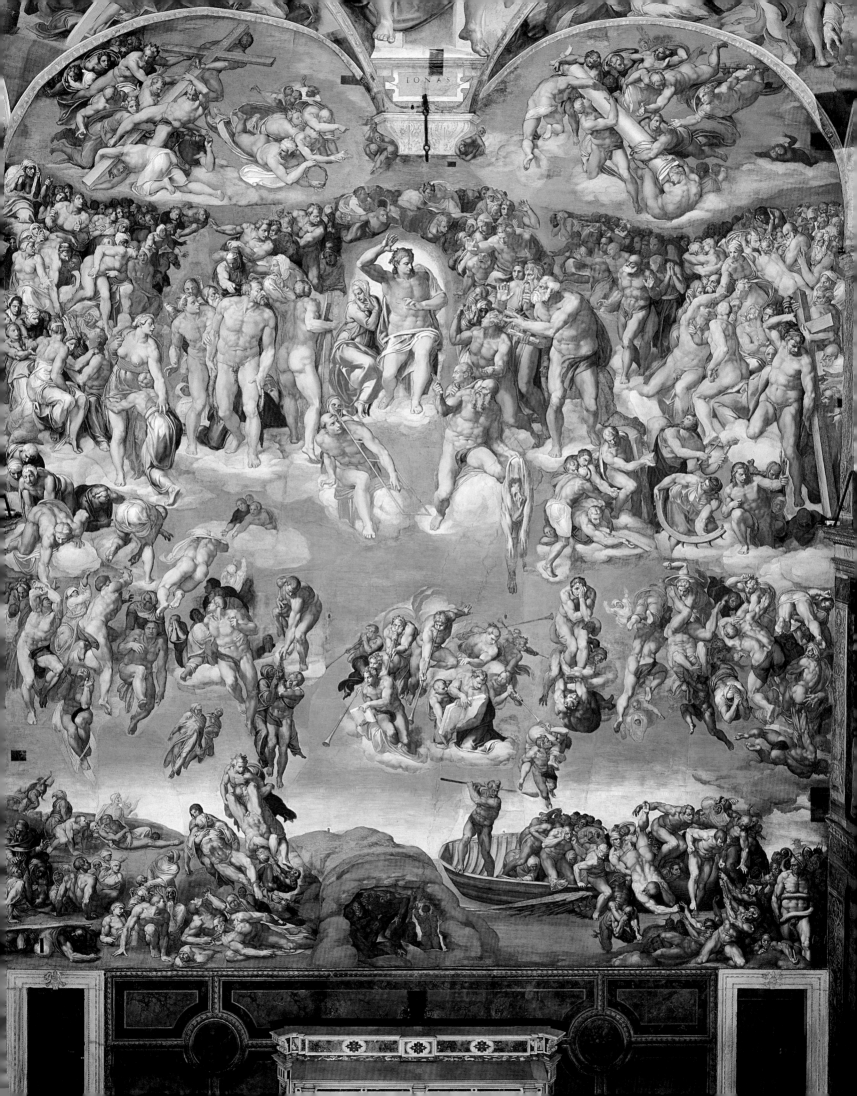

The Last Judgment. More than twenty years after the completion of the vault, in 1536, under the Farnese pope Paul III (1534-1549), Michelangelo, who was now sixty years old, began to fresco the altar wall with the theme of the Last Judgment. It was to be an eternal warning of the transitory nature of life and the universe. In order to paint the *Dies Irae* ("Judgment Day") on the entire wall, Michelangelo had to sacrifice Perugino's 15th century paintings as well as the two lunettes depicting the "Ancestors of Christ" which he himself had frescoed in 1512. The pivot of this magnificent work of art, animated by nearly 400 characters, is the figure of Christ as judge around which the rest of the representation revolves. Next to him only the Virgin Mary, portrayed in an attitude of resigned melancholy, seems removed from the turbulent movement upwards and downwards that involves all the other characters in the scene. The upper area, corresponding to the lunettes, which is also extraneous to the vortex of activity, contains the heavenly world with angels flying about carrying the instruments of Christ's Passion. The motion and attitude of pathos expressed by the circle of saints, apostles and martyrs who surround Christ and the Virgin, convey a sense of anxiety and worry over the forthcoming verdict. It should be observed that Michelangelo painted a sorrowful self-portrait in the folds of the flesh on the face of the martyrdom that St. Bartholomew shows to the Judge. The lower, central part of the fresco is filled with angels heralding the Judgment with their trumpets; on the lefthand side are those climbing up to Heaven and on the righthand side are those being dragged down to Hell. Immediately below, the Resurrection of the Flesh is taking place on the left, whereas, on the right, the damned are being transported in Charon's ship to the underworld's judge, Minos. Once finished, the masterpiece was unveiled on the eve of All Saints' Day in 1541.

Detail of Christ the Judge*: "When the Son of man comes in his glory.., he will separate people one from another as the shepherd separates sheep from goats"* (cf. Matthew 25: 31-33).

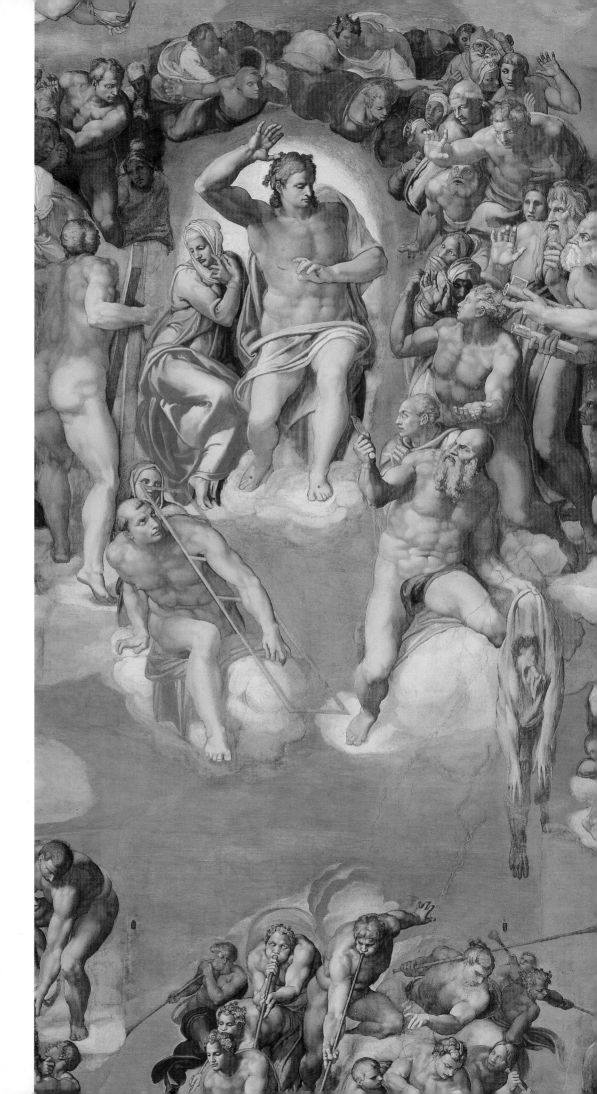

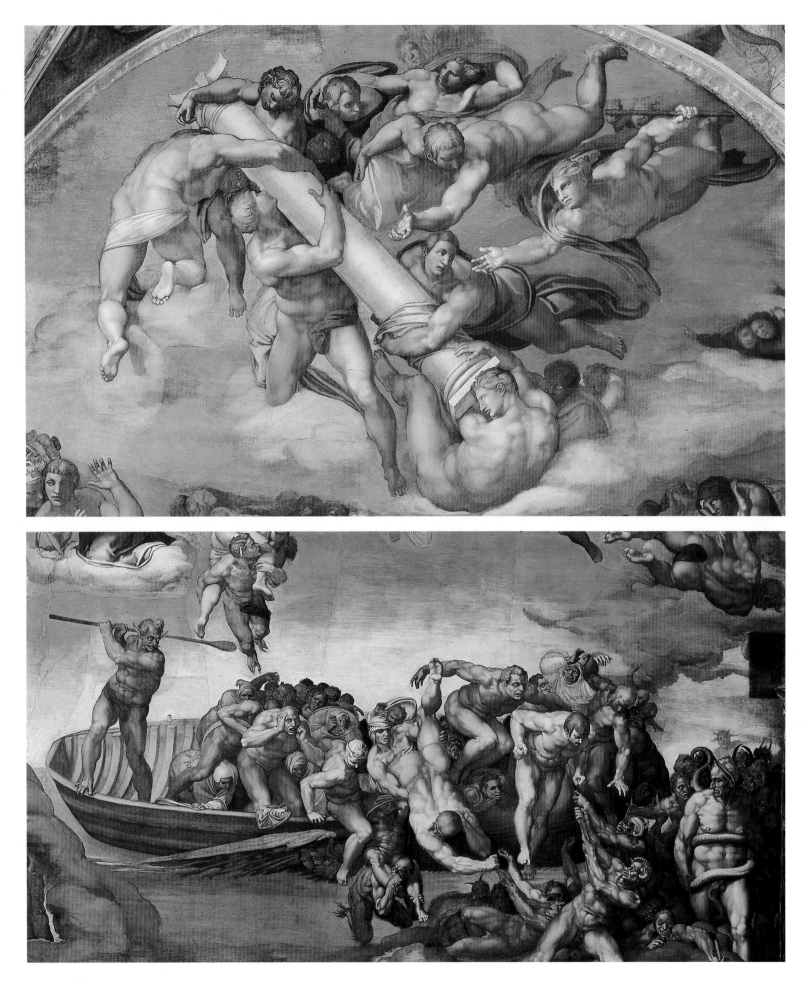

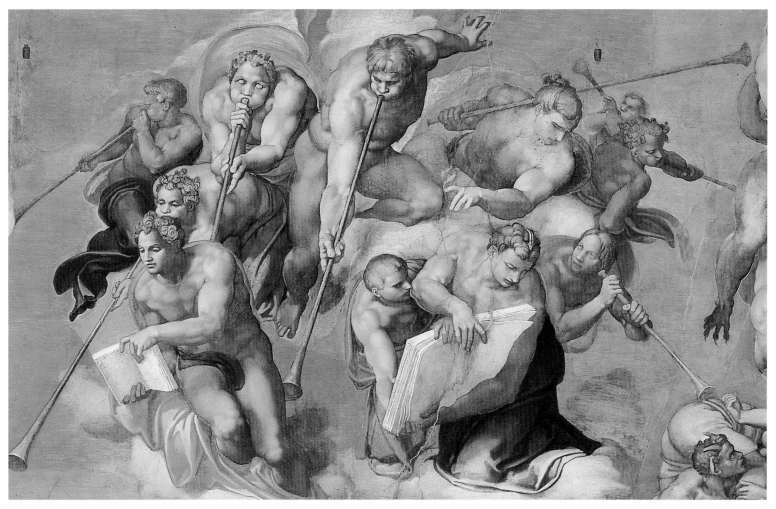

At the center of the lower portion of the fresco, in a position of importance, Michelangelo painted a compact group of angels with trumpets *that herald the end of time and the resurrection of the flesh. Michelangelo represented the words of the liturgical hymn: "Hark! the trumpets blasting forth their thrilling tone, summon all from sepulchral regions before the throne. Now the open book is spread which condemns the quick and dead. Now before the Judge severe, hidden things must all appear. Naught can pass unpunished here." (Tommaso da Celano,* Dies Irae*).*

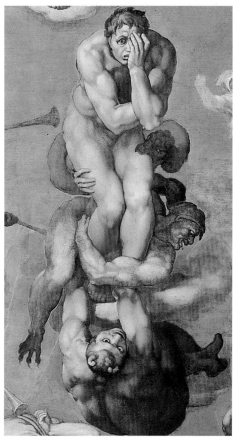

The Last Judgment, detail of one of the damned (on the right).

In the upper part of the Last Judgment *(left, above), Michelangelo depicted groups of wingless angels in flight carrying the instruments of Christ's Passion. In the right lunette, a group of angels is shown in the act of holding up the column of the flagellation. Their bodies, shaped so beautifully by the master, are silhouetted against the background of a sky streaked with clouds. They cluster together in turbulent motion full of apprehension, thus creating the dominant note of the work.*

In the lower right corner of the fresco *(left, below), Michelangelo depicted the scene of hell, obviously inspired by Dante's* Divine Comedy. *The scene is dominated by two mythological figures: the demonic helmsman, Charon and the judge of the damned, Minos. The latter bears the facial features of the master of ceremonies, Biagio da Cesena, one of the first to bitterly criticize the fresco for its excessive number of nudes, claiming that it is "not a work for the chapel of a pope, but for a tavern".*

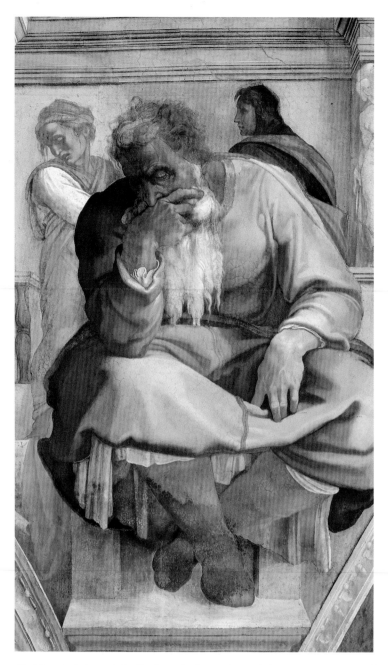

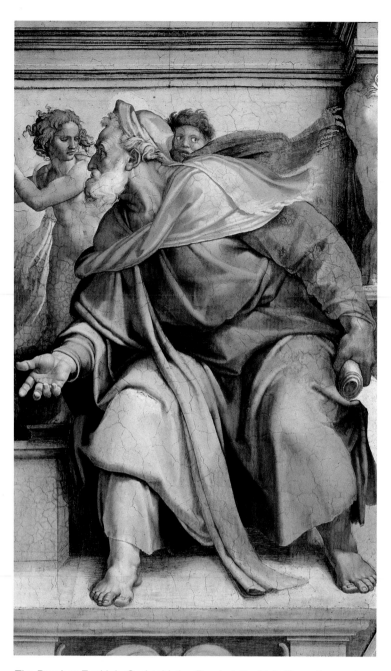

The Prophet Jeremiah. *"In the pit of my stomach how great my agony! Walls of my heart! My heart is throbbing! I cannot keep quiet, for I have heard the trumpet call, the battle cry. Ruin on ruin is the news: the whole land is laid waste... How long must I see the standard and hear the trumpet call?" (cf. Jeremiah 4:19-21). The Prophet of "Lamentations", overcome with pain and oppressed by ill omens, agonizes over the imminent punishment for Jerusalem's unfaithfulness. Some scholars interpret the Seer's bitter and tormented expression to be a more or less symbolic reference to Michelangelo.*

The Prophet Ezekiel. *God told the Prophet Ezekiel: "Son of man, I am sending you to the Israelites, to the rebels who have rebelled against me... Because they are stubborn and obstinate children, I am sending you to them...' When I looked, there was a hand stretching out to me, holding a scroll. He unrolled it in front of me; it was written on, front and back; on it was written 'Lamentations, dirges and cries of grief' "(cf. Ezekiel 2:3-4, 9-10). The spirit of prophecy and that of the priesthood are joined together in the Prophet Ezekiel, whose doctrine is focused on interior renewal. He is portrayed holding a scroll that was given to him by God, and is concentrating all his attention on the words addressed to him by the Lord.*

The Eritrean Sibyl. *Portrayed with a pure, nobile profile, this Sibyl is leafing through a large volume resting on a bookstand. One of the little boys behind her is caught in the act of turning on a lamp, and the other is rubbing his eyes as if he has just awakened.*

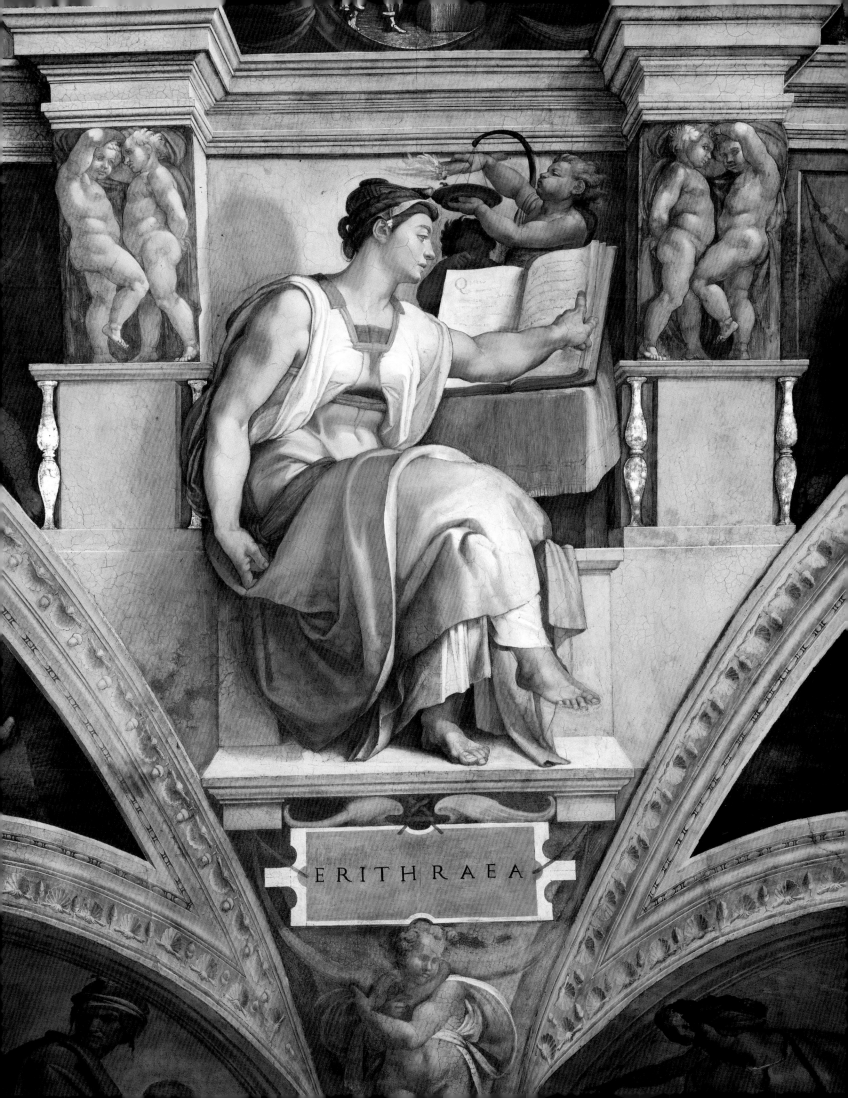

ERITHRAEA

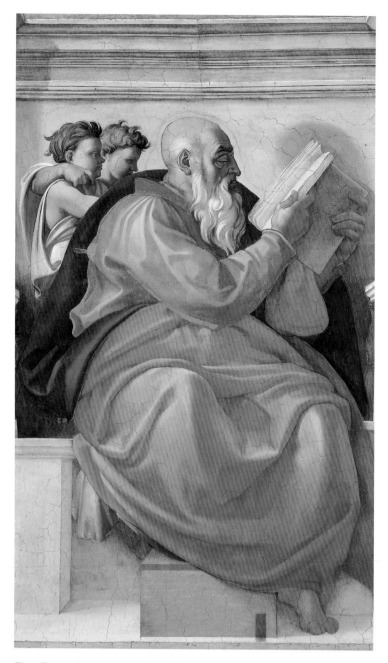

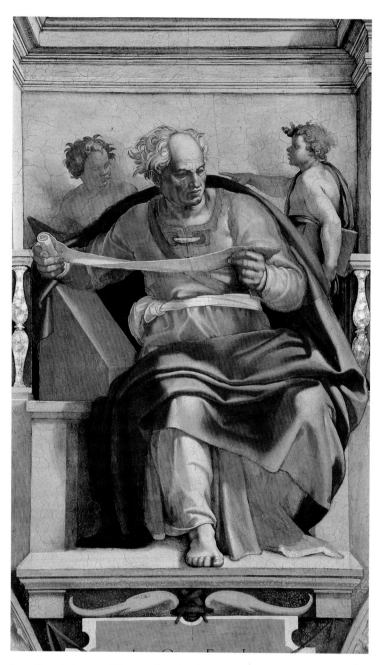

The Prophet Zechariah. *"Rejoice heart and soul, daughter of Zion! Shout for joy, daughter of Jerusalem! Look, your king is approaching, he is vindicated and victorious, humble and riding on a donkey... He will proclaim peace to the nations, his empire will stretch from sea to sea, from the River to the limits of the earth"* (cf. Zechariah 9:9-10). Michelangelo began frescoing the group of Seers with this prophet, who supported the survivors of Jerusalem after the Babylonian captivity by using the word of God. Zechariah is portrayed as a forceful old man in the act of reading.

The Prophet Joel. *The Lord said: "I shall pour out my spirit on all humanity. ... Even on the slaves, men and women... I shall show portents in the sky and on earth, blood and fire and columns of smoke... All who call on the name of Yahweh will be saved..."* (cf. Joel 3:1 foll.). This prophet, his aging face with hollow cheeks furrowed by vigils, is intent upon examining a scroll in order to understand the meaning of the prophecy.

The Delphic Sibyl. *This is the most admired Sibyl of the series due to her physical beauty. She is caught in a moment of intense inspiration. Stylistically, this Sibyl can be linked to Michelangelo's youthful Madonnas.*

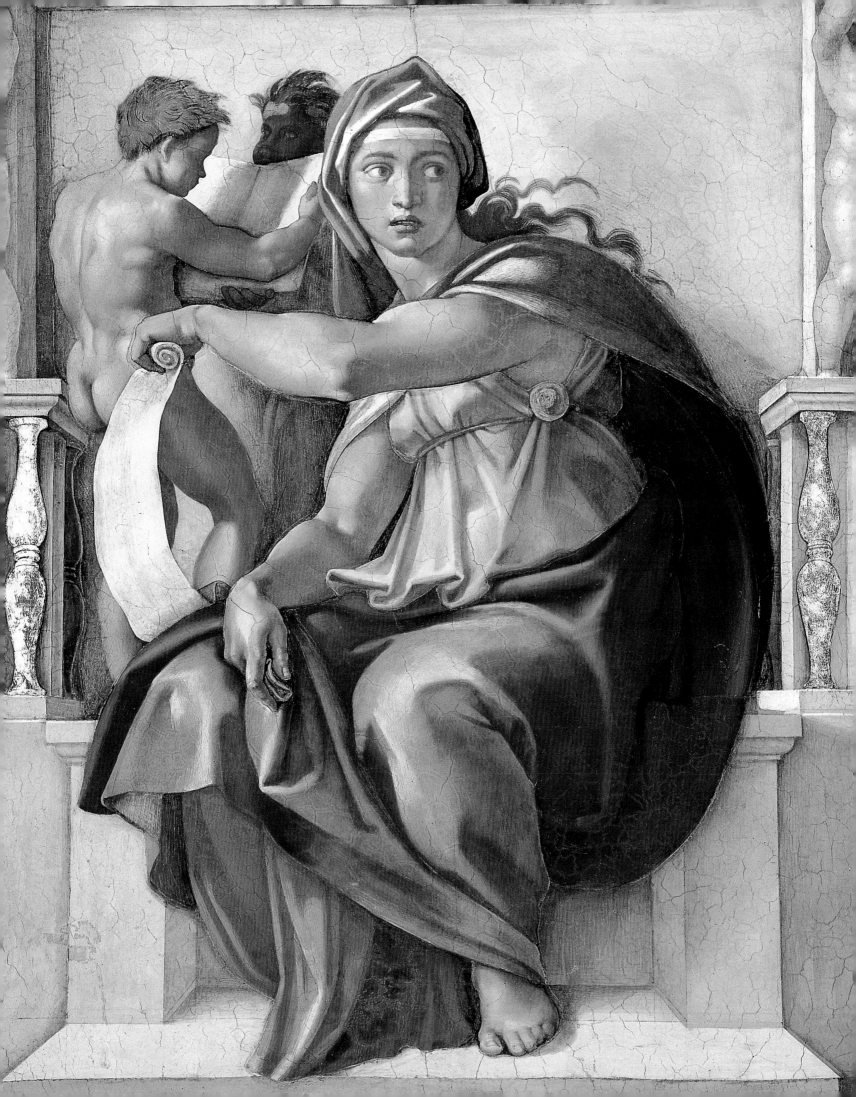

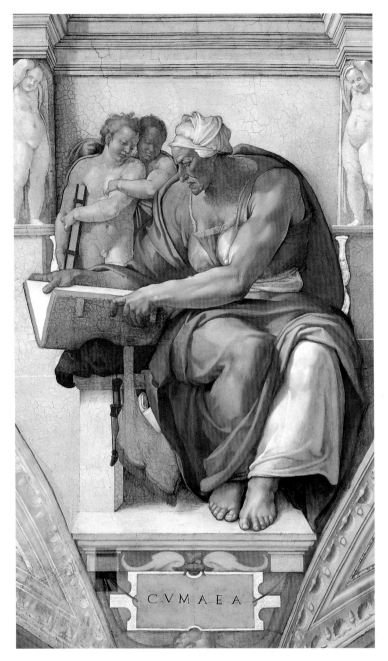

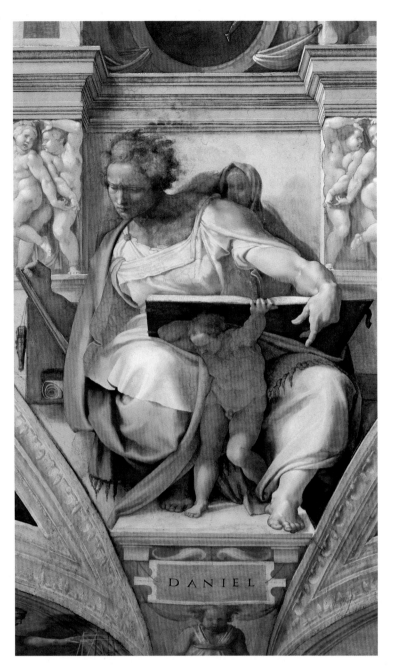

The Cumaean Sibyl. *The face of this huge figure has been ravished by time. This Sibyl is leaning over the open book that she is holding out in front of her with large, powerful hands.*

The Prophet Daniel. *"In the first year of Belshazzar king of Babylon, Daniel had a dream and visions that passed through his head as he lay in bed. He wrote the dream down..." (cf. Daniel 7:1-2). With an expression of intense interior torment on his face, the young prophet is portrayed in the act of writing down his dreams and visions.*

The Prophet Isaiah. *"I then heard the voice of the Lord saying: 'Whom shall I send? Who will go for us?' And I said, 'Here am I, send me" (cf. Isaiah 6:8-9). As the prophet of faith, Isaiah is the most important of the prophets who announced the coming of Jesus Christ the Savior. Michelangelo has caught him in the act of answering God's call.*

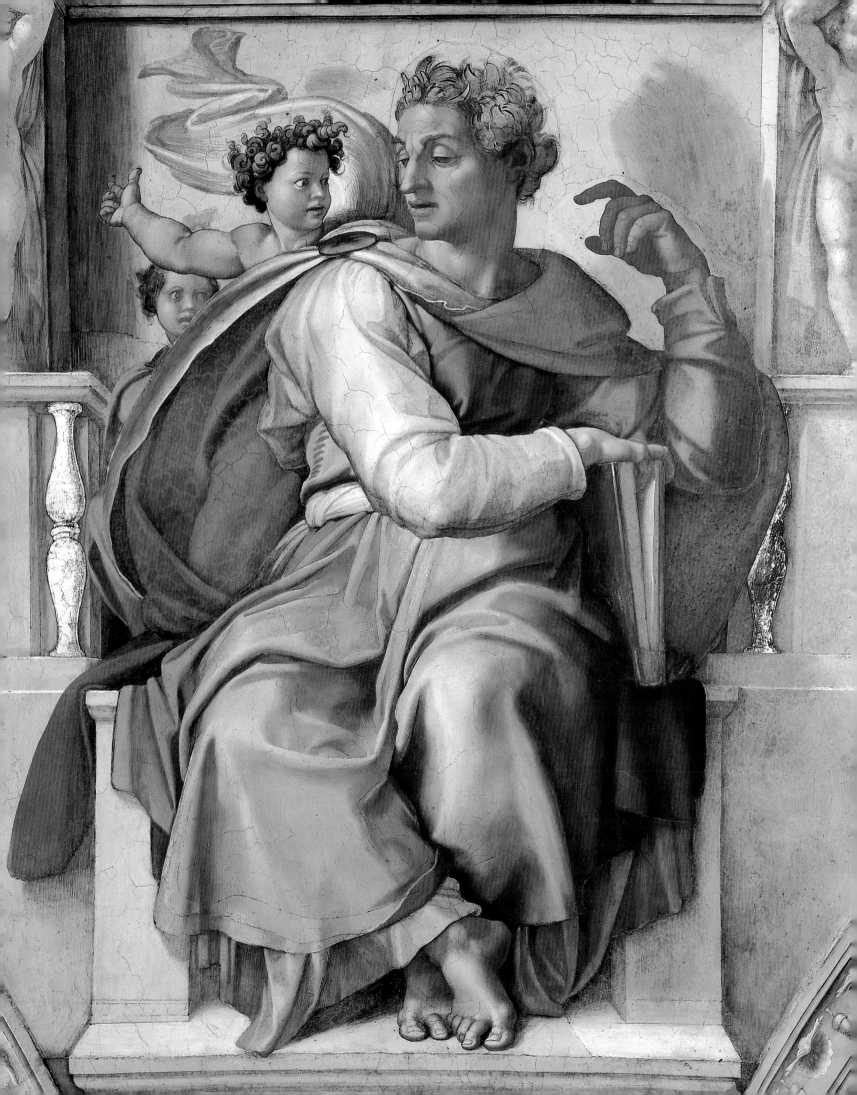

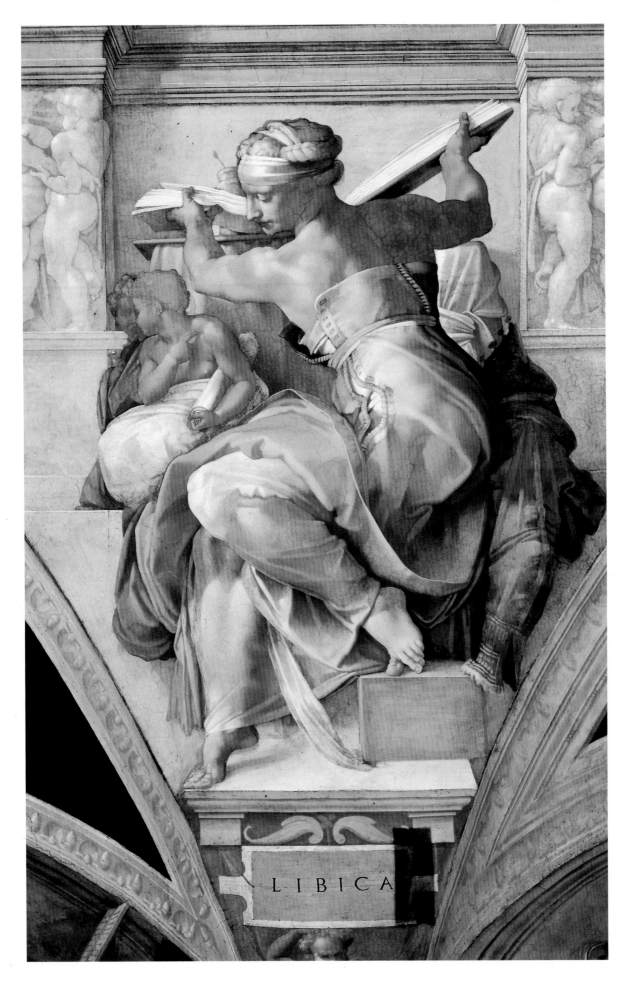

The Libyan Sibyl. *This young Sibyl is portrayed in a complicated motion of turning around, which most scholars have interpreted as the act of closing the large volume she is holding and putting it back on the shelf. It is a most refined and dynamic invention, exhibiting the great artistic maturity reached by Michelangelo in that period.*

LIBICA

The Prophet Jonah. *This is the prophet most frequently portrayed by artistic tradition. His story and the symbolic elements contained within have most certainly inspired artists' imaginations throughout history. On the right, Michelangelo painted the whale who swallowed Jonah and released him three days later. This event is an obvious forecast of the burial and resurrection of Christ. In the Holy Scriptures, his vocation is described as follows: "The word of Yahweh was addressed to Jonah a second time. 'Up!' he said, 'Go to Nineveh, the great city, and preach to it as I shall tell you.' Jonah set out and went to Nineveh in obedience to the word of Yahweh" (cf. Jonah 3:13).*

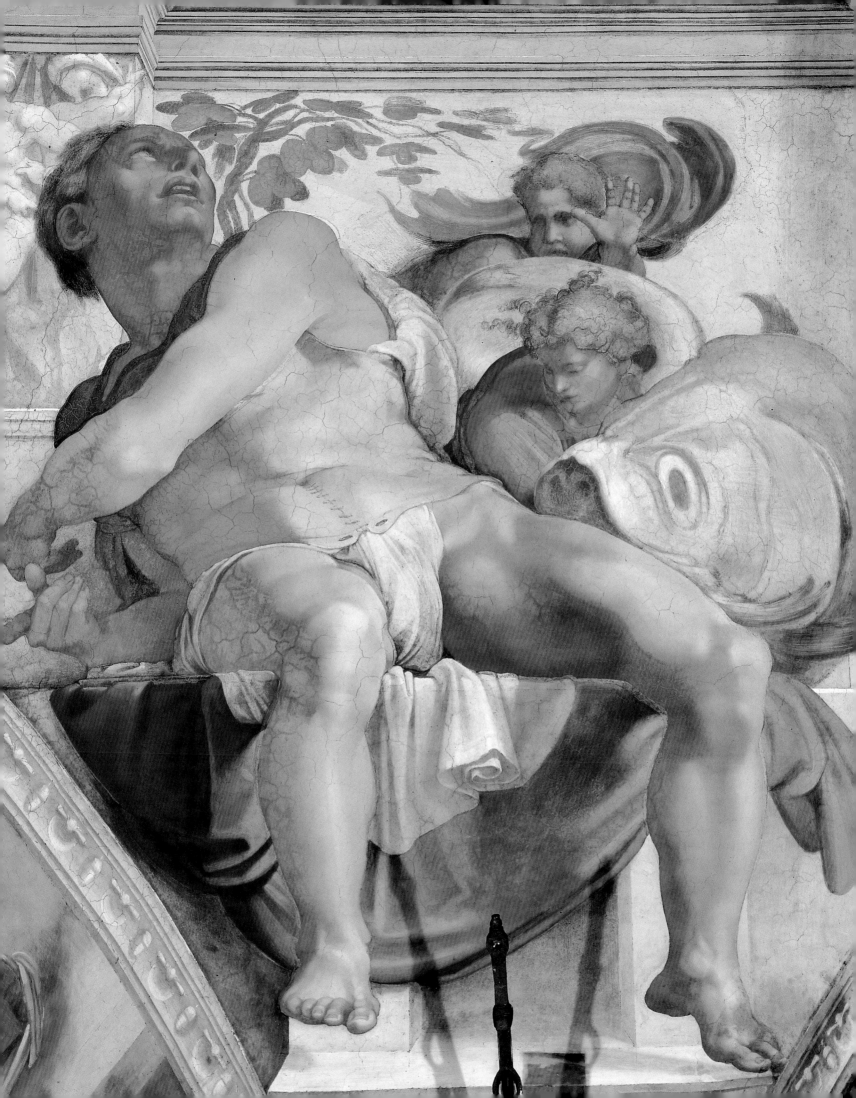

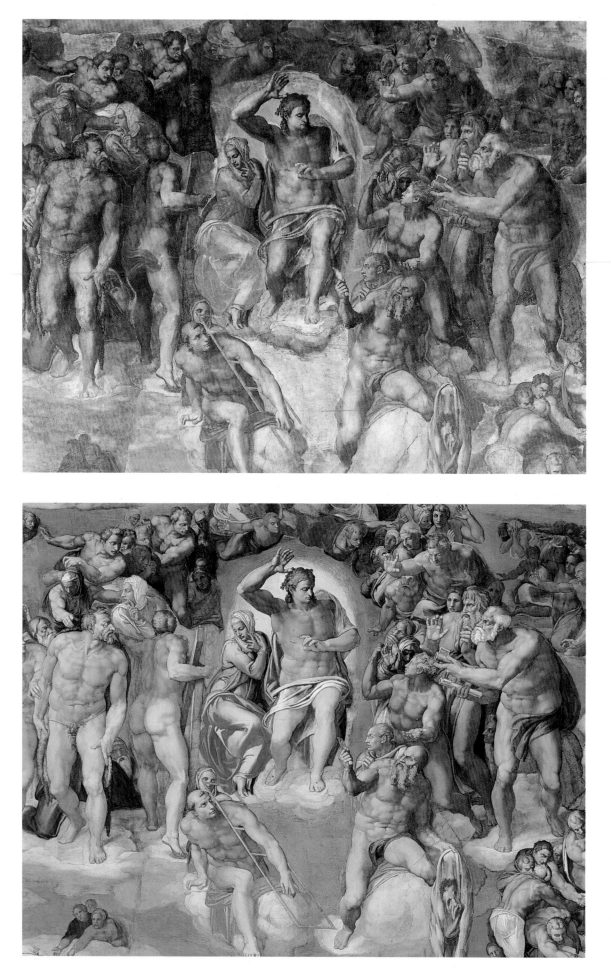

The *cleaning of Michelangelo's frescoes* was begun in 1980, when the operation could no longer be postponed because the glue that had been applied to the frescoes over the centuries (documented for the first time in 1565, but systematically applied over the entire surface between 1710 and 1714) had contracted due to changes in temperature. This contraction caused flakes of paint to be ripped off. Tests carried out on the painted surface demonstrated that the dark brown color of the frescoes was the result of layers of dust and lampblack (from candles and oil lamps) that alternated with the layers of glue. Originally the glue had been applied to the surfaces to cover the salt efflorescence produced by the infiltration of rainwater; later the glue was used to brighten the colors which had been dulled by the dirt. However, the remedy proved to be far worse than the damage; in fact, the glue, a transparent substance made of animal protein, gradually darkened with time. The original colors of the frescoes were restored by repeatedly washing the surfaces with a solution of ammonia bicarbonate, sodium bicarbonate, desogen and carbosilmetilcellulose. The few sections painted *a secco* were cleaned with organic solvents that contain no water. The protection of the frescoes is guaranteed by strict monitoring of the Chapel's microclimate.

Detail of the Last Judgment *before (above) and after (below) restoration.*

The Creation of Adam *before (above) and after (below) restoration. The cleaning clearly revealed the exceptional quality of Michelangelo's fresco technique. Above all it is characterized by his extreme concern for detail (frequently executed with rapid brush strokes applying color) and the uniformity of style which creates the impression that the entire cycle was done entirely by the hand of one artist.*

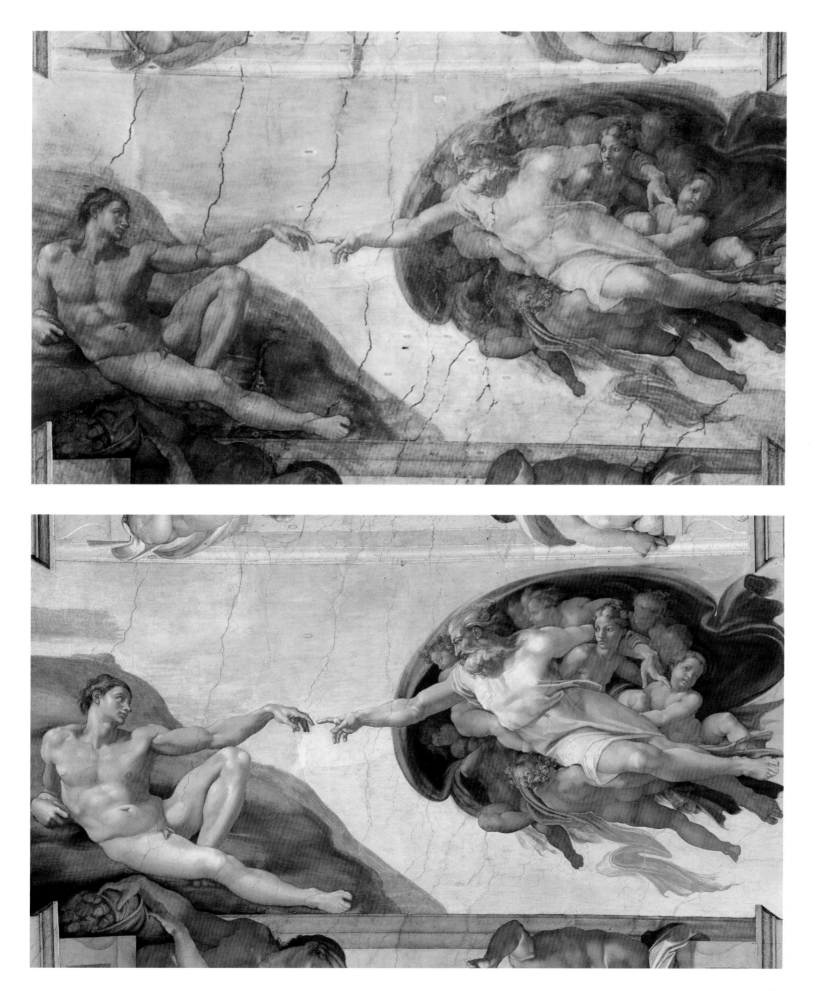

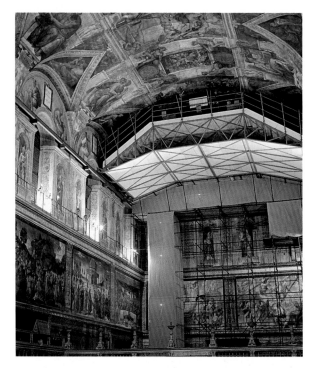

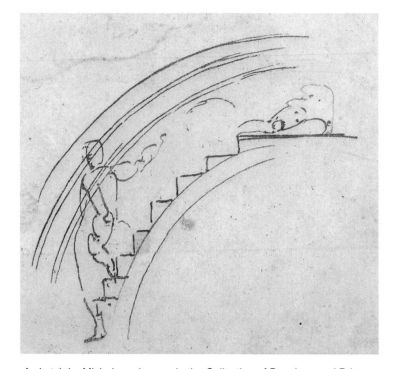

In order to carry out the restoration, a scaffolding similar to the one designed and built by Michelangelo was used. Michelangelo's was fixed and covered one half of the ceiling at a time, whereas this one is shorter and more mobile. The holes in the walls that supported this scaffolding are the same as the original ones used by the artist.

A sketch by Michelangelo, now in the Collection of Drawings and Prints at the Uffizi Gallery in Florence, shows the scaffolding that the artist had built for the Sistine Chapel.

Another sketch by Michelangelo, in the Buonarroti Archive in Florence, is an ironical portrayal of the artist at work.

Restorers at work on the scaffolding in the Sistine Chapel. Shown in profile is Gianluigi Colalucci, technical director; with his back to the camera, Maurizio Rossi; in the background, Fabrizio Mancinelli, scientific director.

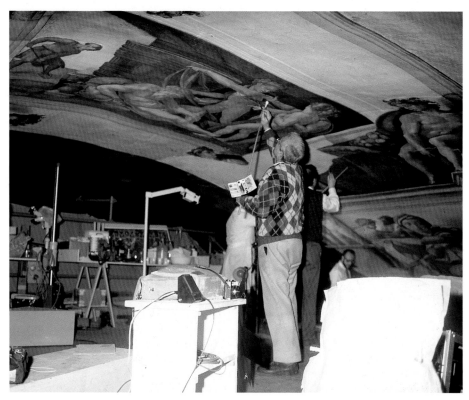

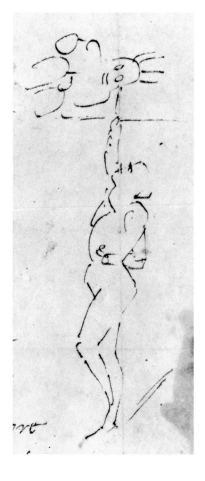

The Borgia Apartments consist of four rooms on the first floor of the north wing of the medieval palace, two rooms next to the Borgia Tower (commissioned by the Borgia pope Alexander VI in 1492 and finished in 1494) and a group of smaller private rooms in the west wing of the building. Bernardino Beth da Perugia, called *il Pinturicchio*, with a large school of assistants, painted the beautiful decorations in the rooms of the Borgia Apartments. The Collection of Modern Sacred Art is exhibited in these apartments and in the rooms beneath the Sistine Chapel.

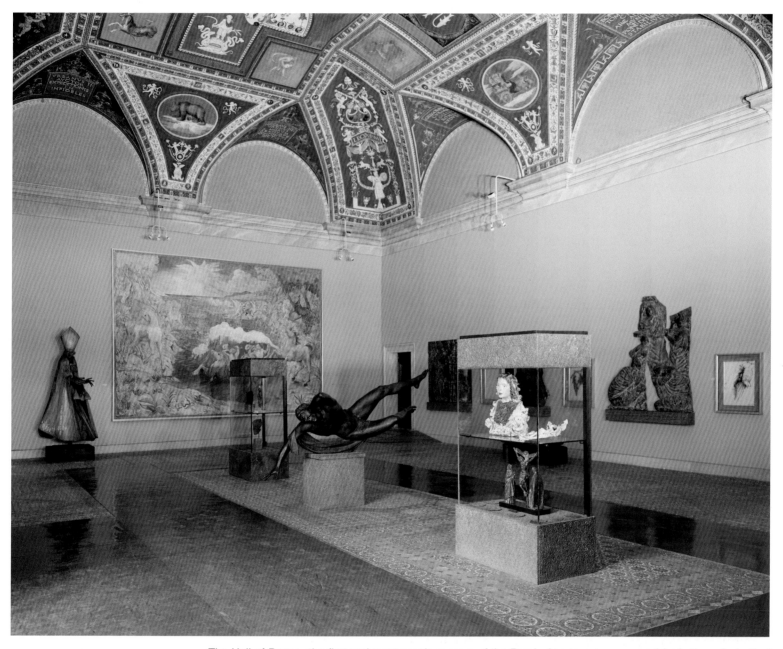

The Hall of Popes, *the first and most spacious room of the Borgia Apartments, was used for both ecclesiastical and secular functions of government. A false vault replaced the original medieval beamed ceiling that collapsed in 1500. It was decorated at the time of Leo X with zodiac signs, planets and constellations, with stuccoes by Giovanni da Udine and grotesques by Perin del Vaga. The artists were inspired by the so-called "golden ceiling" of Nero's* Domus Aurea *near the Colosseum which had only recently been discovered at that time.*

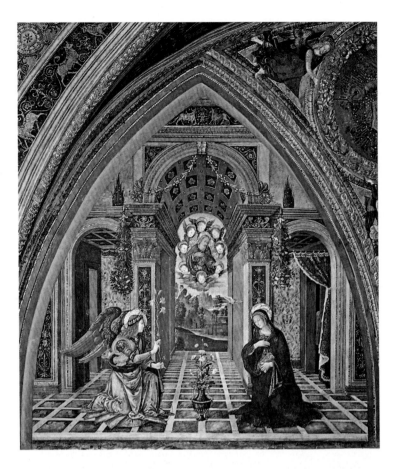

The Hall of Mysteries contains frescoes depicting stories from the lives of the Virgin Mary and Christ. Most of them were painted by the school of Pinturicchio. The fresco of the "Annunciation" (left, above) is an example of the fundamental theme of optimism and naturalism dominating Roman Christian Renaissance art: a cultural heritage that appears to descend naturally from the culture of imperial Rome. In a perspective typical of the Renaissance style, behind the portrayal of the Christian mystery (painted with refined, natural elegance), a classical triumphal arch frames the figure of God the Father, depicted in the sky above a charming country landscape.

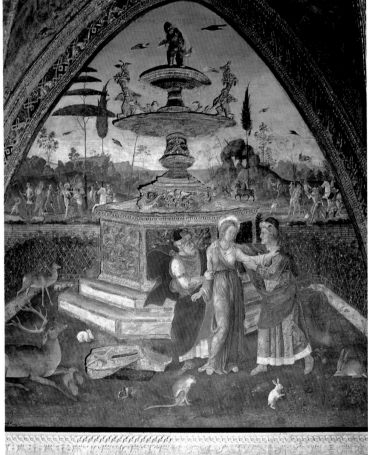

Susannah and the Elders, like all the other frescoes in the Hall of Saints, is the work of Pinturicchio.

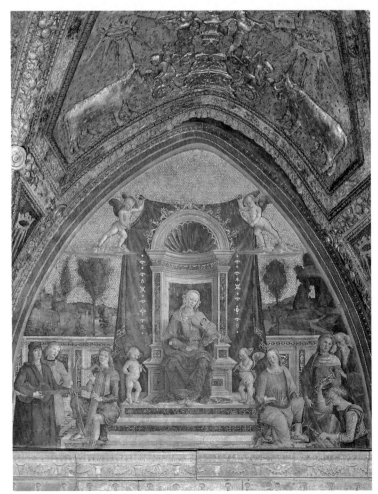

Music (left, below). A tribute to humanistic culture fills the lunettes of the Hall of Liberal Arts, dedicated to the Arts of the Trivium (Literature) and the Quadrivium (Science). The seven Liberal Arts in the Middle Ages were grammar, logic, rhetoric, arithmetic, geometry, music and astronomy.

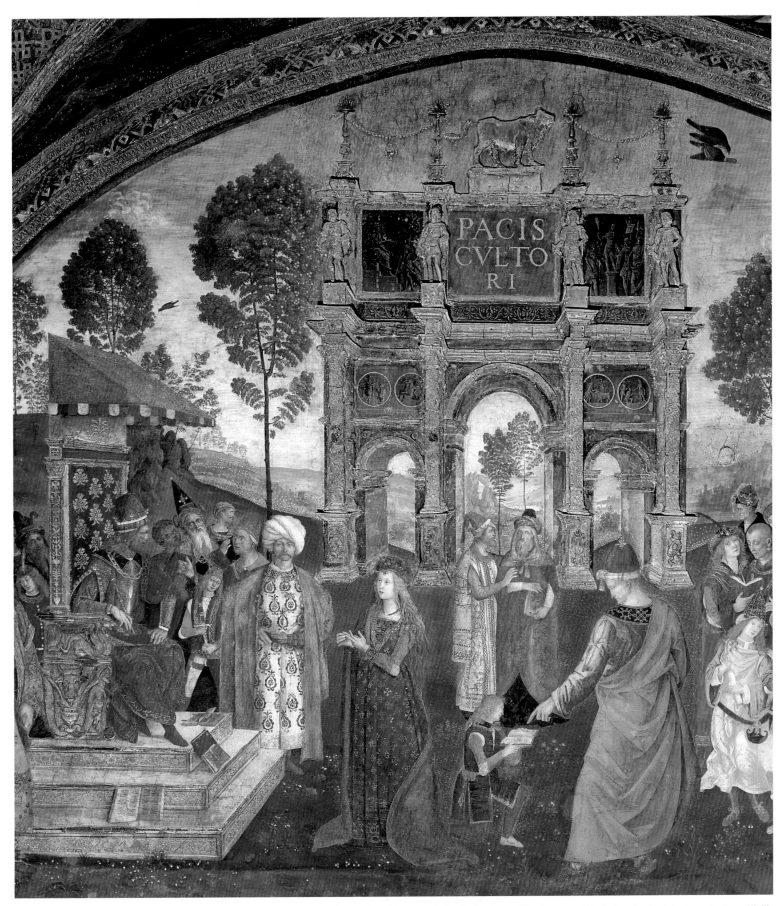

In the Hall of Saints, Pinturicchio's *Dispute of St. Catherine with Emperor Maximian is depicted against an idyllic backdrop, dominated by a Roman triumphal arch that allegorically recalls pagan Rome.*

The text on the arch reads:

PACIS
CVLTO
RI

The Raphael Stanzas (apartments of Julius II Rovere and Leo X Medici). Following the advice of Bramante, the court architect, Pope Julius II called on Raphael to decorate the rooms on the second floor of Nicholas V's wing which he intended to transform into his new private residence. The twenty-five year old artist, who had recently arrived in Rome, began work towards the end of 1508 in the *Stanza of the Signatura* which was to be the Pope's study and library. Here he painted scenes with profound spiritual significance: allegories of faith, reason, ethics, justice and art. In 1512 he began work on the *Stanza of Heliodorus* (named after one of the frescoes), originally the antechamber, which he finished at the end of 1514, in the second year of the reign of Leo X Medici. The subject matter of the frescoes in this room is political: it aims to exalt the spiritual and temporal power of the papacy. The next room, the pope's private dining room, is called the *Stanza of the Borgo Fire* due to subject of its most important fresco. In it, the huge paintings continue the theme begun in the Stanza of Heliodorus: the assertion of spiritual power through political action. This is done by exalting the reigning pope, Leo X, in each scene, although he is always portrayed as one of his two predecessors (both saints) of the same name. The frescoes, painted between 1514 and 1517, are for the most part the work of Raphael's assistants, primarily Giulio Romano and Francesco Penni, who both worked from the master's cartoons. The *Stanza of Constantine*, where official ceremonies and receptions were held, is named after the frescoes which exalt significant moments in the early history of the Church linked to real or legendary episodes in the life of the Emperor Constantine. These decorations were painted by Giulio Romano and Francesco Penni and their assistants between 1517 and 1524.

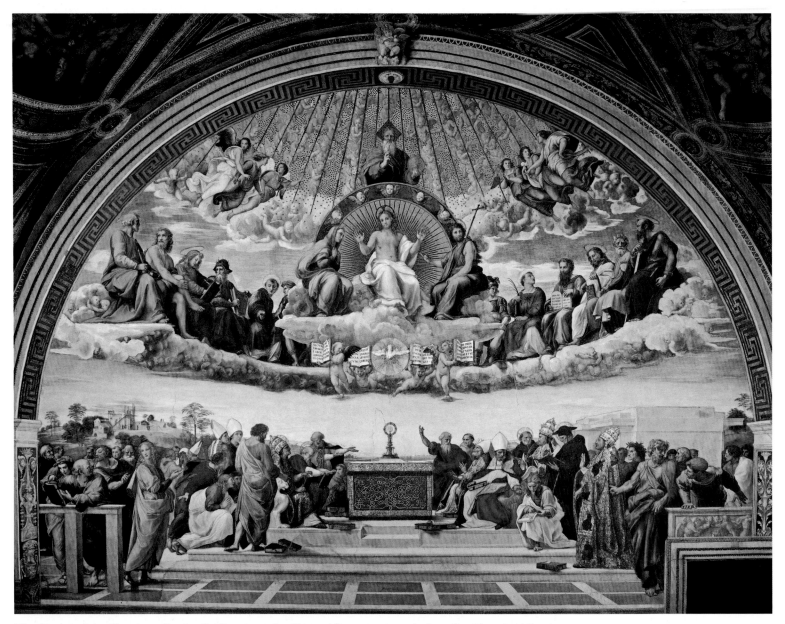

The Stanza of the Signatura. Raphael's Dispute on the Blessed Sacrament *symbolizes the triumph of theology, the supernatural Truth. Four groups of figures on two different levels, clearly separated by a strip of sky, converge on the Eucharist (the figure above) at the center of the painting. On earth, the Church militant is represented by theologians engaged in debate; in heaven, saints, prophets and biblical kings are admitted in the presence of the Trinity that appears vertically above the monstrance. The Holy Spirit is flanked by angels holding the Gospels, whereas Christ is portrayed between the Virgin Mary and John the Baptist.*

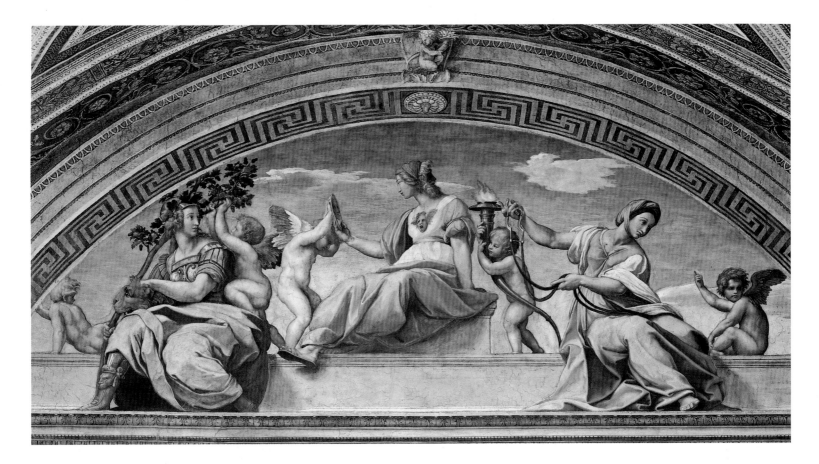

The Stanza of the Signatura. Raphael's Cardinal Virtues (female figures) and Theological Virtues (cherubs). Fortitude is holding an oak branch (symbol of the Della Rovere family), instead of the traditional column, in her hand; Prudence, with two faces, is gazing at her reflection in a mirror; Temperance is holding a pair of reins. Justice, the fourth virtue, is missing here because she is painted on the ceiling. Charity gathers acorns from an oak branch, Hope carries a burning torch and Faith points toward heaven.

The Stanza of the Signatura. Guillaume de Marcillat, master glazier from Verdun, was called to Rome by Bramante to execute the scenes showing the Emperor Justinian Handing the Pandects to Trebonianus (symbol of Civil Law, on the left), and St. Raymond de Peñafort Presenting the Decretals to Gregory IX (symbol of Canon Law, on the right). Gregory IX is portrayed with the features of Julius II.

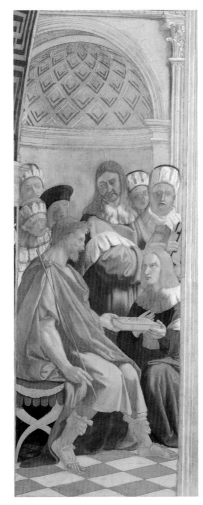

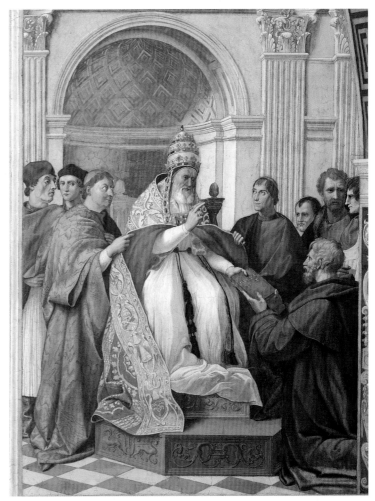

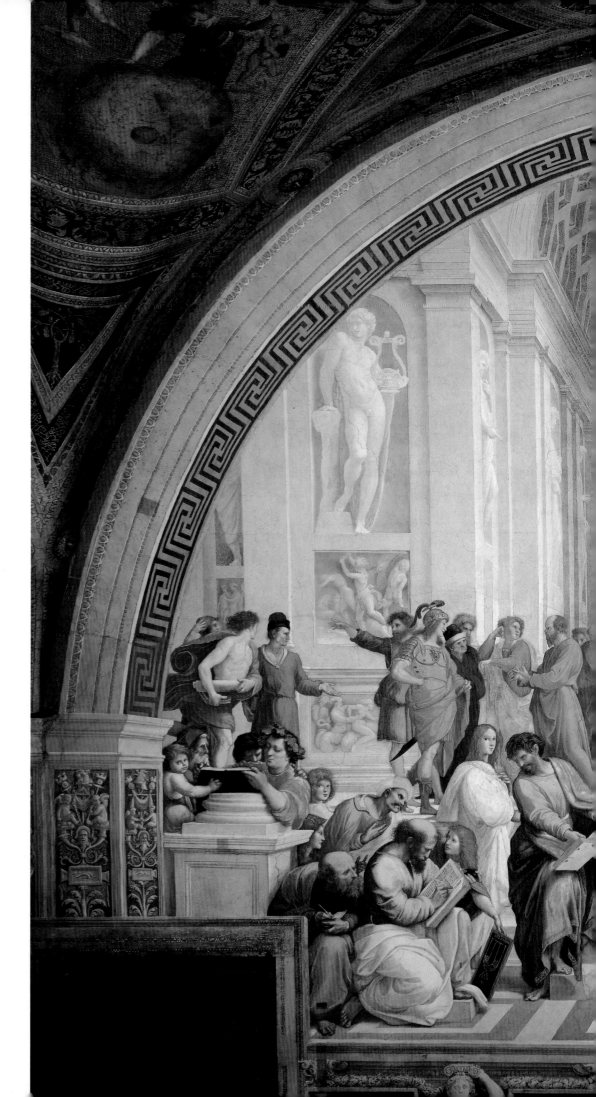

The Stanza of the Signatura. Raphael's "School of Athens" exalts reason, or natural Truth. A gathering of all the major ancient and contemporary thinkers below the vaulted ceiling of a central building topped by a dome alludes to the new St. Peter's Basilica. Raphael's friend Bramante was undoubtedly responsible for suggesting such an architectural setting. Plato, with the facial features of Leonardo, is placed in the center, discoursing with Aristotle. They use their hands to illustrate the debate: with his forefinger, Plato points up-ward to the empyrean of ideas, the source of all knowledge, whereas Aristotle, with the palm of his hand indicating the ground, stresses concrete physical reality. In the foreground, a solitary and dejected Heraclitus, with the face of Michelangelo, is shown meditating on the constantly changing nature of things. Diogenes reclines on the steps in the center of the painting. To the right, leaning over a blackboard is the image of Bramante in the guise of Euclid; and on the far right, Ptolemy and Zoroaster with a globe and celestial sphere, are actually portraits of the artist himself and his friend Sodoma. The monochromes along the base are the work of Perin del Vaga. They were executed during the papacy of Paul III to replace the original wood paneling.

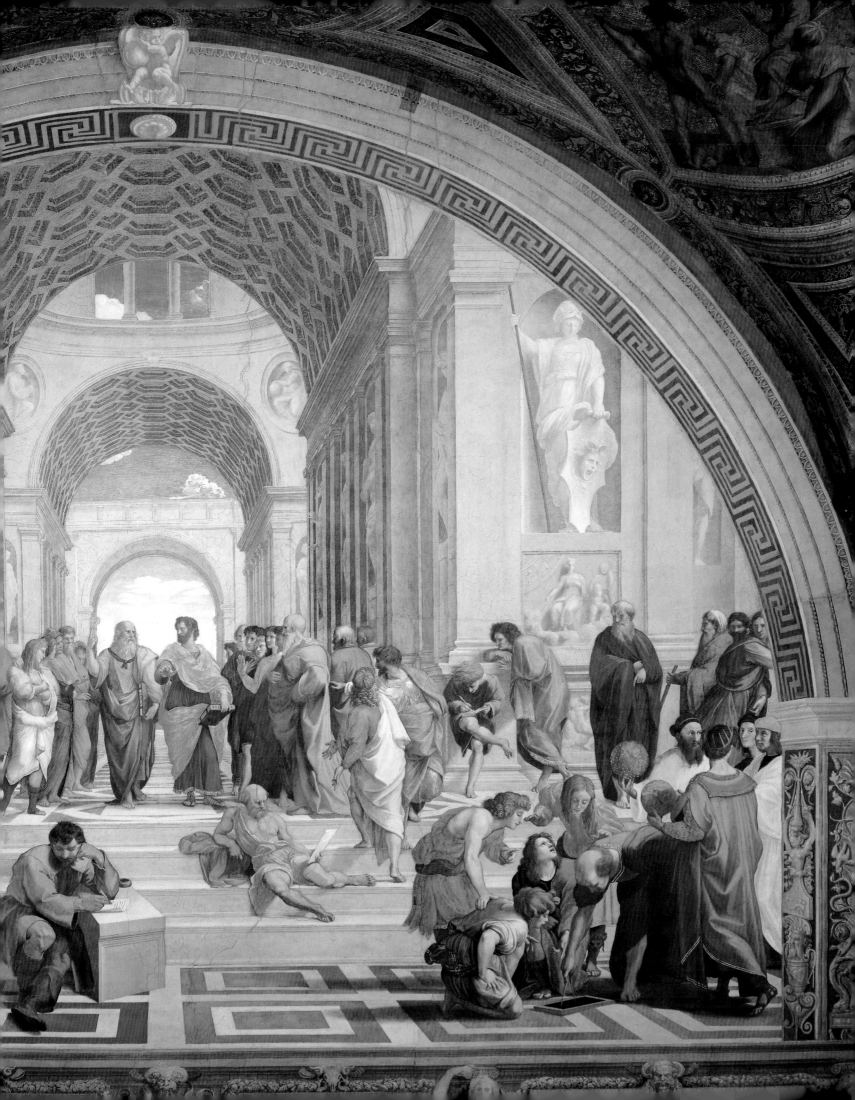

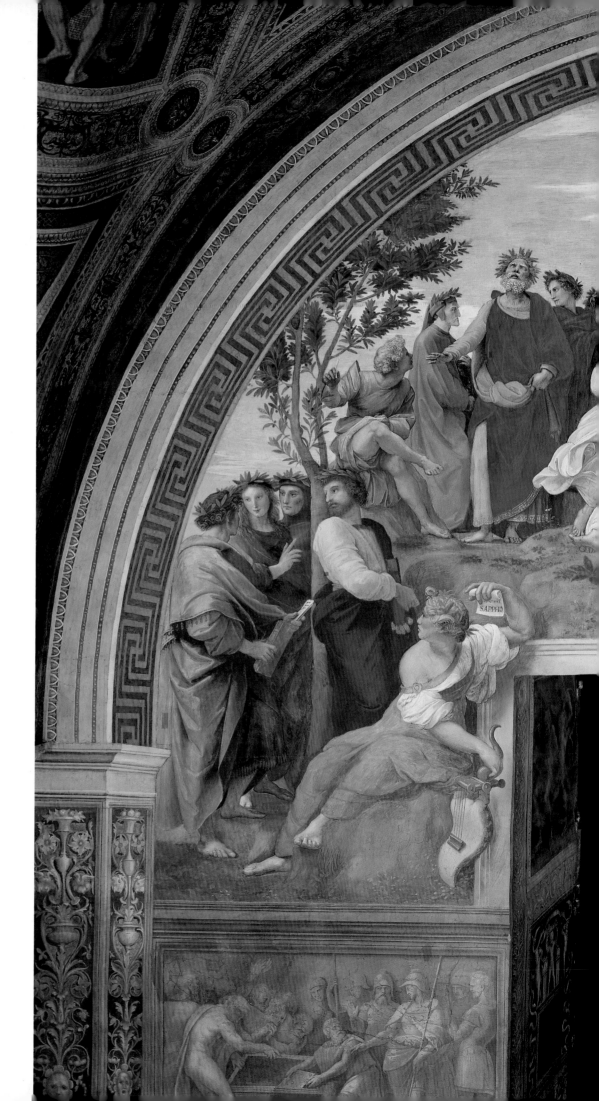

The Stanza of the Signatura. Raphael's Parnassus, *the allegory of beauty, is represented by the images of music and poetry: Apollo holding his lyre, the nine Muses, Epic Poetry (with a horn) and Lyric Poetry (with a cithara) are all depicted in the midst of a gathering of poets.*

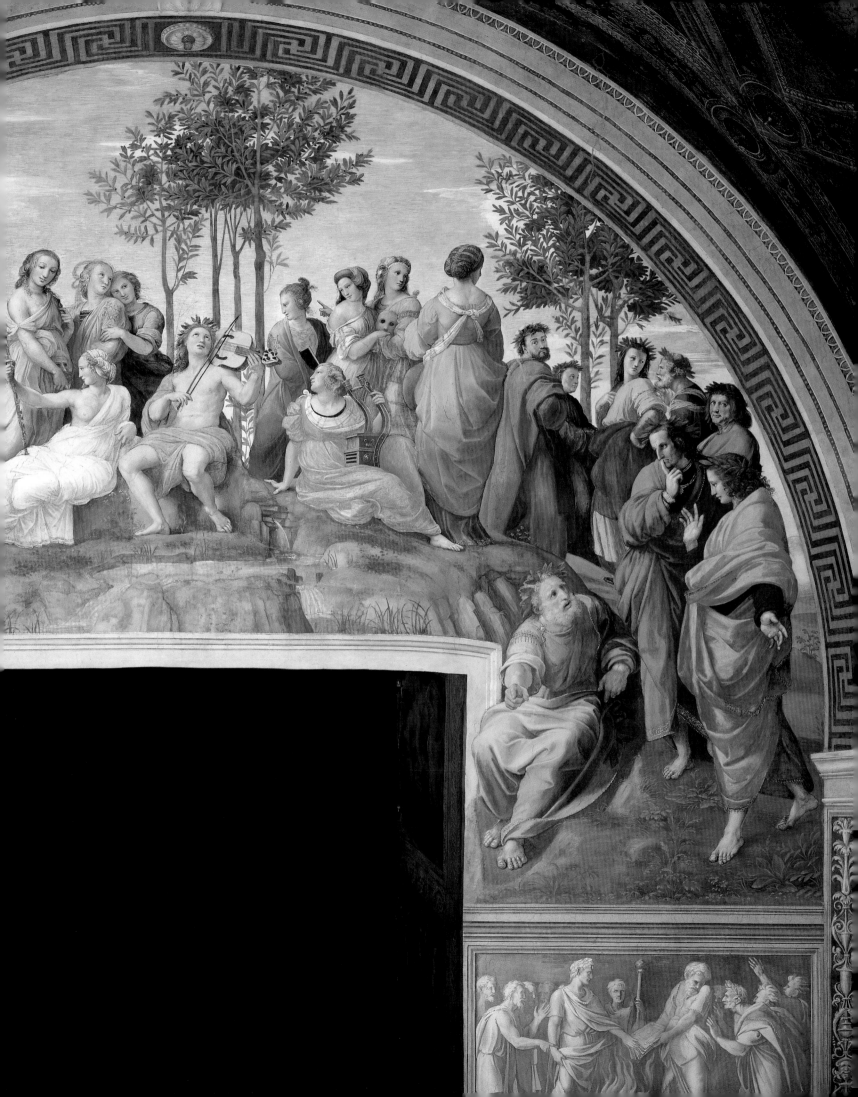

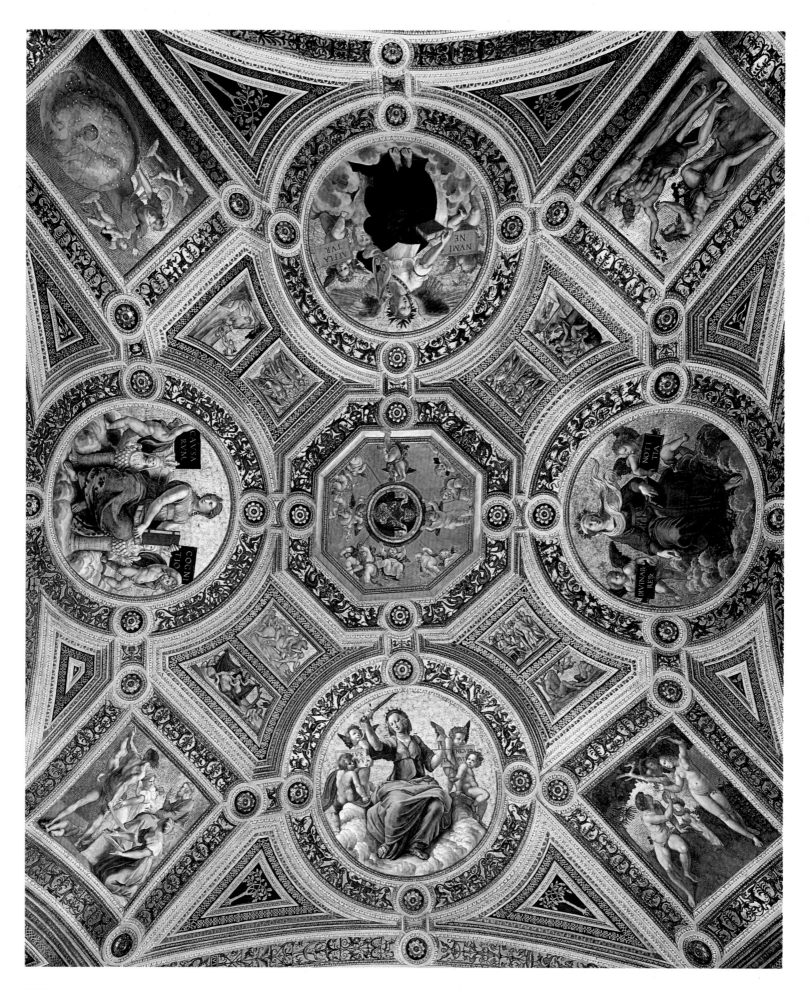

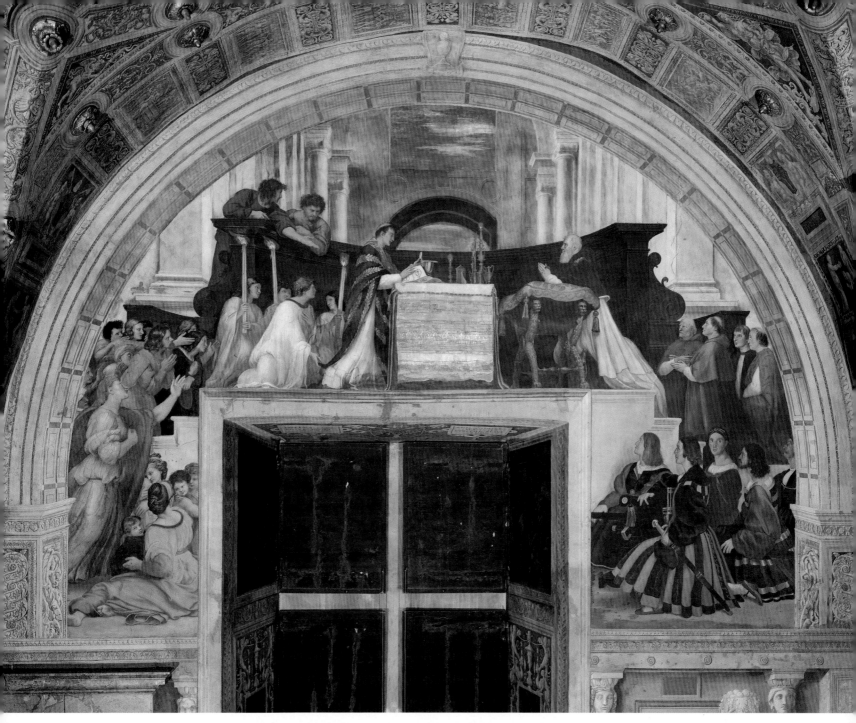

The Stanza of Heliodorus. Raphael's Mass of Bolsena *depicts the 1263 miracle that occurred at Bolsena. A Bohemian priest, who had doubts regarding the mystery of transubstantiation, was celebrating mass when he noticed that the consecrated Host was bleeding. This event was the origin of the feast of Corpus Christi, established in 1264 by Pope Urban IV.*

Ceiling of the Stanza of the Signatura. *The octagon in the center, with winged cherubs holding the papal coat of arms, is surrounded by four medallions with personifications of Theology, Justice, Philosophy and Poetry. At the four corners of the ceiling are rectangular scenes with Adam and Eve, the Judgment of Solomon, Astronomy, and Apollo and Marsyas.*

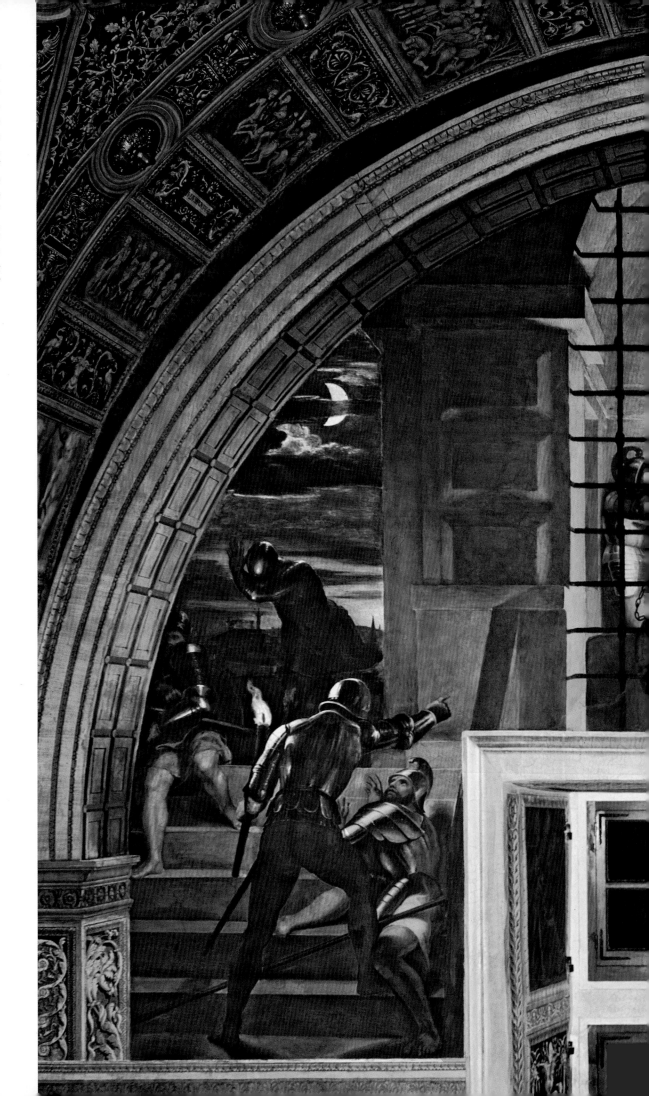

The Stanza of Heliodorus. Raphael's The Freeing of St. Peter. "Peter was sleeping between two soldiers, fastened with two chains, while guards kept watch at the main entrance to the prison. Then suddenly an angel of the Lord stood there, and the cell was filled with light. He tapped Peter on the side and woke him. 'Get up!' he said, 'Hurry!' — and the chains fell from his hands. The angel then said... 'Wrap your cloak round you and follow me'" (Acts 12:6-8).

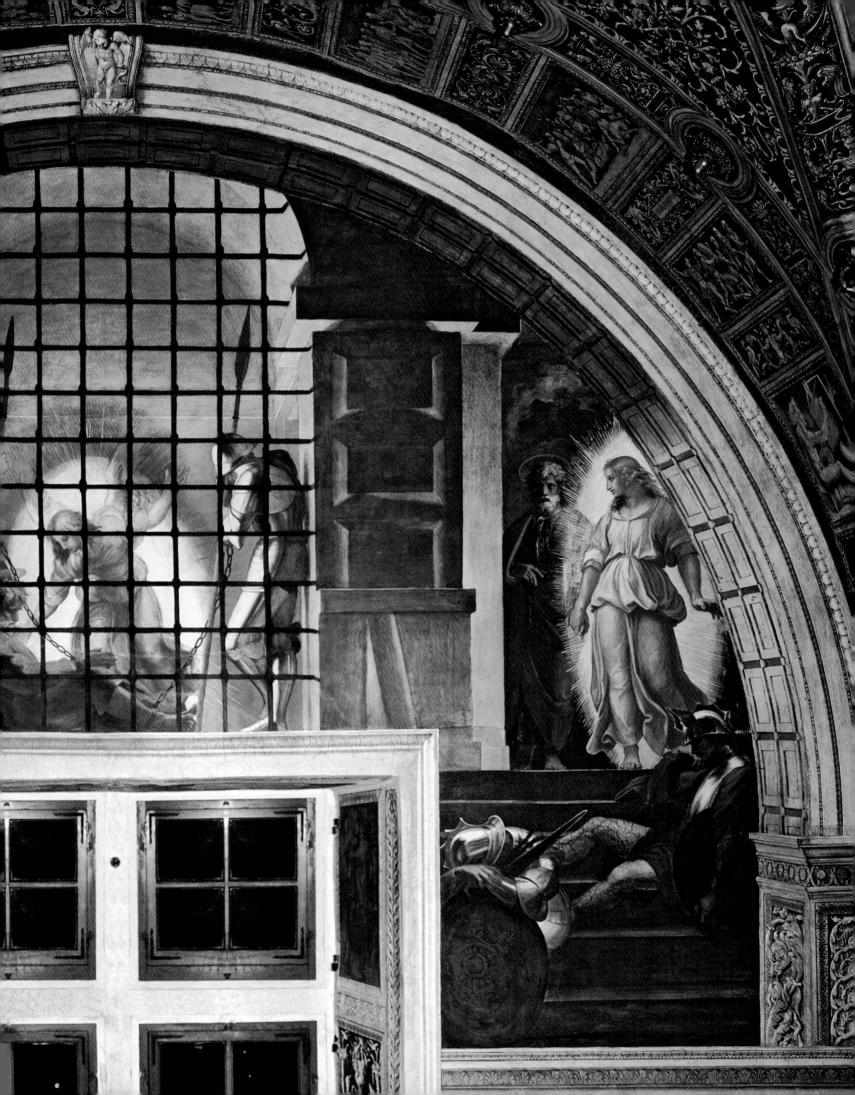

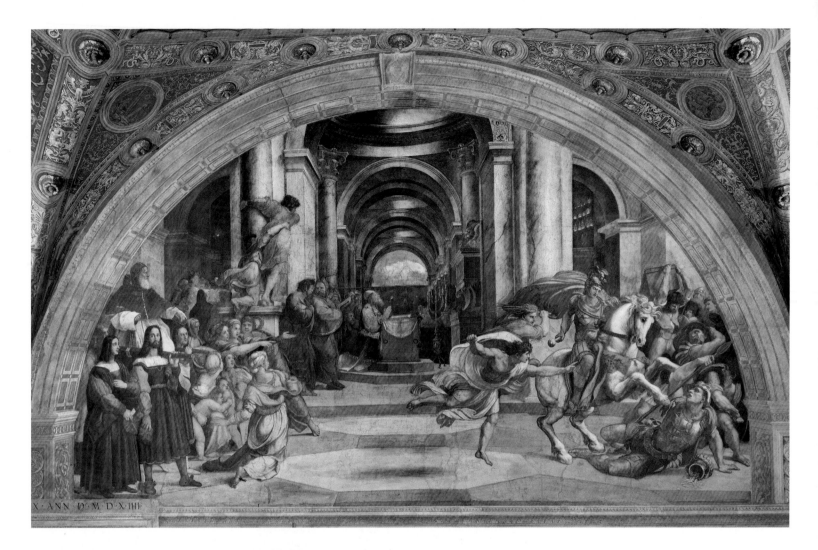

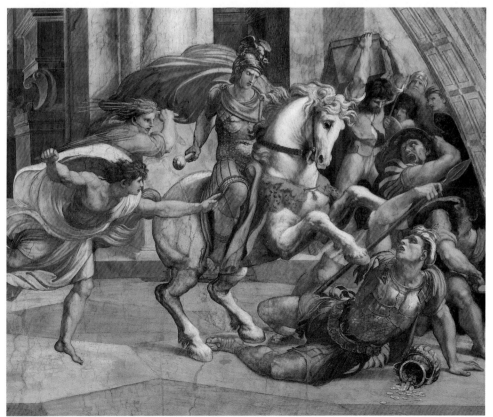

The Stanza of Heliodorus. Raphael's Expulsion of Heliodorus from the Temple *represents the inviolability of Church property. The presence of Julius II, as both head of Church and State, makes the composition an explicit manifesto in favor of the papacy's temporal power*

The Stanza of Heliodorus. Raphael's Expulsion of Heliodorus from the Temple, *detail: "Before their eyes appeared a horse richly caparisoned and carrying a fearsome rider. Rearing violently, it struck at Heliodorus with its forefeet. The rider was seen to be accoutred entirely in gold. Two other young men of outstanding strength and radiant beauty, magnificently apparelled, appeared to him at the same time and, taking their stand on each side of him, flogged him unremittingly, inflicting stroke after stroke. Suddenly Heliodorus fell to the ground, enveloped in thick darkness"* (2 Maccabees 3:25-27).

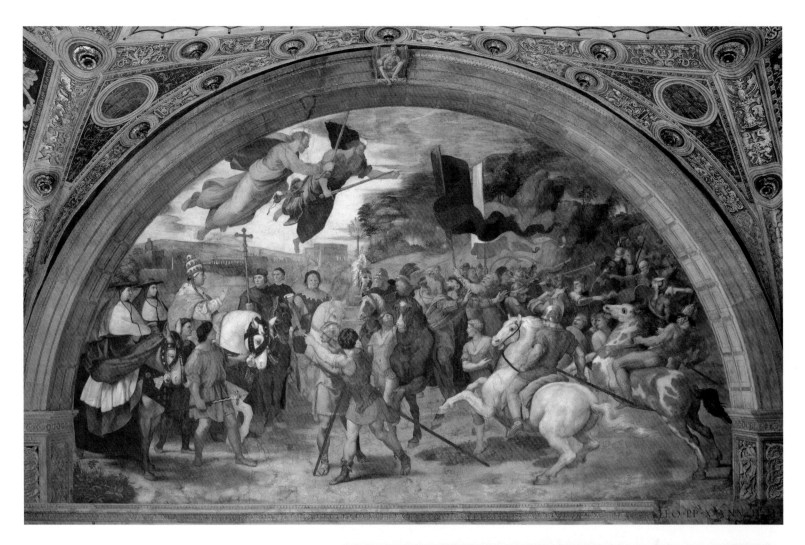

The Stanza of Heliodorus, Raphael and assistants. St. Leo the Great's Meeting with Attila *in 452 is a reference to the supremacy of spiritual over temporal power. Pope Leo X, portrayed in the guise of Leo the Great, appears peaceful in contrast to his forceful predecessor.*

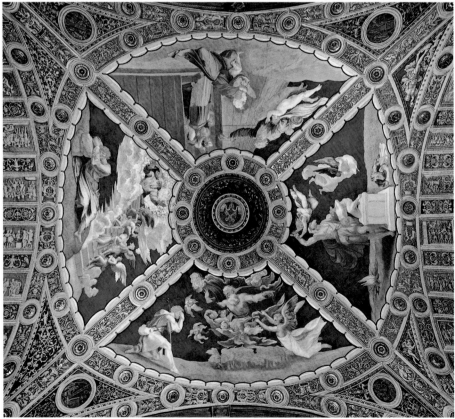

Ceiling of the Stanza of Heliodorus, *Raphael. These episodes from Genesis (the "Sacrifice of Isaac", the "Burning Bush", "Jacob's Ladder", "God Appears to Noah") were probably painted by assistants from cartoons by the master. Noteworthy is the influence of Michelangelo, who had only recently finished the Sistine Chapel ceiling.*

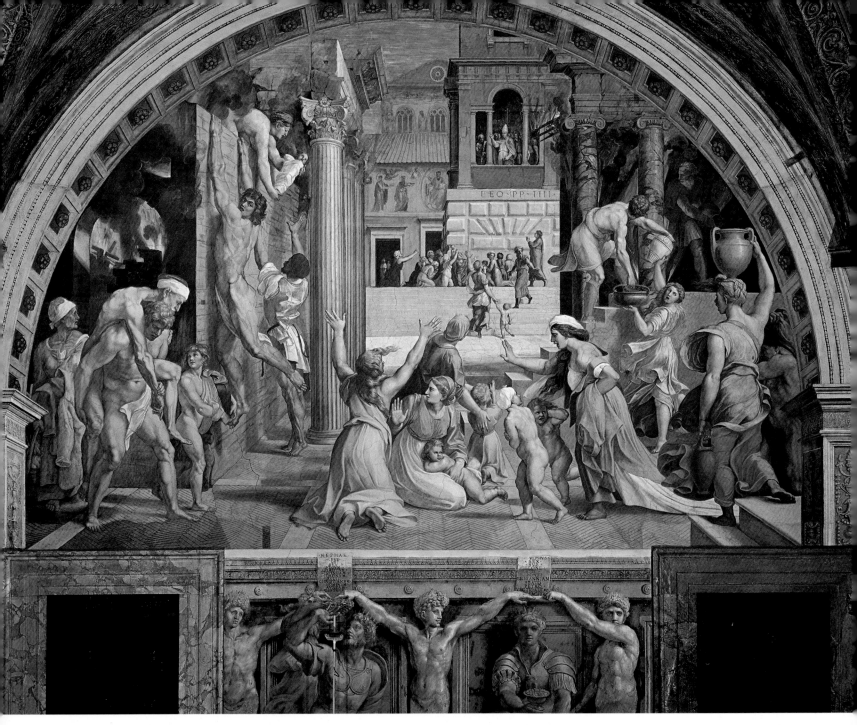

Stanza of the Borgo Fire, school of Raphael. The Fire in the Borgo *commemorates the miracle performed in 847 by Pope Leo IV, the founder of the Leonine city. Raphael has painted the façade of Constantine's Basilica as it appeared before its demolition in 1608. The detail on the left of the picture, depicting Aeneas as he flees from Troy in flames with his elderly father and his young son, is probably the work of Raphael. The decorative band is by Giulio Romano.*

Fire in the Borgo *(detail), in the Stanza of the Borgo Fire, painted by the school of Raphael. The group of women on the left, depicted in their desperate attempt to quench the flames, are the most important, vital figures in this scene.*

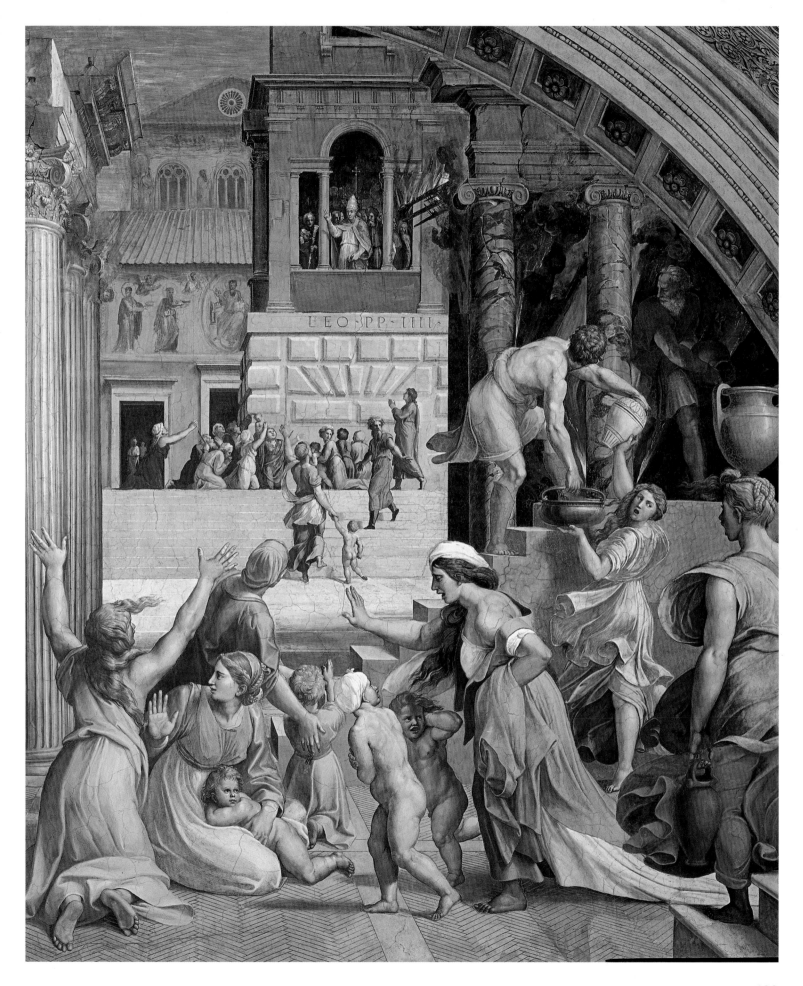

Within the image: LEO · PP · IIII ·

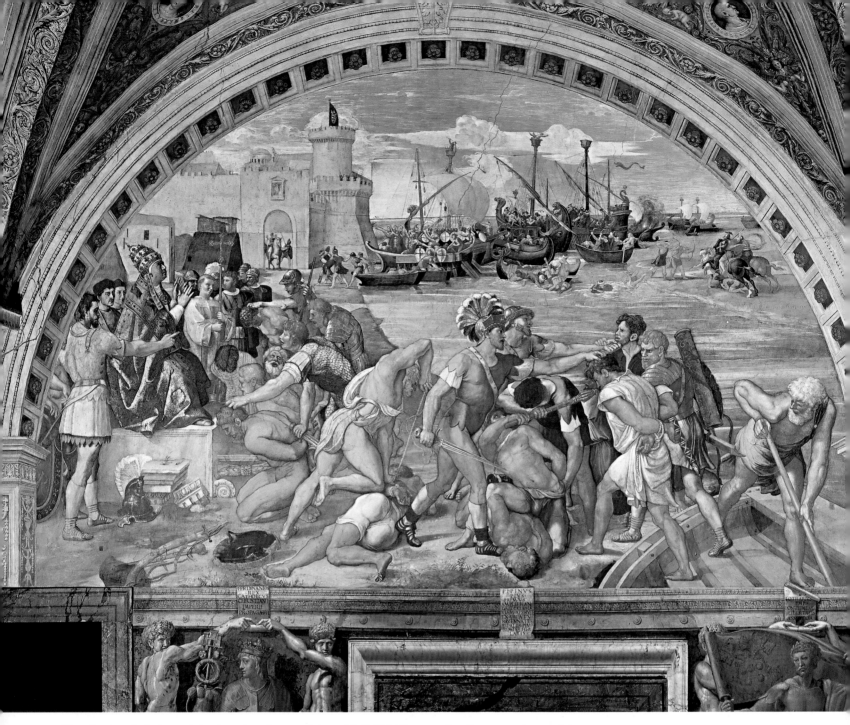

The Battle of Ostia, *celebrating the victory of Leo IV (847-855) over the Saracens, is used here as a reference to Leo X's plan to organize a crusade against the Ottoman empire. The figure of Leo IV is in fact a portrait of Leo X.*

The Ceiling of the Stanza of the Borgo Fire *was painted by Pietro Vannucci, called* il Perugino. *This decoration, consisting of allegories of the Holy Trinity, is the work of Raphael's teacher Perugino, who painted it in 1507-08, before his pupil joined him in Rome.*

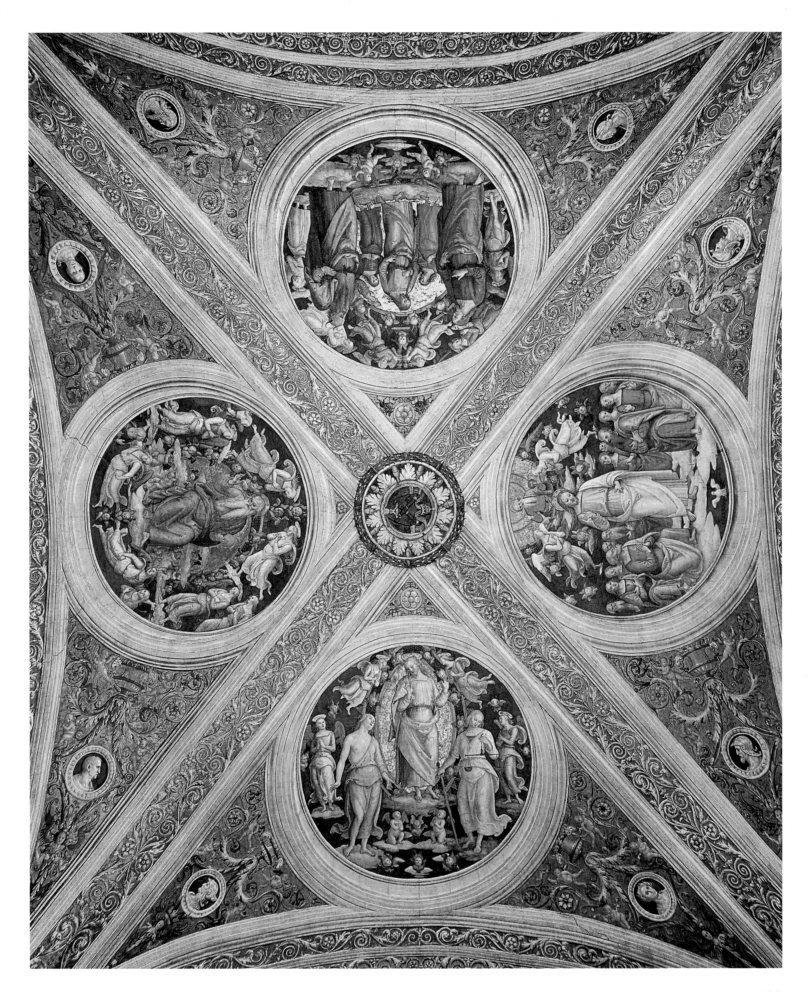

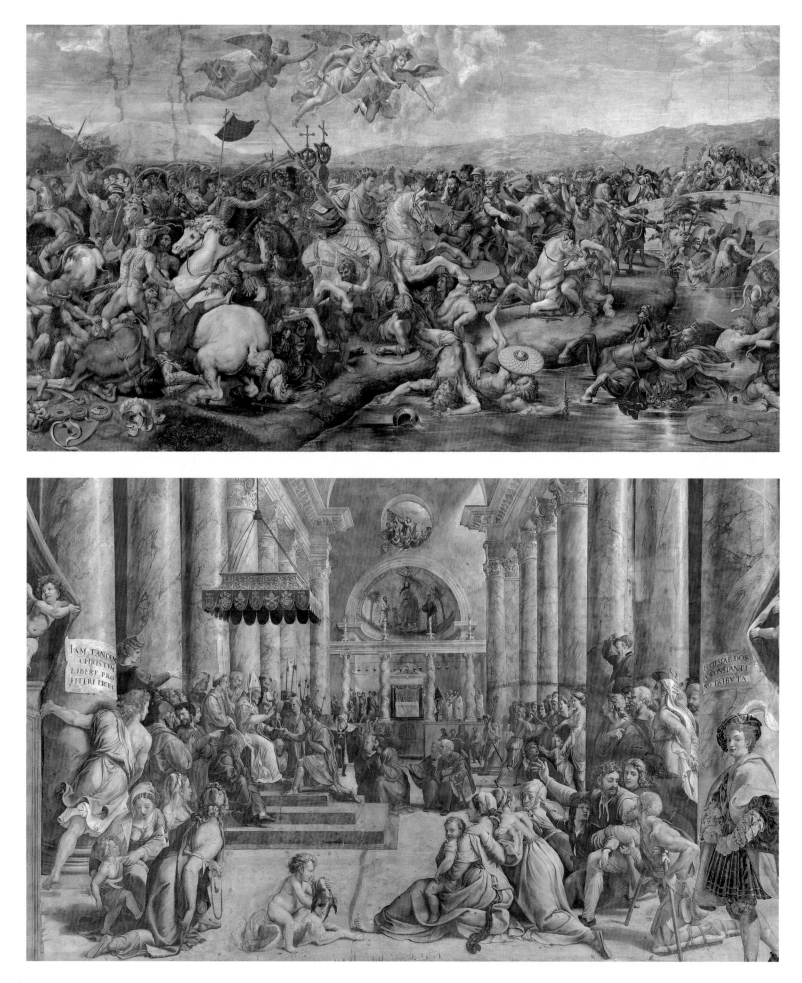

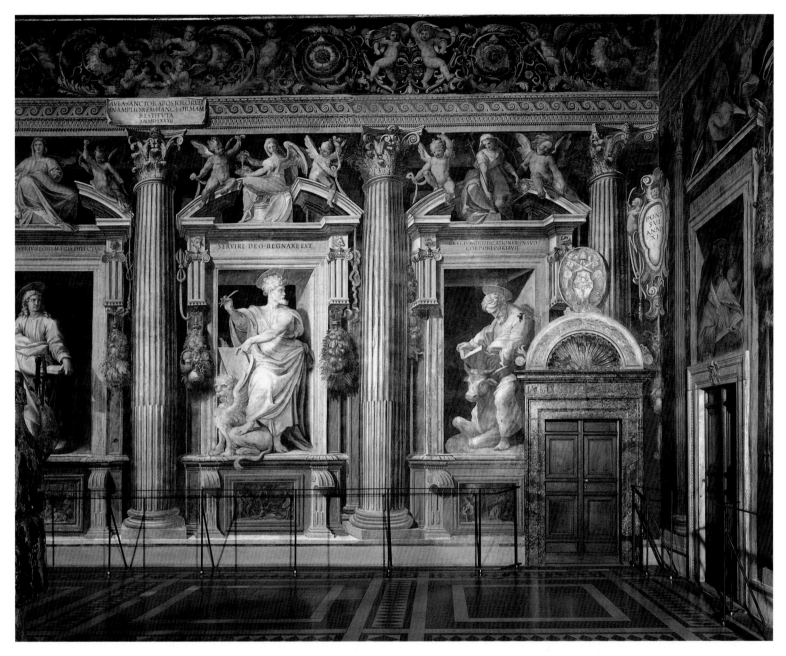

The Hall of the Chiaroscuri, *also called the "Hall of Grooms". This was formerly the papal antechamber, and it was here that public and private ceremonies were held. It was decorated by Raphael's assistants from cartoons by the master, but the frescoes were destroyed in 1558, at the time of Paul V, as part of a plan that was never carried out, to alter the structure of the rooms. A few years later, during the next papacy, Taddeo and Federico Zuccari, assisted by a group of artists, decorated the room, freely restoring the originals with frescoes of the apostles and other saints; this task was completed at the time of Gregory XIII in 1582.*

The Stanza of Constantine, Giulio Romano (left, above). The scene shows the *Battle at the Milvian Bridge on the outskirts of Rome where Constantine, fighting in the name of Christ, defeated the emperor Maxentius, on October 28, 312. After this battle, Christianity was decreed the official religion of the Roman Empire (Edict of Milan, 313).*

The Stanza of Constantine, Giulio Romano and Francesco Penni (left, below). The scene depicts the legendary *Donation of Rome when Constantine presented the city to Pope Sylvester I (in the guise of Clement VII Medici). The altar of St. Peter's, as it appeared before Bramante had the apse of Constantine's Basilica demolished to make room for the new basilica, can be seen in the background. The origins of the papal state date back to 722, at the time of the Lombard domination, when the Duchy of Rome fell under the jurisdiction of the Holy See.*

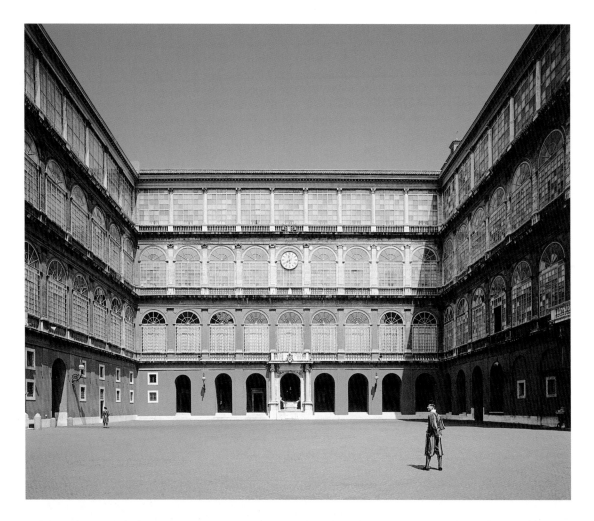

The Loggias of Bramante and Raphael. *The Loggias were added to the eastern façade of the medieval palace of the popes by Donato Bramante who began work here for Julius II probably in 1508. At Bramante's death, on March 11, 1514, construction work had reached the second story of the Loggias. Raphael, who replaced Bramante as supervisor of the project, finished the Second Loggia and crowned the entire construction with a trabeated peristyle in 1519; today this is the entrance to the Secretariat of State. The decoration of the First Loggia (below, left) consists of trompe l'oeil grape arbors and grotesques. It is the work of Giovanni da Udine, one of Raphael's assistants, who finished it in 1519. Many years later (1560-1564), Giovanni da Udine and his assistants also decorated the small vaults of the Third Loggia (below, right) with allegorical pictures, stuccoes and grotesques. The Third Loggia is called the Loggia of Maps: European, Asian and African countries were painted by Antonio Vanosino of Varese from cartoons by Etienne Dupérac.*

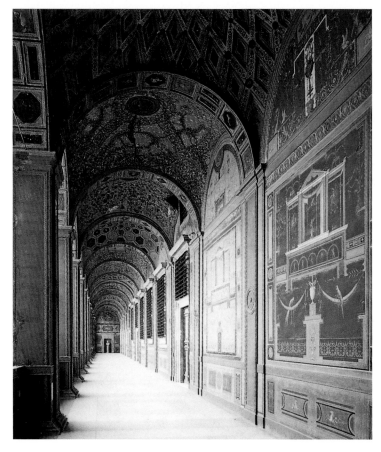

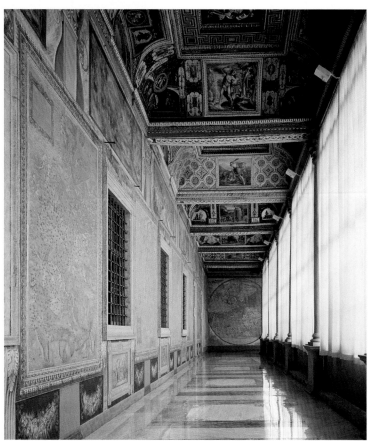

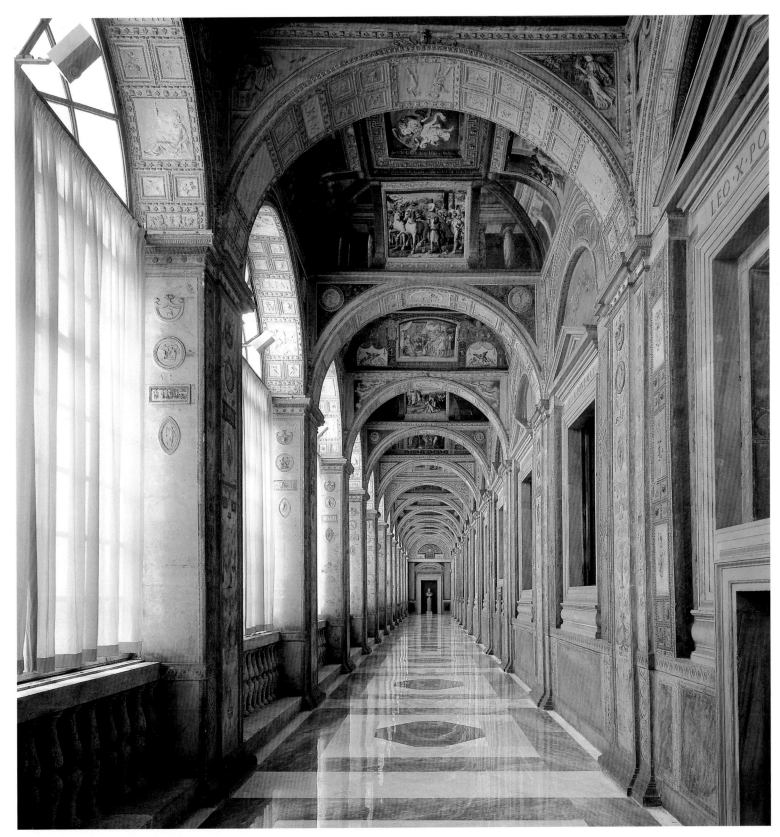

View of the Second Loggia *(towards the north). The decoration of the Loggias of St. Damasus, and the Second Loggia (better known as Raphael's Loggia) in particular, is beyond a doubt dedicated to the glory of Pope Leo X (1513-1521). The internal structure is covered completely with painted grotesques, bas-reliefs and stucco decorations, most of which show the influence of the iconographical repertory of classical art. The type of ceiling designed by Raphael, with a flat central lacunar and five nearly level panels, was ideal for painting pictures. In fact, the scenes are referred to as the Raphael Bible (on the following pages): each of the thirteen vaults of the Loggia contains four frescoes with scenes taken from the Old Testament, with the sole exception of the last one toward the north, that represents scenes from the New Testament.*

The *Raphael Bible*. Four scenes from the Bible are found on the vaults of each of the thirteen bays: the first twelve are from the Old Testament and the thirteenth is from the New Testament.

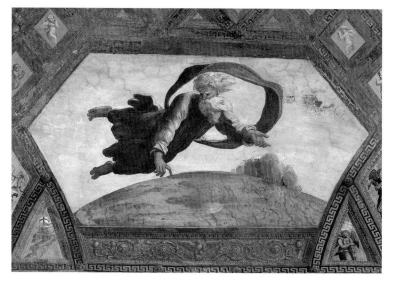

God separates the earth from the waters.

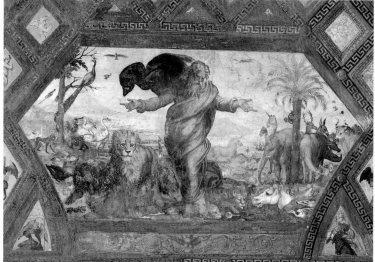

Creation of the animals.

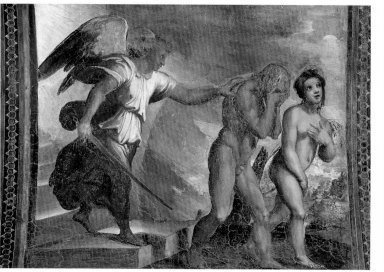

Adam and Eve banished from Eden.

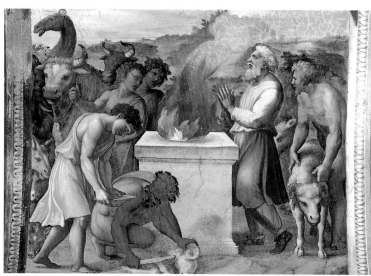

Noah's Sacrifice.

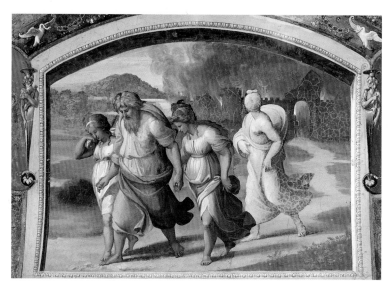

Lot flees from Sodom.

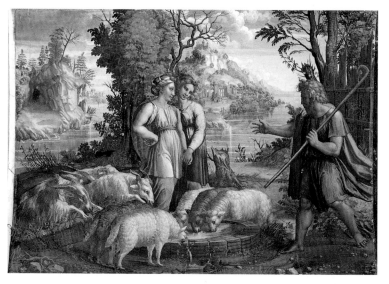

Jacob meets Rachel.

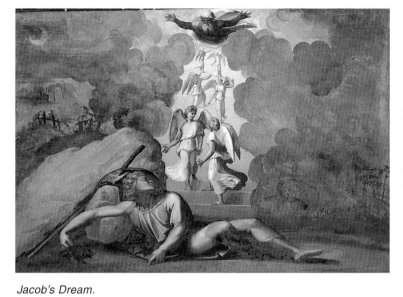

Jacob's Dream.

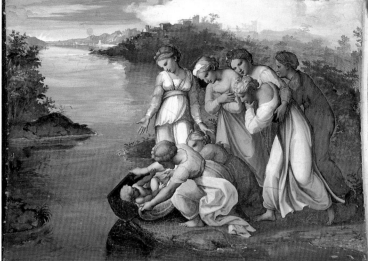

Moses saved from the water.

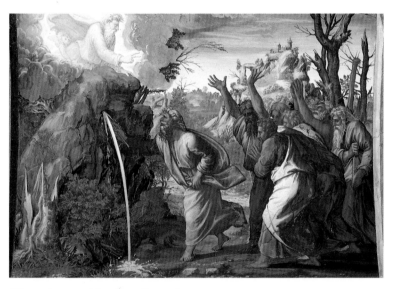

The waters gushing from the rock.

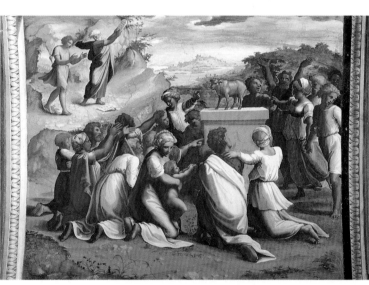

Adoration of the golden calf.

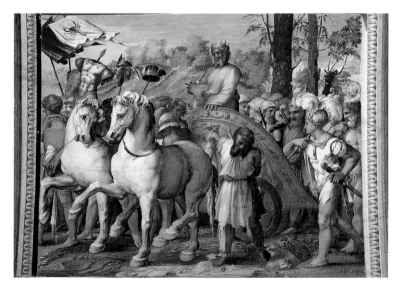

David's Triumph.

Solomon's Judgment.

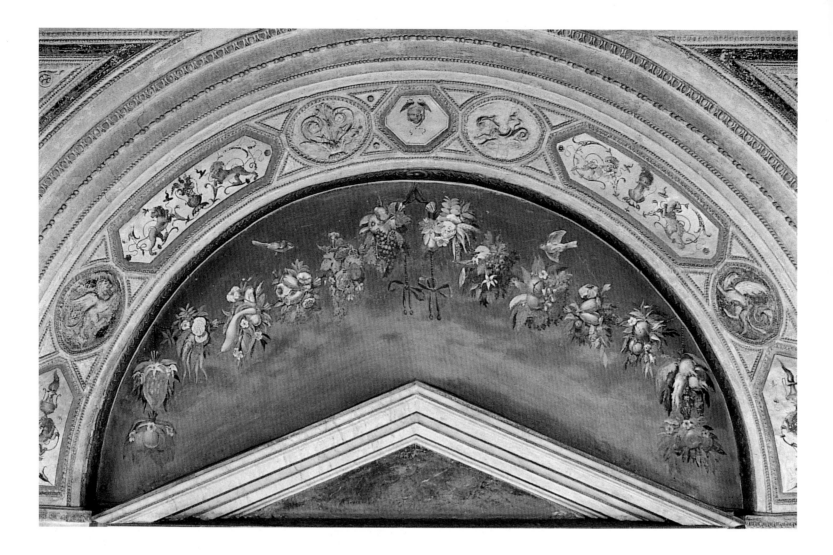

Festoon, *detail of the lunette in the sixth bay of the Second Loggia.*

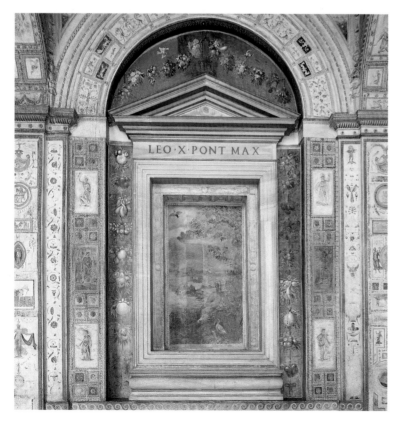

Internal wall *(left) of the second bay of the Second Loggia.*

Pilaster strip *(on the right) between the second and third bay of the Second Loggia, upper section.*

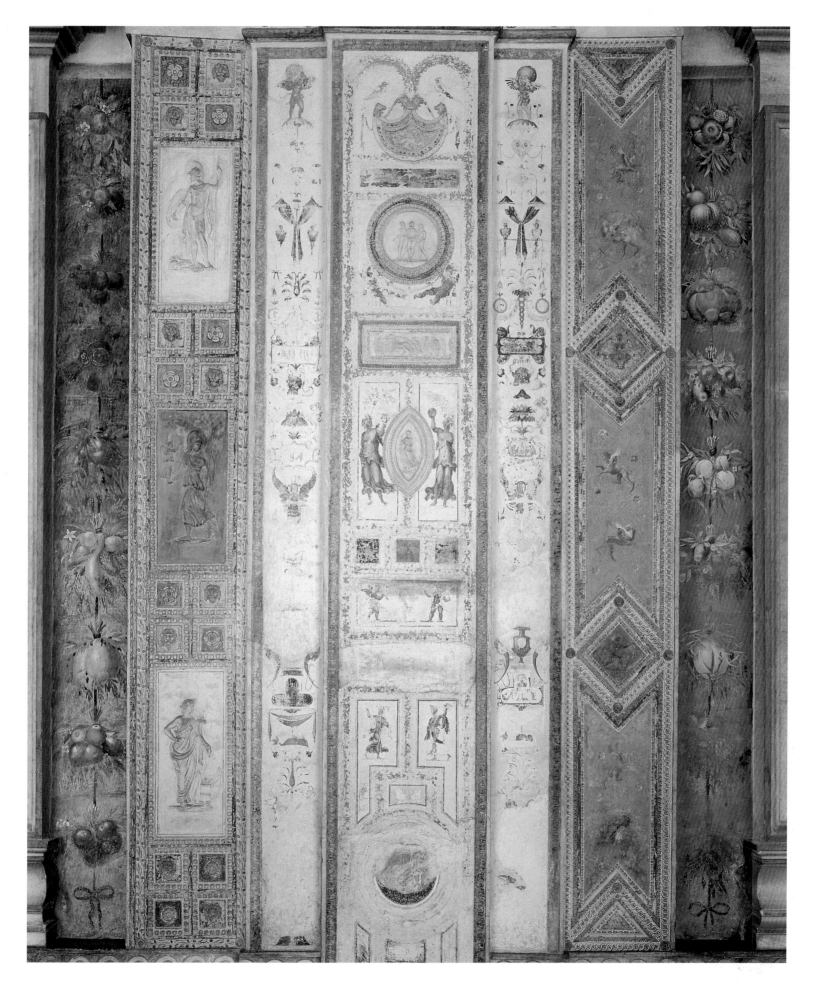

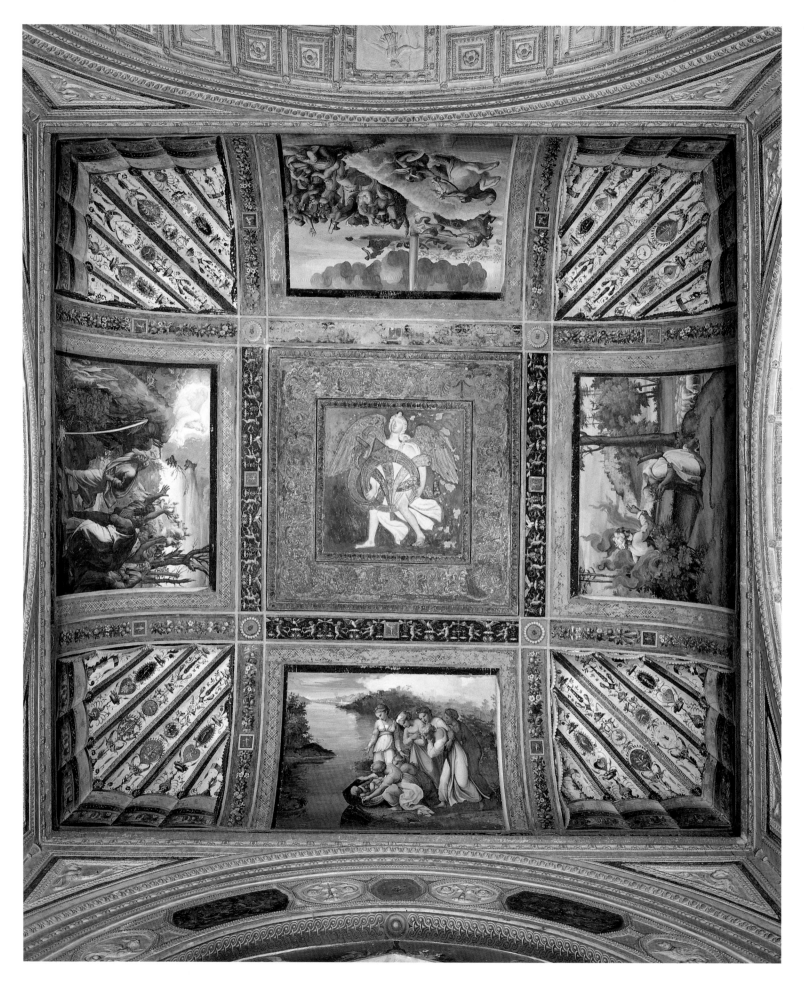

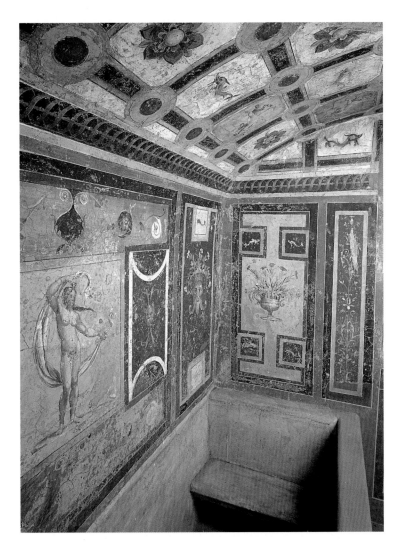

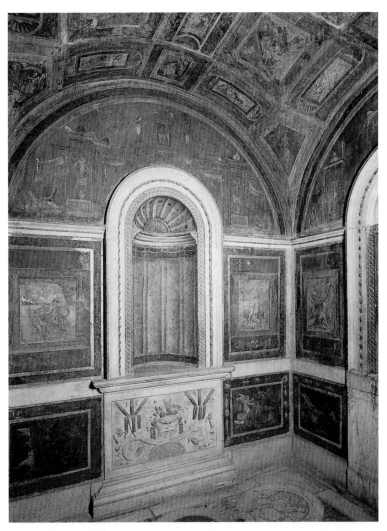

On the first floor of the palace is Clement VII's Stufetta, *the Medici pope's bath chamber (above, left). It is a very small rectangular room, 2.6 by 1.92 meters, and only 2 meters high, decorated with grotesques probably painted by the same artists who assisted Raphael on the frescoes for the Stanza of Constantine.*

The paintings in the Stufetta *(above, right) and the Loggetta (on the following page) of Leo X's close collaborator Cardinal Bernardo Dovizi, called il Bibbiena from the name of his birthplace, were painted by Raphael and his assistants between in 1516 and 1519. Here the master was clearly imitating the style of the decorations from the recently excavated Domus Aurea. These two rooms are on the same floor as Raphael's Third Loggia (the Loggia of Maps), today housing the Secretariat of State.*

The Stufetta *(right) of Cardinal Bernardo Dovizi: detail of the wall paintings.*

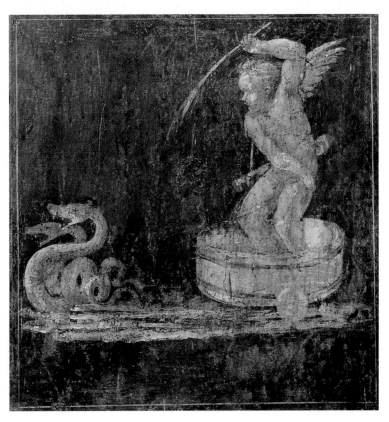

Detail of the vault of the eighth bay. *Stories from the Life of Moses, depicting "Moses Saved from the Water", the "Burning Bush", the "Crossing of the Red Sea ", and the "Prodigy of the Waters gushing from the Rock".*

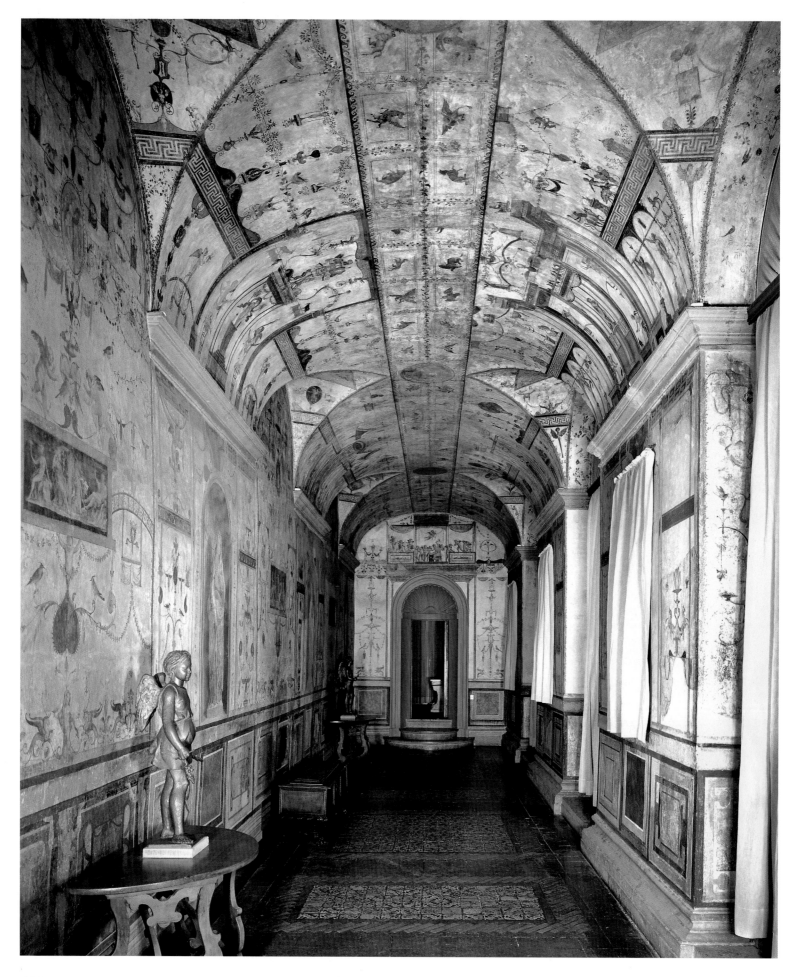

The Secretariat of State *(right)* is housed in the apartments behind the Third Loggia. The Secretariat is the body which implements the decisions taken by the pope and coordinates the ecclesiastical ministries that make up the Roman Curia. Its origins date back to the period of the Council of Trent, which is documented in a fresco by Giovanni Antonio Vanosino. The painting reproduced here *(below, right)* is located on the end wall of the antechamber of the Secretariat of State.

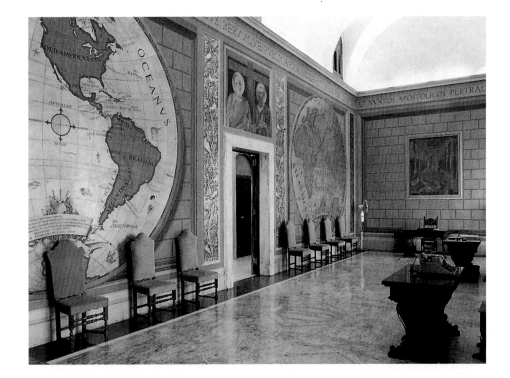

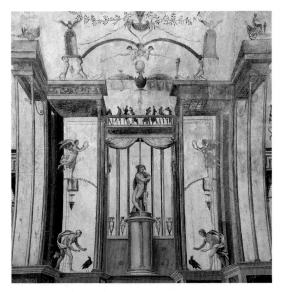

The Loggetta *of Cardinal Bernardo Dovizi, a detail of the grotesques.*

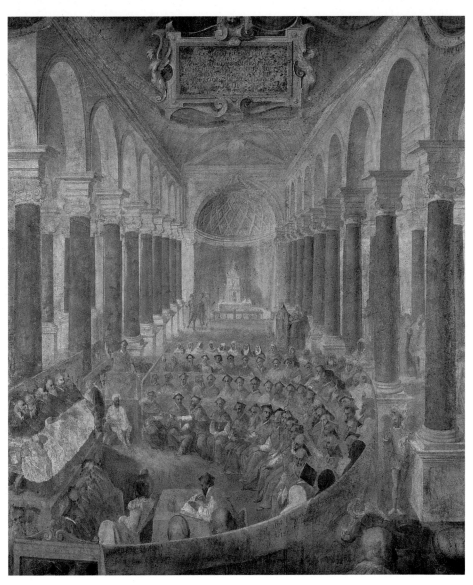

The Loggetta *of Cardinal Bernardo Dovizi, called* il Bibbiena. *The rectangular corridor measures 3.12 by 15.74 meters. It was frescoed by the same artists who were working on the Second Loggia at about that time. Giulio Romano and Perin del Vaga are responsible for the fanciful grotesques that enliven the ceiling and the walls. The remains of Hispano-Moresque majolica tiles on the floor are also noteworthy.*

The "Conversion of Saul" and the "Crucifixion of St. Peter" are the last works Michelangelo ever painted (1542-1550). They are found in the Pauline Chapel, built by Antonio da Sangallo the Younger, as part of the renovation project for the *Sala Regia*.

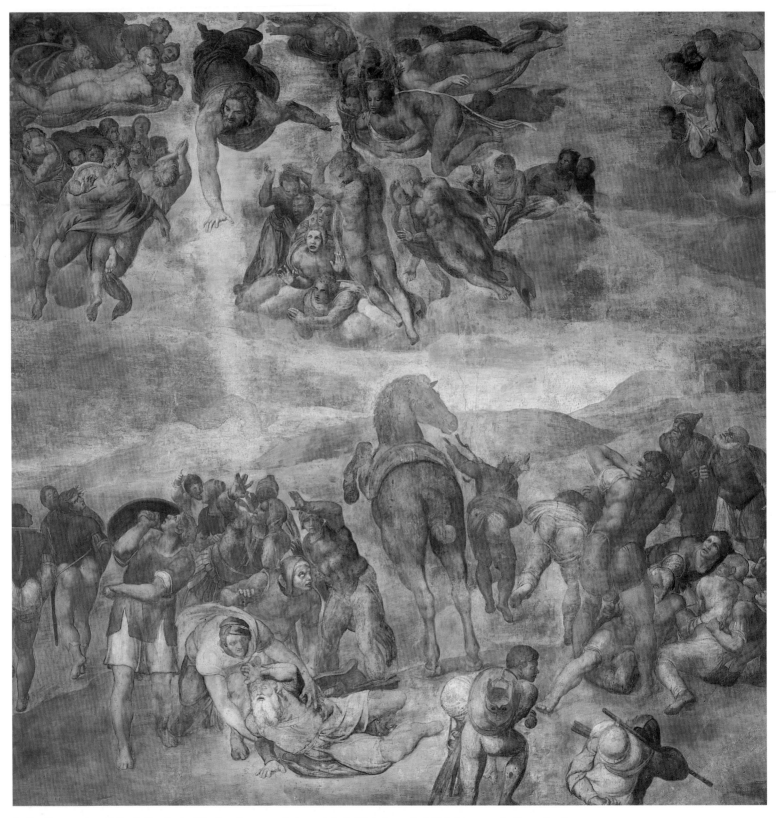

In the Conversion of Saul, *the first of the two frescoes to be painted, Michelangelo faithfully recounts the episode told in the Acts of the Apostles 9: 3-7: "It happened that while he was travelling to Damascus and approaching the city, suddenly a light from heaven shone all round him. He fell to the ground, and then he heard a voice saying, 'Saul, Saul why are you persecuting me?'..."*

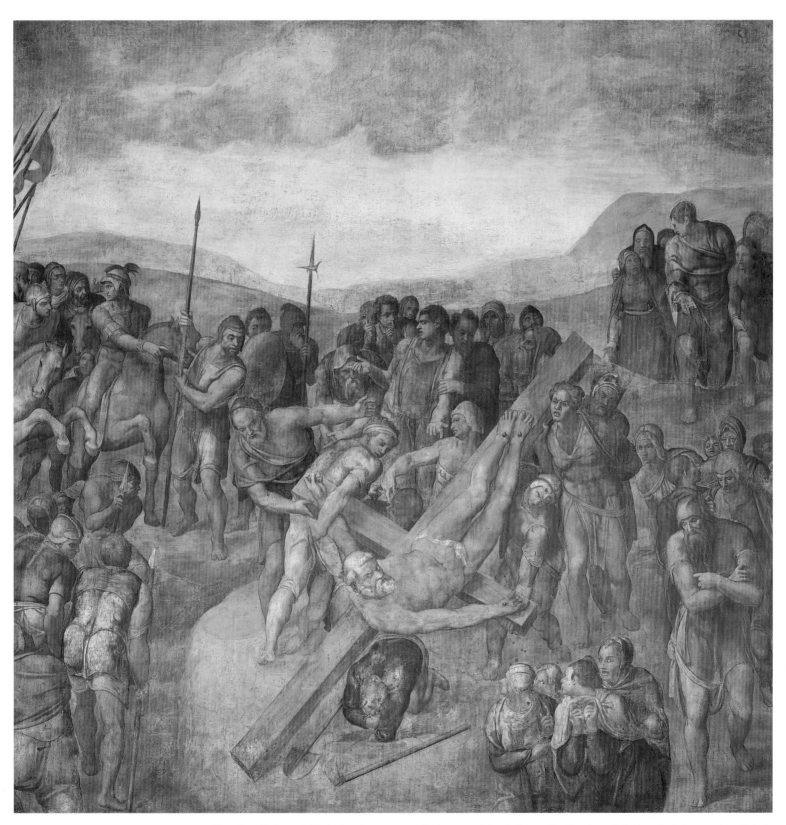

The Crucifixion of St. Peter *is composed of concentric circles, with the Apostle's head at the center. Peter's decision to be crucified upside down, because he considered himself unworthy to die in the same position as Jesus, is faithfully reproduced by Michelangelo. The figure in the lower righthand corner appears to be a self-portrait of the great artist.*

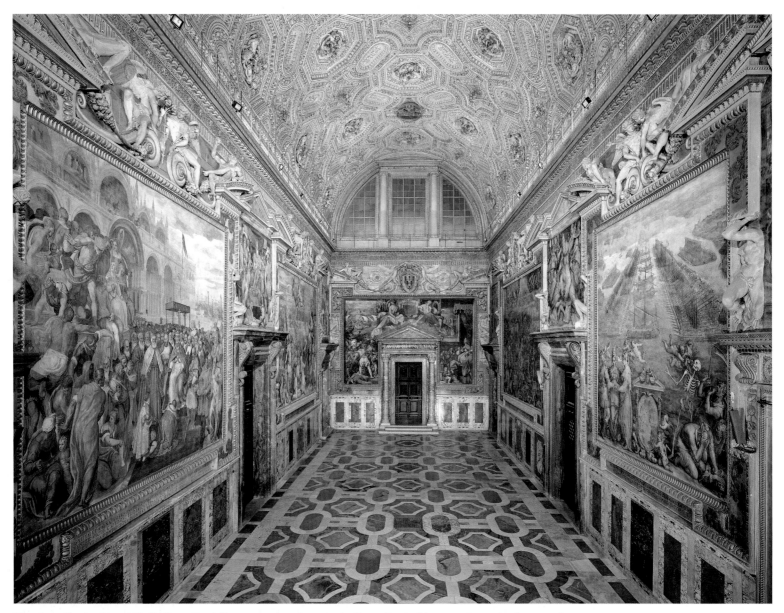

The Sala Regia *(Royal Hall)*. Pope Paul III entrusted to Antonio da Sangallo the Younger the task of renovating and decorating the oldest wing of the medieval palace, the area where official receptions, public consistories and other ceremonies of the papal court were held. The most important hall in this wing is the Sala Regia, a sort of "antechamber" to the Sistine Chapel. The renovation work began early in the spring of 1538. Sangallo eliminated the existing flat ceiling and gave this immense room (approximately 34 by 12 meters) a splendid tunnel-vaulted ceiling (33.6 meters high), decorated with octagonal stucco panels painted by Perin del Vaga. The door in the end wall leads to the Pauline Chapel, whereas the one to the right leads to the Scala Regia (Royal Staircase); in the foreground, the door to the right leads to the Sistine Chapel and the one to the left to the Sala Ducale. The pictorial decoration, begun under Pius IV, includes episodes from the history of the papacy; it was concluded under the reign of Gregory XIII, in 1573, by Giorgio Vasari, Taddeo Zuccari and their assistants.

The Sala Ducale, *also used for official ceremonies, was created by joining together two rooms of the original nucleus of the medieval palace. Bernini designed this transformation during the reign of Alexander VII in the 1660s. Bernini is also the author of the splendid stucco curtain, which is held up by winged cherubs. Most of the pictorial decoration in the room dates from the second half of the 16th century. It was in this room that the pope would wash the feet of twelve beggars dressed up as the Apostles on Holy Thursday.*

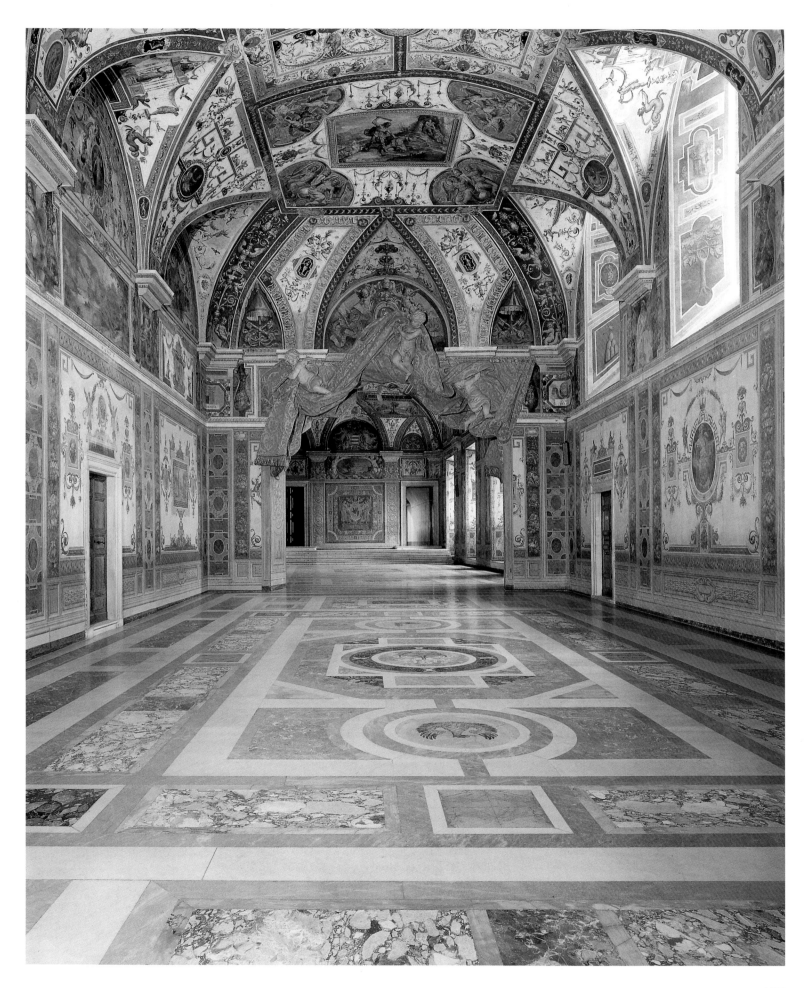

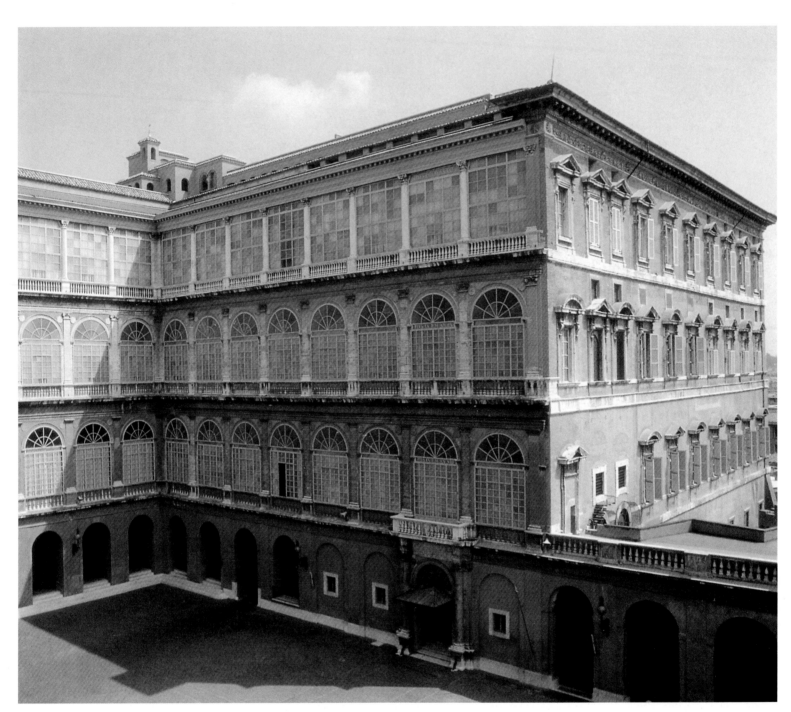

In 1563 Pius IV had the Loggias extended northwards, perpendicular to Bramante's and Raphael's. With this addition, modeled precisely on the original Loggias, he began the transformation of the former "secret garden" of Nicholas V, reserved for the papal court, into the Courtyard of St. Damasus. The construction of this courtyard, begun by Pirro Ligorio, was completed in the reign of Gregory XIII, first by Martino Longhi the Elder and finally by Ottaviano Nonni, called il Mascherino, in the 1570s. At the time of Sixtus V, Domenico Fontana provided the popes with a new residence in the Vatican. Until then they resided in the rather bleak northern apartments of the medieval palace with additions commissioned by Pius V, Julius III and Gregory XIII. The Sistine Palace is a construction with a square-shaped plan (53 by 52.4 meters) overlooking the courtyard of St. Damasus, opposite the medieval-Renaissance one. The three orders of Loggias are similar to the earlier ones, and perhaps were started during the previous pope's reign by Mascherino and Longhi. Fontana began work on April 30, 1589. At the death of Pope Sixtus on August 27, 1590, it was nearly complete; in October 1595, during the reign of Clement VIII Aldobrandini, Taddeo Landini finished the project. However, Pope Clement moved his residence to the Quirinal Palace, where his successors remained until 1870 when Pius IX, after the fall of the Papal State, transferred the residence of the popes back to the building next to St. Peter's.

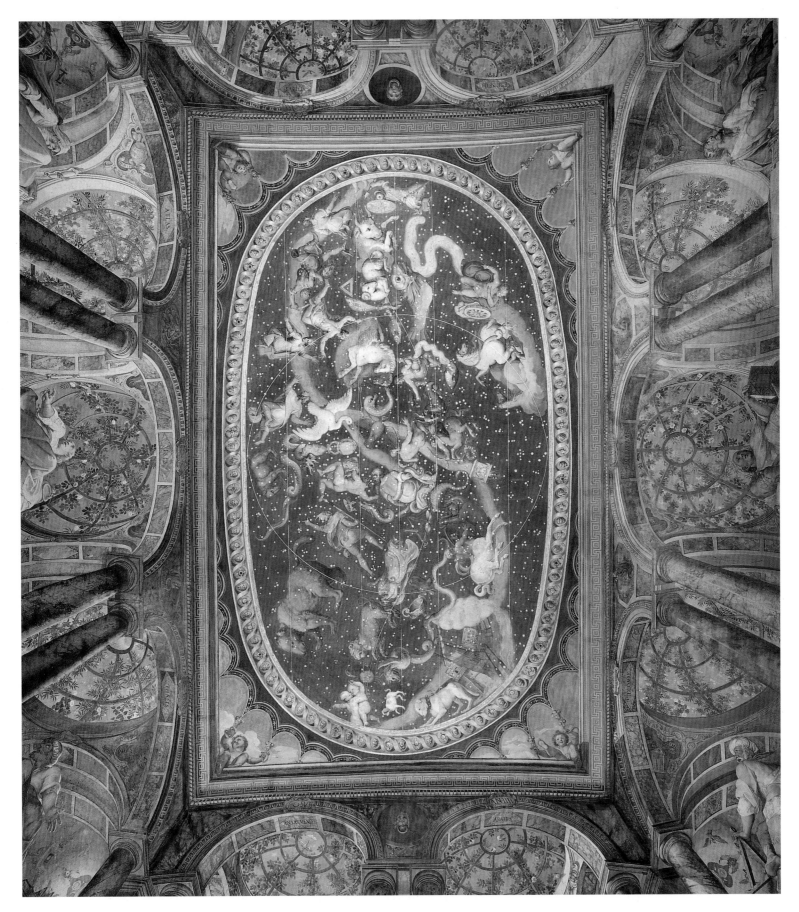

Ceiling of the Sala Bologna, which is named after the fresco reproducing a map of that city. This room corresponds to the Third Loggia of the wing constructed at the time of Gregory XIII. The composition depicting the twelve constellations of the zodiac was painted in 1575 by Giovanni Antonio Vanosino.

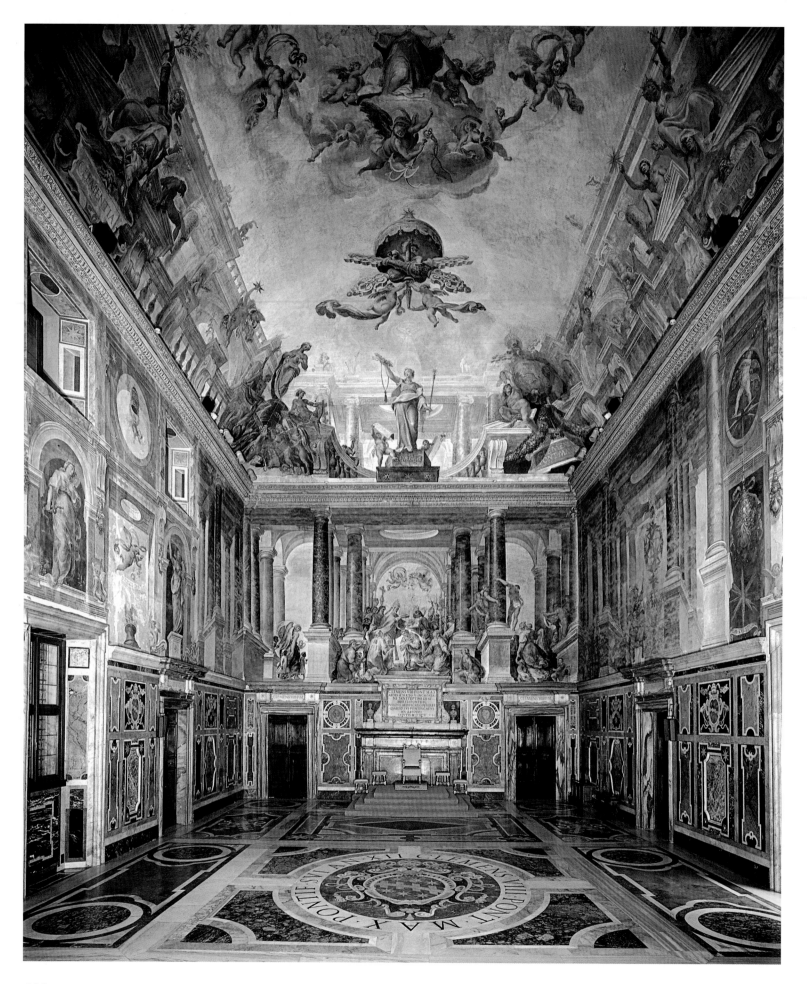

Proceeding through the various rooms of the Appartamento Nobile, *we reach the* Library *where the pope receives the highest authorities from all the foreign countries in the world.*

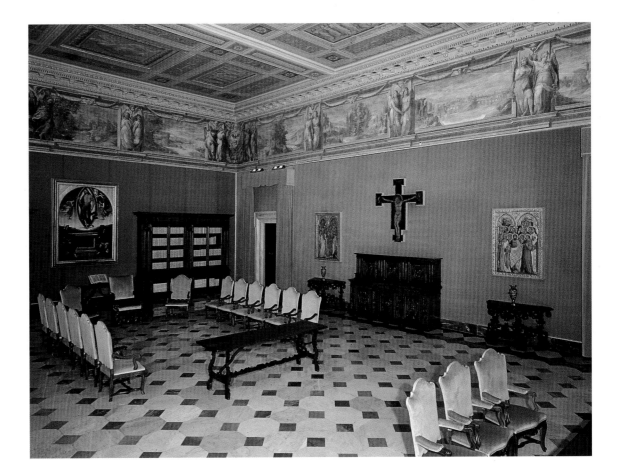

In the Hall of the Consistory *(right), the Pope presides over the assembly of the College of Cardinals to discuss matters related to the government of the church.*

The Clementine Hall, *named after Pope Clement VIII, was designed and built in 1596 by Giovanni Fontana (Domenico's brother) and Giacomo della Porta. It is the magnificent vestibule of the pope's apartments, the* Appartamento Nobile, *on the second floor of the Sistine Palace. The lavish decoration, which is an anticipation of the Baroque style, was carried out in 1600-01 by the brothers Giovanni and Cherubino Alberti.*

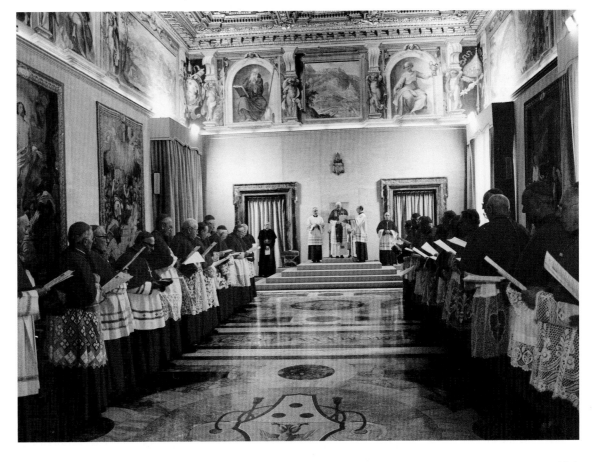

THE MUSEUMS, THE LIBRARY AND THE ARCHIVES

A Noble and Humble Guide

In the Vatican, the historical and the sacred are invariably entwined. Every visit there is an encounter with faith and culture. Inevitably, we end up regretting that we were unable to take in everything, and find ourselves wishing we had stayed longer to contemplate all the beauty that surrounds us.

By now, we have viewed unique masterpieces. Though we haven't been in a museum, we've already seen whole cycles of frescoes which, if added to the works associated with the Vatican's indoor collections, would make it the largest single fresco museum in the world. Such is the weight of the combined works inside Nicholas V's chapel, frescoed by Fra Angelico; the Borgia Apartment painted by Pinturicchio and his school; the Stanzas and Loggias splendidly decorated by Raphael; the Sistine Chapel, where artists like Perugino, Botticelli, Ghirlandaio, Signorelli, Cosimo Rosselli are joined to the mighty Michelangelo.

Indeed, we come out of the apostolic palaces just as dazzled by all this art as if we were walking straight into the glare of a midday sun. Before leaving these rooms, however, we should pause to glance from the loggia connected to the apartment of Julius II. Here, the gruff and abrupt pontiff would look out with pleasure across the long garden that dropped off in gradual descent before rising again to the distant *Palazzetto del Belvedere*. This small and delightful construction had been ordered by Innocent VIII as a place to stop and rest during his long walks.

One day, Pope Julius had one of his sudden inspirations. He called his favorite architect, Bramante, and directed him to make it a reality. The steep declivity between the palace and the belvedere would be divided into three spacious levels connected by highly theatrical staircases. Flanking them would be two broad and parallel corridors more than 300 meters long. Walking through them, it would be possible to pass from one side to the other, always remaining on the same level.

Seeking Divine Perfection

These extensive wings, together with others which would be added subsequently, now house the museums, the library and the Secret Archives of the Vatican. Taken together, the three would confer worldwide fame to the Vatican in the fields of art and science.

For centuries preceding the Renaissance, art and science—in the broadest sense of the terms—were viewed by the Church in separate lights. As Deoclecio Redig de Campos, director of the Vatican Museums throughout the 1970s, observed, "While we owe to the monastic scribes all that has come down to us of the written patrimony of the Ancient World, be it literary, scientific, juridical, or historical, nothing was done to save monuments or works of art. This was particularly true of the sculptures of pre-Christian Rome, which were often precious copies of famous Greek originals already lost."

The reason for these conflicting attitudes can be traced to the fear that classical art, with its dominantly mythological content, might have a harmful effect on the faith and moral behavior of simple people who were ignorant and superstitious. On the other hand, the written texts were available to a small class of the educated elite, and thus could not have the same effect.

But with the coming of Humanism in the 15th century, the popes and Church leaders were able to admire the natural beauty that was evident in pagan art. The breathtaking statues of Greco-Roman antiquity were viewed as unsurpassed examples of how man's creativity could aspire to forging an image of godliness. Ancient art was seen as prefiguring Christianity with its seeking of divine perfection.

Since they knew they were the vicars of Christ on earth, the popes of the Renaissance moreover saw themselves in some way as the heirs of Rome's imperial greatness. An almost palpable current of inspiration flowed through the basilica and through the two wings willed by Julius II—the eastern one built by Bramante and the western one, designed by Pirro Ligorio a half century later.

The Della Rovere pope then placed in a garden (the *Antiquarium*) his personal collection of statues and classical sarcophagi. The garden was located between the northern and eastern wings of the Belvedere and the semicircular columns that connect with the apostolic palace. The first work to be transferred there, in 1506, was nothing less than the celebrated "Laocoon". Five years later in the same courtyard was placed the "Apollo Belvedere", unearthed in 1489 and acquired by Della Rovere while he was still a cardinal. Believed to be a work of ancient Greece, its ideal beauty proved to have a profound influence on the development of artistic style not only in that century but for centuries afterward.

Other celebrated pieces would soon find their way into Julius's sculpture garden: the "Venus Felix", "Ariadne Abandoned", the two statues found lying respectively in the Tiber and in the Nile, the celebrated "Belvedere Torso" that was the preferred model for Michelangelo in conceiving the muscled bodies that we still associate with his art.

Art and Nature

With his "sculpture courtyard," Julius in effect had scattered the seeds for what would one day become the Vatican collection. It would become one of the largest complexes of its type, housing the biggest collection anywhere of classical antiquity. In a sense, his uncle Sixtus IV had beaten him to it in 1471 when he had moved a collection of antique bronze statues from the Lateran Palace to the Capitol Hill (*Campidoglio*), inviting the Roman citizens to view them. In the Vatican, on the other hand, the sculpture garden was accessible only to experts. Julius also decreed that the adjacent *Palazzetto del Belvedere* be used to house young artists then employed at the papal court. That way, he reasoned, they could draw inspiration from the proximity of the Greco-Roman masterpieces. The enjoyment of these art works, immersed in nature, was a concept itself suggested by reading the classic authors. Thus the pope and his guests plunged themselves into an atmosphere of renewed classicism. And from the *palazzetto*, one could descend into the gardens below by way of a delightful winding staircase, enclosed within a tower, begun by Bramante and finished by Pirro Ligorio, known as Bramante's Spiral Staircase.

The promising beginnings of the museums came to a standstill amid the severe atmosphere of the Counter-Reformation. Pius V (1566-72) even considered ridding himself of the entire statue collection, judging it unseemly to keep such "idols" within the Vatican.

But the pendulum swung again in the second half of the eighteenth century with the birth of two new and interrelated sciences: archaeology and art history. The key figures of these movements, respectively, were the German archaeologist Johann Winckelmann, Clement XII's Commissioner for Antiquities, and the abbot Luigi Lanzi. New impulse came with the impressive construction of the Pius-Clementine Museum, which effectively absorbed Julius's arcadian sculpture garden. To this day it remains the nucleus of the entire collection. Its name "Pius-Clementine" derives from two papal patrons: its founder, Clement XIV (1769-74), and the pope who brought it to completion, his successor Pius VI (1775-99). And in contrast to the sixteenth century when the primary criterion was the aesthetic enjoyment of a select few, the new spirit of collecting centered around preventing the further loss of art works and housing them in public buildings where they could be studied.

The establishment of the Pius-Clementine was preceded by that of several smaller museums—all connected with the Vatican Library. These include the "Corridor of Plaques and Memorial Tablets", with its rich collection of ancient funerary inscriptions, both pagan and Christian; the Sacred Museum, willed by Benedict XIV, centered on early Christianity and contained coins, cameos, and the lead seals of the pontiffs; the Vatican's Medal Collection, sacked by the French under Napoleon; the Profane Museum with items not directly connected to the origins of Christianity.

In order to avoid the further loss of art works, Clement XIV began a systematic campaign of acquisitions. He also began to think of constructing a new museum. He settled on the *Palazzetto del Belvedere*, transforming the adjoining sculpture garden into an octagonal courtyard.

Another great leap forward in the development of the Vatican Museums came when Monsignor Gian Angelo Braschi, the closest advisor to Pope Clement XIV, rose to the papal throne as Pius VI. He viewed the arts as an element of great prestige for the Church in measuring itself against other European monarchies. And since space to house all these art works was quickly running out, Pius's remedy was to build a new museum and thus add to the whole.

Museums into the Future

The project, entrusted to Michelangelo Simonetti and his assistant Giulio Camporese, paradoxically began with a decision in radical contrast to the concept of conserving art. In order to lengthen the Statue Gallery, Innocent VIII's chapel with frescoes by Mantegna was destroyed. The various museums were connected by a master staircase which Simonetti used to join the collections of the library to the Hall of the Greek Cross, the sarcophagi of St. Helen and St. Constance, the Round Hall (inspired by the Pantheon), and the Hall of Muses with its "Belvedere Torso" at the center. From here you enter the Clementine Museum by way of the Hall of Animals.

But the new museum, which had an entrance on the Atrium of the Four Gates, remained open only a short time. The iniquitous Treaty of Tolentino (1797), imposed on the Papal States by Napoleon Bonaparte, deprived it of its most famous works. More than 500 wagons were used to carry away the spoils to Paris. What was taken was restored only in part, thanks to the terms of the Congress of Vienna (1814-1815) and to the untiring efforts of the new head of Fine Arts in Rome, Antonio Canova, appointed in 1802.

Canova had the additional task of finding space for the new works which had been acquired in the meantime, in part to fill the void left by the Napoleonic sacking. He knew he also needed to create a new exhibition area for the most famous works when they were returned from France. These included no fewer than three masterpieces of Raphael: "The Transfiguration", the "Crowning of the Virgin" and the "Madonna of Foligno".

The immense Belvedere Courtyard, already divided in two by the wing of Sixtus V's library, became the site of the so-called *Braccio Nuovo* (1822), built in neoclassic style. It changed the south boundary of the Courtyard of the Pine Cone in order to house other noted sculptures such as the "Augustus of Prima Porta" and the "Nile".

The next expansion came with Pope Gregory XVI (1831-1846) who founded both the Etruscan Museum in 1837 and the Egyptian Museum two years later, thus enlarging the field of antiquity beyond the purely Greco-Roman. The same pope established—in 1844, inside the Lateran Palace—the Gregorian Profane Museum. It included statues, sarcophagi and mosaic reliefs for which there was no more space in the Pius-Clementine. Ten years later, Pius IX decided to establish the Christian Museum for housing the discoveries then being made at excavation sites among the catacombs. In 1926, Pius XI founded the Missionary and Ethnological Museum which reflected the activities of the farflung missions among the indigenous cultures of the world.

The three collections of the Lateran Palace were brought within the Vatican complex between 1963 and 1973. They were placed in a wing known as the *Paolina* because it was created

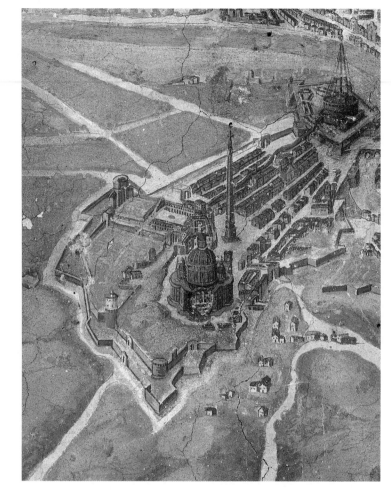

Detail from a scroll depicting the plain of Rome in the map, Latium et Sabina, *one of the forty frescoes in the Gallery of Maps, based on cartoons by the astronomer, Ignazio Danti. In the foreground, the Vatican complex and its surrounding walls are clearly visible. In the background is Castel Sant'Angelo (Hadrian's Tomb).*

The Palazzetto del Belvedere. *At the top of the northern slopes of the Vatican hill, in the area once occupied by Nicholas III's walled gardens, Pope Innocent VIII Cybo had a crenellated loggia built. Called the Loggia del Belvedere, this construction replaced one of the gates of the old walls; it was built between 1484 and 1487 by Jacopo da Pietrasanta from designs by Antonio del Pollaiolo. The pope used it as a resting place during his walks. Later, a few bedrooms were added to its southern side. To the left is the tower of Bramante's Staircase and next to it is Bramante's Corridor, built to link the Palace to the Belvedere at the top of the hill.*

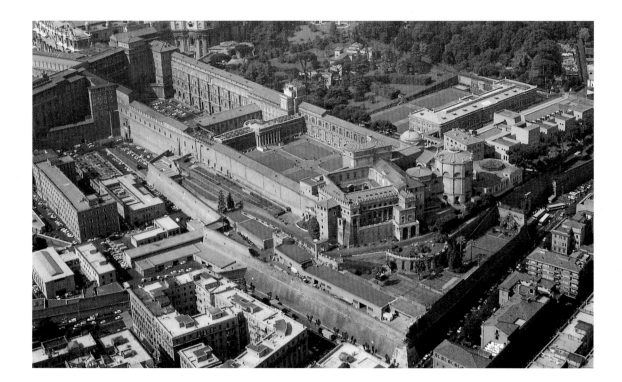

during the pontificate of Paul VI (1963-78). If the *Braccio Nuovo* was ideal for the housing of statues, the *Paolina* Wing can both accommodate new art works as well as lending itself to imaginative rearrangements of its contents.

A Springtime Lasting Centuries

After the recovery of the paintings carried off to France, a new picture gallery was created—first in the Borgia Apartment and subsequently in several other settings before a definitive solution was found. This finally came with the establishment, in 1932, of the Pinacoteca in eclectic style erected on the eastern side of the Pius-Clementine Museum. Virtually all of the works therein have a religious subject. The artists represented run from Giotto to Melozzo da Forlì, from Leonardo to Titian and Veronese. Raphael occupies the main room with his paintings and his tapestries created for the Sistine Chapel.

In the same year, a new entrance to the museums was inaugurated. It is located along the wall that flanks the Viale Vaticano. A broad spiral ramp, designed by Giuseppe Momo, leads up to the various collections. In the basement area beneath the square garden facing the Pinacoteca, Paul VI founded the Carriage Museum—a fascinating collection of nineteenth century carriages used by the popes, as well as the first automobiles employed to transport Pius XI and Pius XII.

The most recent addition to this already extensive series of collections is the Religious Modern Art Collection, spread out between the Borgia Apartment and other areas. The 740 works include such artists as Matisse, Rouault, Chagall, Moore, Martini, Greco, Manzù, Ferrazzi, and Carrà. Everything there was offered in homage to Paul VI. No better response to the rhetorical question expressed by that pope: "Is religious art merely the fruit of a bygone and outdated season of the human spirit, or is it something belonging to our days, in which religion seems to have lost so much of its magical inspirational role?"

The more than 40,000 square meters of the twelve museums that constitute the Vatican complex cover a route fully seven kilometers long. Every year, more than three million visitors can see for themselves that, in the words of Bishop Giovanni Fallani, "the history of religious art is the story of a springtime lasting centuries, one that has so many high points that it seems ever to renew itself." The magnificence of all this art served a specific purpose for the popes, particularly during the

Middle Ages and the Renaissance. For them it was a teaching instrument, a manifest proof of the greatness of religious faith. It was something anyone could see with his own eyes.

The endless corridors of art within the Vatican have an invigorating effect on today's religious pilgrim. There is a natural give and take between the spiritual life and the aesthetic one. In these rooms too, the visitor who is a believer has reason to reaffirm his Catholicism. Inside the basilica, he experiences the liturgical community through the presence of his brethren, all of the same faith, coming from all parts of the globe. In the figure of the pope, he is able to perceive the universal paternity of Christ's vicar on earth. And here in the museums, these magnificent creations of art serve to remind him that nothing that is human is alien to the Christian: neither thought, science, art, politics or the activities that make up one's daily labor.

The Apostolic Library

The Vatican's Apostolic Library is another important aspect of this catholicity. Leaving aside the pontifical libraries which were in operation under the popes and the Curia until the fourteenth century, let's have a look at the one which is open to all scholars who apply to study its extraordinary contents. It contains every field of knowledge that was cultivated by the Humanists, rather like the library at San Marco's in Florence. The person who conceived it was a Humanist pope we have already encountered: Nicholas V (1447-55). Though he was not rich, he was able to buy or have copied such a wealth of manuscripts that by the time he came to Rome he had already assembled a notable collection. At the time of his death, Nicholas's personal "library" contained 800 Latin codices, 353 Greek ones, in addition to 56 others found in his bedroom. Taken together, these were the seeds of a future Vatican Library which he had in fact dreamed about. "It should be a spacious hail," he wrote, "illuminated with large windows and open to all scholars."

The library actually came into being under Sixtus IV, at which time the number of codices had swollen to 2,527. Officially it was inaugurated on June 15, 1475 under the direction of the scholarly Bartolomeo Sacchi (1421-81) known as *il Platina*. His nomination was immortalized in a painting by Melozzo da Forlì. The new institution occupied four rooms on the ground floor of the north wing of the Parrot courtyard—an area previously used as a wine cellar and as a place to store grain. Interestingly, the same rooms were utilized in 1967 and 1969 for the first two bishops' synods following Vatican Council II.

In 1587 the library was moved by order of Sixtus V. Not only was the area dangerously damp, but space was running out because of the numerous acquisitions and the growing number of printed volumes which followed Gutenberg's invention of the printing press in 1455. Though a number of conservative-minded humanists opposed the invention, it soon carried the day and swept all before it.

Sixtus gave the commission to the pontifical architect Domenico Fontana to construct a new library between the two long corridors in the Belvedere courtyard. This eliminated the theatrical staircase that led up to the first of two landings. All of the rooms of the new library were covered in frescoes. The hall named for Sixtus V, with its vast ceiling, walls and pilasters—all frescoed—remains a striking vision for anyone visiting the museums. The most representative of the Mannerist painters at the close of the 16th century depicted there the most famous libraries of the ancient world as well as the ecumenical councils. On the pilasters we can see the inventors of the various alphabets and types of writing, preceded by "Adam and Christ", and "the Way, the Life and the Truth"; the lunettes celebrate many of the ambitious building projects of Sixtus V.

Once again, a shortage of space required alterations and changes. The plans sketched out by Leo XIII (1878-1903) to facilitate a better conservation of manuscripts and printed works were on such a scale that one could legitimately speak of a third Vatican library.

Among the library's celebrated prefects, we should cite Achille Ratti who in 1922 became pope with the name Pius XI. The library is considered one of the most modern, wide-ranging and well-equipped in the world. The collection contains more than 75,000 codices in manuscript and approximately 8,200 incunabula, i.e., the earliest printed texts. The total number of works in the collection is 800,000.

Through it all, the library has remained faithful to the mission as envisioned by Sixtus IV. In a papal bull dated 1475, he declared his intention of founding a public library that would be "of pride to the Church Militant, and of benefit to scholars."

The Secret Archives

The Belvedere courtyard also leads to the Secret Archives, recognized as one of the most outstanding and important archives in the world. It was founded in 1612 as the Central Archives of the Church. As might be imagined, much of its contents actually date back centuries prior to its founding. As examples, there are the two collections of letters (fifth and sixth centuries) belonging to St. Leo the Great and St. Gregory the Great; a diploma given to the Emperor Otto II (962) written in gold on purple velum. From the time of Innocent III (1198-1216) is a collection of Vatican Registers, consisting largely of papal bulls. The 2,047 volumes add up to what is considered one of the principal sources of information regarding the history of Europe.

No less important are the 353 volumes of the "Avignon Registers", entailing a wealth of information regarding the permanence in that city during the "Babylonian Captivity". That particular collection is enriched by the celebrated set of golden seals, the largest of its type anywhere. There are 68 of them —from that of Frederick Barbarossa (1164) to that of Charles VI Hapsburg (1723). Outstanding among the precious mementos are the petition to Pope Clement VII asking for the annulment of Henry VIII's first marriage (1530); a love letter from the same monarch to Anne Boleyn; the accord stipulating the abdication of Queen Christina of Sweden, authenticated with no fewer than 306 seals.

The Archive is called "secret" because there was a time when the term meant "private", and in fact it served "first of all and principally the Roman Pontiff and the Holy See." However, everything in it has been available to scholars from the time of Benedict XV's pontificate, that is to say since 1922. John Paul II wrote that the Vatican Archive may be thought of as "an extraordinary book which contains within its pages—be they dark or luminous, rousing or dramatic—the records of a centuries long human endeavor, to which the Church and our whole civilization are both heirs and continuers."

Once again, shortage of space required an inventive solution. A large extension to the archives was dug beneath the Courtyard of the Pine Cone. Inaugurated by John Paul II in 1980, it is a veritable anti-nuclear bunker built entirely in reinforced concrete on two floors. All together, the extension measures 31,000 square meters and contains no fewer than 43 kilometers of shelves.

Vatican Astronomy Even Before Galileo

Religioni ac bonis artibus (for Religion and the Arts) was written plainly on the prospectus of the *Collegio Romano*, the greatest scholastic institution of its day, founded by Gregory XIII at the end of the sixteenth century. And the "arts" meant more than the figurative arts, the libraries and the archives. The Vatican has long been active in the sciences in the most modern sense of the term. Even half a century prior to the "Galileo Affair", science scored a significant victory only a stone's throw from the papal residence. The result was the reformation of the old Julian Calendar, renamed (for Pope Gregory XIII) the Gregorian Calendar. The decree was signed on February 24, 1582.

Pope Gregory had ordered the construction of a tower ("the Tower of the Winds") on the western end of the Belvedere. The sundial placed there enabled Ignazio Danti to demonstrate that the spring equinox no longer occurred on March 21 but on the 11th. Following these corroborations, Gregory moved to readjust the calendar according to calculations provided earlier by the brothers Luigi and Antonio Lilio, both scientists. Thanks to this joint effort, the equinox would once again coincide with the traditional date.

Three centuries later, in 1891, Leo XIII founded the Vatican Observatory in the Tower of the Winds. After 1906, it was transferred to the stone keep inside the Gardens (the present-day seat of the Vatican Radio) and subsequently to Castel Gandolfo in 1932 because of the excessive nighttime illumination of the city of Rome. By observing the skies above the Vatican, a group of Jesuit astronomers under the direction of Fr. Johannes G. Hagen was able to compile a 10-volume catalog which registered the position of half a million stars.

Nowadays, their colleagues and fellow priests scrutinize the firmament from a new observatory located in the mountains of Arizona in the United States. So Vatican City has continued to welcome science in a spirit of broadmindedness whatever their faith or political ideology.

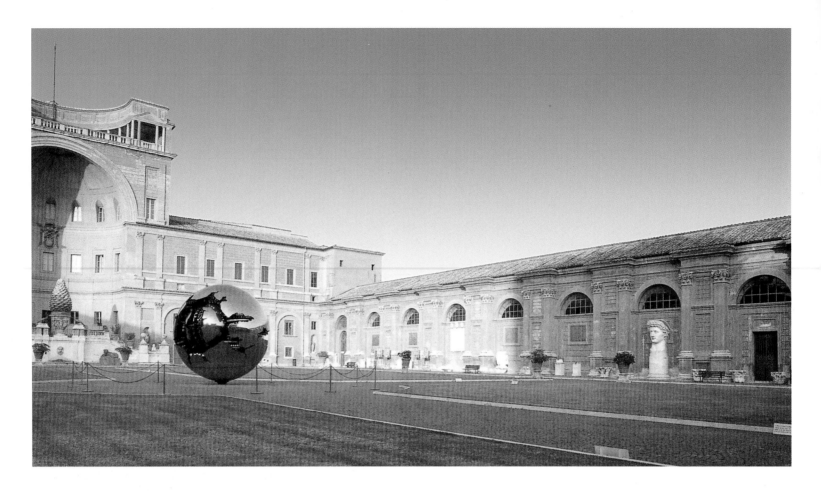

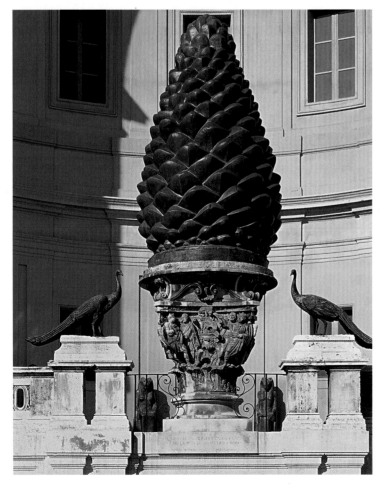

The last stretch of Bramante's Belvedere Corridor is the only one which has remained unaltered. It opens onto the Courtyard of the Pine Cone, the uppermost level of the original three-tiered "theater", designed by Bramante. Today, the gallery houses the Chiaramonti Museum.

The monumental Pine Cone in gilt bronze, originally a Roman fountain dating from the 1st or 2nd century A.D., formerly stood in the center of the outdoor atrium of the original St. Peter's, where it had probably been placed as early as the 8th century. Earlier on, it had stood in the Campus Martius in the district of Rome that is still known as the Pigna, or pine cone. In 1608, when the present basilica was built, the pine cone was moved to the courtyard that was then named after it. On either side are copies of Roman bronze peacocks, dating from Hadrian's period; the originals of these statues are in the Braccio Nuovo gallery of the museums. The capital that supports the pine cone has a relief decoration with referees and Roman athletes (222-235 A.D.).

The Nicchione della Pigna ("large niche of the pine cone"). In 1551 Michelangelo replaced Bramante's original circular stairway, partially destroyed by the exedra, with the flights of steps present today. On the sides of the fountain are two Egyptian lions (Dynasty 30, 4th century B.C.); the statues placed around the semicircle are also Egyptian.

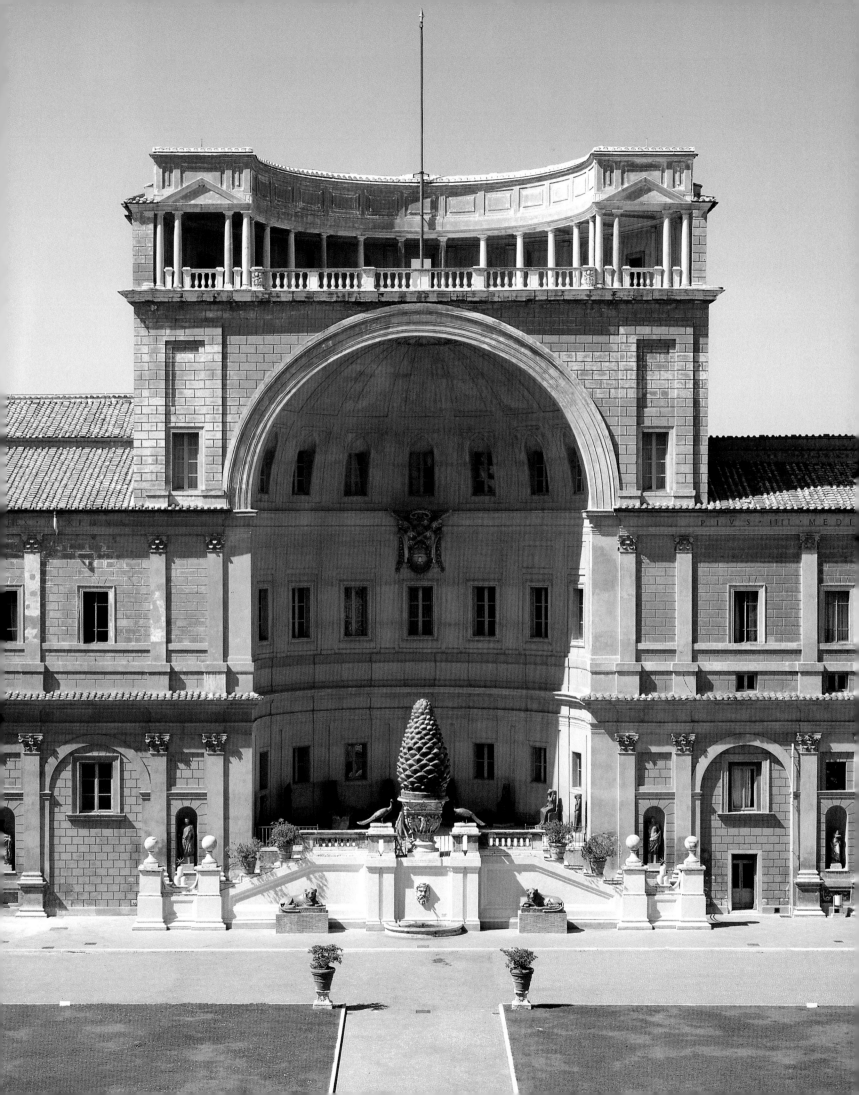

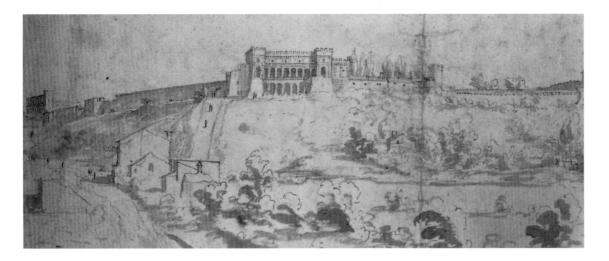

The Palazzetto del Belvedere as it appeared in 1535. The original of this drawing by Maarten van Heemskerck is in the Berlin Kupferstichkabinett.

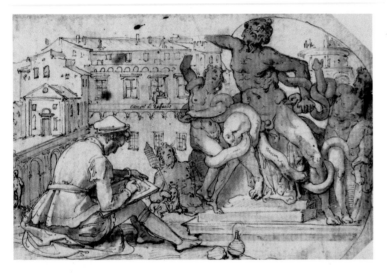

Julius II turned Innocent VIII's Palazzetto into a lodging place for artists. The Antiquarium in the gardens below soon became a school where contemporary sculptors could compete with the classical masters. In this mid-16th century drawing (left) from the Prints and Drawings Collection of the Uffizi in Florence, Federico Zuccari portrays his brother Taddeo at work copying the classical statues in the Belvedere. In the background Bramante's Corridor and the papal palace.

Julius II's Antiquarium (below). In the area between the exedra of the immense Belvedere three-tiered "theater" and Innocent VIII's Palazzetto, Julius II placed the classical statues of his private collection. It became the original core of the Vatican Museums and was added to by his successors until Pius V (1566-1572) decided that these pagan statues were "idols" and thus unsuitable for the pope's residence: closing off the gardens, the sculptures were packed up. We know what Julius II's Antiquarium looked like thanks to a painting by Hendrik van Kleef done in 1559, today in the Musées Royaux d'Art et d'Histoire in Brussels.

On March 5, 1565, on the occasion of the wedding between Annibale Altemps and Ortensia Borromeo, Pope Pius IV organized a splendid joust (below) in the Belvedere Courtyard which had just been completed. An unknown 16th century painter depicted the celebrations; this painting is on display at the Museo di Roma.

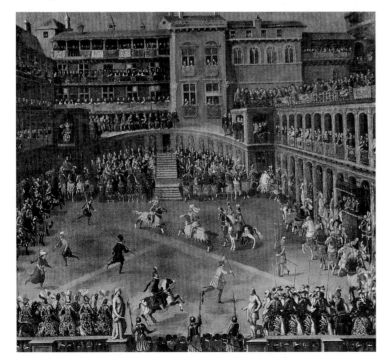

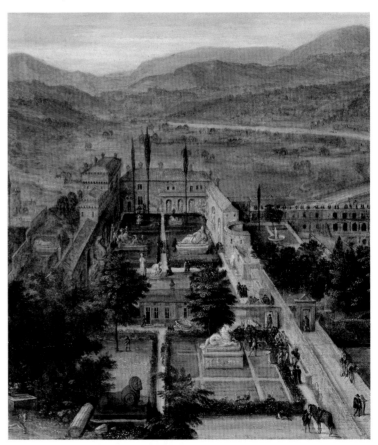

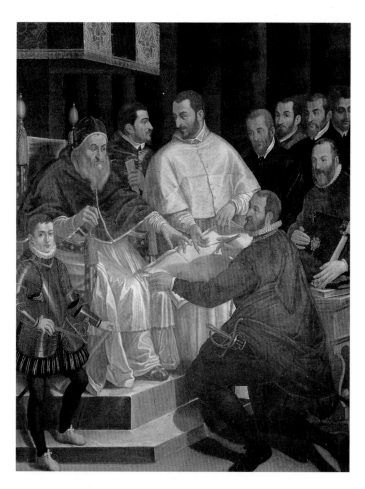

In just over a year, between May 1587 and September 1588, Domenico Fontana designed and constructed a new wing across the Belvedere Courtyard for Sixtus V. It was built on the site of Bramante's first stairway and was designed to house the Vatican Library. Under the artistic direction of Cesare Nebbia and Giovanni Guerra, in just two years (1588-90) several artists executed the pictorial program drawn up by Federico Ranaldi, prefect of the library, and Silvio Antoniano, secretary of the Sacred College of Cardinals.

In the Sistine Hall, *the library's original reading room, the lavish pictorial decoration includes scenes of the Ecumenical Councils, ancient libraries, portraits of the inventors of the art of writing and episodes from the papacy of Sixtus V, shown here as he reviews Fontana's drawings for the new building (left).*

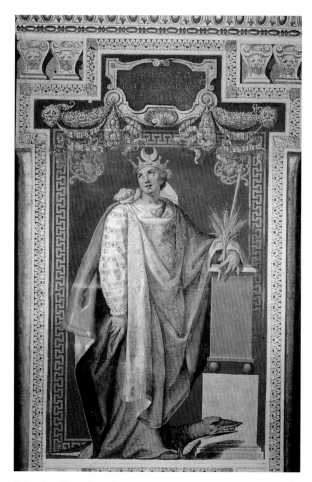

Isis, the Egyptian deity, is portrayed here as one of the inventors of the letters of the alphabet.

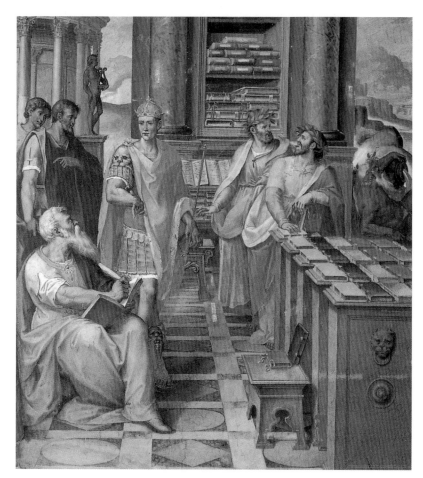

The painting on the left shows the Emperor Augustus, founder of the Biblioteca Palatina *(Palatine Library) among some literati of his time.*

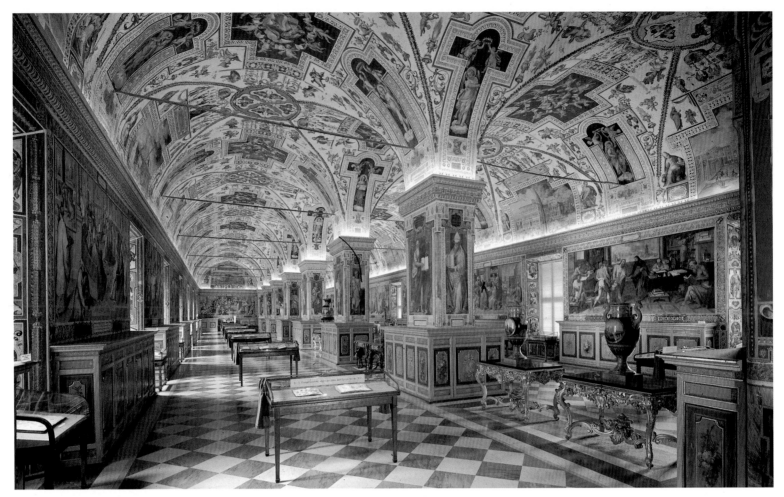

View of the Sistine Hall, the reading room of Sixtus V's Library: a hall with two aisles, its ceiling is supported at the center by seven columns. Sixtus V commissioned Domenico Fontana to build this wing of the library between 1587 and 1589.

Fresco depicting the Second Council of Constantinople (553).

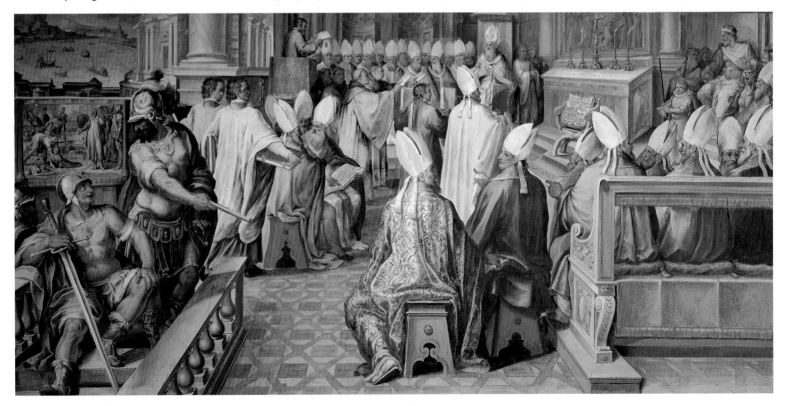

The origins of the Vatican's Secret Archives go back many centuries, but it was only formally established as an institution on January 31, 1612, when it was set up in the new wing of the Vatican Library. It contains official documents concerning the government of the universal Church. These rooms, designed from the very beginning to house the Secret Archives, still contain its original furniture. They are decorated with episodes from the diplomatic history of the Church.

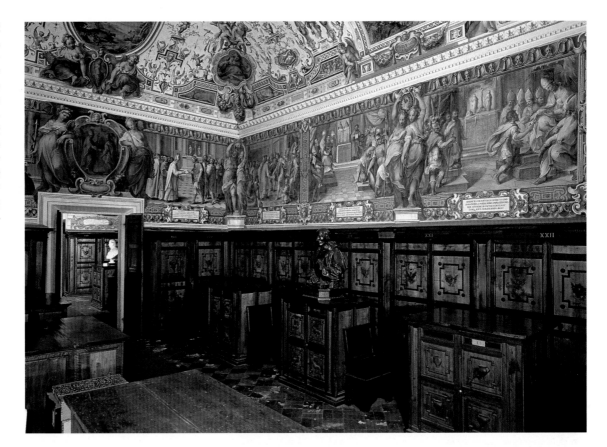

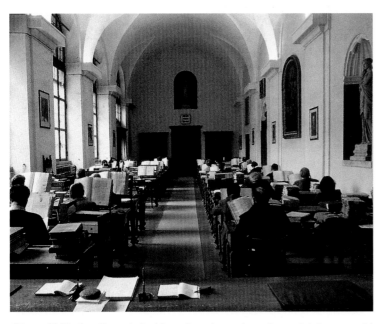

Since 1880 the Secret Archives has been transformed into a world renowned scientific institution for historical research. A special reading room is provided for scholars.

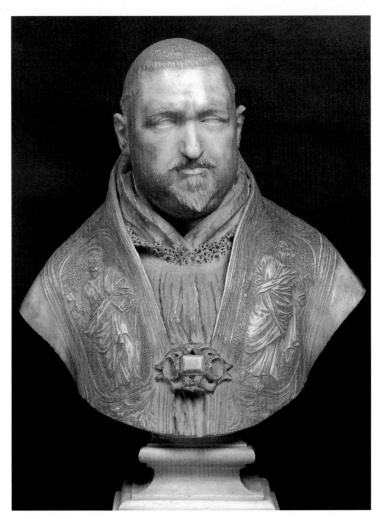

The Borghese pope Paul V, portrayed here by Bernini (Borghese Gallery, Rome), founded the Central Archives of the Church in 1612. It was called the "Secret" Archives because, like the archives of all sovereigns at that time, it was considered private even though it contained documents belonging to the State.

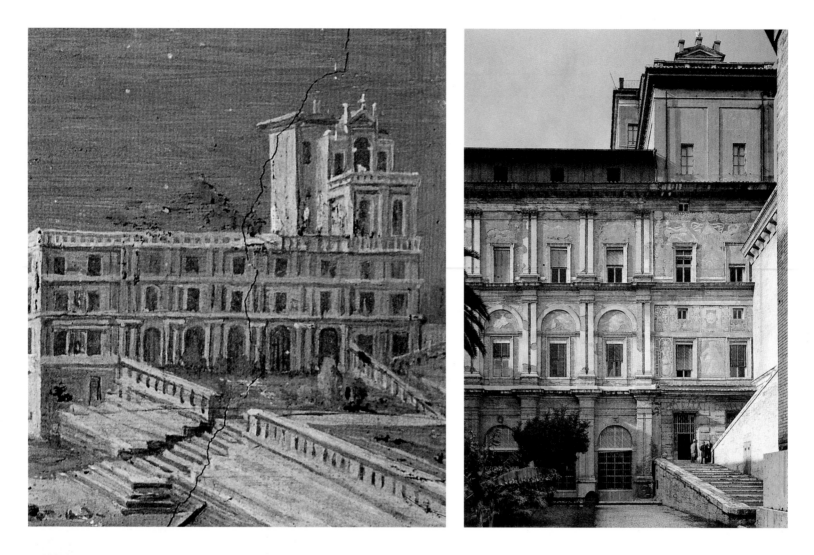

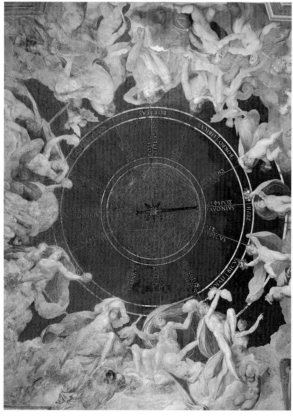

Pope Gregory XIII commissioned the construction (1578-1580) of the Tower of Winds, (above left in a 16th century fresco painted at the time of its construction). It was built by Ottaviano Mascherino, and designed as a sundial by Ignazio Danti in order to provide scientific evidence for the necessity of reforming the Julian calendar. This resulted in the "Gregorian" calendar (February 24, 1582), which is still in use today.

The ceiling of the Hall of the Sundial (left) is entirely taken up by the anemoscope designed by Ignazio Danti. The fresco decoration, with numerous figures (cherubs, young boys and old men) symbolizing the winds, was painted by Mathias Bril in 1581 to surround the wind rose.

Ignazio Danti explains to Gregory XIII why it is necessary to reform the Julian calendar. This panel was painted in 1582, and is on display at the State Archives of Siena.

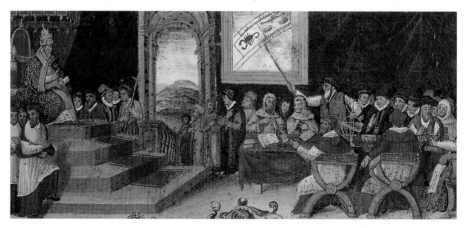

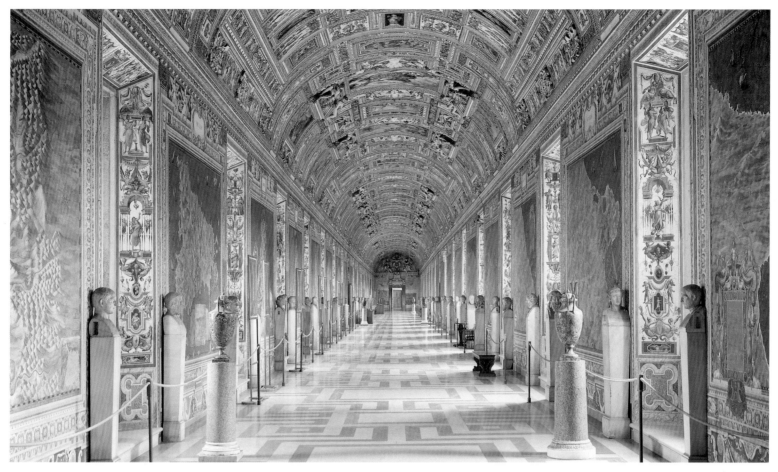

The della Rovere pope Sixtus IV founded the Vatican's Apostolic Library with a papal bull dated June 15, 1475. It was set up on the ground floor of the northern wing of the papal palace, which until then had been used as a wine cellar or granary. The library's origins go back to Nicholas V's collection of 834 Latin codes, an exceptional number for that time. The scene below depicts Sixtus IV visiting the library open to scholars. Opposite the pope is Cardinal Giuliano della Rovere, the future Pope Julius II; behind Sixtus IV is Bartolomeo Platina, the first librarian. The fresco was painted by an unknown 15th century artist in the Sistine Hall of the Ospedale di Santo Spirito (Hospital of the Holy Spirit). At that time, the papal library contained 2,527 Greek and Latin manuscripts.

The Gallery of Maps (above) is connected to the Tower of Winds, and was built by the same architect. It is decorated with forty maps reproduced from cartoons by the astronomer Ignazio Danti. The stucco and fresco decoration of the ceiling, a fine example of Mannerist art, was executed in 1583 by a group of artists working under the direction of Cesare Nebbia and Girolamo Muziano.

Detail of one of the maps depicting Italy in ancient times, drawn from a cartoon by Ignazio Danti.

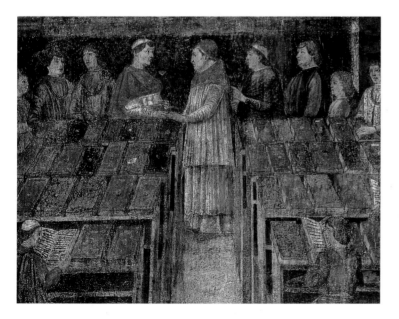

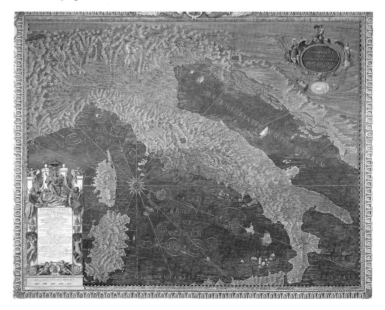

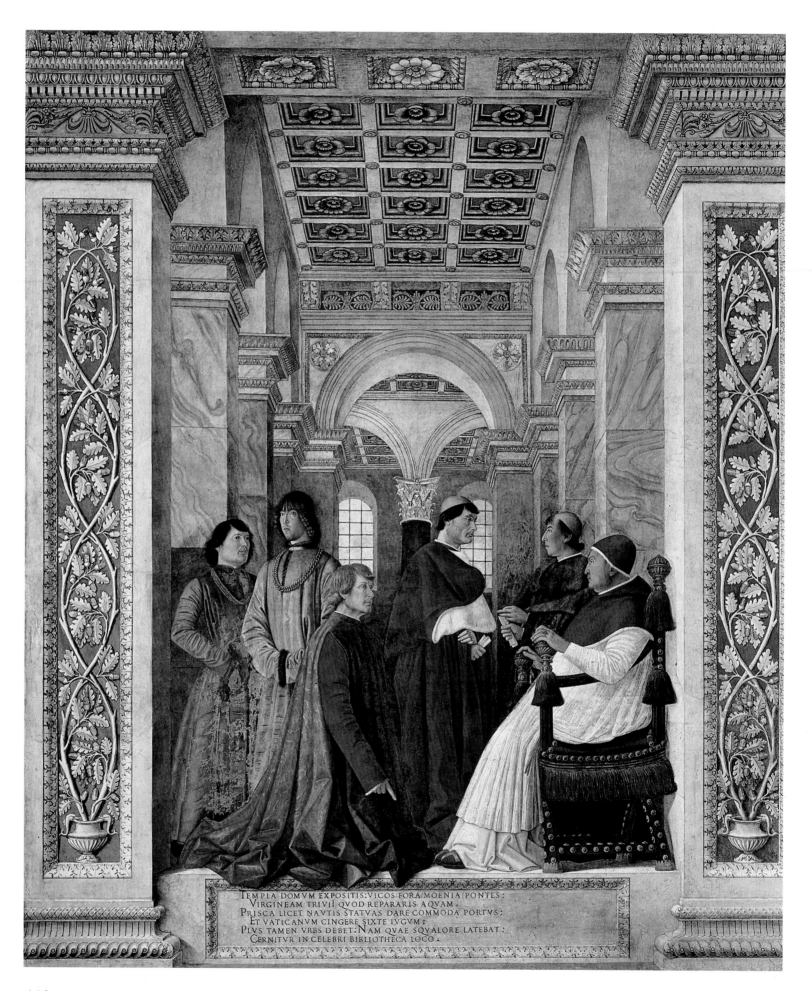

TEMPLA DOMVM EXPOSITIS:VICOS:FORA MOENIA PONTES:
VIRGINEAM TRIVII QVOD REPARARIS AQVAM.
PRISCA LICET NAVTIS STATVAS DARE COMMODA PORTVS:
ET VATICANVM CINGERE SIXTE IVGVM:
PLVS TAMEN VRBS DEBET:NAM QVAE SQVALORE LATEBAT:
CERNITVR IN CELEBRI BIBLIOTHECA LOCO.

Melozzo da Forlì's "Sixtus IV nominates Bartolomeo Platina prefect of the Vatican Library", painted in 1477. The fresco commemorates the foundation of the library and the nomination of its first prefect, Bartolomeo Platina. It was originally painted on the northern wall of the Latin Library, but was detached in 1825, and transferred to canvas; it has been on display in the Pinacoteca (picture gallery) since 1833. Sixtus IV is sitting on his throne with Platina kneeling in front of him. Next to the pope are his two nephews, Cardinals Pietro Riario and Giuliano della Rovere (who will later become pope with the name, Julius II). In this scene, an ordinary event takes on a heroic dimension and history models itself after the grandeur of ancient Rome. Classicism with its wide architectural perspective is combined with expressive portraits of the main characters' facial features.

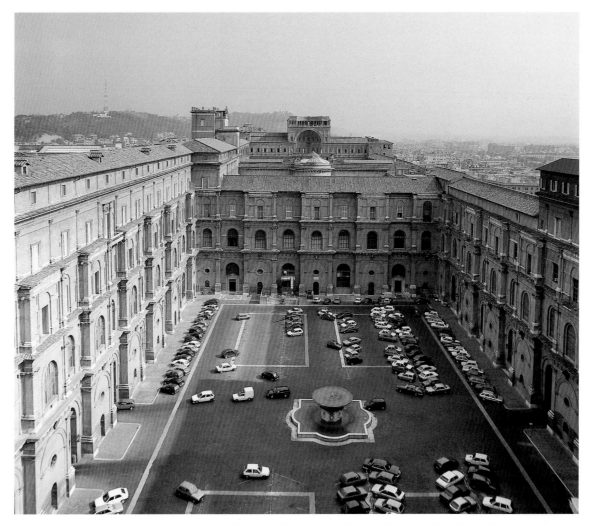

The present-day Belvedere Courtyard with the wing of the Sistine Library. Pirro Ligorio's superimposed corridors can be seen on the left; the Tower of Winds and the Nicchione della Pigna are clearly visible in the background.

Perin del Vaga's fresco in Castel Sant'Angelo (Hadrian's Tomb), painted between 1537 and 1541, permits us to see how the lowest of the three levels of the Belvedere Courtyard was used to stage theatrical performances. Although this fresco is not an accurate reconstruction of the two lower levels, it gives us a precise view of the upper one with Bramante's Exedra and Innocent VIII's Palazzetto del Belvedere behind it.

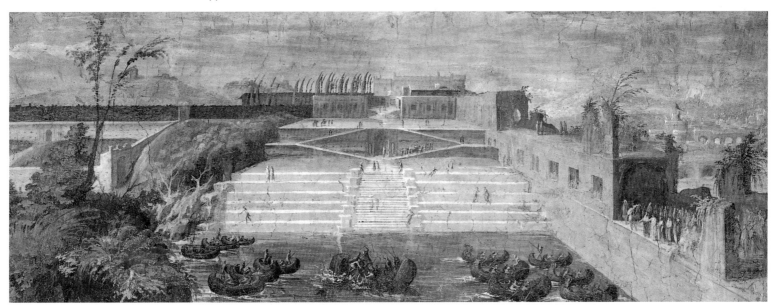

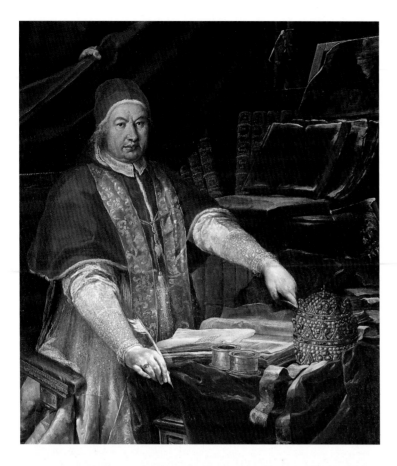

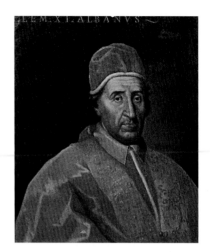

In 1756 Benedict XIV Lambertini *founded the Sacred Museum of the Vatican Library to house the archaeological finds from the early Christian era. He is depicted here in a portrait by Giuseppe Maria Crespi on display in the Vatican Pinacoteca.*

In 1703 Clement XI Albani *founded the first museum in the Vatican, the Ecclesiastical Museum, but its collections were soon dispersed. This portrait of Clement XI by an unknown artist belongs to the National Museum of Art in Stockholm.*

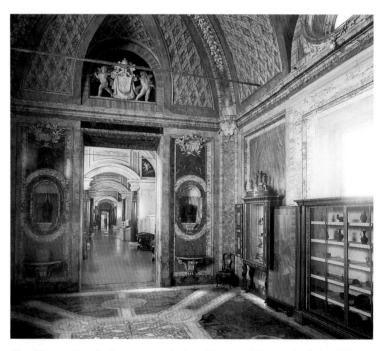

The Clementine Gallery, *named after Clement XII, was built in 1732 by closing the arcades of the portico at the northern end of Bramante's western corridor. In the foreground, the Profane Museum.*

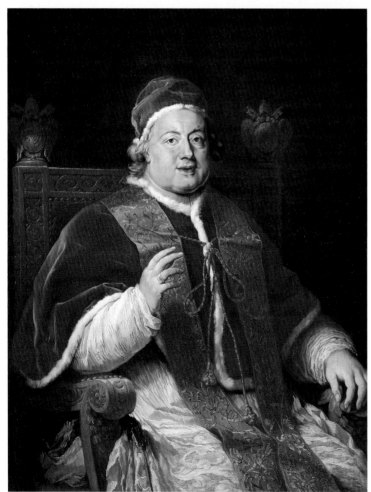

In 1767 Clement XIII Rezzonico *set up the Profane Museum at the northern end of the Clementine Gallery; in it he conserved all the non-Christian objects belonging to the Vatican's collections of antiquities, including ancient coins. This portrait in the Vatican Pinacoteca is by an unknown 18th century artist.*

The *Sacred Museum* is housed in three rooms at the southern end of the Western Corridor and contains early Christian archaeological finds.

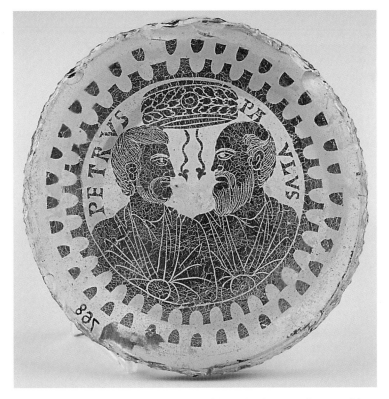

Saints Peter and Paul, *carved in gold foil at the bottom of a cup. Glass objects of this type were often found inside the walls of the catacombs.*

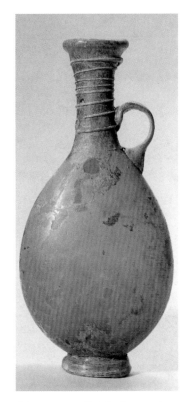

Glass cruet. *Originally used as containers for ointments or perfume, cruets were often transformed into sacred relics.*

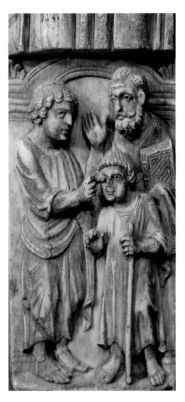

Healing of a Blind Man, *a scene often used as a metaphor for conversion to the faith, is a decoration on an ancient pyx (small cylindrical vessel) belonging to an early Christian oculist, detail.*

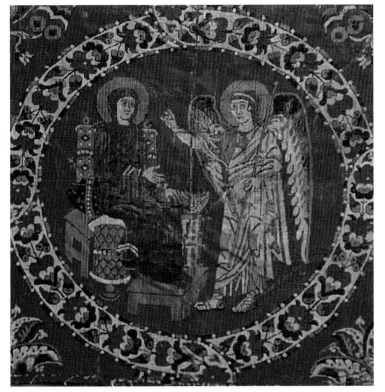

A piece of silk from the Christian Orient, probably Syria, dating from the 8th-9th century, depicts the Annunciation.

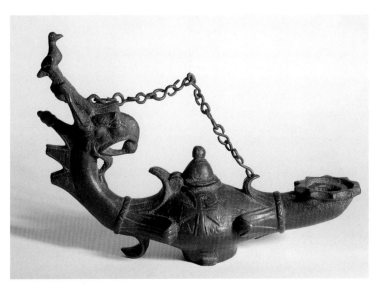

Oil lamp *in the shape of a griffin, with Christ's monogram (3rd-4th century A.D.).*

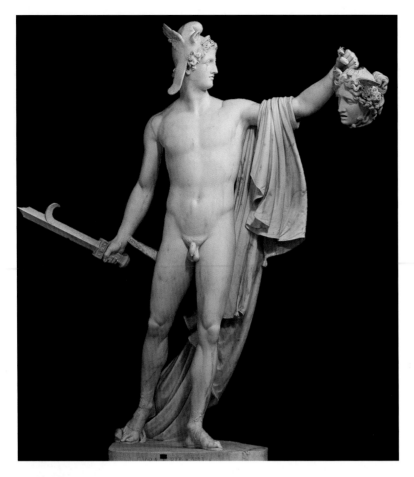

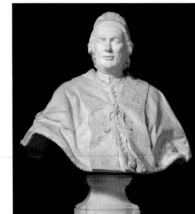

Perseus *by Antonio Canova, acquired by Pius VII in 1802 to replace the "Belvedere Apollo" that Napoleon had taken to Paris in 1797 after plundering Rome.*

Clement XIV Ganganelli, *founder of the Clementine Museum. This marble bust by an unknown 18th century sculptor is in the Pius-Clementine Museum.*

The Octagonal Courtyard *was built by Michelangelo Simonetti in 1772-73, during Clement XIV's papacy, in the little garden that had previously housed Julius II's Antiquarium. The courtyard echoes the shape of the former 16th century garden; but was designed as an enclosed space in which the only reminders that it was once an open garden are the flower pots planted with azaleas and the fountain with aquatic plants.*

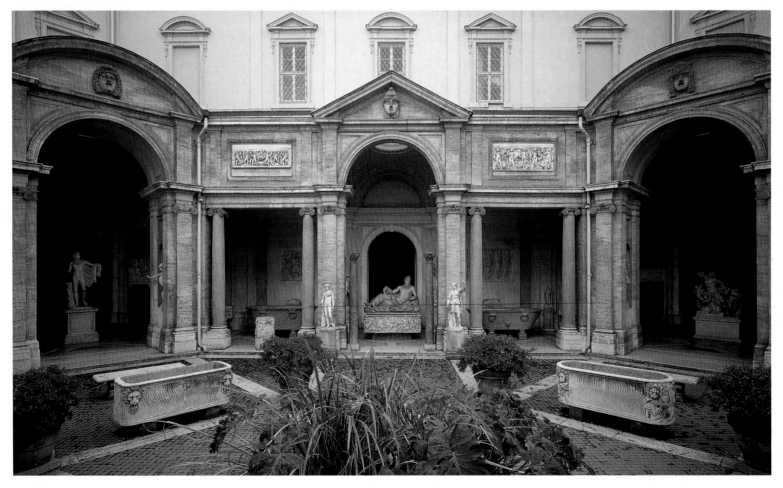

Apoxyomenos. *Found in Traste-vere (Rome) in 1849, this marble statue is a 1st century A.D. Roman copy of a bronze Greek original by Lysippus dated around 320 B.C. The Greek athlete is shown brushing off the perspiration from his arm.*

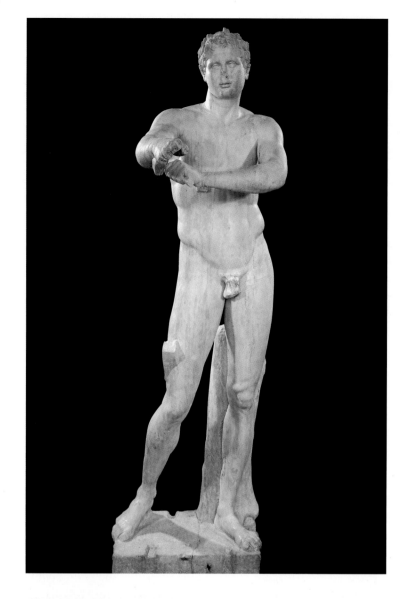

The Belvedere Apollo *(on page 152). Historical documents show that this renowned statue was conserved in the Belvedere in 1509, and was the most important statue in Julius II's Antiquarium. For many centuries it remained an aesthetic model for all sculptors, until the rediscovery of Parthenon reliefs proved that it was a 2nd century Roman copy of a bronze sculpture by a 4th century B.C. artist from Attica.*

The River Tigris *(below). Recently placed in the Octagonal Courtyard, this copy of a Hellenistic sculpture dates from Hadrian's time. When it was found, the statue was missing its head, right arm and left hand; the replacements were carved under the direct supervision of Michelangelo. Paul III had it brought to the Belvedere.*

Laocoon *(on page 153). This sculpture tells the final part of the story of the Trojan priest who was condemned to a horrible death by Pallas Athena for opposing the entrance of the Trojan horse from the Greek army. It was discovered on January 14, 1506 on the site where Emperor Titus's palace once stood, exactly where Pliny the Elder, the Latin writer, had described it in the 1st century A.D. Giuliano da Sangallo and Michelangelo saw the sculpture as it was being excavated and urged Julius II to buy it. When it was transferred to the Vatican, all the bells in Rome rang out and the event was celebrated publicly. The statue was considered an original work by sculptors from Rhodes executed at the beginning of the Christian era. It was already famous in Roman times for its extraordinary power of expression, and from the moment of its excavation inspired artists of the time, including Michelangelo, to equal its emotional force. Laocoon was considered an ancestor of the Roman tribes, because as a result of his warnings, the Trojan hero Aeneas, ancestor of Romulus, fled Tray to find refuge on the coast of Latium, the region where Rome was later founded. Some scholars have recently suggested that the statue may in fact be a copy of a bronze original cast in Pergamum in the 2nd century B.C.*

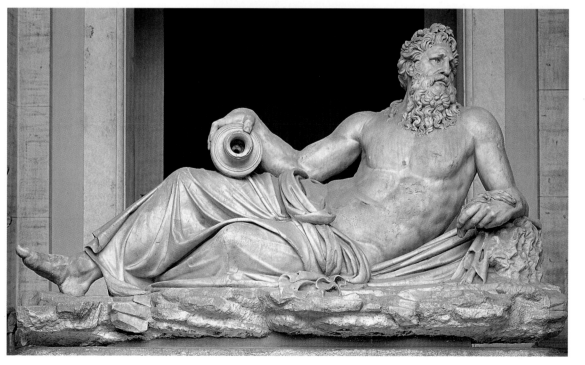

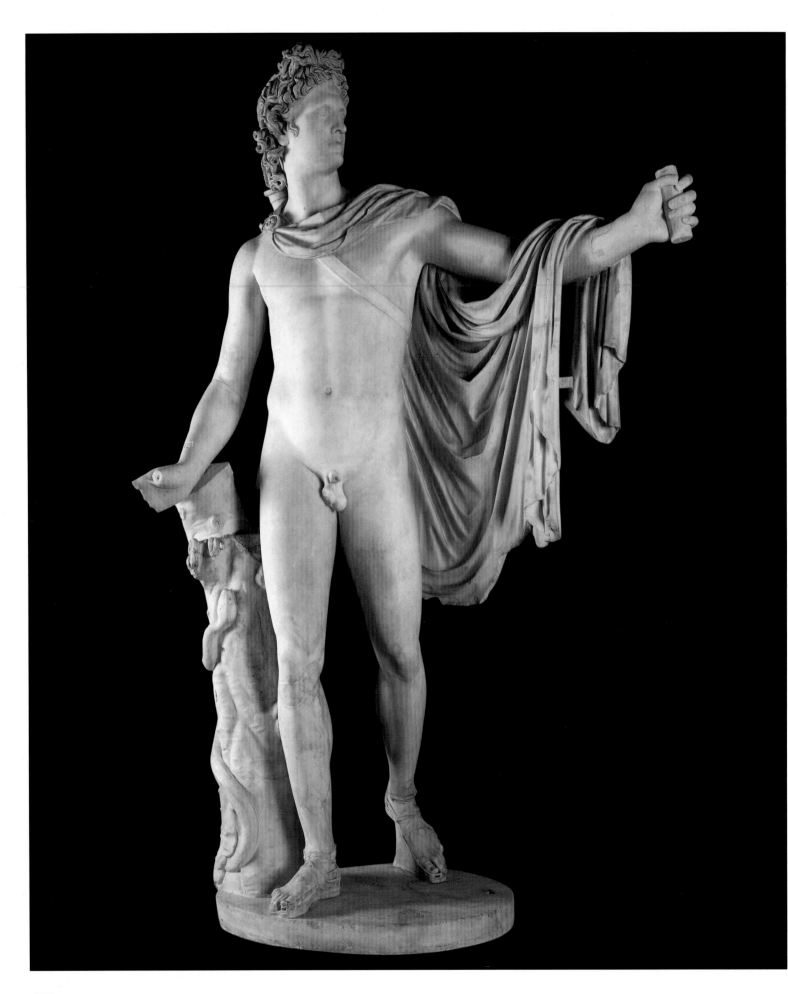

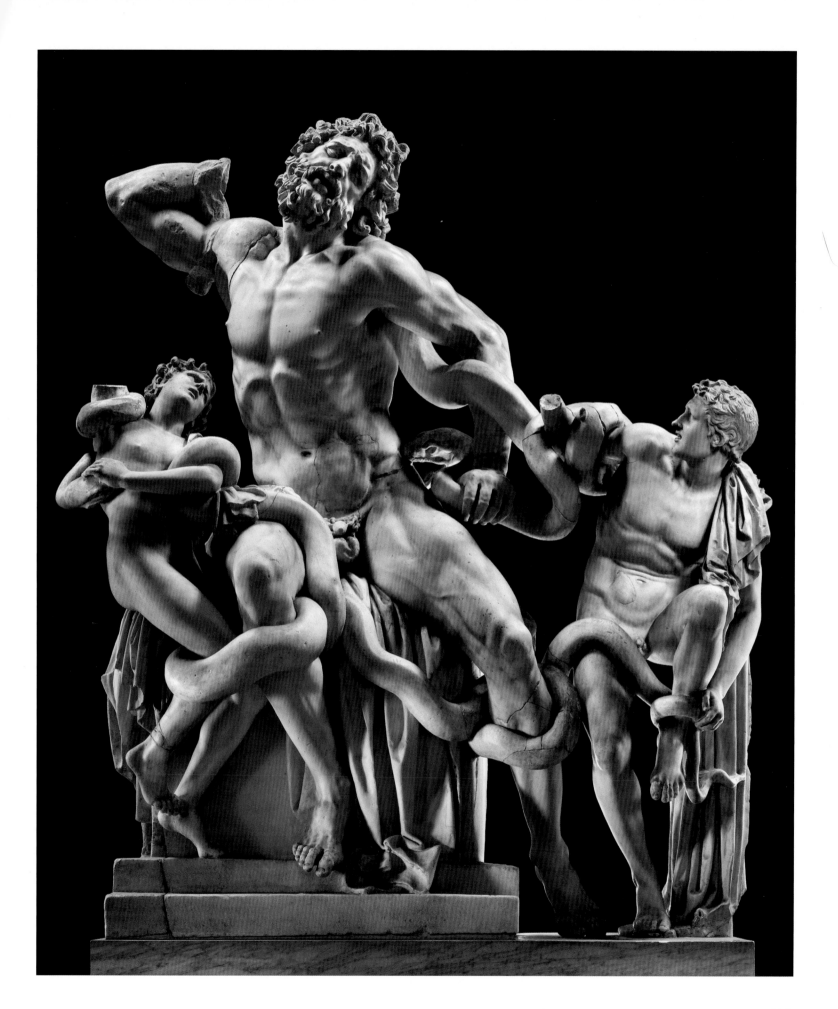

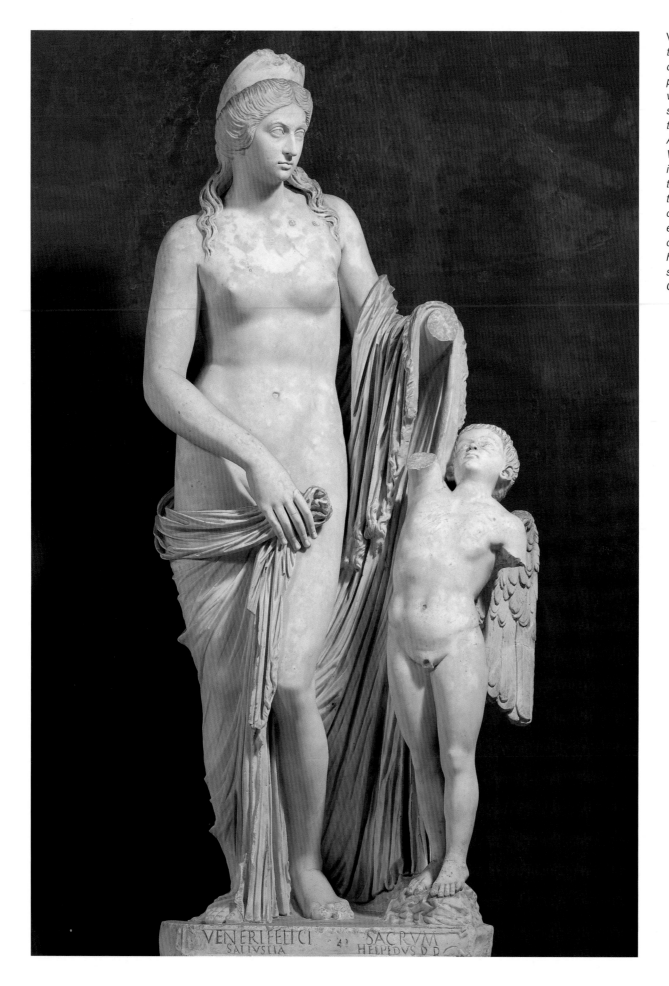

Venus Felix. *By 1509 this statue already occupied a prominent position in the Belvedere garden alongside "Laocoon" and the "Belvedere Apollo". A Roman version of a Venus by Praxiteles dating from the mid-4th century B.C., the face of this statue is a portrait of a 2nd century empress: either Faustina, the wife of Marcus Aurelius, or her daughter-in-law Crispina, the wife of Commodus.*

VENERI FELICI   SACRVM
SALVSTIA   HELPIDVS D.D

Hermes. *Found near Castel Sant'Angelo, this sculpture was added to the collection in the Garden of Statues by the Farnese pope Paul III in 1543. It was greatly admired by all the artists of the time and for centuries was considered a model of perfect human proportions. It is a copy executed in Hadrian's time of a 4th century B.C. Greek bronze.*

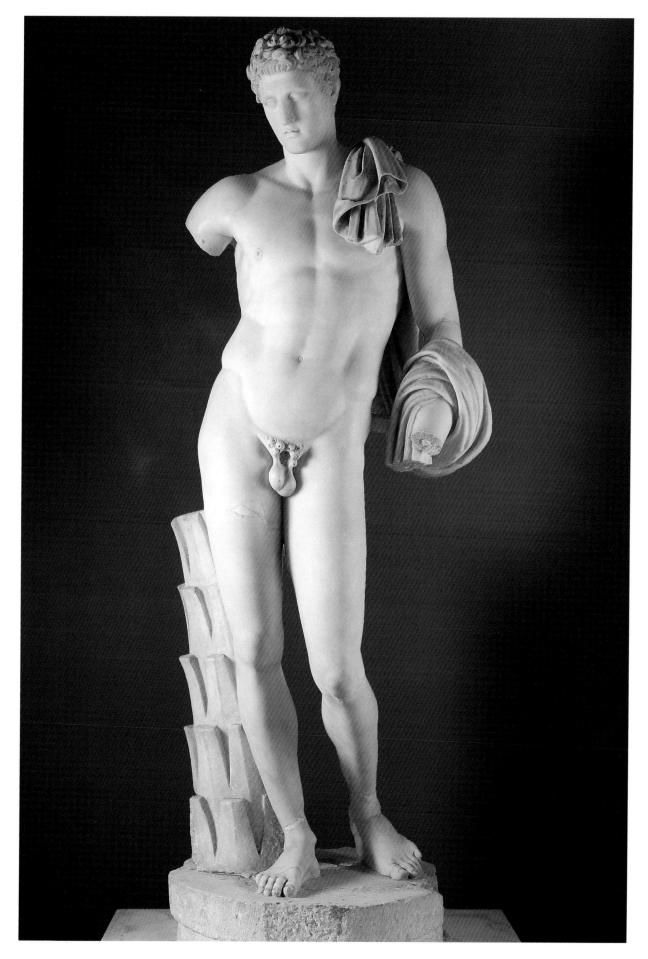

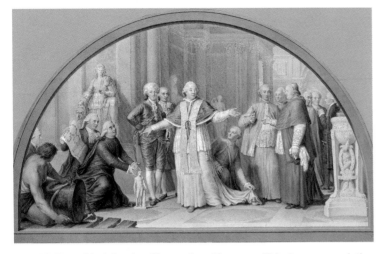

Pius VI Braschi visits the Clementine Museum. *This tempera painting by Stefano Piale (1783) is found in the Vatican Museums. Shown kneeling on the left are Giambattista Visconti, Commissioner for Antiquities and the museum's first "President", the architect Simonetti and the sculptor Gaspare Sibilla, one of the restorers of the museum's classical statues (detail below). The painting commemorates Pius VI's decision on May 12, 1776 to continue work on the construction of the new rooms for the collections. The Pius-Clementine Museum, which probably opened in 1784, was virtually completed by 1786 and, despite Simonetti's death in 1787, its contents were all on exhibit by 1792. The Museum's first guide book, compiled by Pasquale Massi, "guardian" of the museum, also dates back to 1792.*

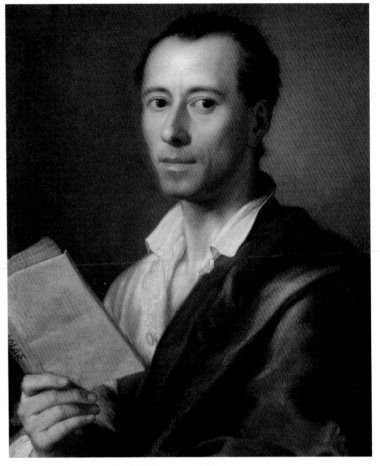

Johann Joachim Winckelmann *in a portrait by Anton Raphael Mengs in the Metropolitan Museum of Art. The great German archaeologist was one of the leading scholars who played a fundamental role in the formation of what was to become the Vatican Museums. He arrived in Rome in 1755 and was nominated Prefect for Antiquities by Clement XIII in 1763.*

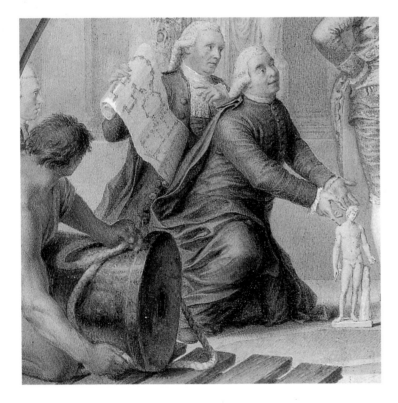

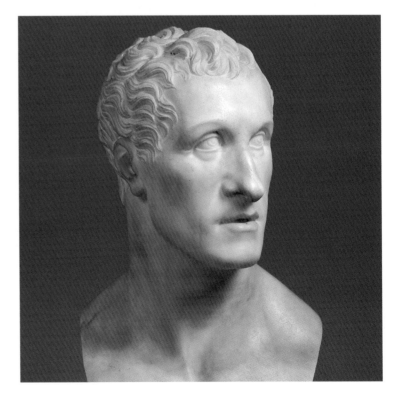

This portrait of Antonio Canova *sculpted by his friend Antonio d'Este in 1832 from a plaster model is found in the Office of the Director of the Vatican Museums. Together with abbot Carlo Fea, the Venetian sculptor, nominated Inspector General of Fine Arts by Pius VII in 1802, initiated a campaign to recover the works of art that had been taken to Paris after the Napoleonic sacking.*

The Gallery of Statues *(1772)* *in the loggia of the Palazzetto* *del Belvedere is the most* *important room of the original* Clementine Museum. *Designed* *in the late Baroque style, it is* *the work of Alessandro Dori.*

The Hall of Busts *(below, left)* *was set up at one end of the* *gallery in the late 18th centu-* *ry. Portraits of Julius Caesar* *and the Roman Emperors* *Augustus, Marcus Aurelius,* *Lucius Venus and Antoninus* *Pius are on exhibit here. Part* *of the Belvedere collection* *since 1512, Ariadne (below,* *right) was placed at the other* *end of the Gallery of Statues,* *which was enlarged in 1776* *by Michelangelo Simonetti. It* *is a Roman copy dating from* *the 2ⁿᵈ century A.D. of a 2ⁿᵈ* *century B.C. original from* *Pergamum.*

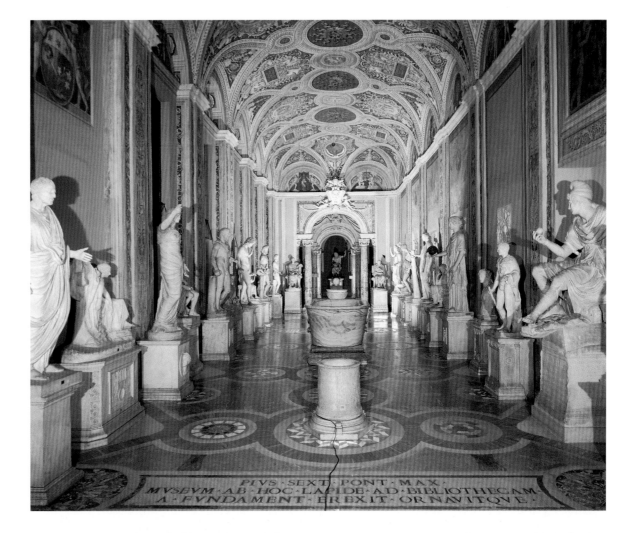

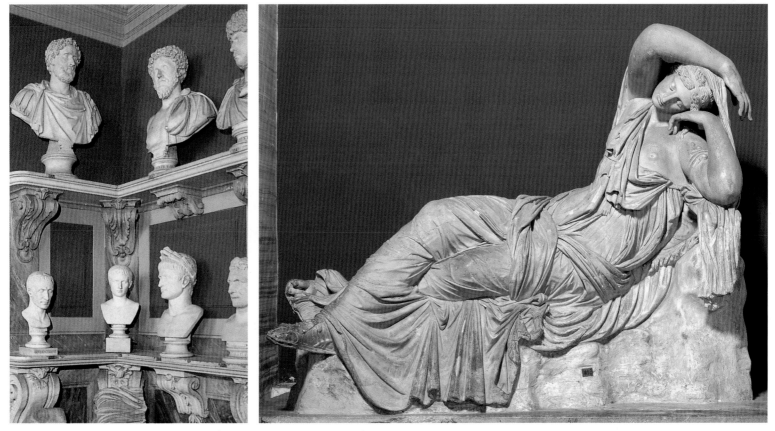

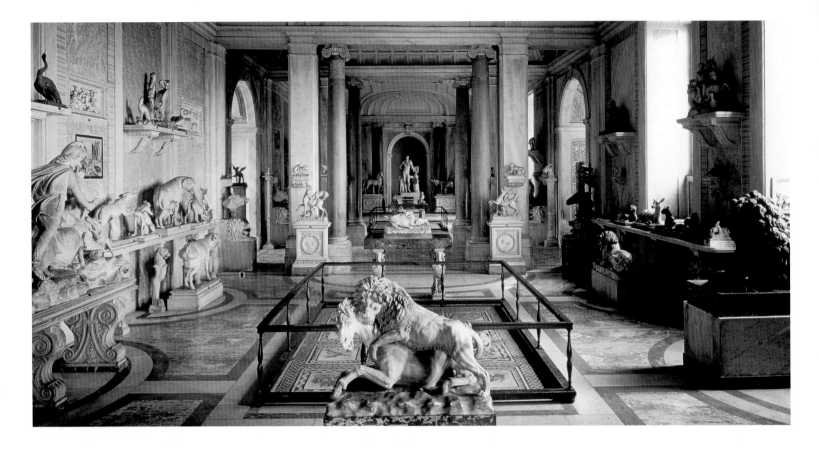

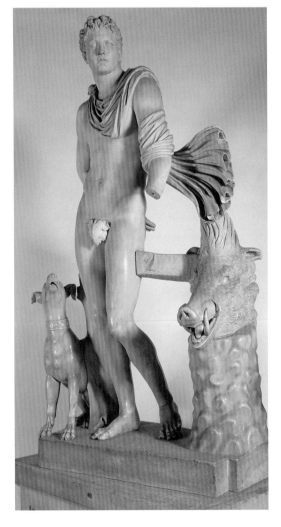

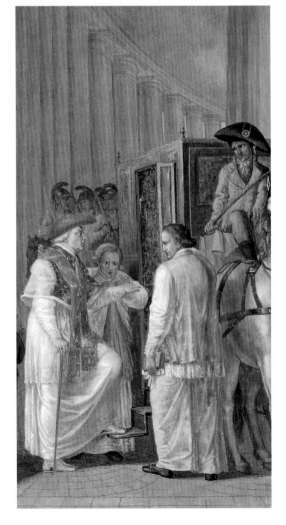

The Hall of Animals *(above)*. The splendid Meleager *(detail, left)* is in a niche at the end of the room. Bought by Clement XIV, it was already famous and considered one of the most beautiful statues in Rome from the mid-16th century. It is a Roman copy, probably dating from the 1st century A.D., of a 4th century B.C. Greek original attributed to Skopas.

After the proclamation of the Roman Republic and the occupation by French troops, on February 17, 1798, Pope Pius VI was forced into exile. He would die on August 29th of the following year in Valence, France. This 1818 fresco in the Clementine Gallery of the Vatican Library is probably the work of Domenico Del Frate.

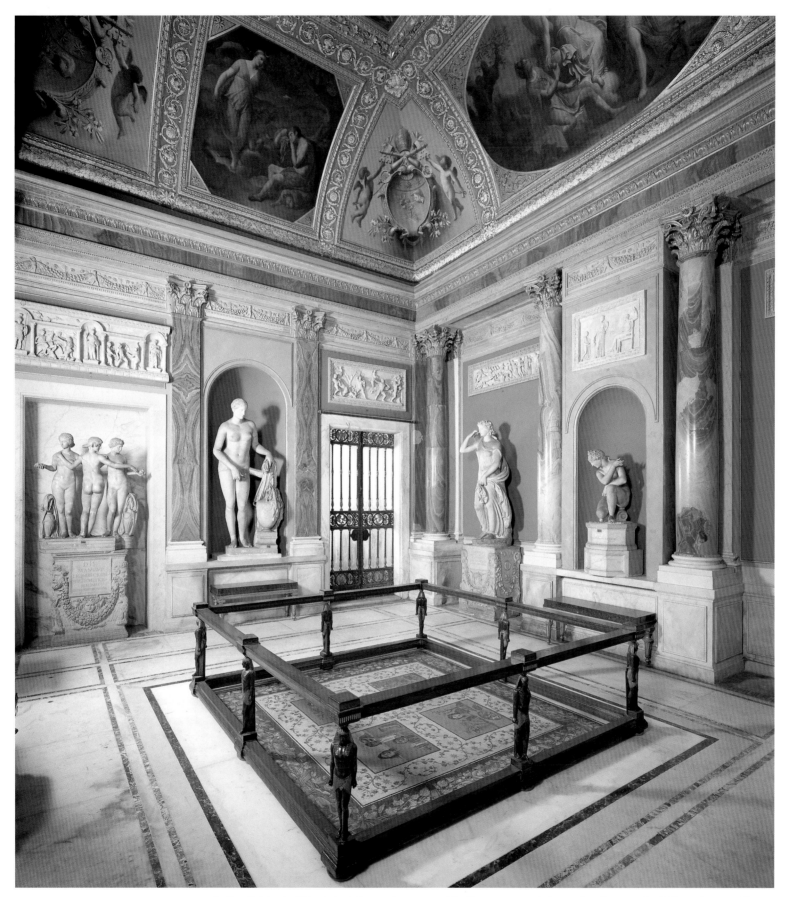

In the Cabinet of Masks, *statues are arranged for the purpose of decorating the room's 18th century ambiance. The most important work is the* Cnidian Aphrodite, *a Roman copy of a statue by Praxiteles. In 1791-92, Domenico De Angelis decorated the ceiling with oil paintings of mythological scenes. The room is named after the Roman floor mosaic depicting theater masks.*

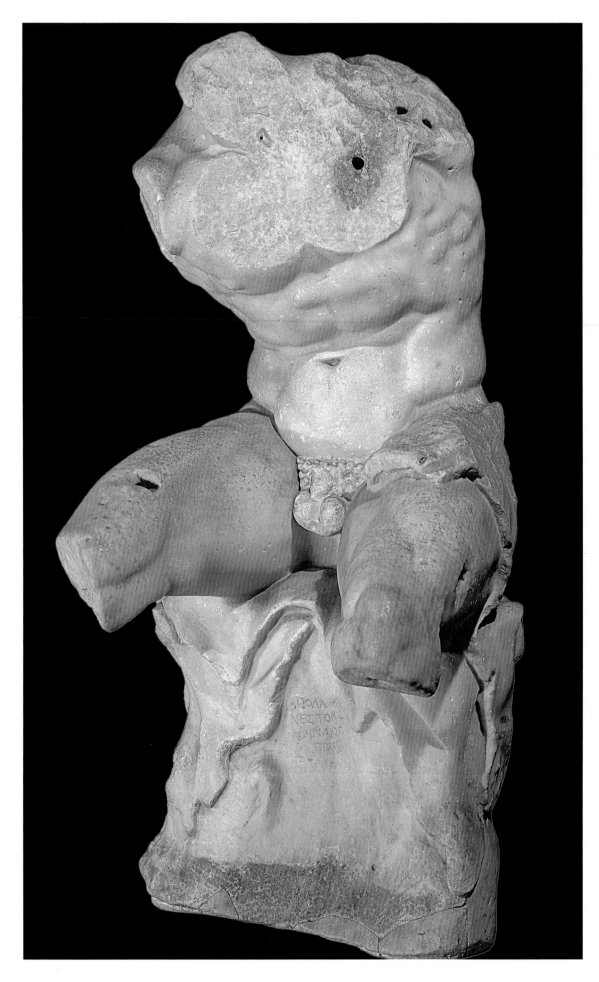

The Belvedere Torso was brought to the Belvedere by Clement VII and greatly admired by Michelangelo. By tradition, it was considered a fragment of an image depicting Hercules, although there is no concrete evidence to support this theory. The marble sculpture was carved by Apollonius, a 1st century B.C. Athenian artist who is also the likely author of the original of the Verospi Jupiter.

The Hall of Muses *contains a group of marble sculptures of Apollo and the Muses that were found in 1775 during the excavations of a Roman villa near Tivoli; they are Roman copies of Greek originals dating from the time of Hadrian in the first century A.D. Between 1782 and 1787 this room was decorated by Tommaso Conca with frescoes relating stories of Apollo and the Muses.*

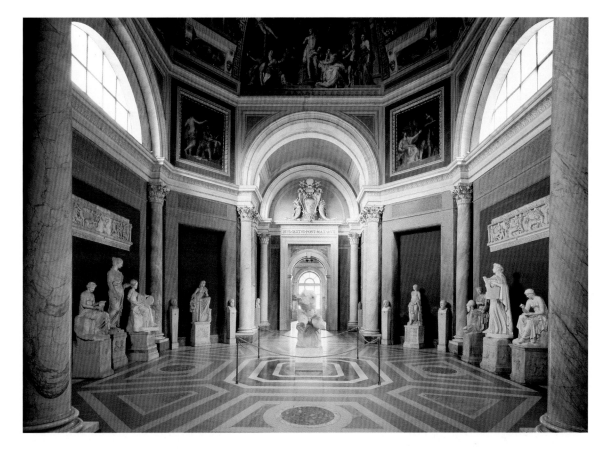

Thalia *(right), the muse of comedy. The comic mask, the pastoral staff and the drum in the muse's hands were added in the 18th century to replace the original ones that had been lost.*

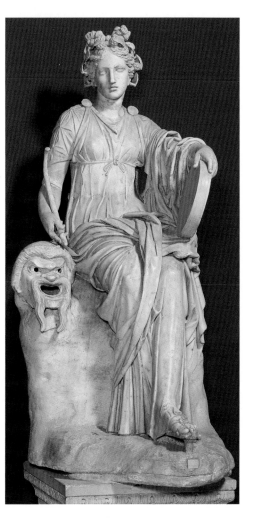 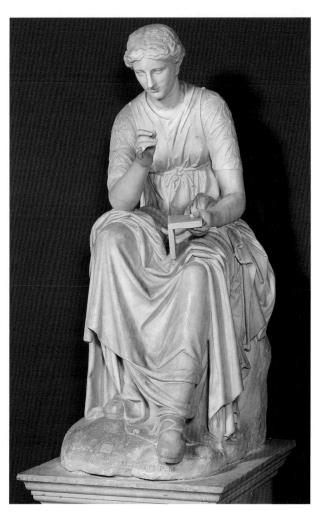

Calliope, *the muse of epic poetry, was found without a head; the sculptor Gaspare Sibilla took a female head dating from the early Imperial period and attached it to the bust of the muse.*

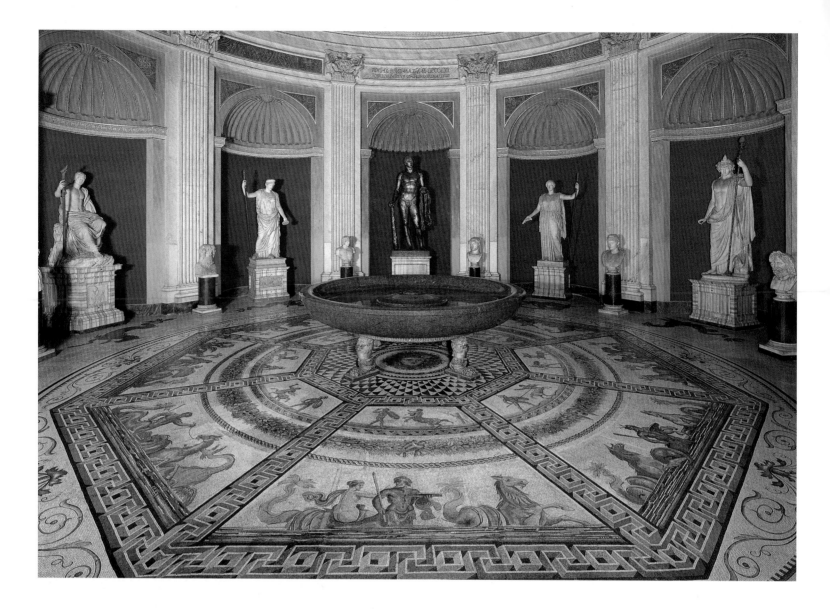

The Round Hall *is Simonetti's masterpiece: for the exhibition of classical statuary, he was obviously inspired by the Pantheon.*

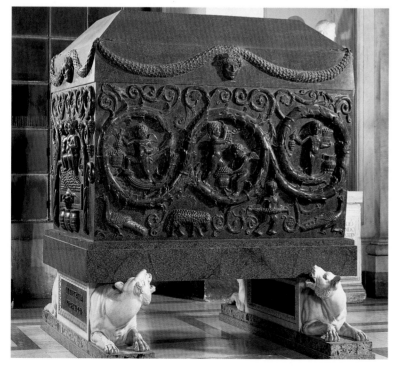

Constantina's sarcophagus. *Sculpted around 340 in Egypt for the daughter of Constantine, this immense porphyry sarcophagus (225 cm. high) is decorated with scenes of grape harvesting, the Christian symbol of life.*

The Simonetti Stairway, *finished in 1788-89 after the architect's death, was built to lead to the Pius-Clementine Museum. The front of the stairway corresponds to the entrance wall of the Hall of the Greek Cross, and looks like a grandiose backdrop designed for a lavish stage set. Beyond the side entablatures of the Serlian arch, the flights of stairs leading up to the Gallery of Candelabras and to the Etruscan Museum are visible. The flight of the main stairway is surmounted by a sloping barrel-vaulted coffered ceiling. On either side of the entrance stand two carved sphinxes from the Imperial period.*

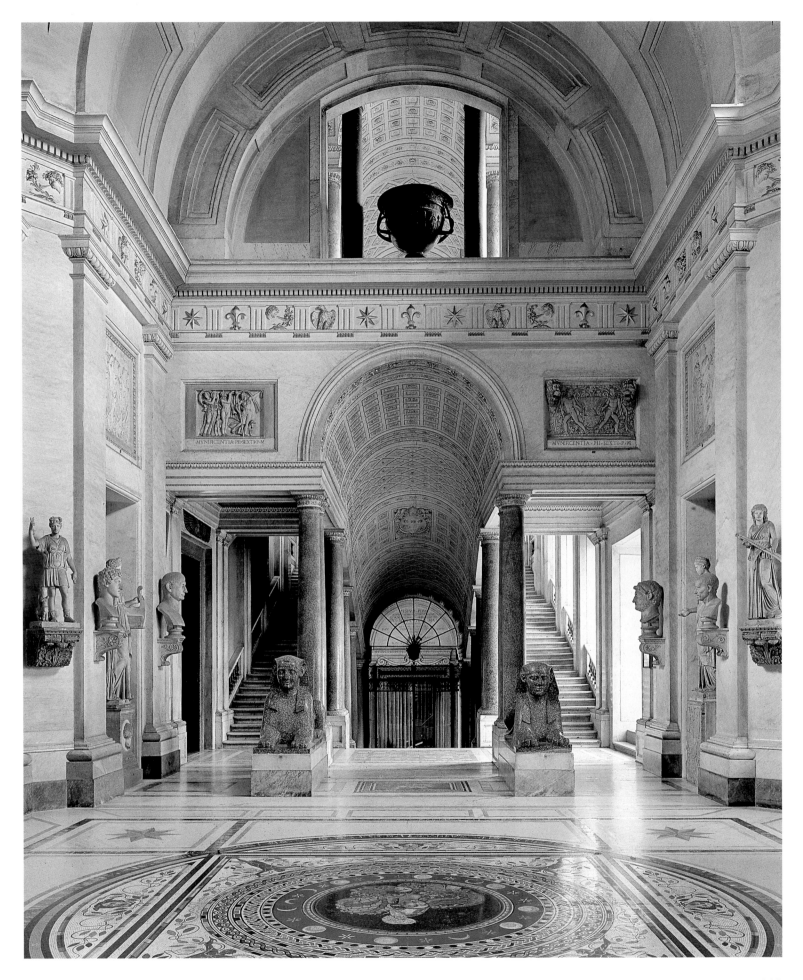

The *Gregorian Etruscan Museum*. Founded by Gregory XVI on February 2, 1837, this museum is located on the top floor of the *Nicchione della Pigna*. It contains items excavated by private archaeological expeditions licensed by the Papal State working in southern Etrurian necropolises in the last century. Due to a legal claim, the papacy reserved the right of preemption on what was found. In 1935 Benedetto Guglielmi donated his collection of archaeological finds from Vulci to the Vatican, and in 1968 Mario Astarita donated his splendid collection of antique glassware and ceramics to Pope Paul VI.

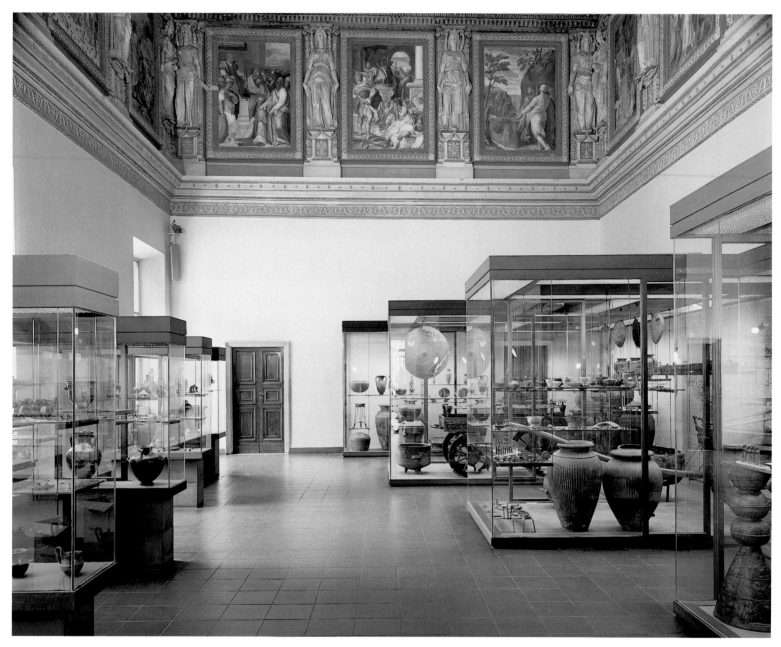

The Hall of Regolini Galassi *contains archaeological finds from the 7th century B.C. tomb named for the two archaeologists, Regolini and Galassi, who discovered it south of Cerveteri in 1836. The new layout of the exhibition was realized by Francesco Buranelli.*

The collection of Greek vases from the tombs of southern Etruria is on exhibit in the Lower Hemicycle of the Etruscan Museum. Of particular importance is the amphora with black figures (left) signed by Attic potter and ceramist, Exekias (530 B.C.). Achilles and Ajax playing a game of mora is depicted on one of the two sides.

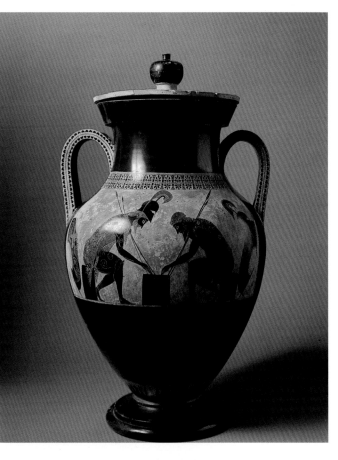

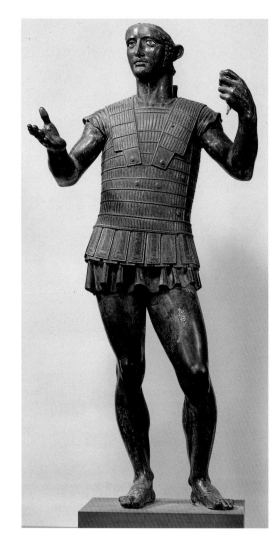

Found near Todi in 1835, Mars is a bronze cast dating from the late 5th century B.C.

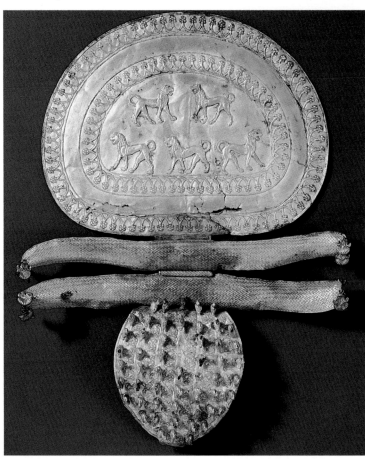

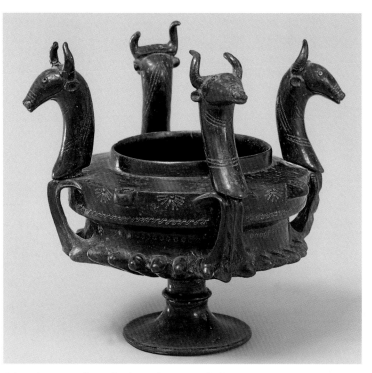

Gold fibula, *from the 7th century B.C., the oriental period of Etruscan culture.*

A bucchero pyx from the late 7th century B.C.

The so-called Hall of Terracottas *is a large room that recreates a suggestive space quite similar to the sacred areas of antiquity where an external wall* (temenos) *enclosed the high platform on which the temple stood, with a more or less large square in front of it for votive offerings and altars for the performance of religious ceremonies.*

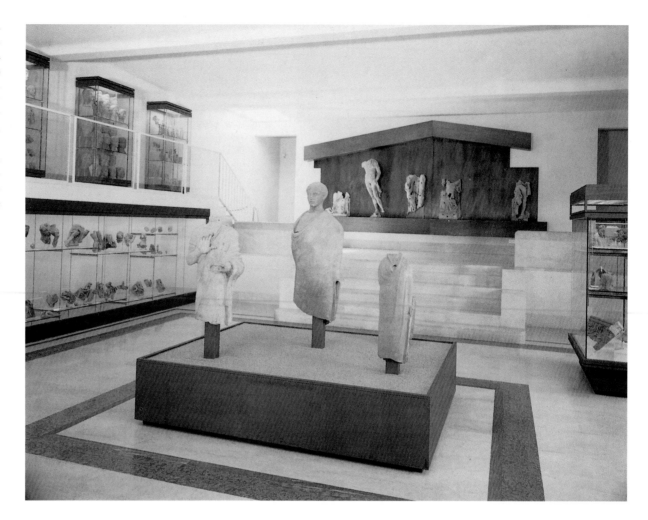

The *Gregorian Egyptian Museum* was opened on February 2, 1839. It is housed on the first floor of the *Nicchione della Pigna* below the Etruscan museum. In the third room there is a reconstruction of part of the decoration from the Canopic *Serapeum* (below) from Hadrian's villa in Tivoli.

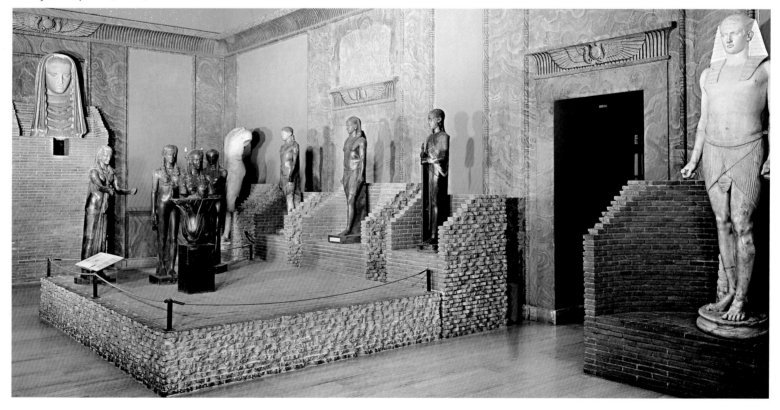

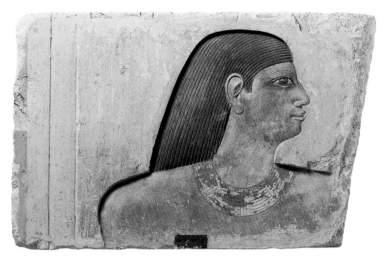

Sandstone fragment with a young man's head
(Dynasty 6, about 2250 B.C.).

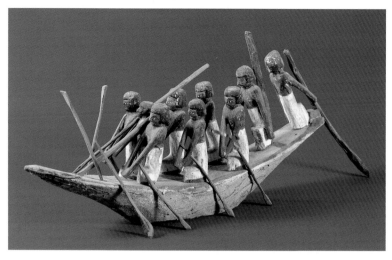

*Wooden model of a typical Nilotic boat
(Dynasty 11 and 12, 2040-1780 B.C.).*

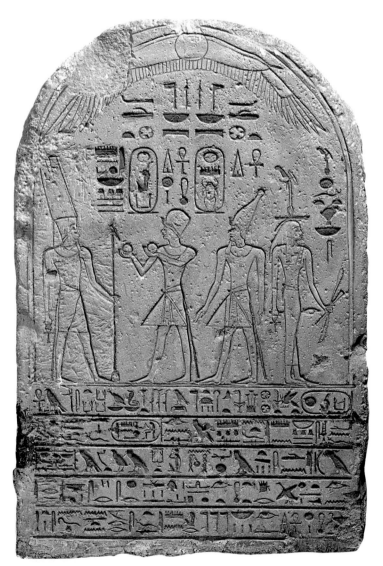

Sandstone stele showing Queen Hatshepsut, *together with her son,
Thutmose III, offering a sacrifice to the god Amon (Dynasty 18,
about 1400 B.C.).*

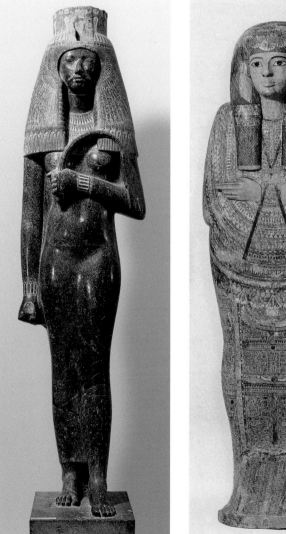

Colossal granite statue of Tuia, *the
mother of Rameses II (Dynasty 19,
about 1250 B.C.).*

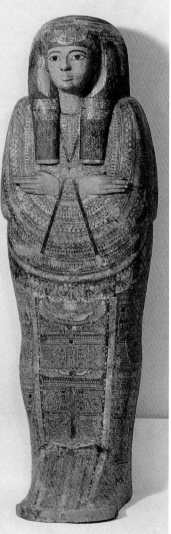

*Painted sarcophagus for
a mummy (Dynasty 22,
930-800 B.C.).*

In 1838, under the Cappellari pope Gregory XVI, the collection of tapestries was put on display in the present-day *Gallery of Tapestries*. The core of the collection consisted of ten tapestries, called the *Scuola Vecchia* or "Old School" tapestries, woven at the time of Leo X by Pieter van Aelst in Brussels from cartoons by Raphael and his assistants (the cartoons, illustrating stories from the lives of Peter and Paul, are today in the Victoria and Albert Museum, London), and another eleven tapestries depicting stories from the New Testament ("New School"), woven in the same Flemish factory at the time of Clement VII. They were originally meant to hang in the Sistine Chapel, below the frescoes. The Old School tapestries were exhibited for the first time on December 26, 1519 and the others in 1531. Put up for auction by the French in 1799, they were bought back by the Secretary of State, Cardinal Ercole Consalvi at the antique market in Leghorn in 1808.

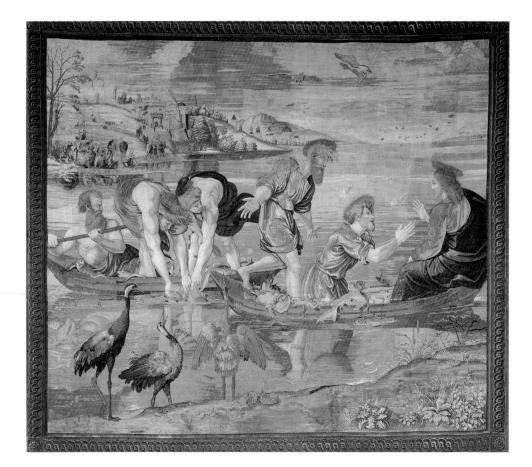

Old School of Raphael, Miraculous Draft of Fish.

New School of Raphael, Resurrection.

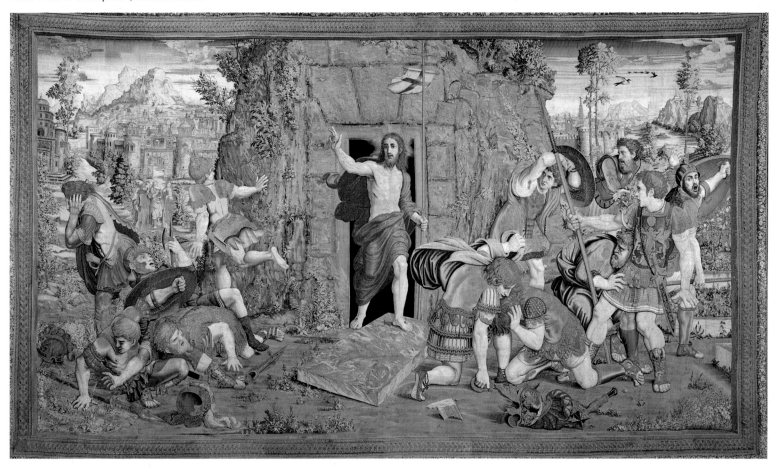

The Gallery of Candelabra *was constructed in 1785-88 by Simonetti and his assistant Giuseppe Camporese, who finished it after the master's death. It was built by closing in a loggia that dated from Clement XIII's papacy, and was intended to house antiquities smaller than the ones seen in the previous rooms.*

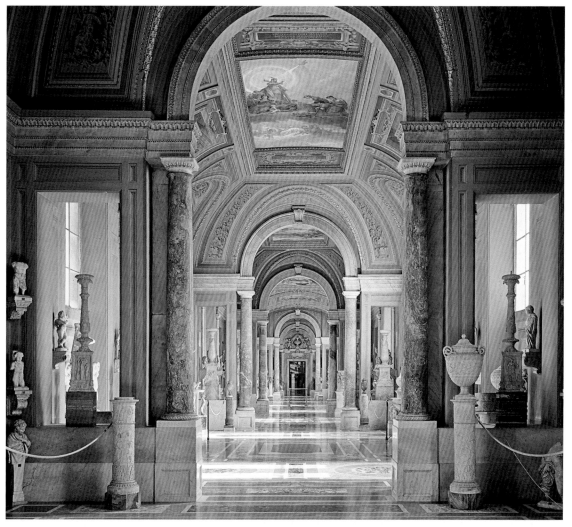

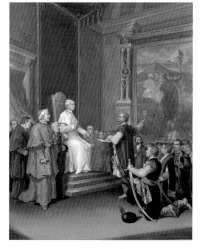

In a panel on the ceiling of the Gallery of Candelabra, Domenico Torti has depicted the Polish mission offering to Leo XIII a painting by Jan Matejko on September 14, 1883. The painting shows John III Sobieski freeing Vienna from the Turkish siege (1683). The huge canvas is now in the Sobieski Hall in the Borgia Tower.

The Hall of the Biga *(right)*, finished in 1792-93, occupies the floor above the Atrium of Four Gates, on the same level as the Gallery of Candelabra. In the center of the room, the marble group of the same name was assembled by the sculptor Francesco Antonio Franzoni (responsible for the horses and wheels). This is a typical example of the trend of "restoring antiques" that was so popular at the time. The body of the chariot is a Roman sculpture from the first century A.D.

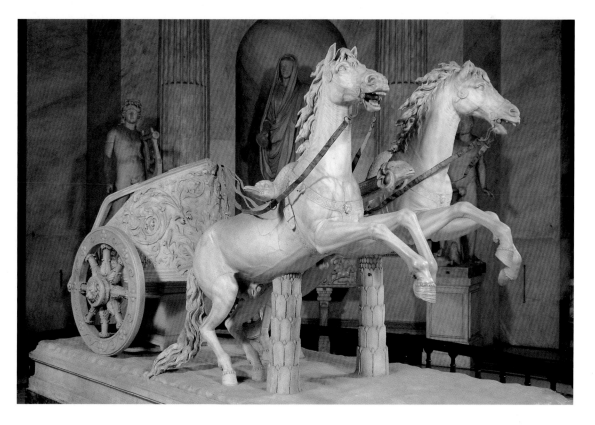

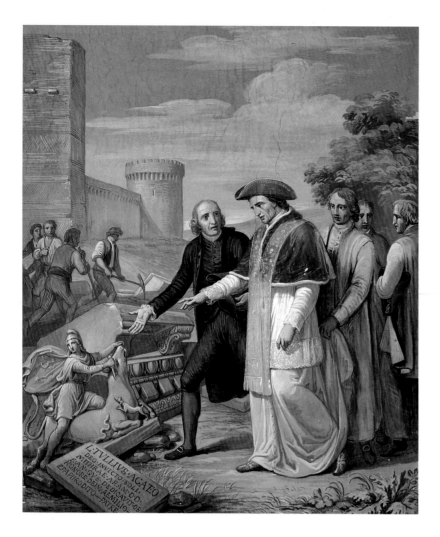

After the fall of the Roman Republic and the retreat of the French troops, the newly elected Chiaramonti pope Pius VII *returned to Rome on July 3, 1800. As part of his reorganization of the Papal State, the pope also began the reconstruction of the collections of works of art which had suffered huge losses after the Napoleonic plundering (the Tolentino Peace Treaty on February 19, 1797). In this 1818 fresco by Domenico Del Frate in the Clementine Gallery, the pope is seen talking with abbot Carlo Fea, Commissioner for Antiquities on the site of an archaeological dig at Ostia Antica.*

The Chiaramonti Museum *(next page, above)*, set up and partially financed by Canova in 1805-07, is in the northern wing of Bramante's Belvedere Corridor. It contains archaeological finds added to the collections after the French invasion.

The Lapidary Gallery *(next page, below)*, with Christian and pagan inscriptions displayed along the walls, is housed in the wing of Bramante's Belvedere Corridor. It was set up by Gaetano Marini at the time of Pius VII. During the last century, the corridor was the entrance to the museums and the library.

Canova commissioned Francesco Hayez to paint the scene of the return to Rome of the works of art that had been confiscated from the Papal States by the French Republic after the Treaty of Tolentino in a lunette in the Chiaramonti Museum. In the foreground, Sir William Hamilton, the Undersecretary of the British Foreign Office, who worked tirelessly for the restitution of these works of art; also in the foreground, the statue of the River Tiber which stayed in Paris as Pius VII's gift to the restored French monarchy. In the background, Monte Mario not far from the Vatican.

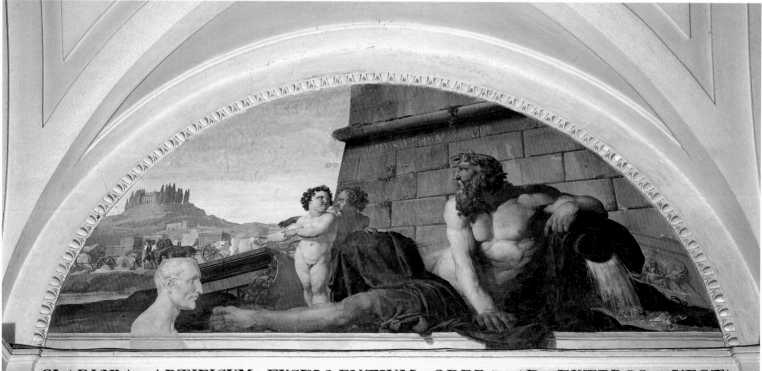

CLARIORA · ARTIFICVM · EXCELLENTIVM · OPERA · AD EXTEROS · AVECTA
VRBI · RECVPERATA

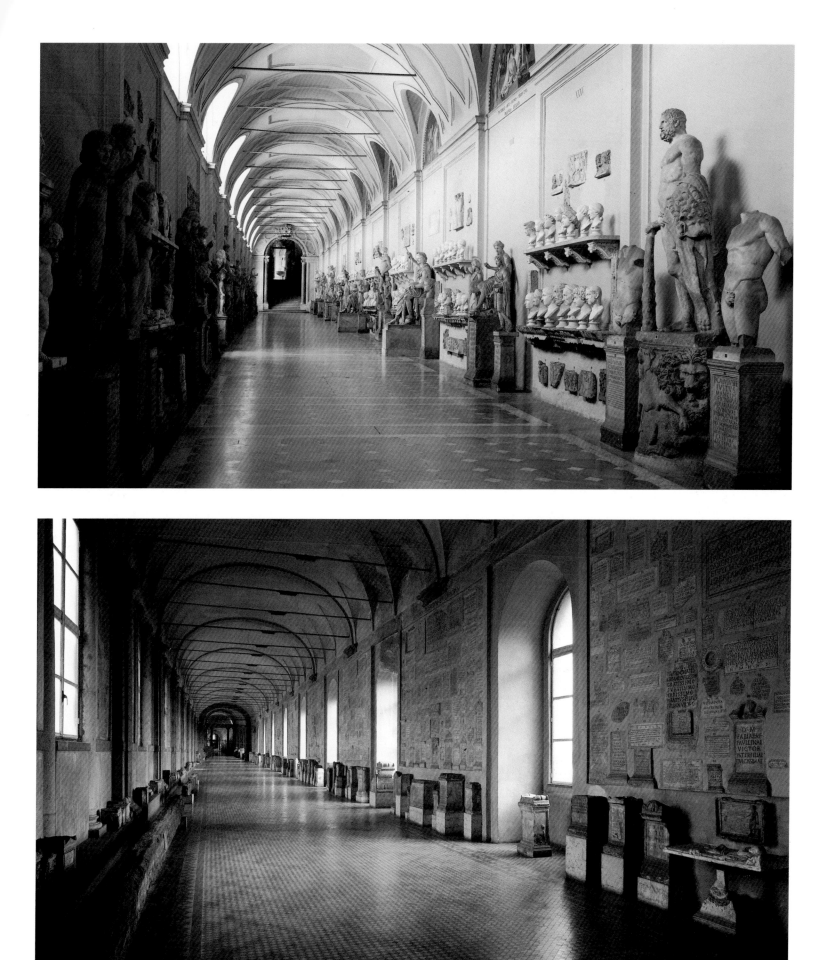

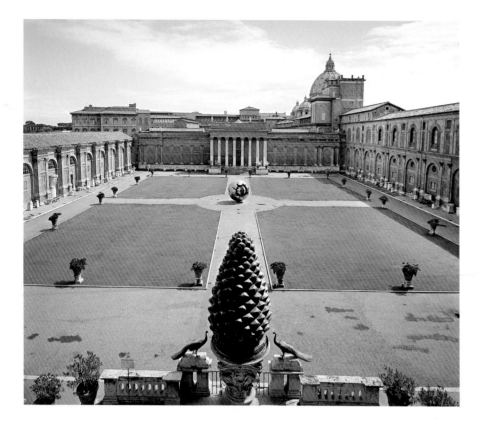

The Braccio Nuovo *(exterior and interior)* was built in the neo-classical style by Raffaele Stern in 1817-22 to house new acquisitions and the statue of the River Nile. The "New Wing" was built on the southern side of the Courtyard of the Pine Cone; it joins the long Bramante Corridor to the gallery of the Vatican Apostolic Library on the other side.

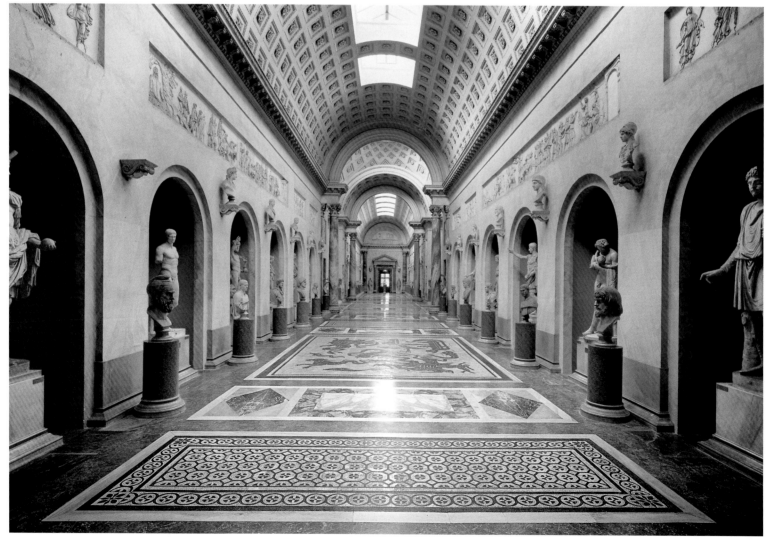

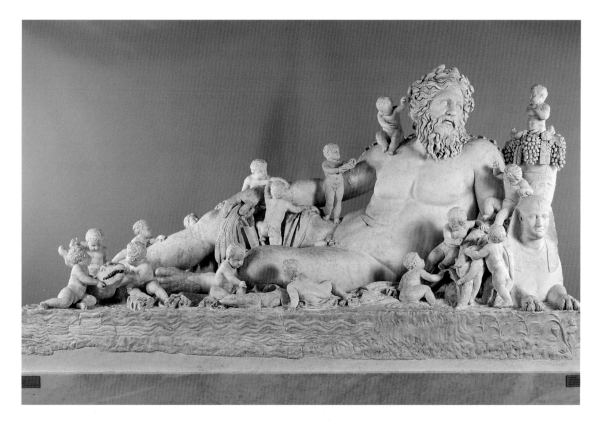

The River Nile. This colossal marble sculpture (162 cm. high), returned from France following the Congress of Vienna, formerly stood in Julius II's Antiquarium in the Sculpture Gardens, where it was presumably placed by Leo X in about 1513. It is a Roman statue from the 1st century A.D., probably carved from a Hellenistic model.

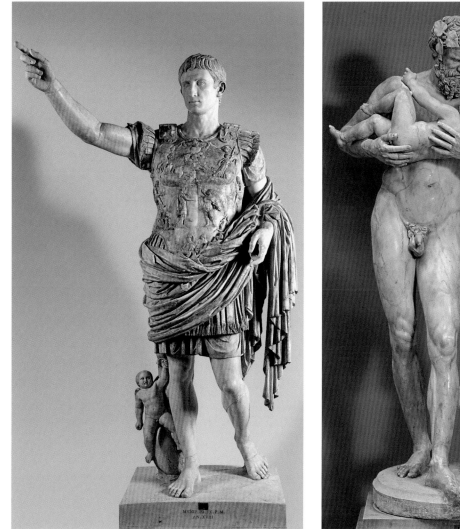

Augustus of Prima Porta. *The statue of the first Roman Emperor, who died in 14 A.D., was found during the last century among the ruins of the villa belonging to his wife Livia, at Prima Porta on the outskirts of Rome. This is probably a copy, made for the widow, of an official bronze statue cast shortly after the year 20 B.C.*

Silenus with infant Dionysus. *A Roman copy of a Greek original by a follower of Lysippus (about 300 B.C.).*

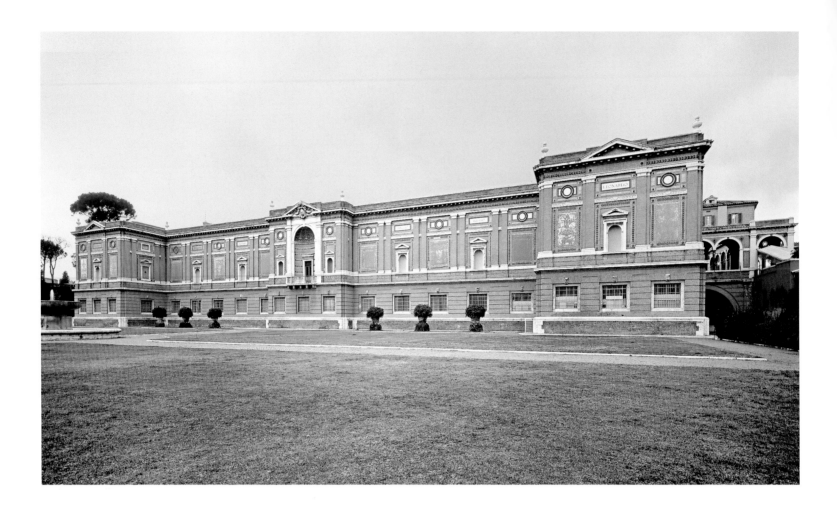

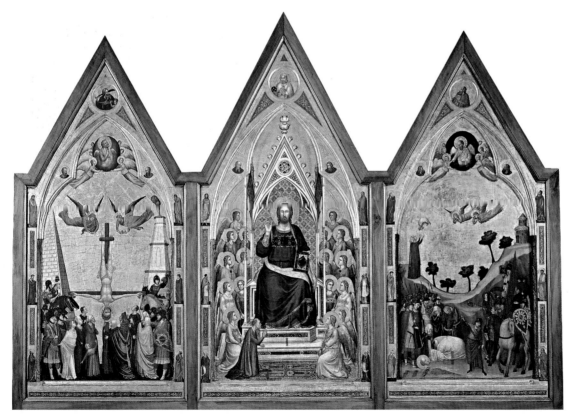

The origins of the Vatican's Pinacoteca *can be traced to the picture gallery which Pius VI had opened in 1790 in what is now the Gallery of Tapestries. Nevertheless, the institution of the Pinacoteca dates to the agreements reached at the Congress of Vienna in 1814-15, when the Holy See promised to put on display in a single place all the paintings that would be returned by the French (1815-16); these works of art had been taken away to France as a result of the Tolentino Peace Treaty (1797) which the pope had been obliged to sign. Of the 506 paintings that the occupying forces took away, only 249 were returned. The final display of the paintings, arranged according to chronological and historical principles in the building designed specifically for this purpose by Luca Beltrami (begun in 1929), was inaugurated by Pius XI Ratti on October 27, 1932.*

Giotto and his assistants painted this triptych of "Christ Enthroned" with Peter and Paul, also known as the Stefaneschi Triptych, *around 1315 for the high altar of the old St. Peter's.*

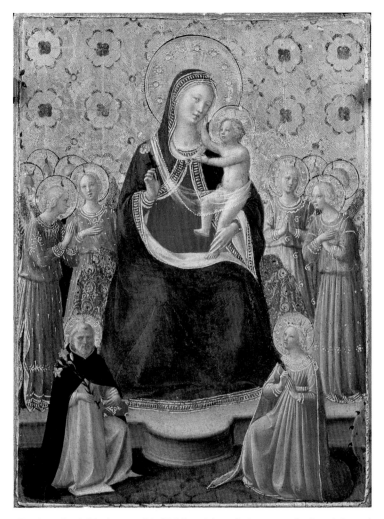

Fra Angelico's Madonna with Child and Angels between St. Dominic and St. Catherine of Alexandria *(ca 1435). Giovanni da Fiesole, called Blessed Fra Angelico, was ordained a priest between 1423 and 1425 at the convent of St. Dominic in Fiesole. This panel, exhibited in the Pinacoteca since 1877, seems to suggest a direct knowledge of the art of miniatures, thus confirming the paternity of Fra Angelico. The painting is of the highest quality, executed with brush point on a gilt pastiglia plaster background with an etched floral pattern.*

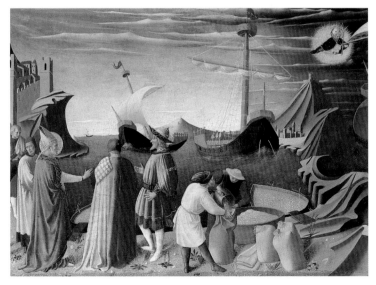

Blessed Fra Angelico's St. Nicholas receives wheat from the imperial messenger *and (on the right)* St. Nicholas saves a ship at sea *(1447-1450).*

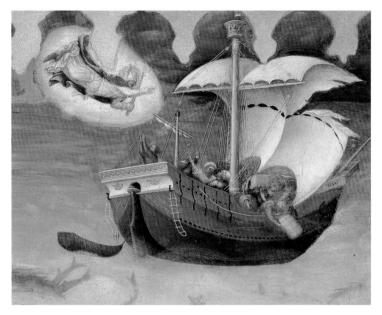

Gentile da Fabriano, St. Nicholas Saves a Ship at Sea, *a predella panel dating from 1425.*

Melozzo da Forlì's Angel with Viola *is a fragment of a detached fresco painted around 1480, originally in the apse of the Basilica dei Santissimi Apostoli.*

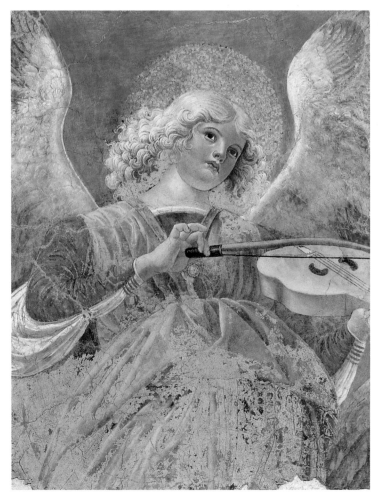

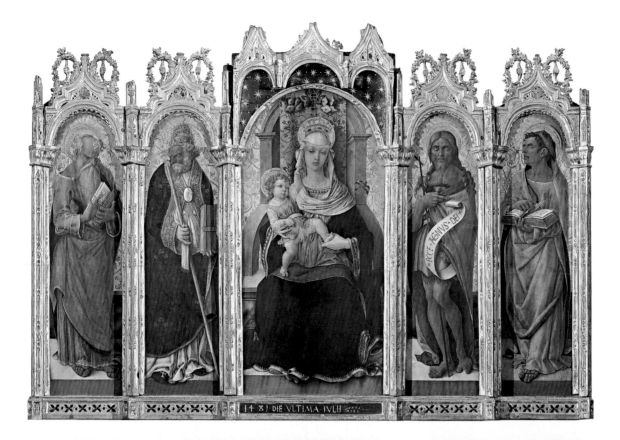

Vittore Crivelli's Madonna and Child with Four Saints (1481) is also called the "Polyptych of Grottammare". The brother of the more famous artist, Carlo Crivelli, Vittore collaborated with Carlo on various works of greater importance. He diligently worked to spread his brother's style in many polyptychs like this one, painted for churches in the countryside of the Marches region.

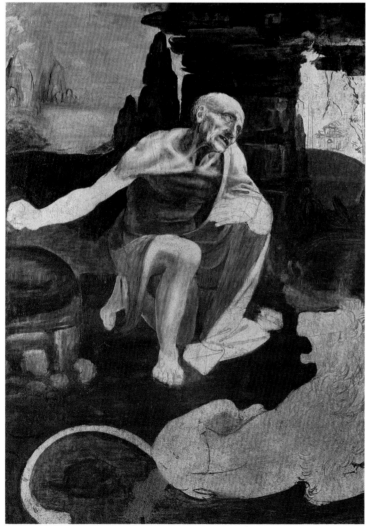

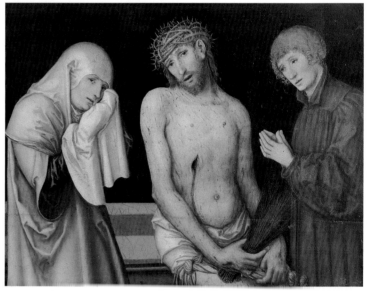

Lucas Cranach the Elder's Pietà is probably one of the German artist's (1472-1533) later works.

Leonardo da Vinci's St. Jerome is an unfinished work dating from the master's early maturity, at the beginning of the 1480s.

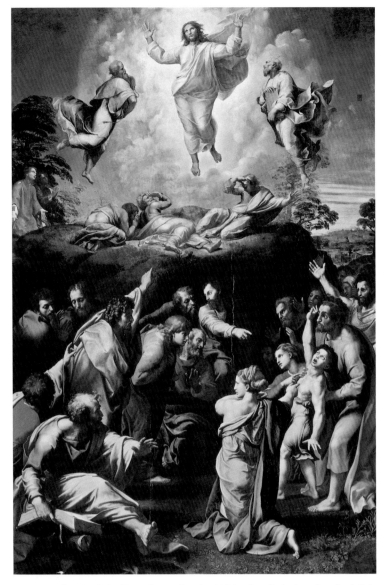

Raphael finished the Transfiguration *in 1520, shortly before he died; it is regarded as his artistic testament.*

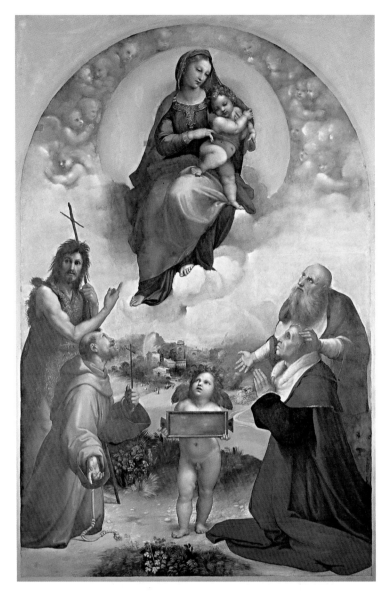

Raphael painted the Madonna of Foligno *for the Church of S. Maria in Aracoeli in Rome in approximately 1511, and it was taken to Foligno after 1564.*

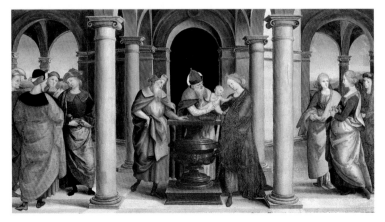

Raphael's Circumcision, *a predella panel, is one of his earlier works (ca. 1502).*

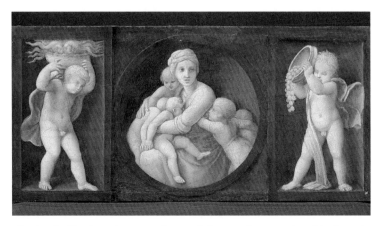

Raphael's Charity, *also part of a predella panel, was painted in Perugia in 1507, the year before the artist moved to Rome.*

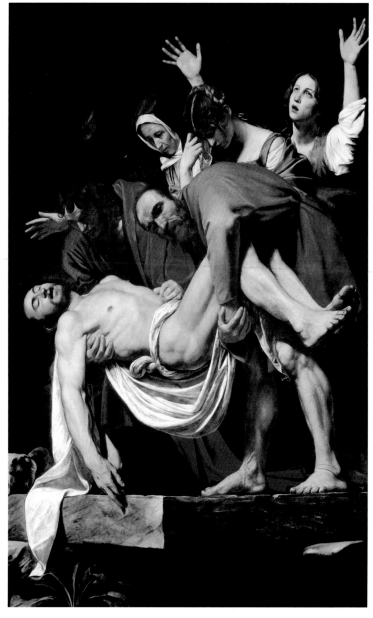

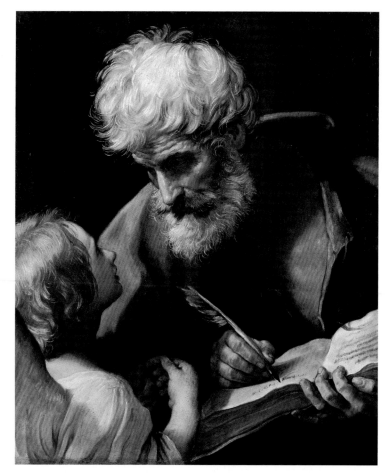

Guido Reni's St. Matthew and the Angel *was painted between 1635-1640 when the Bolognese artist had reached full maturity.*

Caravaggio's Deposition *was painted around 1602-04 when the artist from Lombardy was living in Rome.*

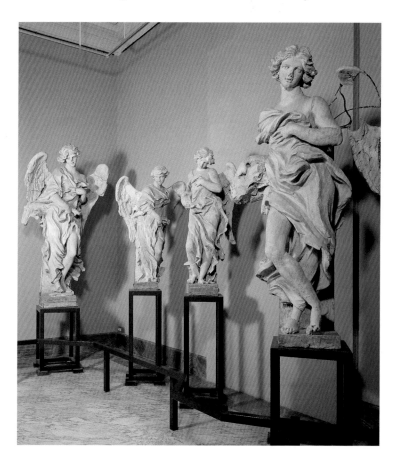

In the penultimate room of the Pinacoteca are the plaster casts *that Bernini used for the Doctors of the Church and the Angels on his cathedra of St Peter in Glory in St. Peter's basilica (1660s).*

The most recent construction *in the Vatican Museums, designed by the Passarelli brothers and built by the* Governatorato's *technical services behind the Pinacoteca, was opened to the public on June 15, 1970. It houses the collections of the Gregorian Profane, the Pius-Christian and the Missionary and Ethnological Museums, originally located in the Lateran Palace and transferred to the Vatican by John XXIII Roncalli in 1962. For the most part, the Gregorian Profane Museum includes items found in 19th century archaeological expeditions in the Papal States.*

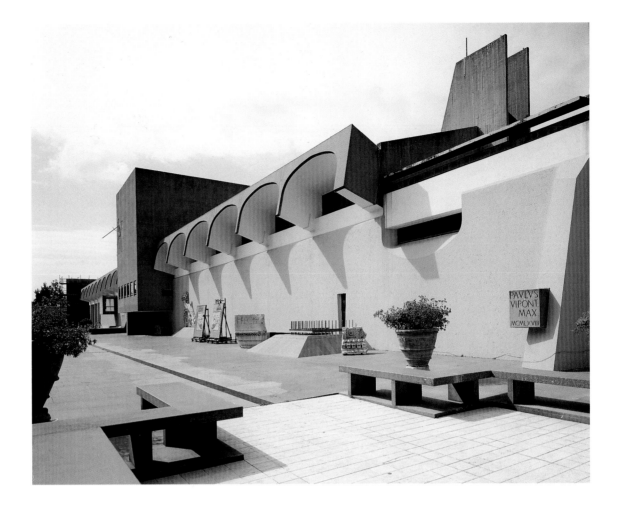

The *Fleeing Niobid, known as the "Chiaramonti Niobid" because it was formerly in the museum of that name, is probably the work of a 2nd century B.C. Attic artist.*

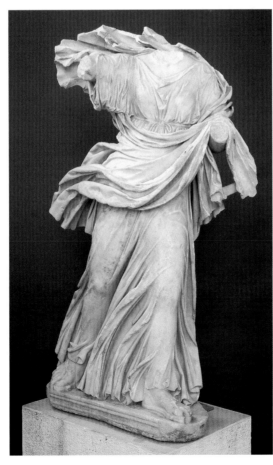

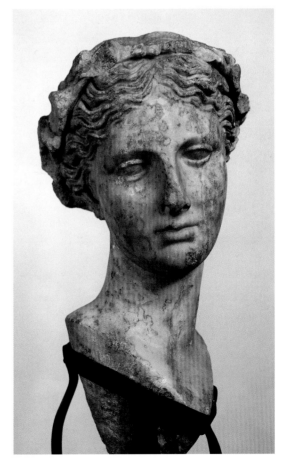

A Greek-inspired Roman head from the second century A.D. attributed to Thalia, muse of comedy, was found under the Lateran Seminary in Rome.

The *Gregorian Profane Museum* was founded by Gregory XVI in 1844 in the Lateran Palace, and transferred to the Vatican by John XXIII in 1962. It houses a collection of antiquities from excavations and archaeological finds made in the Papal States.

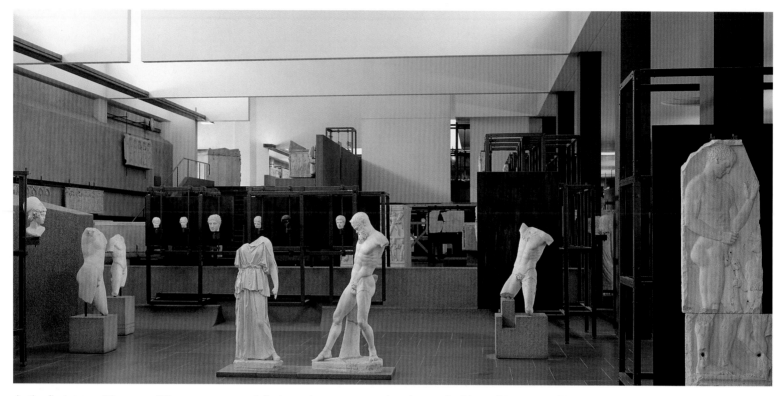

In the first room, Athena *and* Marsyas *were modelled on a bronze group of sculptures by Myron (450-440 B.C.). The headless figure of Athena is a cast of a Roman marble statue; the original head belonging to the statue of the goddess is displayed on the left. The Marsyas is a Roman copy in marble dating from 134 A.D. To the right, the* Palestrita *(an Attic marble sculpture of an athlete dating from the mid-5th century B.C.) is a part of the collection of original Greek sculpture.*

The Departure of Domitian *is a commemorative relief in which the face of the emperor (81-96 A.D.) was erased and replaced by the features of his successor, Nerva, because Domitian was condemned by the Senate to damnatio memoriae after his death.*

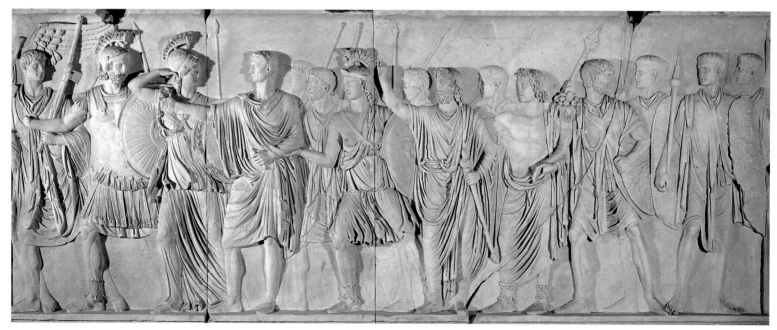

The *Pius Christian Museum* was founded by Pius IX in 1854 in the Lateran Palace, and was transferred to the Vatican at the same time as the Gregorian Profane Museum. It contains archaeological finds from excavations carried out during the last century in the early Christian catacombs as well as items formerly in churches in Rome and in the Sacred Museum in the Library. It was opened to the public on June 15, 1970.

This fragment of a Boeotian funerary stele, *dating from about 430 B.C., was clearly influenced by the Parthenon reliefs; it is part of the collection of original Greek sculpture.*

The Sarcophagus *(below), shaped like a bathtub, depicts a shepherd with the deceased couple on either side of him (late 3rd century).*

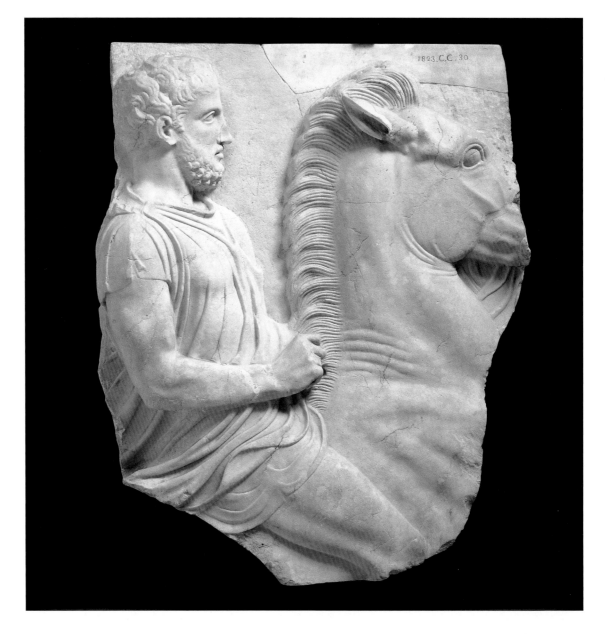

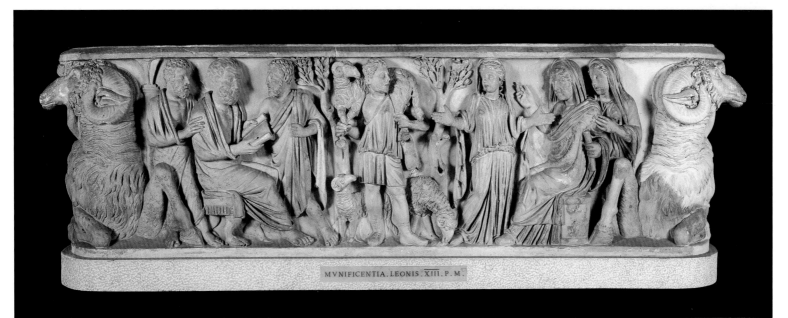

MVNIFICENTIA. LEONIS. XIII. P. M.

The *Missionary and Ethno-logical Museum* was founded by Pius XI in the Lateran Palace on November 12, 1926, when the temporary exhibition on display in the Vatican for the occasion of the Jubilee the previous year was transformed into a permanent collection. At present the Museum, which was inaugurated in 1973, is housed in the basement of the most recent wing of the Vatican Museums. It contains extra-European works of art and other religious items, pertaining to both Christianity and other religions.

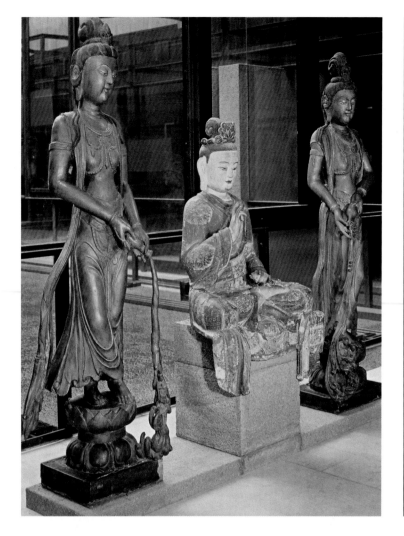

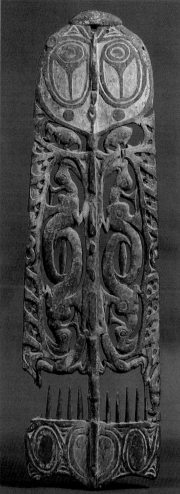

Buddha preaching *between two Taoist deities (China: the Buddha comes from Beijing; the other two figures from Shanxi; Ta Ming dynasty, 1368-1644).*

Kamboragea, *Papuan* water deity (New Guinea, 19 th century).

Vili *ritual mask* (Congo, early 20 th century).

The Aruacos fertility deity *shaped like a jaguar (Colombia, Sierra Nevada de Santa Marta, 17 th century).*

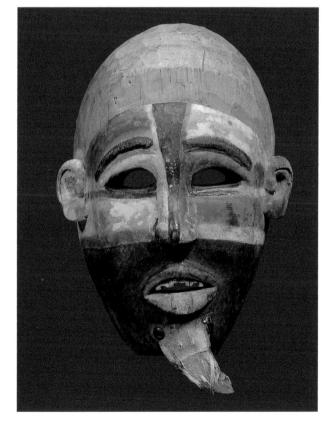

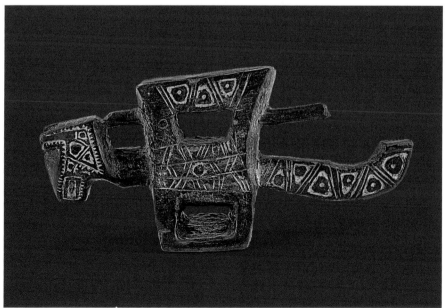

The *Religious Modern Art Collection* is derived from the Contemporary Art Department that was opened in the Pinacoteca in 1960. Following Paul VI Montini's appeal to artists in the Sistine Chapel on May 7, 1967, the collection of contemporary art by the Vatican was greatly increased through the efforts of Monsignor Pasquale Macchi, the pope's secretary. The collection, then containing 542 pieces, was inaugurated by Paul VI on June 23, 1973 and inserted among the main collections of the Vatican Museums.

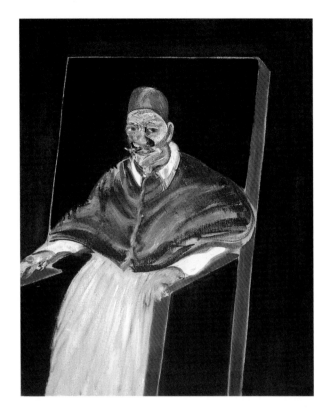

Francis Bacon's
Study for Velàzquez's
Pope *(1961)*.

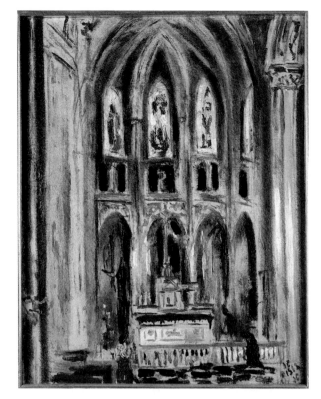

Filippo De Pisis'
Church Interior *(1926)*.

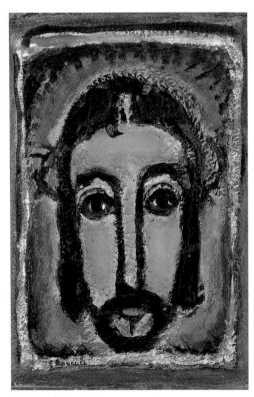

Georges Rouault's
Ecce Homo *(1946)*.

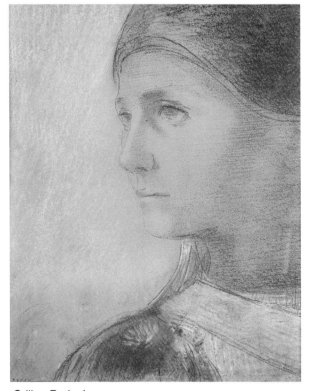

Odilon Redon's
Joan of Arc.

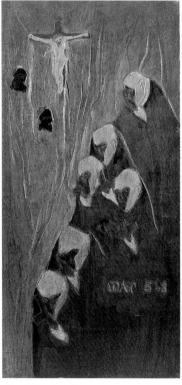

Paul Gauguin's
Religious Panel *(ca. 1892)*.

Gino Severini's
Dance of Death *(1964)*.

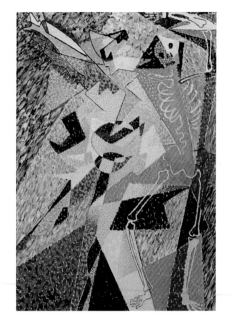

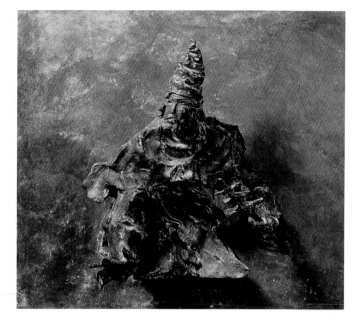

Lucio Fontana's
Martin V *(1951-2)*.

Emil Nolde's
Priest *(1939-45)*.

The Carriage Museum *was assembled beginning in 1968 and—together with many items associated with the Pontifical Military Corps—opened as a Historical Museum in 1973. Since 1987 it has been a separate section of the Historical Museum in the Lateran Palace. It contains 19th-century carriages and sedans belonging to popes, and the first motorcars owned by Popes Pius XI and Pius XII, such as the 1930 Mercedes Benz.*

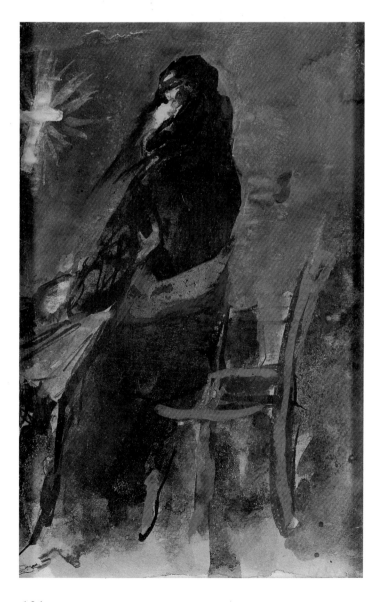

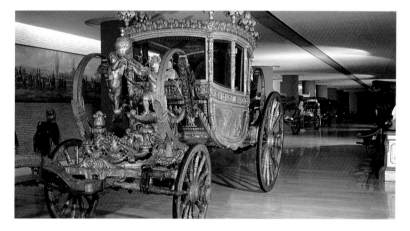

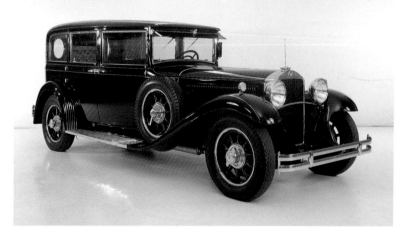

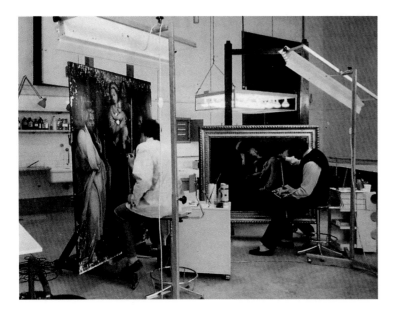

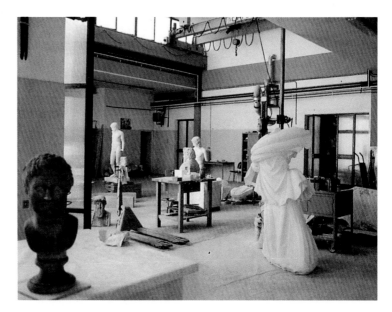

The Restoration Laboratory of the Vatican Museums (above,on the left), founded in 1925, is located in the building that houses the Pinacoteca. It is under the supervision of the Director of the Museums and employs people in various specialized areas (paintings, bronzes, terracotta, wood, ceramics). Attached to it is the Department for Scientific Research and Application. In 1984, the Marble Restoration Laboratory (above,on the right) was founded next to the Pius-Clementine Museum, it is fitted with the most modern technology and equipped to produce casts of the statues.

The Laboratory for the Restoration of Tapestries (below) (1926), has been entrusted by the Museum administration to the Franciscan Missionary Sisters of Mary, who work in collaboration with the Restoration Laboratory staff.

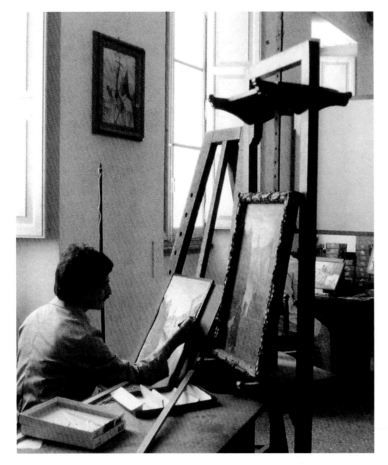

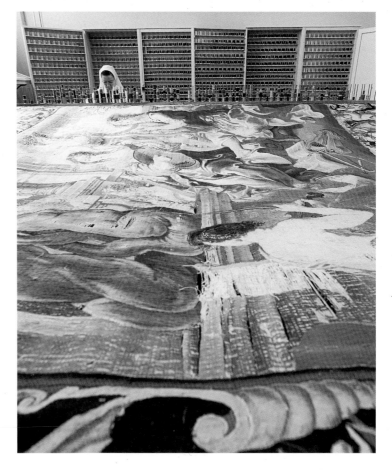

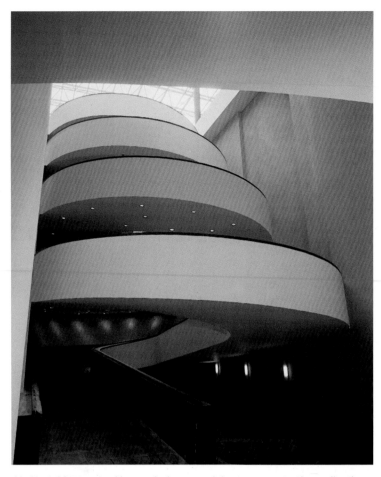

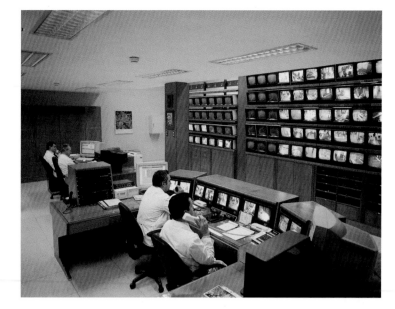

A sophisticated closed-circuit television system monitors visitors, who number around four million a year.

Vatican Museums. New spiral ramp giving access to the collections (2000).

On 7 February 2000, Pope John Paul II inaugurated the new entrance to the Vatican Museums, which had been created in a bastion of the Vatican walls next to the old entrance built in 1932 by Giuseppe Momo. The 1932 entrance is now used as the exit. A great spiral ramp leads visitors to the Atrio delle Corazze where they find directions indicating the locations of the various collections of the Museums.

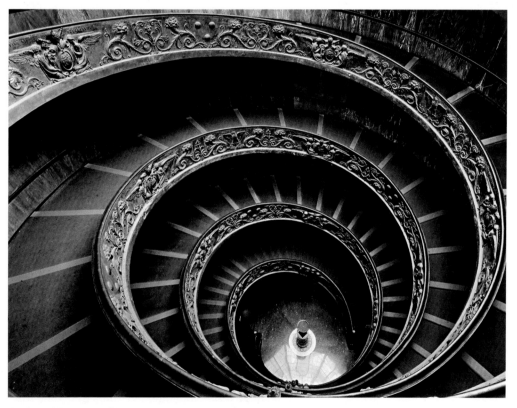

Vatican Museums. Giuseppe Momo, spiral ramp (1932).

Among the services offered to visitors are two currency-exchange offices, one near the entrance (right), the other at the end of the Museum itinerary.

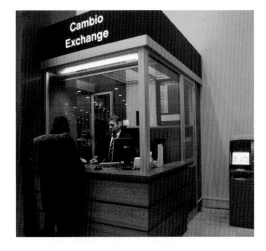

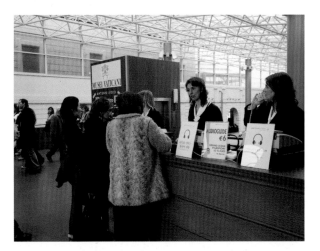

It is possible to hire a multi-lingual audio guide, specifically created for the various sectors of the Museums to guarantee a complete and well-informed visit.

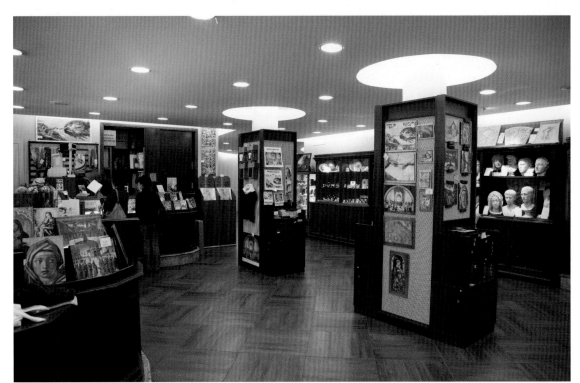

Several sales desks offer a wide range of tourist guides and art books in various languages, as well as reproductions inspired by pieces in the Vatican collections.

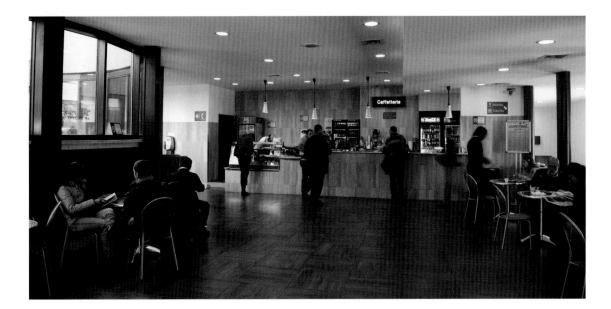

A caffetteria and a restaurant-pizzeria with a view over the gardens and the dome of St. Peter's cater to the needs of Museum visitors.

THE CITY

An Ordinary Workday

Along with the solemn and religious side of the Vatican, which we've had occasion to observe and admire, there is the ordinary everyday Vatican as well. Beyond the Leonine Walls there is more going on than the contemplation of artistic masterpieces and the important decision-making that regulates the life of the Universal Church. A humble and relatively uneventful daily life is also taking place. Side by side with the cardinals and the prelates is their household staff—comprised of religious, relatives or housekeepers—who pass through the St. Anne Gates every morning to do the shopping in the tiny "commercial quarter" of the pontifical city.

In other words, along with the diplomats, the monsignors and other important figures on business within the tiny state, there is a small army of ushers, workers and artisans without whom the Vatican would cease to function. Interestingly, if you count up priests, nuns and laity, it is the latter category which outnumbers the sum of the former by more than two to one. In fact, alongside 710 priests and 393 nuns, there are no fewer than 2,587 laypeople working for the Vatican.

An example of the singular juxtaposition that is often the case within the Vatican can be seen in the large tower of Nicholas V. Only three floors (an elevator ride) from the very rooms where the pope lives we find the tellers' windows of a bank! Could there be a greater abyss than the one that separates the pope's pastoral concern for his flock from the financial astuteness that must guide the directors of the Institute for Religious Works? And yet (it should be said), the money in this case is destined for religious causes and to further missionary works around the world.

Down on the first floor of the Apostolic Palace are the offices of the Administration for the Patrimony of the Apostolic See; and on the other side of the St. Damasus courtyard the special unit that manages the Holy See's finances.

Only a few yards from the tower, on the other side of Via Sant'Anna, is the food commissary. Access is granted to those who have a special identity card, something extended only to Vatican employees, pensioners and their families, as well as a few Catholic organizations.

There's a gasoline pump beneath Michelangelo's apse, and not far from that can be seen the edge of a fenced off vegetable garden. It's a homey touch, something you might more readily associate with the countryside than with the inside of the Vatican. However, that simple vegetable patch isn't there to confer an exotic touch in contrast to the grand formal gardens that surround it. No, its actual purpose is to provide fresh vegetables for the pontifical dining room.

If from within the basilica majestic intonations can occasionally be heard, or else outbursts of heavenly music from the Sistine Choir or humble psalms sung by the canons of the chapter, you're as likely to hear the screeching of electric saws in a nearby carpenter's shop. Such is the cohabitation in this part of the tiny city-state. And if distinguished diplomats from all over the world are silently at work amid Raphael's frescoes on the third loggia, down on the ground floor the modest *Floreria Apostolica* goes quietly about its business of storing furnishings for the apartments of the pope and the cardinals.

An Extended Family

The Vatican is a tiny state which guarantees freedom and sovereignty to a spiritual power that embraces the whole world. In fact, the Vatican adds up to an amazing concentration of services. There's a hotel, a bank, food stores, greenhouses where flowers and plants are produced to beautify the basilica, a train station, first aid station, pharmacy, printing press, newspaper office, radio station, and helicopter port. So while the pope is engaged with the problems of the world on the second and third floors of the Apostolic Palace, a quiet provincial city down below goes about its daily routine.

Someone examining this village in the terms usually applied to a country would be surprised at some of the conclusions to be drawn. For one thing, everything in the Vatican is public property. Every activity depends directly upon the State. You could say that there is no free market. No private citizen may open a shop. Only four types of commerce are allowed: foodstuffs, clothing, gasoline and tobacco.

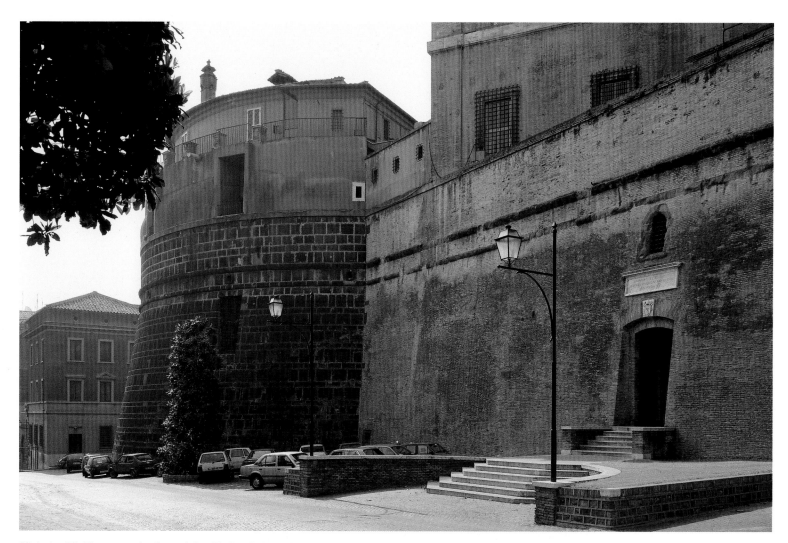

Nicholas V's Tower, *at the foot of the Sistine Palace, is the largest tower of the medieval Leonine walls. It was rebuilt in part during the reign of Nicholas V.*

The Vatican is, in fact, a State the size of a small town or of a medium-sized business. Perhaps more accurately, it is like an extended family in which everybody knows everybody else. The Pope has full legislative, executive and judicial powers, as granted him by the first article of the Fundamental Law of State which came into effect on 22 February 2001 (substituting the law of 7 June 1929).

Nevertheless, everything about this tiny city-state favors more intimate relations among its parties. The real motive for this greater familiarity is that everyone there, in a profound sense, is a collaborator of the pope; they are all there to help him in his role as universal pastor. That's why we said earlier that the Vatican is like an extended family. So much so, in fact, that the doors are closed in the

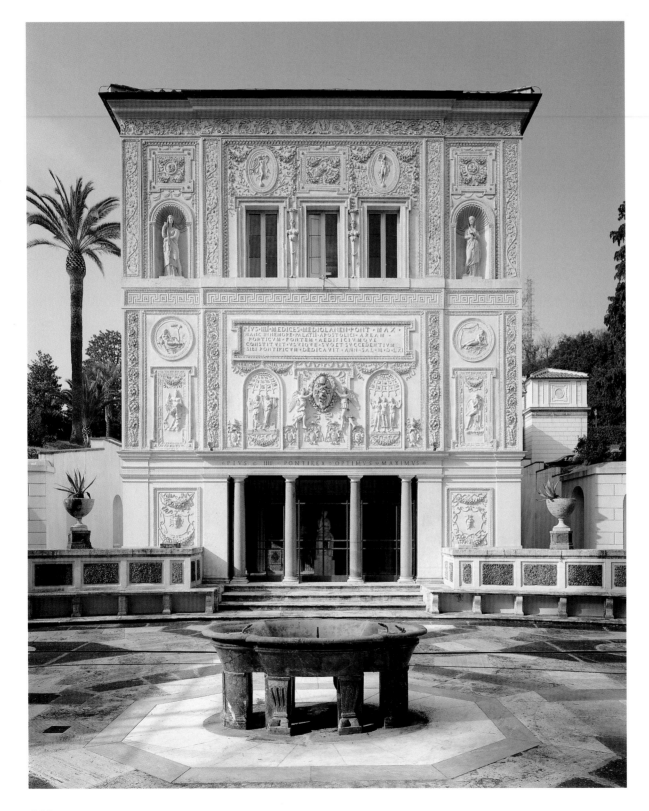

The Casina of Pius IV.
Pirro Ligorio built a new
refuge for Pope Pius IV's
moments of leisure in the
gardens. It consists of two
small buildings: a villa with
a loggia opposite it con-
nected by an elliptical
courtyard. The entrance to
the courtyard is between
two aedicules located at
the top of curved stair-
ways. A lavish decoration
of seashells, mosaics and
stuccoes with mytholog-
cal subjects and small
frescoes covers the
façades and the interiors.

evening, and the St. Anne Gates—closed halfway at 8 pm—are locked up at midnight. During the day, no one can enter any part of Vatican City without a precise reason.

The whole of this city-state belongs to the world's cultural patrimony. Its sovereignty, as John Paul II told the United Nations on October 3, 1979, "is motivated by the fact of the papacy, which must carry out its mission amid total liberty." A state, then, in the service of the pope's freedom. Strangely enough, only in the past two decades have there been place-names (streets, etc.) inside the Vatican. The decision to have them at all was made by Paul VI in 1972. And yet, the first stones in this cluster of buildings absolutely unique in the world were the bricks used to cover Peter's tomb in the years between 64-67 A.D. And the city itself must be considered more than sixteen centuries old—that is, from the time of the construction of Constantine's basilica, followed shortly by the building of hospices and chapels. Nowadays within the tiny city-state there are 78 place-names to be found scattered among its 108 acres: 41 streets, 23 squares and 14 courtyards.

A Tour Among the Gardens

We should certainly begin with a highlight: the *Villa Pia*, an absolute Renaissance gem located in the midst of the papal gardens. Known also as the *Casina di Pio IV*, this delightful structure consists of a loggia and a small dwelling place, and bridges the transition between the museums and the rest of the tiny city-state. In this century, the *Casina* has been put at the disposal of the Pontifical Academy of Sciences, as if to seal the union between the arts and sciences under papal auspices.

Built by Pirro Ligorio for Pope Pius IV (1559-65), the *Casina* is connected to an elliptical courtyard. The entrance to the courtyard is between two aediculas located at the top of curved stairways.

Such a novelty was architecturally audacious for its time. Nowadays we see the *Casina* as a typical and very attractive example of Mannerist architecture in Italy, a precursor of the baroque taste to come. A lavish decoration of seashells, mosaics and stuccoes on mythological subjects,

together with small frescoes illustrating episodes from the life of Moses, cover the façades and the interiors. Permeating everything is a curious mixture of mythology and sacred history. Indeed, alongside the muses and pagan divinities we find the Annunciation and the Holy Family.

If while planning the west wing of the Belvedere courtyard or the building that continued the loggias on the north side of the St. Damasus courtyard, Pirro Ligorio found himself conditioned by Bramante's earlier work, the *Casina* offered free reign to his considerable, even bizarre fantasy. Here he treats architecture as though it was an endless keyboard to be played upon at will. Everything is carried out in his highly personal style and with complete security.

In 1922, a new building in classic style was added to the back part of the villa in order to accommodate the Pontifical Academy of Sciences, which Pius XI determined to relaunch with new vigor. The Academy would be composed of 80 authorities, chosen by the pope from among the most distinguished scientists and mathematicians the world over. The architectural addition may not have been the most successful from an aesthetic point of view, but its position and surrounding landscape make this scientific institute unique in the world. The same building houses the Pontifical Academy for Social Sciences, founded in 1994 by John Paul II.

An Enchanted Wood Filled with Splashing Fountains

Climbing up from Pius IV's *Casina* toward the top of Vatican Hill, we come next to the "Gardener's House". It encompasses the ruins of a medieval tower, perhaps once part of the walls built by Innocent III. Further up we can see a statue of St. Peter, part of a much larger monument planned to commemorate the First Vatican Council. From here we must strike out in the direction of the splendid *Fontana dell'Aquilone* (Eagle Fountain). It was built by the Flemish architect Jan Van Santen (a name italianized to Giovanni Vasanzio) to mark the fact that the Borghese pope Paul V had restored and enlarged the Emperor Trajan's aqueduct so that water could be brought from Lake Bracciano. In fact, this particular supply was named *Acqua Paola* in his honor.

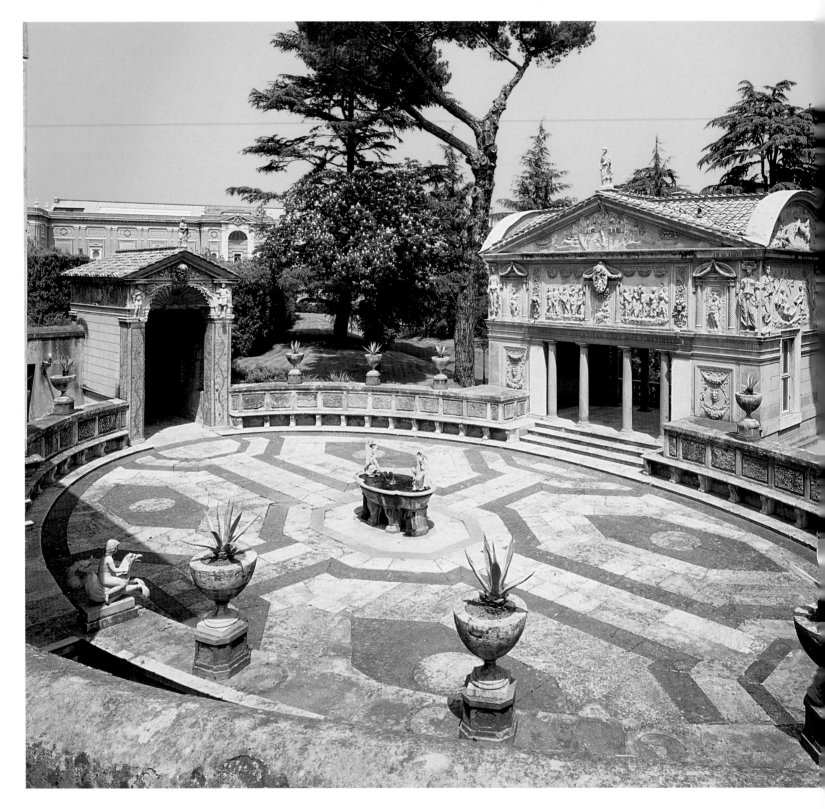

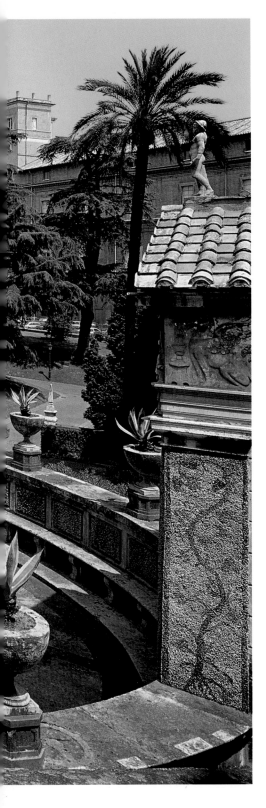

The Casina of Pius IV. Also called the "Nymphaeum", the interior courtyard is oval-shaped and joins together the four architectural structures of the villa.

The commemorative fountain derives its name from the huge eagle positioned at the back, overlooking the basin. The fountain itself was conceived as an immense rocky grotto with two small cavities beside it. In front of the grotto is a wide semicircular basin in which marine creatures and dragons cavort among the waters that cascade down from the back of the fountain.

The eagle and the dragon are the heraldic symbols of the Borghese family. Paul V, who was active in beautifying the gardens, also gave Vasanzio the commission to build the nearby *Fontana delle Torri*, so called because of the two towers with battlements and dragons framing the rocky backdrop. It is also known as the Fountain of the Sacrament owing to the fact that its shape and the play of the waters suggest an altar with a monstrance displayed among the candles.

But we haven't completed our tour of Vatican fountains until we've seen the famous "Galley Fountain". It too was built during Paul V's pontificate, though by Carlo Maderno, and is located at the foot of Bramante's staircase and to the east of Innocent VIII's *palazzetto*. Some forty years later the fountain got its present-day name when Clement IX (1667-69) arranged to have a sailing ship made of copper and lead placed in its basin. Perhaps designed by Vasanzio, it was fitted out with cannons that shoot water. No doubt the pontiff had in mind his predecessor Urban VIII, who had dictated—not without some irony—the text for a plaque asserting that "the war machinery of the popes produces not flames but sweet water which extinguish the fires of strife."

Incidentally, if one of the undoubted glories of Rome are its numerous fountains, much of the merit must go to the popes. The three fountains in Piazza Navona, the celebrated Trevi Fountain, the *Fontanone* on the Janiculum, the Tortoise Fountain, the Triton Fountain and many others—all owe their existence to papal largesse. They are not merely a source of water, but of enduring enchantment to successive generations.

If it happens to be a hot day within the walls of the Vatican, there's more to cool us than the freshness of fountains. An ancient wood comprising some 4.9 acres is filled with leafy holm oaks, bitter oaks, durmast oaks, cypresses and even a majestic beech—the latter normally found at only 800 meters' altitude.

In one particular period, the 44.5 acres of gardens within the Vatican became for the popes very familiar terrain indeed. For a total of 69 years they remained "prisoners", exiled inside the Vatican, from September 20, 1870 until February 11, 1929 during which the temporal power of the papacy was extinguished by the newly formed Italian state.

Leo XIII would come here twice a day, and indeed he spent his holidays here as well. No one had a greater passion for gardening than Leo. Here, at least, was a place where he could imagine he had regained the freedom of a nobleman living on his country estate. In his novel "Rome," the French author Emile Zola placed Leo XIII in the midst of "the loveliest garden in the world." In fact, the pope had olive trees planted there, as well as a small vineyard, and he even had nets placed among the trees to snare birds (which he then let go).

At the Top of the Hill

Near the woods is a large tower built right into the medieval walls erected by Leo IV. It was here that Leo XIII moved during the summer months; and for greater comfort he had a small *palazzetto* built next to it. From here he had a view within the Vatican facing south, and outside the Vatican in the direction of Monte Mario. And the view was directed toward the stars when Pius X (1903-14) moved the Observatory there, where it remained from 1906-31. Since 1932, it has been located inside the Pontifical Palace at Castel Gandolfo.

Now the building houses the headquarters and various studios of the Vatican Radio. Programs in 42 languages reach every continent thanks to two towers, respectively 79 and 107 meters high and equipped with rotating antennas, located at Santa Maria di Galeria, 24 kilometers north of Rome.

Only 250 meters from the tower is the Marconi Broadcasting Center, designed by Gugliemo Marconi himself and inaugurated with a famous radio message by Pius XI on February 12, 1931. The pope spoke into an octagonal microphone held by four clips mounted within a steel circle—still conserved as a memento at Vatican Radio headquarters.

Among those present that day was the Secretary of State, Cardinal Eugenio Pacelli, later Pius XII, who was to do so much to favor the development of this new technology. Vatican Radio's first transmitter was made by the Marconi Society in London. The Franklin antenna, which rises behind Michelangelo's cupola, was considered an amazing feat of technology for its time.

Not far from the tower, a small square building next to the vegetable garden underwent a radical transformation a few years ago. Until then the residence of the director of Vatican Radio, it was converted into a small monastery for nuns wholly devoted to prayer and penance. Presently there are eight Poor Clares from different countries who pray every day for the pope and his ministry. Every five years, nuns from other orders come to take their place. The monastery, it goes without saying, is a hidden source of spiritual grace.

Every now and again in our stroll through the gardens we come upon statues of the Virgin and the Saints. One of the more interesting is the reproduction of the *Madonna della Guardia,* donated by the citizens of Genoa to their illustrious countryman Benedict XV (1914-22). And further along, where there is a lengthy gap in the ancient walls, we come upon the grotto of the Madonna of Lourdes, a gift from French Catholics to Leo XIII. Though everything is on a slightly smaller scale than at Massabielle, the altar is the same one that stood in front of the "grotto of the apparitions" for the first hundred years. There are other gifts from abroad: the statues of Our Lady of Guadalupe, St. Theresa of the Child Jesus and that of St. Bernard. The most recent to arrive are a statue of the Madonna of Czestochowa, situated at the edge of the heliport; and a beautiful ceramic relief by Renata Minuto *Mater Misericordiae,* given by the Catholics of the Italian city of Savona in 1995.

From the Heliport With Missionary Enthusiasm

Built in 1976 atop the bastion that stands on the highest point of Vatican Hill, the heliport is the point of departure for all the pope's missionary journeys.

Apropos bastions and battlements, the whole of Vatican City (with the exception of the Basilica and the section extending from the Charlemagne wing to the

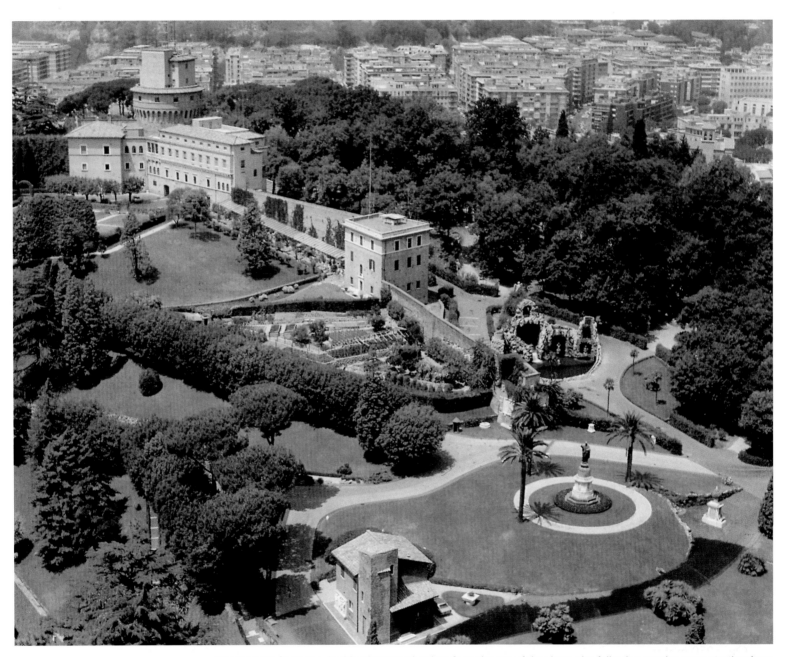

The Vatican Gardens. *In this photograph taken from the top of the dome the following can be seen starting from below: the Gardener's House with a medieval fortified tower connected to the original nucleus of the pope's residence; the bronze statue of St. Peter, a monument that commemorates Vatican Council I; the Eagle Fountain; the small palazzetto built for Leo XIII's leisure time (now occupied by the administrative offices of the Vatican Radio).*

Palazzo S. Uffizio) is enclosed within massive walls topped by imposing bastions. All of them were built in the period between the pontificates of Paul III and Urban VIII—that is, from 1540 to 1640. Given the extreme shortage of space within the Vatican, even the terraces above these ramparts are frequently utilized. The Belvedere bastion serves an unusual purpose: there is a tennis court there, which may be reached via the Viale dello Sport, which runs alongside Innocent VIII's *palazzetto* and the Bramante staircase. Another rampart houses the spacious *Vignaccia* warehouses. Almost directly across from them, positioned significantly along the Viale San Benedetto, co-patron of Europe, stands a singular memento: a fragment of the Berlin Wall. It is 3.6 meters high, 1.2 wide and weighs 2,600 kilos. It was given to John Paul II in recognition of his crucially important moral role in the process that led to the fall of Communism.

From the heliport, which is the highest point within the Vatican, we begin the descent. One of the first things we encounter is the Tower of St. John. During the pontificate of John XXIII (1958-63), it was modernized and fitted out with a private apartment spread out over four floors and connected by an elevator. The pope would occasionally go there to spend several days in solitude. The tower itself was part of the Vatican's very first defense system, put in place by Leo IV in 848.

John Paul II stayed there for a couple of weeks immediately following his election to the papacy in 1978. At the time, his private apartment was being prepared in the Apostolic Palace.

The tower was also home to the exiled Hungarian Cardinal Mindszenty, and, during their visits to the Vatican, three patriarchs of Constantinople: Athenagoras, Dimitrios and Bartholomaios. It has also housed several sovereigns and heads of state.

Michelangelo's vast cupola looms over us amid the intense green of the lawns and gardens of the Vatican. The source of such greenery, noticeable even during the summer heat, is an underground network of tubes that allow for constant watering.

Coming upon the railroad station with its neoclassic lines, we are likely to think the whole thing is more for show than actual necessity. And yet, in this little depot

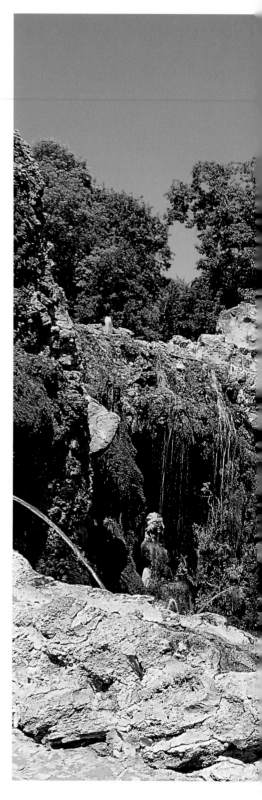

The Eagle Fountain. *Paul V was particularly interested in the decoration of the Vatican Gardens and commissioned several fountains, including the two most important which are illustrated here. They were designed by Jan van Santen, called* il Vasanzio *by Italians, who decorated them with eagles and dragons, the emblem of the Borghese family.*

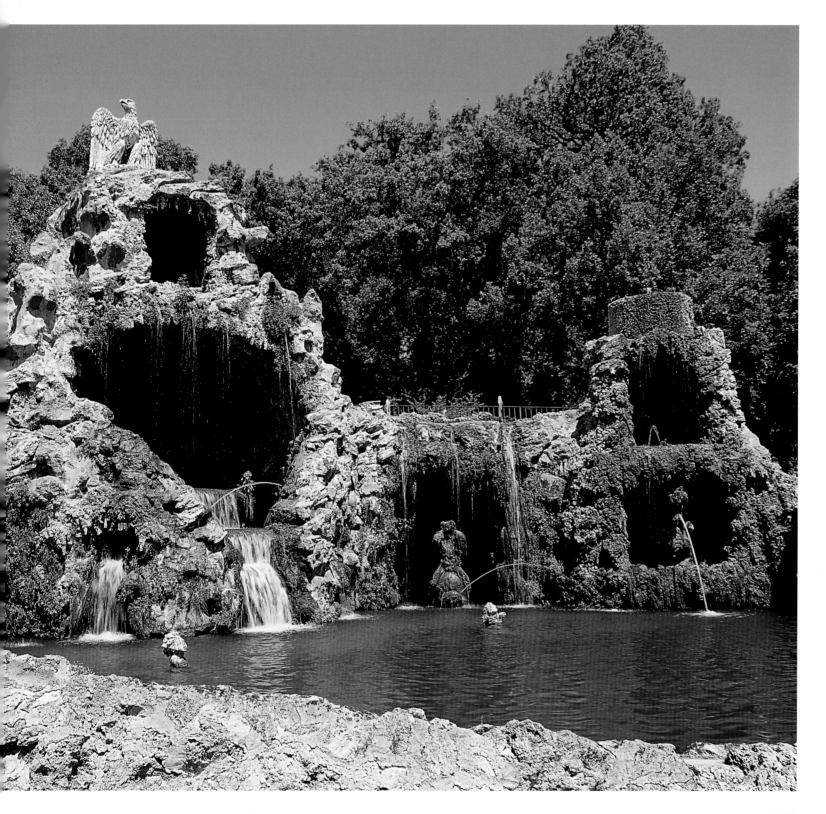

there are more than 2,000 arrivals a year of freight from Italy and other countries. It's amazing to think that there is literally an "iron curtain" separating the Vatican from Italy—in this case a sliding iron door that is electrically powered. The section of the rail line that belongs to the Vatican is 861.78 meters long.

Though for freight only, an exception was made for John XXIII on the occasion of his trip to Assisi and Loreto on October 4, 1962. That was a week before the opening of Vatican Council II. John Paul II also boarded a train in special circumstances on November 8, 1979 when he travelled to convey his blessings to train workers on their national day.

The Ethiopian College, together with the Teutonic College, enjoys the extraordinary privilege of being located within the walls of the Vatican. The former seminary is heir to the ancient hospice once connected to the church of Santo Stefano degli Abissini, which goes back to the ninth century. It is one of only nine early Christian churches with a semicircular crypt in the manner of St. Peter's. The seminary was built to receive the Abyssinians who came to Rome around the year 1400.

The Teutonic College and its connected graveyard also has an ancient history, going back to Roman pilgrimages by Catholics from German-speaking lands. The college descends from the *schola francorum* built in 799 by Charlemagne. To be precise, the college and the graveyard are located just inside the borders of the Vatican, between St. Peter's Basilica and the Nervi Auditorium for papal audiences. Obviously, this whole area is considered extraterritorial property.

With its great size, the *Palazzo del Governatorato* dominates everything half way up Vatican Hill. Built toward the end of the 1920's, it is the administrative heart of the tiny state that was created by the Lateran Treaty. Among other things, it houses the Pontifical Commission for the Vatican City State, together with all the offices dependent upon it. In front of the building, plants in season are arranged to faithfully recreate the crest of the reigning pope.

Further to the left we can see the Mosaic Studio which continues the tradition (going back to 1557) begun with mosaic decorations in the basilica. Enamels classified according to 28,000 shades of color are distributed throughout 10,000 boxes, each with three compartments.

Further down, on the huge Piazza S. Marta, we can see the building which houses both the Tribunal and the headquarters of the Vatican's security service. More than a hundred watchmen, in fact, guarantee public safety during the various papal ceremonies. The piazza itself takes it name from the *Ospizio di S. Marta,* which is the Vatican's hotel. Until recently it was divided into two parts: one wing with about forty mini-apartments for prelates in the Curia, and another wing for receiving groups of pilgrims during the summer. The second wing was torn down and in its place was constructed a building which can house 120 cardinals, bishops and prelates stopping off briefly in the Vatican. When there are future conclaves, it is understood that the cardinal-electors will reside in this building while going to vote in the Sistine Chapel.

In order to get to the commercial part of the city, we have to first walk up the Via delle Fondamenta which runs alongside the apse of the basilica. This will bring us to Piazza del Forno so called because it was once the location of the *forno apostolico* (Apostolic bakery). This little square is positioned at the intersection of no fewer than five roads, and practically faces one of the main entrances to the sacred palaces. When Rome was captured in 1870, it was on this square that the Republican and Papal forces faced each other, because this point marked the border.

Once past the door to the *Palazzo Vaticano* and inside the Sentinella courtyard, one can descend via the so-called "Big Grotto" into the Belvedere courtyard. It is an unusual tunnel that passes beneath the west wing of the museum. From the Belvedere courtyard it is possible to admire—this time from below—the "exedra" (open, columned semicircle) at the foot of the papal palace. It was there that Machiavelli's play *Mandragola* was performed for the first time, and where, in 1565, a colorful tournament was organized on the occasion of the marriage of two young relatives of Pius IV, Annibale Altemps and Ortensia Borromeo.

The Fountain of the Sacrament *stands on the spot formerly occupied by one of the gates of the Leonine City walls; two false towers were built on either side to mark this fact. The fountain gets its name from the pattern made by the water, because the jets are designed so as to suggest the shape of six candles surrounding an altar.*

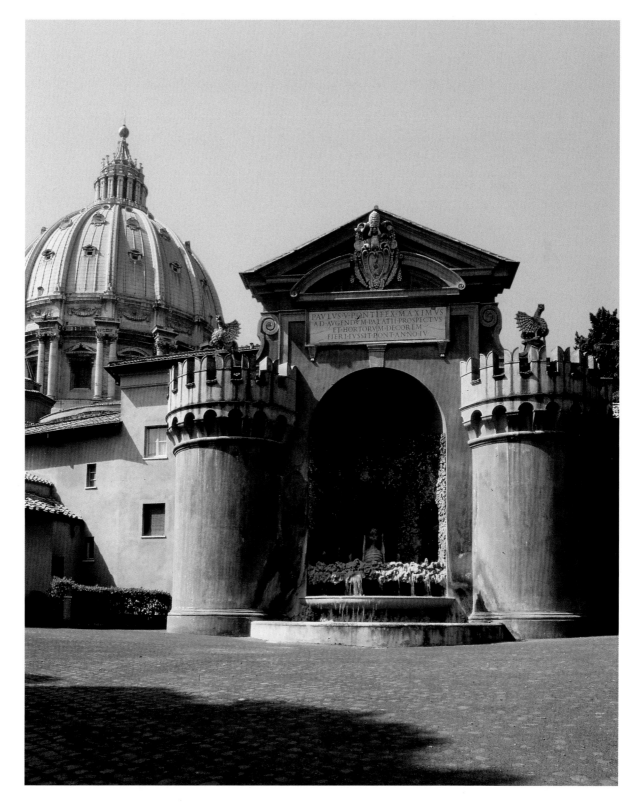

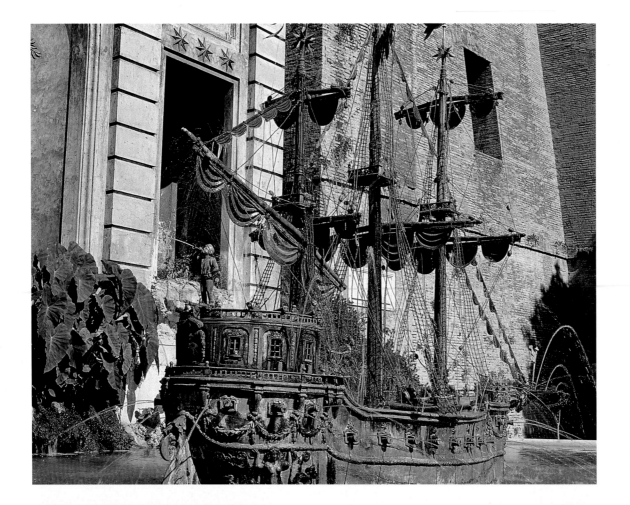

The Galley Fountain *was commissioned by Paul V to be placed at the foot of Bramante's stairway. It became known as the Galley Fountain when Clement IX (1667-69) added the lead cast of a ship.*

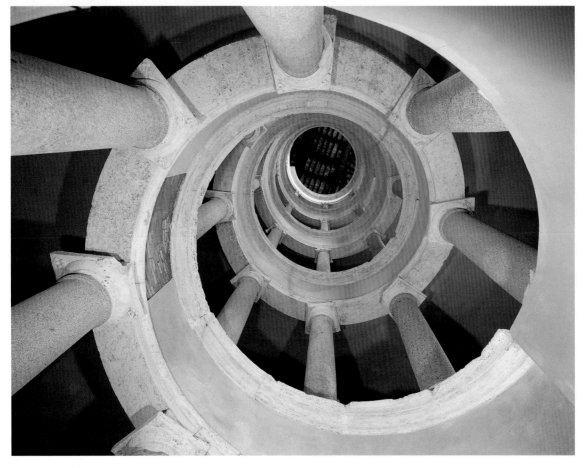

The Spiral Staircase, *closed within a tower next to Innocent VIII's palazzetto, connects the Belvedere to the gardens below. Designed and begun by Bramante probably towards the end of 1511, it was finished by Pirro Ligorio in 1564.*

The Commercial Quarter

Once past the Bramante wing, we come upon several essential Vatican services, starting with the central post office. Over four million letters and fifteen million postcards are handled here every year. There are separate mail sacks for the various offices within the Vatican, one of which is marked "Holy Father". The pope, in fact, receives more than 2,000 letters a day.

Alongside the post office is the multi-lingual Vatican printing press, nowadays completely computerized. It is the direct descendent of the venerable *Stamperia Vaticana*, founded by Sixtus V in 1587. In its storeroom antique lead typesetting is still kept in fifteen languages. Run by the Salesians, the printing press produces publications in thirty languages. There is even a "secret" section of the workshop where pontifical documents are published. The six to eight persons who work in this section are sworn to silence regarding the contents of the texts they are printing.

At the site of the present-day headquarters of the printing press there was once a foundry for the fusion of heavy metals and the production of artillery. Modernized in the first half of the sixteenth century under Pope Urban VIII, the foundry produced among other things the statue of Napoleon in Place Vendome in Paris, the angel atop Castel Sant'Angelo, and the statue of the Virgin Mary in Piazza di Spagna.

The nearby *Libreria Editrice Vaticana* can take credit for the first edition of sacred books produced by Aldo Manuzio (1450-1516) and his sons. Now it is an up-to-date publishing house specializing in the printing of the papal documents and proceedings, and also those of the Holy See in general.

Founded in 1861, *L'Osservatore Romano* is the oldest newspaper published in Rome. In addition to the daily edition, six weekly versions are produced in as many languages; there is also a monthly edition printed in Polish. The most recent member of the Vatican's media family is the *Centro Televisivo Vaticano* which was established to "develop the presence of the life of the Church through the use of audio-visual technology".

Right next to the post office are the medical facilities and out-patient offices. About sixty specialists and general practitioners, a dozen professional nurses and four technicians in the diagnostic unit are on call. For the benefit of pilgrims, there is also a first-aid station that can handle up to twelve persons. The Vatican pharmacy, under the direction of the Fatebenefratelli Order, is famous for stocking medicines that are not on sale even in Italy.

Once past the food commissary, which we've spoken of earlier, we come to the Vatican's motor park. It is located on the same property where the papal stables stood at the beginning of the century. It consists of 58 cars, 27 vans and trucks, 6 buses and 7 special vehicles. Throughout the Vatican there are also 81 lifts and freight elevators. Beneath the motor park, an ancient burial ground was discovered in 1956 while workers were laying the foundation for the present construction. Evidently, it is part of the necropolis that extended along the Via Trionfale. The most interesting aspect of this particular burial ground—of which about 240 square meters were unearthed—is that it is virtually intact, rather like the one beneath the St. Peter's basilica.

"O Roma Felix"

This brings us to the end of the commercial and industrial area of the tiny city-state. The name Via del Pellegrino (pilgrim) reminds us that it was the last section of the ancient Via Francigena, trod by generations of pilgrims coming from northern Italy and the rest of Europe. At the halfway point they would begin singing "O Roma Felix", an ancient hymn which spoke of Rome as the land "bathed in the blood of the apostles Peter and Paul."

The church of San Pellegrino was founded probably by Leo III at the beginning of the ninth century. Next to it stood a hospice which for centuries during the medieval period received pilgrims bound for the basilica. This leads us to Via Sant'Anna, at the end of which is the busiest entrance to the Vatican, the St. Anne Gates. On the left side just before coming to the gate is the parish church for all residents of the Vatican, dedicated to *Sant'Anna dei Palafrenieri.* The *palafrenieri* were the grooms and footmen who took care of the horses belonging to the pope and his court. In fact, the stables were once located in the immediate vicinity. The church itself was built on the design of Jacopo Barozzi, more famous as Vignola.

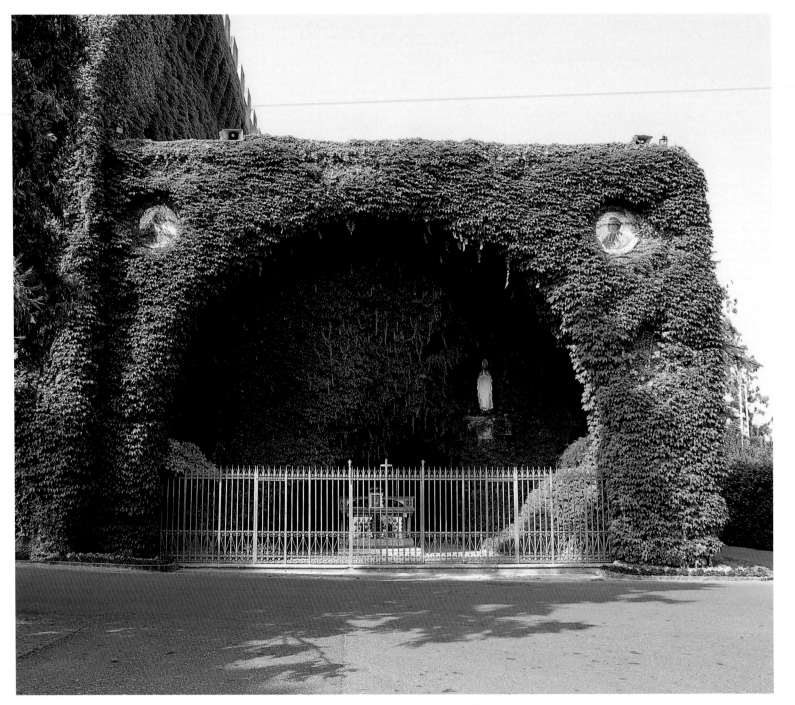

The Lourdes Grotto *is a faithful reproduction of the* Grotte de Massabielle near Lourdes. *In 1902 the French gave it to Leo XIII, who is depicted in the mosaic above left; on the right is a portrait of bishop Schopfer of Tarbes Lourdes. The altar is the original one from Lourdes, a gift to John XXIII in 1958 on the occasion of the centennial of the apparition of the Madonna of Lourdes.*

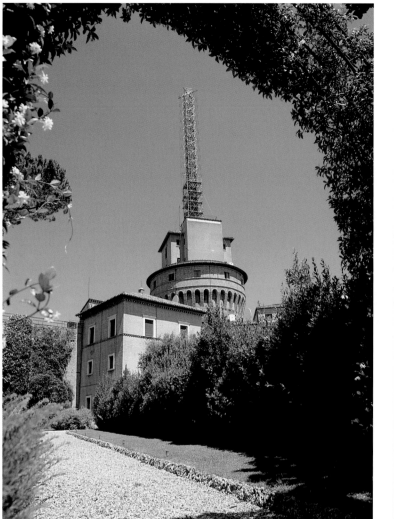

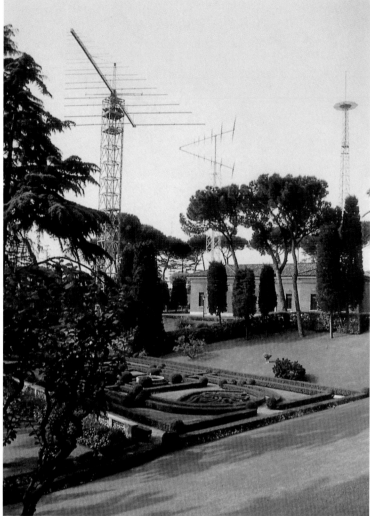

The Palazzetto *of Leo XIII and the Leonine Tower (above, left), today housing the Administrative Offices of the* Vatican Radio, *were built along Leo IV's medieval wall.*

The building housing the Marconi Broadcasting Center *(above, right), still in use, was planned by Guglielmo Marconi and inaugurated by Pope Pius XI on February 12, 1931 with a message that was broadcast worldwide.*

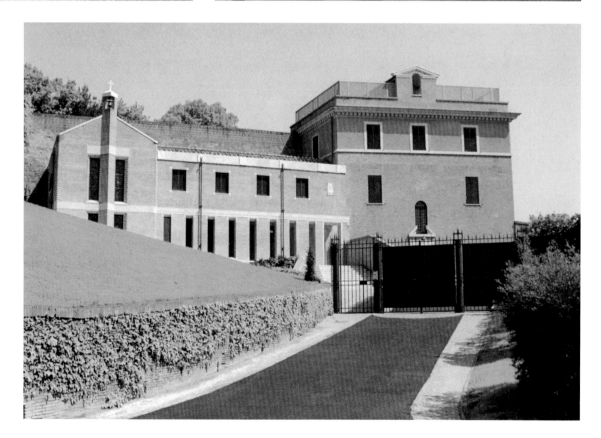

The Mater Ecclesiae Monastery *of the poor Clares was recently founded between the botanical garden and the pope's vegetable garden.*

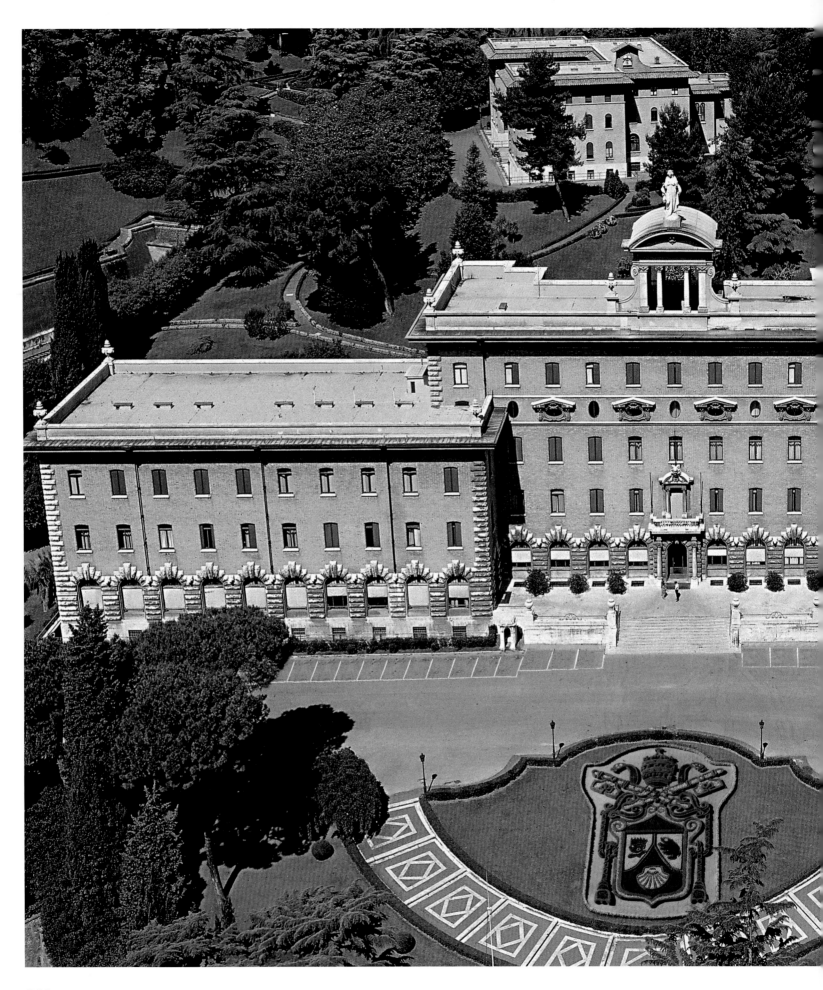

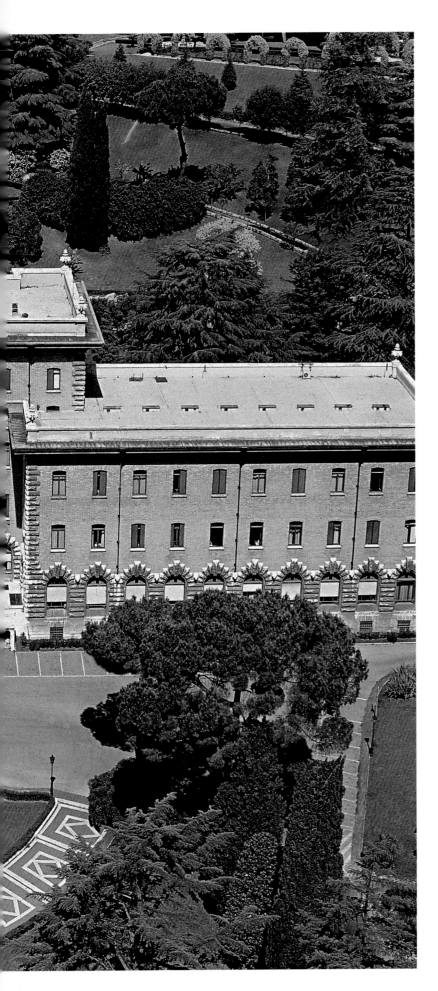

The last section of Via Francigena led to what is today the Swiss courtyard. There we find the barracks with its 100 apartments for the guards whose principal task is to "keep constant watch over the safety of the Holy Father and his residence". The idea of having a guard made up entirely of Swiss soldiers was that of the Della Rovere pope, Julius II. In addition to setting in motion the construction of a new St. Peter's, commissioning Michelangelo to do the frescoes for the Sistine Ceiling, and calling Raphael to decorate the Stanzas, this is the fourth great initiative for which Giuliano Della Rovere will always be remembered. The guard, dressed in its celebrated uniform of yellow, red and blue stripes, number 100 strong, of which 70 are halberd bearers. These are the battle-axes with pikes mounted on a handle fully six feet long. The guards themselves come from all the cantons of Switzerland.

Closing off the courtyard is the famous "Porta Sancti Petri", the most important access to the Vatican in medieval times. It is the portal through which pilgrims reached their goal: the basilica with the most precious relics of all Christianity. For them, it was the conclusion of a long journey with the risk of illness or attacks by bandits.

The present-day gate of St. Peter, unfortunately hidden by the northern part of the colonnade on the piazza, maintains all its impressiveness. The gate as we see it now dates from 1492, during the pontificate of Alexander VI. At one time it was called "Porta Viridaria" because the gardens of the pope were located there. It is located along Leo IV's wall connecting the Apostolic Palace to Castel Sant'Angelo. This wall, 800 meters long, is known as the *passetto* (passageway) because, thanks to a walkway at the top, one could go all the way from the basilica and the apostolic palace to the fortress.

Thanks to this elevated connecting link and to the sacrifice of 147 Swiss Guards, Clement VII was able to reach the safety of Castel Sant'Angelo on May 6, 1527, thus evading capture during the Sack of Rome.

The Palazzo del Governatorato *is so-called because it houses the Governorate, i.e., the group of organizations that exercise executive power within Vatican City State. All those services essential to the day-to-day workings of the small State are administered from the Governatorato: the issuing of postage stamps and the minting of coins, the running of the railway (used for the transport of freight), the papal Villa at Castelgandolfo and the Observatory next to it.*

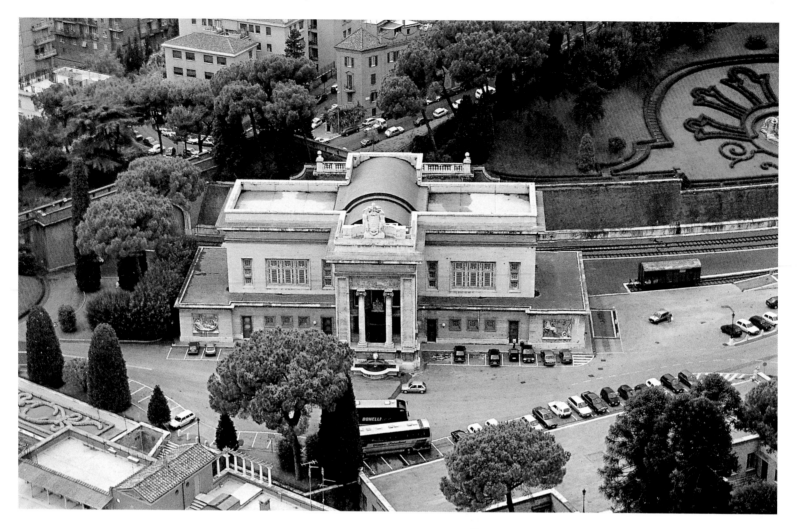

The Railroad Station *built by Giuseppe Momo immediately after the foundation of the Vatican State in 1929. A large iron gate separates the Vatican and Italian railways.*

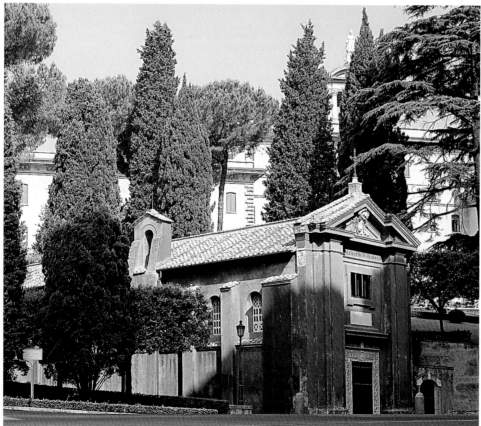

S. Stefano degli Abissini, *the Vatican's oldest church, has a portal with a beautiful marble frieze on top.*

The Church of Sant'Anna, *a construction with a central plan, was designed by Jacopo Barozzi, called* il Vignola, *in 1572 for the Confraternity of the Court Grooms. Today it serves as the Vatican City parish church. The St. Anne Gate, sentineled by the Swiss Guards wearing fatigues rather than their service uniform, is the service entrance to the Vatican.*

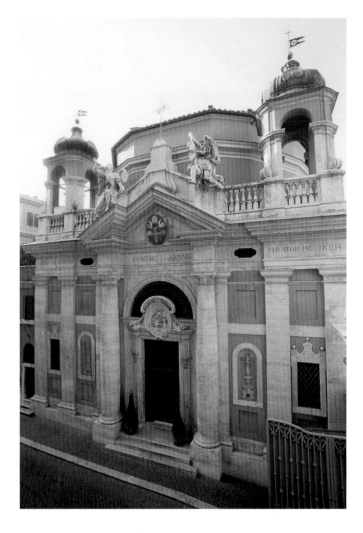

The Chiesa di San Pellegrino, *or Church of the Holy Pilgrim, is located on the present-day Via del Pellegrino which used to be the last stretch of the Via Francigena, the main medieval road connecting Rome to the North and the road used by pilgrims to enter the city. The votive chapel probably dates from the time of Leo III (795-816). The fragment of a fresco depicting "Christ Blessing" in the conch of the apse is the oldest fresco in the Vatican (aside from the decoration of the tombs in the necropolis): it dates from the early 9th century. The saints on either side of Christ are 17th century copies of 14th century figures. From 1653 the church was administered by the Swiss Guard, who buried their dead in the little cemetery. Since the first half of this century it has become the church of the* Corpo di Gendarmeria.

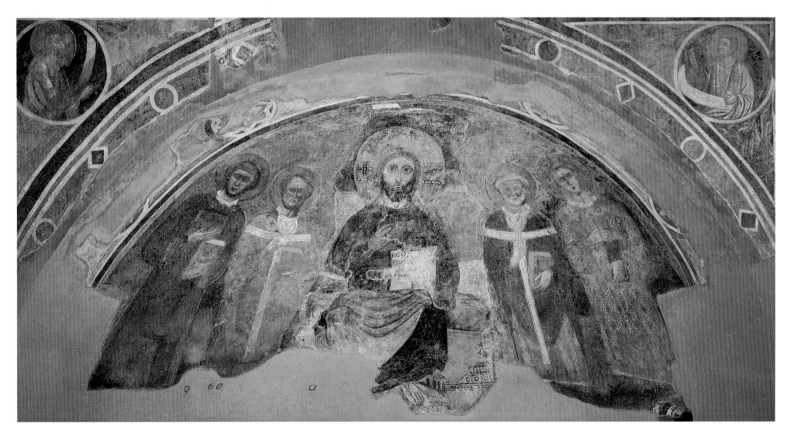

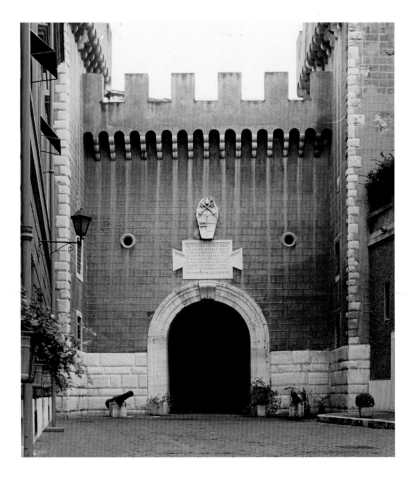

St. Peter's Gate. *The gate we see today is a reconstruction (dating from 1492 and the pontificate of Alexander VI) of the ancient door that connected via Francigena with the Basilica's main square. It was also called the Porta Viridaria because the Vatican Gardens originally stretched to the nearby viridarium ("garden surrounded by columns").*

The so-called labyrinth, characteristic of Italian gardens, is located behind the Ethiopian College; the dome of St. Peter's can be seen in the background.

The Swiss Guard celebrates Memorial Day on May 6, the day on which, in 1527, the Swiss sacrificed their lives to save Medici pope Clement VII from Emperor Charles V's Lansquenets. Clement V/I escaped to safety in Castel Sant'Angelo thanks to the secret passetto ("passageway") which runs along the Leonine Walls. The military corps was instituted by Julius II on January 21, 1506. Its barracks are housed in two buildings at the foot of Nicholas V's Tower, the last segment of the Via Francigena (the present-day Swiss Courtyard) which ends at St. Peter's Gate. The Swiss Guard still wear the 16th century uniforms in the colors of the Medici dynasty: blue, yellow and red. The corps of the Swiss Guard protect the Pope, the Apostolic Palace and all entrances to the Vatican.

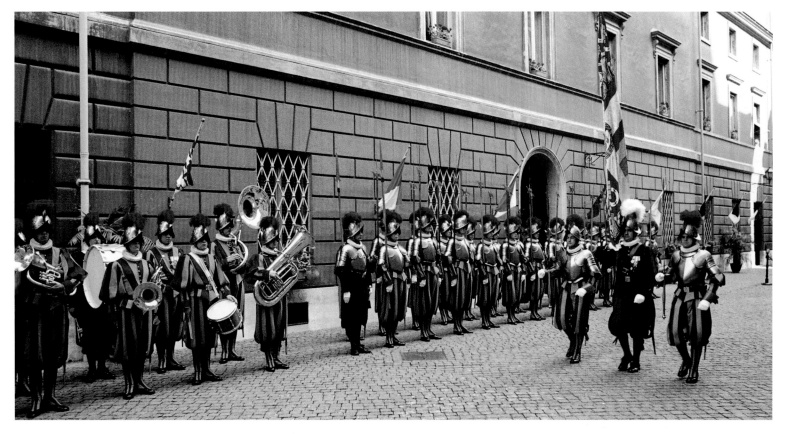

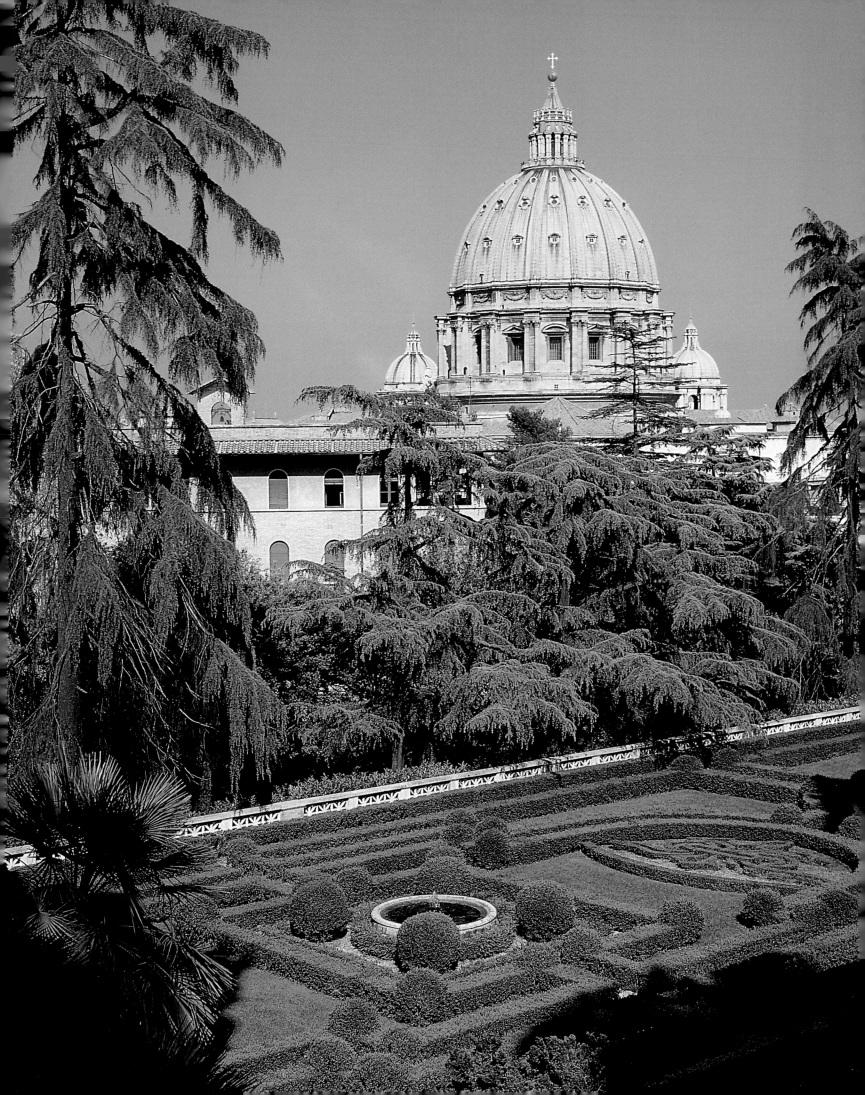

THE PIAZZA

A Natural Scenario for the Faith

Our itinerary through the Vatican has frequently turned into a religious pilgrimage to holy places. We're now back at our starting point, in the incomparable St. Peter's Square, with the advantage of being better able to grasp the full force of these monuments. We understand now the connective thread through it all—from the sepulchre of the apostle to the city-state all around it—and this knowledge will give us a better understanding of the whole.

Enclosed within the embrace of the Bernini colonnade with its 284 massive columns laid out in four rows, we can see why it has been defined "the most beautiful square in the world, located in front of the greatest temple of Christianity." Few places anywhere can convey the emotion we feel standing in this vast amphitheater, enclosed within the gigantic colonnade. And it is impossible to walk across it, even after doing it hundreds of times, without being struck by its stupendous theatricality. It is at once simple and grandiose, stirring and yet infinitely peaceful, both ancient and modern. Not surprisingly, the square is considered the most inspired creation of all the many things Bernini left in the Vatican.

Nor is artistic amazement the only thing we experience in this unique piazza. Our deepest religious feelings find here a natural scenario for their expression. Now that we have traveled around the Vatican, we are better able to comprehend three profound realities: the Catholic Church, the pope, the Vatican city-state. Here too, as earlier inside the Basilica, we can perceive the architectural expression of Christianity.

The massive square is divided into two parts. The first is formed by a huge oval, 196 meters wide and 148 long, carried out by Gian Lorenzo Bernini under the pontificate of Alexander VII, between 1656 and 1667. The ellipse is comprised of two semicircles joined by a central rectangular area. Bernini chose to close off the curved part of the square with an imposing colonnade in the doric order. The colonnade confers such a sense of solemn grandeur that it both moves and subdues the viewer. The 284 columns in travertine marble, each 16 meters tall and arranged in rows four deep, create three galleries. Above the colonnade, which is 18.5 meters tall, stand 96 statues, each 3.20 meters

high. All around the piazza, they form a crown of martyrs, confessors, virgins and hermits—all sculpted by disciples of Bernini and on designs made by the master.

At the far end, the colonnades join onto two long, slightly splayed porticos that run all the way to the Basilica; they create a trapezoidal shaped parvis which gives the impression that the façade is closer to the square than it really is. On the balustrade are 44 more statues, seeming almost to participate in the procession of pilgrims come to Rome. That brings to 140 the number of saints who appear to be directing—from the lofty heights of the loggia—the long lines of advancing pilgrims below.

In order to close the monumental amphitheater, Bernini had planned another wing on the colonnade. Leaving sufficient space laterally, it would have continued the curve of the other two, thus completing his marvelous piazza.

For more than three centuries this spectacular setting has served as a prologue to the Basilica. On more than one occasion during the year it becomes an enormous open-air church or else a vast hall for meetings between the newly-arrived pilgrims and the successor of Peter. The idea, in fact, of welcoming within a spacious "common home" vast numbers of people is implicitly suggested by the two wide arms of the colonnade. With his semi-circular creation, Bernini succeeded in reproducing the "motherly embrace" that had been asked of him. For it had been written, in 1600, in the Chigi codex: "St. Peter's, being virtually the matrix of all other churches, should have a portico which could receive within its open and maternal arms not only Catholics to confirm them in their faith, and heretics to reunite them with the Church, but even infidels to illuminate them as to the True Faith."

A Mute Witness to Martyrdom

If we go to the center of the piazza, we will find the most precious element in this whole vast panorama: the obelisk. To begin with, it is inestimably valuable from a point of view of history and archeology. The second largest obelisk in all Rome, it is nearly 2,000 years old inasmuch as its construction was ordered by Caius Cornelius Gallo,

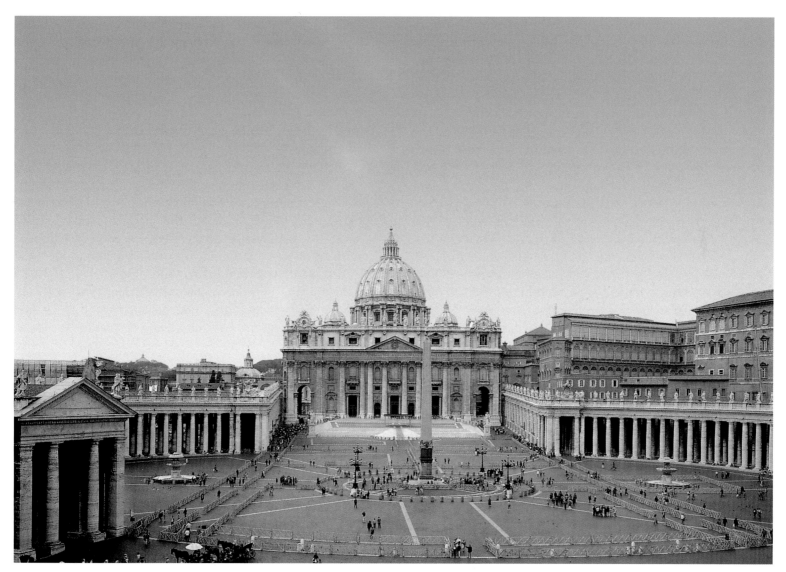

A view of St. Peter's Square, Bernini's colonnade and the obelisk, the "silent witness" of Peter's martyrdom.

Roman prefect of Egypt. But it is even more important from a religious point of view. For this monolith was nothing less than "mute witness" to the martyrdom of St. Peter. According to an ancient tradition, the apostle was crucified *iuxta obeliscum*, that is to say "close to the obelisk." We know that the obelisk stood on the *spina* of the Circus of Gaius and Nero. It was there that Peter, together with 980 of the first martyrs, professed his faith even in the face of death. The monolith of red Oriental granite, 25 meters long and weighing 327 tons, was brought from Alexandria in Egypt on an enormous raft to satisfy the Emperor Caligula's desire of beautifying his private Circus. It was in front of this "spire"—as they called it in medieval times—that the first mass executions of Christians took place. Perhaps the obelisk was illuminated by bodies set aflame. It was certainly mute witness to the ferocious persecution of the followers of Christ. No other monument could better commemorate the tragic beginnings of the Christian community in Rome.

Now it celebrates the triumph of the Cross. It exalts the sacrifice of the martyrs and the glory of the papacy. For more than fifteen centuries it has stood there, an element of continuity between ancient Rome, *caput mundi* under the pagan Empire, and the new Rome, still *caput mundi* thanks to the primacy of the pope. While everything was changing about it, the obelisk stood where it was. To its right, Constantine's Basilica rose, surrounded by hospices and small chapels.

Though more than one pope thought of having it transported in front of the Basilica, all projects came to nothing due to the difficulties involved. Even Michelangelo was of the opinion that it was impossible. But Sixtus V, never one to be daunted by obstacles, saw his dream realized thanks to the engineering genius of his architect Domenico Fontana.

The immense job, which required the demolition of a number of houses and the opening of a gap in the ancient sacristy, began on April 30, 1586. It would require 52 work days to be completed. The plan called for the employment of five powerful levers, 47 winches, 140 horses and 900 men. It wasn't actually finished until September 10 because work was halted during the summer. The whole arduous operation is depicted in a fresco inside the Vatican Library.

From then on, the obelisk would exalt the victory of Christianity over paganism. The four inscriptions placed at the base of the monolith by Sixtus V say as much. The bronze ball which, according to a medieval legend, contained the ashes of Julius Caesar, was removed from the peak of the obelisk. In its place was put a relic of the True Cross.

Two Windows Which Face the World

Standing by the obelisk, we can look up toward two particular windows that face the square. One is at the center of the church façade; the other, on the third floor of the apostolic palace, is that of the pope's private study. Whenever these two windows open, Christ's Vicar is speaking to the people gathered in the piazza and to all those who hear him throughout the world.

It is from the central loggia of the Basilica that the election of a new pope is announced. It is here that he first appears, and speaks for the first time to the whole world. Likewise, this is where he imparts his benediction at Christmas and Easter, speaking *Urbi et Orbi*—to the city and the world—and giving his blessing in more than 50 languages to all the continents via satellite television.

Every Sunday at noon, on the other hand, the pope recites the Angelus and speaks briefly from the other "window on the world". It is then that this stupendous oval-shaped amphitheater truly becomes the piazza toward which all the peoples of the earth turn their gaze. At that moment, Bernini's creation is open not only to Catholics but to all men of good will who wish to receive an authentic message that comes from God and is directed to the very core of their existence.

The piazza is the symbol of the papal message. Here, above the tomb of Peter, we are put in touch with the apostolic roots of the Church of Rome, which in turn are connected directly to Christ. Inside the Basilica, we listen and pray along with the great assembly gathered around the Universal Pastor of the Church. In the piazza we are not only received but sent out again into the world. Just as the "open arms" are poised to accept us, they are similarly relaxed so as to release us as well. This inward and outward motion—so similar to the systole and diastole of the human heart—is an apt metaphor for the beating heart of Christ's Church.

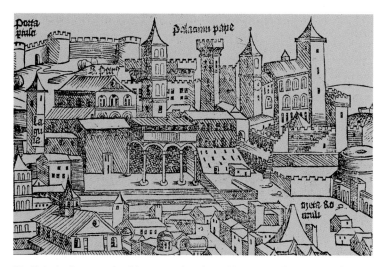

St. Peter's Square. *In this engraving from Hartmann Schedel's "Chronicle of the World", printed in 1493, we can see the old basilica of St. Peter's, the medieval Loggia from which the popes imparted their blessing, and the bell tower. Built in the 8th century, the bell tower was demolished in 1610.*

A Beautiful Journey Not Yet Ended!

There is yet another meeting place within the Vatican. We are speaking of the "Auditorium Paul VI". Every Wednesday, thousands upon thousands see the pope there, hear his message and are reconfirmed in their faith.

This great hall is the most recent architectural masterpiece to be added to all the others within the Vatican. The idea was the bold initiative of Pope Paul VI (1963-78) who gave the commission to Pier Luigi Nervi. The famous engineer had the daunting task of creating a vast functional building in the immediate vicinity of the Basilica. Inaugurated in 1971, the auditorium contains 6,300 seats as well as large areas of free space. Indeed, the seating capacity may be increased to 12,000 with all spectators enjoying good sight lines and impeccable acoustics. In inaugurating the new building, Paul VI explained that such a costly undertaking was necessary to guarantee a suitable place of encounter between the pope and visitors from the world over.

The brilliant structural connection between the ceiling and its concave support, the great parabolic vaulting, the immaculate sight lines toward the stage, the advanced systems of illumination—these and many other elements place the construction among the most successful achievements of contemporary architecture. The sober grandeur of Nervi's interior is greatly enhanced by the oval windows by Giovanni Hajnal and by the "Resurrection" of Pericle Fazzini—an imposing work in bronze and brass located behind the papal throne. Within the same building there is a smaller auditorium for congresses and meetings. Since 1971, the Bishops' Synods have taken place there.

A different type of welcome within the walls of the Vatican is offered to the homeless and disinherited at the nearby *Casa Dono di Maria*. Every day, hundreds of people are fed there. Thanks to the small residence that the pope put at

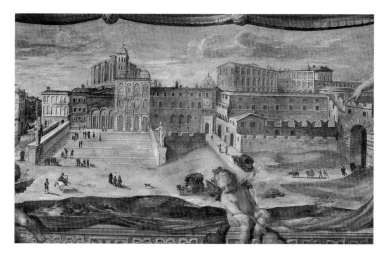

St. Peter's Square *in a fresco in the Apartment of Julius III. The painting, executed in 1564-65, shows the construction of the dome at the stage it had reached at the time of Michelangelo's death and also the unfinished Loggia delle Benedizioni, which was begun at the time of Pius II and enlarged several times until the papacy of Julius II.*

Another fresco of St. Peter's Square *in the Apartment of Julius III, dating from the papacy of Urban VIII, shows the bell towers designed by Bernini. The one to the left was begun in 1641 but then demolished in 1644, because it was feared that it might cause damage to the façade of the basilica. To the right of the basilica is the entrance to the palaces built at the time of Paul V; the Bronze Doors were commissioned especially for this entrance.*

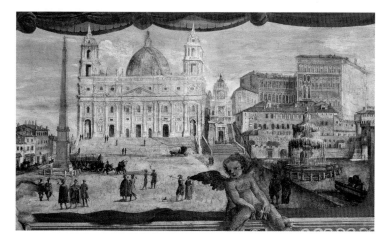

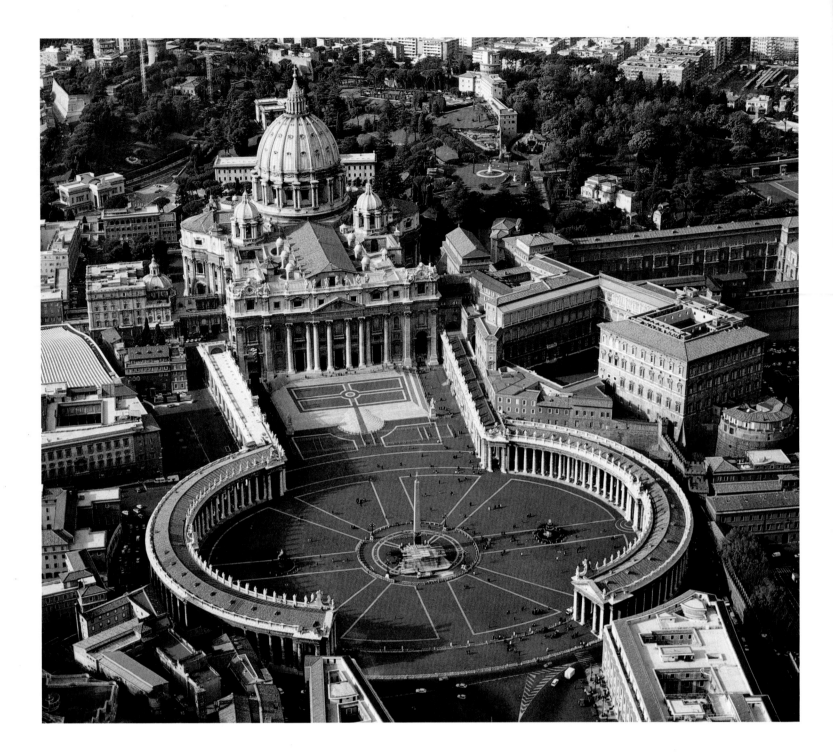

St. Peter's Square. *Gian Lorenzo Bernini worked on the design and construction of St. Peter's Square from 1656 to 1667. He was able to elongate the basilica by adding corridors and colonnades, and by making the entrance to the square the focal point of the whole architectural complex, he reduced the visual impact of the façade so that the dome would appear lighter. To the left, the 17th century Palace of the Sant'Uffizio (Holy Office), which houses the Congregation for the Doctrine of the Faith; immediately behind it, the roof of the Hall of Papal Audiences, inaugurated by Paul VI on June 30, 1971. Between the latter and the basilica stands the Teutonic College; according to tradition this institution was originally established by Charlemagne, who founded a hospice for Frankish pilgrims. Behind it is the 19th century Palazzo della Canonica and the Basilica's Sacristy topped by a dome. To the right of the Basilica is the Sistine Chapel, the Apostolic Palaces, and the barracks of the Swiss Guards.*

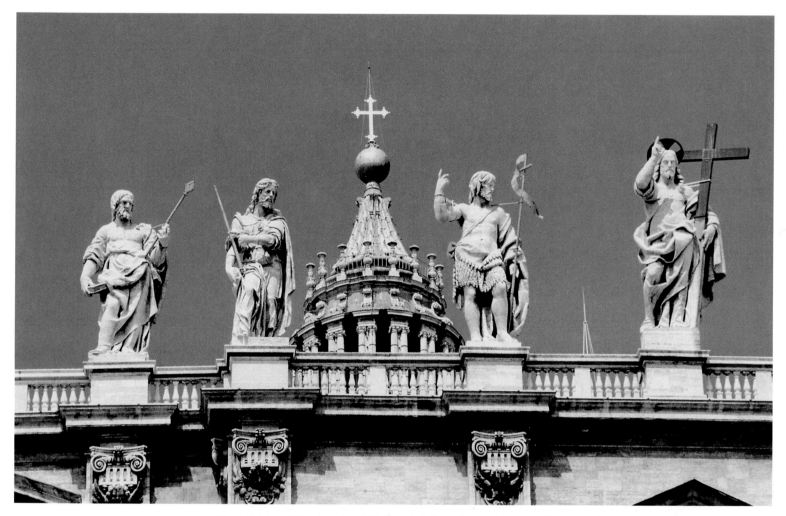

Along the top of the façade of St. Peter's is a series of statues. At the center is the statue of Christ Resurrected, a hand raised in blessing. He is flanked by the apostles. The place of Judas Iscariot, who betrayed Jesus, is taken by a statue of St. John the Baptist, the Messiah's cousin.

the disposal of the sisters of Mother Theresa of Calcutta, at least seventy homeless women have a place to stay.

A further type of welcome or reception—through prayer and contemplation—takes place at the monastery of contemplatives further up Vatican Hill. There, the most fervent prayers of the pope and the entire Church Militant are the subject of intense meditation. It is significant that this spiritual exercise should take place midway between the tomb of the apostle and the home of his successor.

As the long shadows of the evening set in, it is to the windows of the Apostolic Palace that we now turn our gaze.

Those windows, which remain illuminated late into the night, bear witness to the tireless mission of its occupant. They also communicate the notion of a family in which it is possible to follow, at a distance, the labors of the head of the family. Concluding his study of the city, Bishop Fallani wrote: "Our dialogue must be interrupted here, but not concluded altogether. It is not unlike what occurs in a museum, when a custodian interrupts our contemplation with the words: 'Closing time!' For the traveler who has diligently visited whole basilicas and gazed on works of art may well write to his family that the trip, while surely wonderful, has not yet ended!

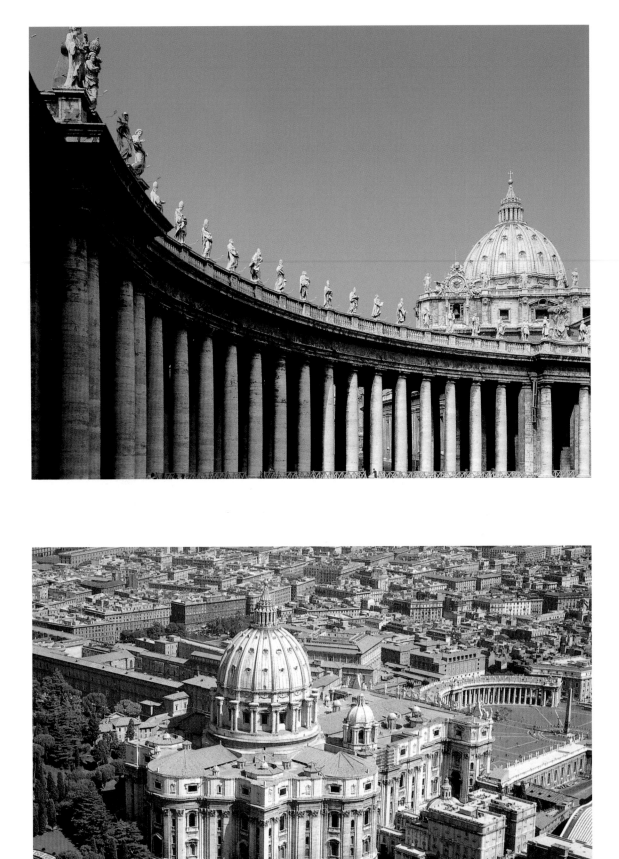

The 140 Saints, each one over three meters high, arranged along the balustrade of the square's two semicircles and the two rectilinear wings of the parvis, were sculpted by Bernini's assistants.

The apse of the southern transept *is the only one that Michelangelo finished in all its detail; it was used as a model for the completion of the other two.*

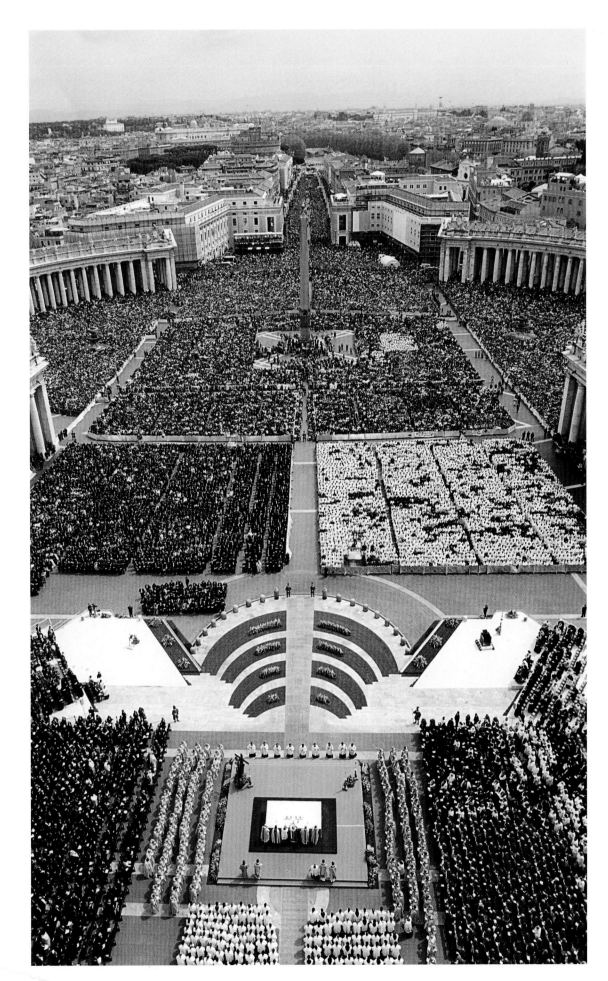

The ceremony inaugurating the pontificate of Pope Benedict XVI (24 April 2005). Cardinal Joseph Ratzinger was elected Pope on 19 April 2005.

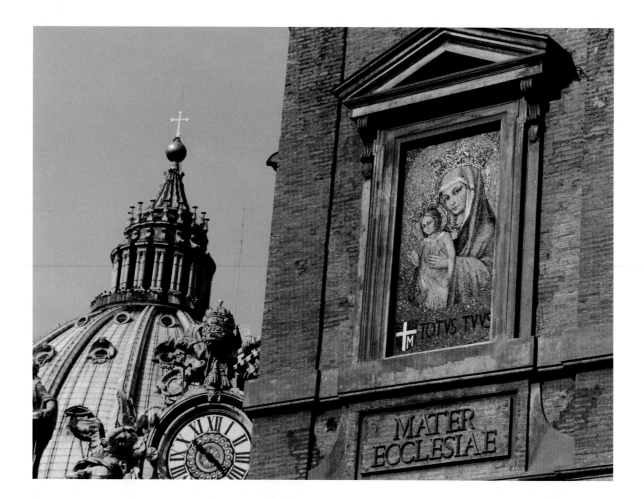

The mosaic of the Virgin Mary and the Christ child was placed overlooking St. Peter's square at the request of Pope John Paul II. It commemorates the attempt to assassinate the pope which took place on May 13, 1981, while he entered the square to begin a general audience. The pope has publically proclaimed his belief that he was saved from death through the intervention of Mary. The Latin inscription Totus Tuus ("Totally Yours") was the pope's motto, and was inserted in Pope John Paul II's coat of arms. Underneath is the inscription Mater Ecclesiae ("Mother of the Church") that expresses faith in Mary's motherly care for the church.

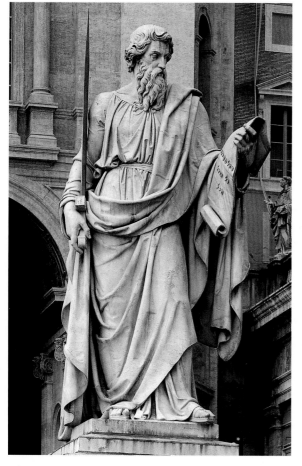

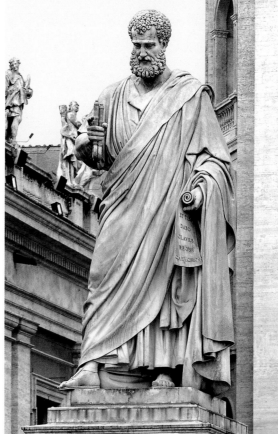

The impressive statues of St. Paul and St. Peter which flank the approach to the Basilica serve as a reminder to the visitor that both saints were martyred in the city of Rome. St. Peter holds the keys which symbolize the spiritual authority which he received from Jesus. St. Paul holds a sword, a reminder of his death on the Via Ostiense. As a Roman citizen, he was killed by decapitation. St. Paul also holds a scroll, a tribute to his important missionary efforts to establish new Christian communities. The statues were placed in the square by Pope Pius IX (1846-1878), in the late nineteenth century.

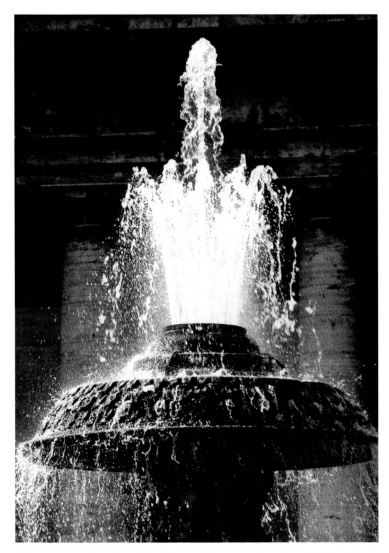

A fountain designed by Bernini provides a gracious break in the linear architecture of the piazza in front of the Basilica. A second identical fountain was added later on the opposite side of the square to provide symmetry.

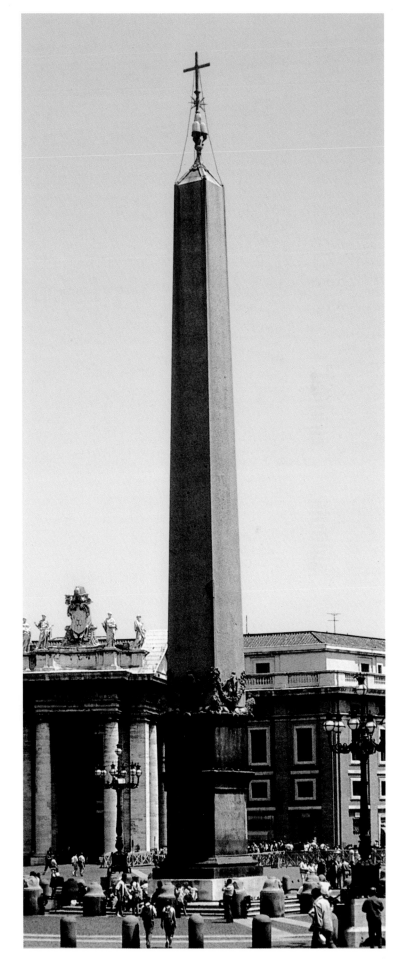

Brought from Heliopolis (Egypt) in 37 B.C. and used in the circus of Caligula near the Vatican hill, the granite obelisk was transferred to its present site in front of St. Peter's in 1586. On April 30th of that year, Pope Sixtus V (1585-1590) supervised the erection of the obelisk, which required 900 men and 140 horses to haul into place. On the top of the monument, the pope placed a relic of the cross on which Jesus had been crucified.

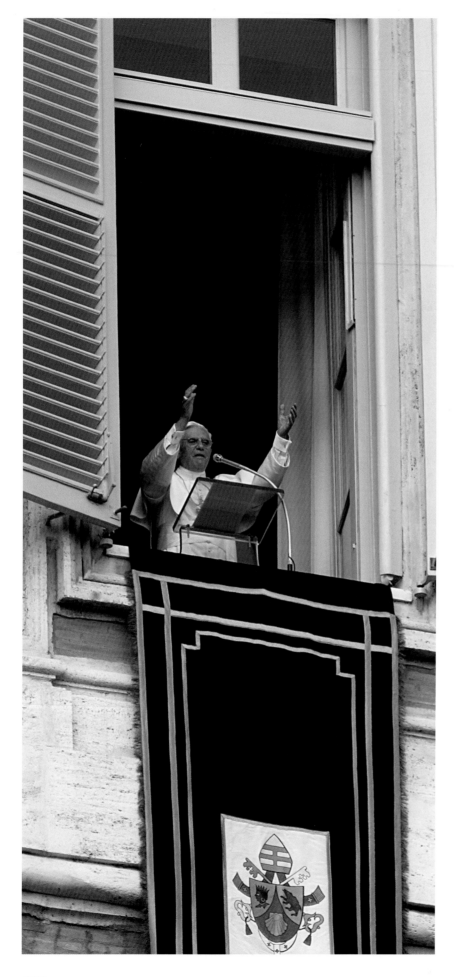

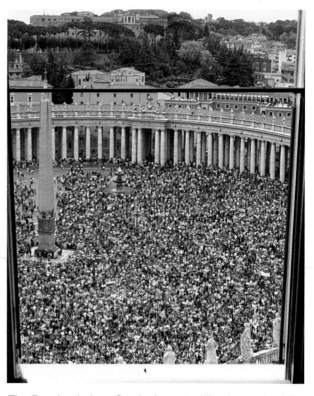

The Pope's window. *Continuing a tradition begun by John XXIII, every Sunday at noon the Pope appears at the window of his private study on the third floor of the Palace to say the Angelus together with the faithful gathered in St. Peter's Square below.*

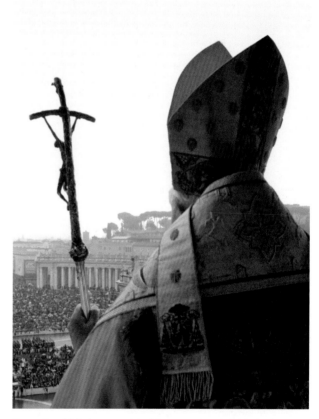

Benedict XVI *imparts his blessing from the* Loggia delle Benedizioni *on Christmas Day.*

BIBLIOGRAPHY

There is an enormous bibliography connected with the Vatican, embracing the history of the papacy and its religious and artistic patrimony.

A good overview compiled by specialists in the field can be found in *Il Vaticano e Roma Cristiana*, published by the Libreria Editrice Vaticana in 1975. Two other indispensable volumes, respectively on the Palaces of the Vatican and the Vatican Museums, were compiled and edited by two of the most authoritative directors of the Vatican museums in the past century. They are Deoclecio Redig de Campos's *I Palazzi Vaticani* (1967, published by Cappelli in Bologna) and Carlo Pietrangeli's *I Musei Vaticani, Cinque Secoli di Storia*, published in 1985 by Quasar in Rome.

Rather difficult to find but precious for all the information it contains on the largest church in Christendom is Genesio Turcio's *La Basilica di San Pietro* published by Sansoni in Florence in 1945. An engaging historical panorama can be found in Ennio Francia's *Storia della Costruzione del Nuovo San Pietro* (De Luca, Rome, 1977). Eva-Maria Jung Inglessis has done a skillful job with her *San Pietro* in the edition dedicated to the pontifical galleries and museums, published in 1978. And very handy indeed is Michele Basso's *Guida alla Necropoli Vaticana*, published by the Fabbrica di S. Pietro in Vaticano, 1986.

Packed with information and written by competent authors working under the general editorship of Prof. Pietrangeli, are the excellent little guides in the series *Guide del Vaticano* (Palombi, Rome, 1989). An excellent overview of Michelangelo and Raphael, brought out in 1994, is the Musei Vaticani publication *Michelangelo e Raffaello in Vaticano*.

Regarding the restoration of the Sistine Ceiling, a volume worth noting is *La Cappella Sistina. La Volta Restaurata: il Trionfo del Colore*, published in 1992 by the Istituto Geografico De Agostini, Novara. Among other things, it contains contributions by those responsible for the delicate restoration: Fabrizio Mancinelli, Gianluigi Colalucci and Nazareno Gabrielli.

Vatican enthusiasts interested in books filled with illustrations and unusual snapshots will warm to Carlo Pietrangeli and Fabrizio Mancinelli's *Vaticano, Città e Giardini*, published by Musei Vaticani in 1985. Another publication worth citing is the joint work of Giovanni Fallani (unbeatable for his combination of artistic knowledge, sound historical grounding and religious sensibility) and Folco Quilici: *Vaticano*, published by Esso Italiana in 1984. Nor should we overlook *Viaggio in Vaticano* with a text by Bart McDowell and photographs by James L. Stanfield, published in 1991 by the National Geographic Society. Finally, journalist Jean Neuvecelle teamed up with photographer Walter Imber to produce the excellent *Vaticano a Porte Aperte*, Edizioni Mondo.

Two French cardinals who lived for decades inside the Vatican have left us the best of their extensive knowledge and keen observations in no fewer than three separate publications. Jacques Martin wrote *Il Vaticano Sconosciuto* (Libreria Editrice Vaticana, 1990); while Paul Poupard gave us *Conoscenza del Vaticano* and *Pellegrinaggio a Roma*, both published by Piemme, Casale Monferrato, 1983.

An approach to the subject that is both historical and "ideological", full of depth and insight, can be found in *Il Vaticano o le Frontiere della Grazia* by Philippe Levillain and François Uginet, published by Rizzoli (Milan, 1985).

LIST OF POPES MENTIONED IN THE TEXT

Peter
Victor I (189-199)
Urban I (222-230)
Sylvester I (314-335)
Damasus (366-384)
Leo I (440-461)
Symmachus (498-514)
Gregory I (590-604)
Leo III (795-816)
Gregory IV (827-844)
Leo IV (847-855)
John VIII (872-882)
Callixtus II (1119-1124), *Guido di Borgogna*
Eugene III (1145-1153), *Bernardo dei Paganelli*
Innocent III (1198-1216), *Lotario dei conti di Segni*
Gregory IX (1227-1241), *Ugolino dei conti di Segni*
Innocent IV (1243-1254), *Sinibaldo Fieschi*
Nicholas III (1277-1280), *Giovanni Gaetano Orsini*
Boniface VIII (1294-1303), *Benedetto Caetani*
Clement V (1305-1314), *Bertrand de Got*
Clement VI (1342-1352), *Pierre Roger*
Gregory XI (1370-1378), *Pierre Roger de Beaufort*
Martin V (1417-1431), *Oddone Colonna*
Eugene IV (1431-1447), *Gabriele Condulmer*
Nicholas V (1447-1455), *Tommaso Parentucelli*
Pius II (1458-1464), *Enea Silvio Piccolomini*
Sixtus IV (1471-1484), *Francesco della Rovere*
Innocent VIII (1484-1492), *Giovan Battista Cibo*
Alexander VI (1492-1503), *Rodrigo de Borja*
Julius II (1503-1513), *Giuliano della Rovere*
Leo X (1513-1521), *Giovanni de' Medici*
Clement VII (1523-1534), *Giulio de' Medici*

Paul III (1534-1549), *Alessandro Farnese*
Julius III (1550-1555), *G.M. Ciocchi del Monte*
Paul IV (1555-1559), *Gian Pietro Carafa*
Pius IV (1559-1565), *Giovan Angelo de' Medici*
Pius V (1566-1572), *Antonio Ghislieri*
Gregory XIII (1572-1585), *Ugo Boncompagni*
Sixtus V (1585-1590), *Felice Peretti*
Clement VIII (1592-1605), *Ippolito Aldobrandini*
Paul V (1605-1621), *Camillo Borghese*
Urban VIII (1623-1644), *Maffeo Barberini*
Innocent X (1644-1655), *G.B. Pamphilj*
Alexander VII (1655-1667), *Fabio Chigi*
Clement IX (1667-1669), *Giulio Rospigliosi*
Clement XI (1700-1721), *G. Francesco Albani*
Clement XII (1730-1740), *Lorenzo Corsini*
Benedict XIV (1740-1758), *Prospero Lambertini*
Clement XIII (1758-1769), *Carlo Rezzonico*
Clement XIV (1769-1774), *G. Vincenzo Antonio Ganganelli*
Pius VI (1775-1799), *G. Angelo Braschi*
Pius VII (1800-1823), *Barnaba Chiaramonti*
Gregory XVI (1831-1846), *Bartolomeo Alberto Cappellari*
Pius IX (1846-1878), *Giovanni M. Mastai Ferretti*
Leo XIII (1878-1903), *Gioacchino Pecci*
Pius X (1903-1914), *Giuseppe Sarto*
Benedict XV (1914-1922), *Giacomo della Chiesa*
Pius XI (1922-1939), *Achille Ratti*
Pius XII (1939-1958), *Eugenio Pacelli*
John XXIII (1958-1963), *Angelo Roncalli*
Paul VI (1963-1978), *Giovanni Battista Montini*
John Paul I (1978), *Albino Luciani*
John Paul II (1978-2005), *Karol Wojtyła*
Benedict XVI (2005), *Joseph Ratzinger*

CONTENTS

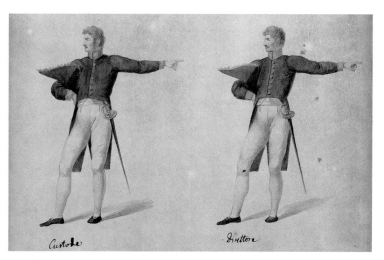

*The Guardian and the Director of the Vatican Museums in 1815
(from the Historical Archives of the Vatican Museums).*

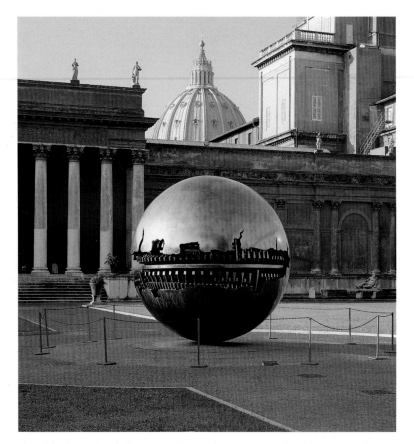

Arnaldo Pomodoro's Sphere within Sphere *was realized in bronze for the Vatican Museums in 1990. It stands in the middle of the Courtyard of the Pine Cone and measures 4 meters in diameter.*